FAMILY NAMES
AND THEIR STORY

FAMILY NAMES AND THEIR STORY

BY

S. BARING-GOULD, M.A.

AUTHOR OF "THE TRAGEDY OF THE CÆSARS," "CURIOUS MYTHS OF THE MIDDLE AGES," &C.

> "I do beseech you
> (Chiefly that I may set it in my prayers)
> What is your name?"
> *Tempest*, Act III., Sc. 1

CLEARFIELD

Originally Published
London, 1910

Reprinted
Genealogical Publishing Company
Baltimore, 1968

Reprinted for
Clearfield Company, Inc. by
Genealogical Publishing Co., Inc.
Baltimore, Maryland
1996

International Standard Book Number: 0-8063-0023-X

Library of Congress Catalog Card Number 68-54868

Made in the United States of America

PREFACE

MR. M. A. LOWER was the first in modern times to break ground in the domain of family nomenclature—in 1842, when he published his first edition of " English Surnames." There were in it many mistakes, and the work was tentative. A better book of his was " Patronymica Britannica," a dictionary of family names that appeared in 1860.

But the share of scientific research first entered the soil with Canon Isaac Taylor's " Words and Places," 1864.

Since then there have been various works on the subject, some good, some bad, some instructive, others misleading; there have been treatises on Irish and Scottish, and on particular county names. Mr. R. Ferguson, in his " English Surnames and their Place in the Teutonic Family," 1858, and " Surnames as a Science," 1883, and " The Teutonic Name-System applied to Family Names in France, England, and Germany," 1864, went too far in deriving most surnames from Teutonic roots, led thereto by Forstemann's " Altdeutsches Namenbuch " (Nordhausen, 1856), a vast work that has been condensed by Heintze in " Die Deutschen Familiennamen " (Halle, 1882).[1] Mr. Bardsley, in his " English Surnames," dealt almost wholly with those found in the

[1] There is also Dr. F. Tetzner's "Namenbuch" (Leipzig, 1893). The most exhaustive German work on names is Pott, " Personennamen,'', (Leipzig, 1859).

PREFACE

Hundred Rolls, 1273, and other documents of the thirteenth and fourteenth centuries. Dr. Barber, in "British Family Names" (London, 1894), gives perhaps excessive pre-eminence to Scandinavian and Flemish names, to such an extent that he derives the family name *Bevan* from the Flemish Bevenot, whereas it stands for Ap Evan. *Carter*, according to him, comes from the Norse Köttr, and *Child* from skjöldr, a shield. *Shepherd* he cannot deduce from a sheep-herd, but derives it from a place called Chebbard. The book has, therefore, to be used with caution. "Ludus Patronymicus; or, The Etymology of Curious Surnames," by Richard Stephen Charnock, 1868, as the author is a scholar, may be consulted with advantage.

"Homes of Family Names in Great Britain," by H. Bingham Guppy, M.B., 1890, is a scholarly work, the result of much research, and evincing a wide knowledge of names, if not of their meanings. Its great value is in the location of family names. There are many other books whose titles and the names of their authors I refrain from giving, as they are often misleading—the blind leading the blind into pitfalls.

In treading the mazes of English nomenclature, one is surrounded by such pitfalls; it is like the road to Plessis Castle, according to Scott in "Quentin Durward": "Every yard of this ground is rendered dangerous by snares and traps and caltrops, and pitfalls deep enough to bury you in for ever." One has to walk warily. It is noticeable enough where others have slipped and fallen in or been caught; and I cannot flatter myself that I have myself wholly escaped. But it must be borne in mind that some names may have distinct derivations, though identical in sound and spelling. For instance, *Tozer* signifies one who dresses cloth in a fulling-mill with teazles, to bring up the nap. But at the Revocation

PREFACE

of the Edict of Nantes, a family of *Thorzeau*, Huguenots, settled in Plymouth, let fall the *r* out of their name, and accommodated it to Tozer. The *Dacres* no doubt in some cases derive from a crusading ancestor who won distinction at Acre, but in most instances take their name from a village near Penrith so-called; and a Ranulph de Dacre, co. Cumberland, who figures in the " Placita quo Waranto," in the reign of Edward I., certainly was designated after this village.

What is the true origin of the surname *Kaye* ? Sir Kay was one of the Knights of the Round Table, and King Arthur's Seneschal; and the romances of the Middle Ages furnished names adopted by people in England and in France. But John del Kai, Sheriff of London in 1207, obviously took his name from the Quay, near which he lived. And Kay is a common pronunciation of Key, and a man who had a key for his shop-sign may have by this means acquired his name. How can we decide whether the family of *Kewe* derives from the parish of that name or from a Cook? The same individual is described in the Parliamentary Writs for 1301 and 1302 as William le Keu and William Cocus.

Some names are supposed to be derived from seasons, as *Noel, Pask, Lammas;* it may be so in some cases, but Noel may come from Noailles, or be a form of Nigel; and when one finds the same man registered in 1273 as Richard Lammesse, and Richard de Lammesse, and when one knows that there is a parish of Lammas in Norfolk, one is disposed to doubt the temporal derivation of some of these names. But a good many such season-names were given to foundlings. A *Leach* is unquestionably a physician, and the horrible creature that was formerly supplied to suck one's blood was so named because it served as a useful doctor in cases of inflammation. But the surname *Blackleach* does not

PREFACE

derive from one of these. Such an entry in the Hundred Rolls for 1273 as that of William le Leche undoubtedly describes a physician. But Henry del Lache, in 1397, indicates that Henry lived by a Lache, or lake, or pool; and Blackleach means the man living at or by Blackpool.

"What variety of herbs soever are shuffled together in the dish," says Montaigne, "yet the whole mass is swallowed up in one name of a salad. In like manner, under the consideration of names, I will make a hodge-podge of differing articles."

CONTENTS

CHAPTER	PAGE
I. INTRODUCTORY	13
II. THE TATTOO AND TRIBAL NAME	28
III. SIRE-NAMES	38
IV. TOTEMISM AND NAMES	74
V. THE CASTLE AND THE MANOR	99
VI. THE VILLAGE	114
VII. THE TOWN : TRADE-NAMES	126
VIII. PLACE-NAMES	154
IX. ANGLO-SAXON NAMES : DOMESDAY	184
X. SCANDINAVIAN NAMES : THE "LIBER VITÆ"	191
XI. THE ROLL OF BATTLE ABBEY	199
XII. FRENCH NAMES : I. EARLY	248
XIII. FRENCH NAMES : II. THE HUGUENOT REFUGEES	277
XIV. NICK- AND DESCRIPTIVE NAMES	295
XV. PREFIXES AND SUFFIXES	318
XVI. NAME STORIES	328
XVII. THE EVOLUTION AND DISINTEGRATION OF SURNAMES	345
XVIII. SCOTTISH AND IRISH SURNAMES	370
XIX. CHANGED NAMES	390
XX. COMPOUND NAMES	402

xi

CONTENTS

	PAGE
APPENDIX TO CHAPTER IX.: ANGLO-SAXON AND DANISH NAMES IN DOMESDAY	408
APPENDIX I. TO CHAPTER X.: SCANDINAVIAN NAMES	410
APPENDIX II. TO CHAPTER X.: SURNAMES OF THE FIFTEENTH CENTURY IN THE "LIBER VITÆ"	412
APPENDIX TO CHAPTER XI.: LIST OF THOSE WHO ATTENDED WILLIAM THE CONQUEROR TO ENGLAND, ACCORDING TO THE "ROMAN DE ROU"	412
APPENDIX TO CHAPTER XII.: HUGUENOT IMMIGRANTS' SUBSCRIPTIONS TO A LOYAL ADDRESS, 1744	414

FAMILY NAMES
AND THEIR STORY

CHAPTER I

INTRODUCTORY

WE cannot deduce our English surnames from the nomenclature of any single people, for the English of to-day are an amalgam of many races that have been fused into one. We have among us British names as Wynne (white); Hoel, that has become Howell; Caradog, now Craddock; Morgan, Madoc, now Madox; Gruffydd, that has become Griffith; and perhaps Coel, that is now Cole.

There are Saxon names as well—Algar; Joll; Eadmund, become Edmunds; Godwin, now Goodwin; Godric, now Goodridge.

Mr. R. Ferguson wrote three books on the subject of Anglo-Saxon names, and their survival in English nomenclature. But a great gap intervenes between the use of Anglo-Saxon names before the Conquest and the adoption of surnames by the conquered; and Anglo-Saxon Christian names, as shall be shown later on, died almost completely out before the assumption of family nomenclature became general; and their existence among us is due to a cause to be noted in the sequel.

Scandinavian surnames based upon personal designations are more numerous in England, but these come nearly all, if not all, from ancient Northumbria, which included Yorkshire.

INTRODUCTORY

There the descendants of the old Danish and Norse settlers clung to their ancient nomenclature later than elsewhere—indeed, till the fashion of adopting surnames prevailed. We have such names. Bard has become Barth, unless it be a contraction, as is probable, of Bartholomew; Jökull yields Jekyll, Halfdan is now Haldane, Sweyn is Swayne, Olafr yields Oliver—but this comes to us through Normandy. Ragnar is now Rayner, and this, again, comes in a roundabout fashion through the Regnier of the Conqueror. Hávarð is Howard, Hjorvarð is Harvey, Steinarr we recognize in Stoner, Ketill is Kettle, Grimm is Grymes, Hámund is Hammond, Friðestan is Featherstone, Thorfin is Turpin. But it is in Yorkshire, East Anglia, Durham, and Northumberland, that these are mainly found. Elsewhere, if we trace them, it will usually be found that the families bearing these names have at some time come into other parts of England from the ancient Northumbria or from Lincoln. We have, indeed, elsewhere names that came originally from Norway, but they have somewhat altered their form by transmission through Normandy. These latter names are numerous, for it was with the Conqueror that family nomenclature may be said to have had its beginning in our land. Of such I shall have to say more hereafter.

Then, again, we have Flemish names, not only the surnames Fleming or Flamank, but also such as Catt; Phayre, which is still common in Belgium; Bowdler and Buller, both derived from Boulers or Bollers, one of the principal fiefs in Flanders. Baldwin de Bollers received from Henry I. the barony of Montgomery and the hand of his niece, Sybilla de Falaise. But most Flemish names are of late introduction, not earlier than the sixteenth century. In Pembrokeshire, where was planted a colony in the reign of Henry I., there are none. *Flinders* is from Flanders, *Clutterbuck* is Cloeterboeke, and *Cobbledick* may be from Koppeldijck, *Mossop* from the Dutch Masdorp, *Vandeleur* is undoubtedly Van de Laer, and *Fullalove* is from Vollenhove. But the Dutch and Flemish names are not numerous.

There are also among us Germans and Jews. In fact, we

INTRODUCTORY

have in our island a vast heap of names, and it is no easy matter to sort them out according to their various origins.

Let us take the largest county in England, the old Deira, Yorkshire. The original population were Celtic, and even after the Angle Conquest the kingdom of Elmet remained to the Britons, seated among the Western Hills, and stretching as far as Leeds. Yorkshire and the whole country to the north, to the Firth of Forth, the Scottish Lowlands, were subjugated by the Angles from Schleswig, a people one in blood with the Danes of Zealand, with only slight dialectic differences in their speech. Scandinavian Saga asserts that the Kings of Zealand claimed suzerainty and exacted taxes from Northumbria from an early period, and that there was a constant influx of Danes into it during many generations. But it was not till 790 that Yorkshire was invaded in hostile form from Denmark. In 876 King Halfdan settled the country, apportioning the land among his Danish followers. The Danes, moreover, spread into Mercia—that is, the Midlands—and numerous place-names there show that they not only conquered it temporarily, but that they also settled down there permanently. Lincolnshire also was peopled by Danish settlers, and they not only gave names to places, but retained their Scandinavian personal designations, to transmit them to the present day.

The population of Yorkshire underwent great changes during the twelfth century. " As the various industries grew up, they invited skilled workmen from different parts. Not only the Normans, but Flemings in the twelfth century and Germans in the fourteenth, came into the country. The mines at Alston were worked about 1350 by a party from Cologne, under Tillman, and the great German colony under Hochstetten, in the time of Elizabeth, made a notable addition to the Lake District population. Even in the fourteenth century, as can be seen from the poll-tax returns of Yorkshire, names suggest immigration from various parts of England, from Scotland and Ireland, and from France."[1]

[1] Collingwood, "Scandinavian England." S.P.C.K., 1909.

INTRODUCTORY

What was true of Yorkshire was true of the rest of England.

When the Jutes, Saxons, and Angles, invaded and subjugated the land, they did not come to light their own fires and clean their own boots, but to take their ease as masters, and turn the natives into hewers of wood, drawers of water, and tillers of the soil, for their advantage. Nowhere, save at Anderida, can there have been wholesale extermination of the inhabitants. Conquerors would no more think of wiping out the working population than they would of killing all the sheep and oxen. The fighting man was not so eager to lay aside spear and sword for plough and oxgoad, as to deprive himself of the men who could drive the plough and the oxen for him, while he lounged and caroused at home.

At the Norman Conquest there was even less loss of life among the natives. Only in Northumbria was there devastation and wholesale slaughter, for there only was the restlessness deemed to be otherwise incurable. Elsewhere the old freeholders were dispossessed of their freeholds, but suffered in many cases to remain on as tenant farmers. When a great Baron had 100 or 170 manors given to him, he could neither occupy them himself nor place his retainers in them at once, for he needed his Norman men-at-arms about him in his castle to watch and keep in control the subjugated English. He could not afford to disperse them over the country. He was compelled to leave in the several manors men who understood the soil, the ways of the country, and who would pay him an annual rent.

In time, however, he would establish his superannuated servants in these manors and farms, as he filled their places about his person with younger men from abroad, and by this manner much Norman blood, carrying with it Norman nomenclature, was dispersed over the land. Where we encounter a Peters and a Pierce, a James and a Jacques, we know that the first descend from an English and the latter from a French ancestor.

Many of the Norman names which have been foisted into

INTRODUCTORY

the Roll of Battle Abbey are those of men that never fought at Hastings, but came over later to better their fortunes under Henry I., or still later under the Angevin Kings.

Indeed, during 300 years of English grip on Normandy, Maine, Anjou, and Guienne, there was incessant flux and reflux between England and France, and many a knight and man-at-arms of French blood, who had served under the banners of English nobles during the wars in France, was rewarded with a grant of land in England, and a little homestead in which he could hang up his battered arms and rest his grey head.

Isabella of France, the wife of Edward II., introduced in her train many persons bearing surnames hitherto unknown in England.

And they came to stay.

Even at the time of the Conquest there were Flemings in England. Later on an eruption of the sea compelled them to abandon their dwellings, now covered by "the deep and rolling Zuyder Zee," and many wanderers sought refuge in England and were allowed to inhabit the Scottish borderlands. Not long afterwards, about 1107-08, Henry I. removed the colony to the Welsh south coast, and gave up to them the fertile district since called "Little England beyond Wales," which had been wrested from the Cymri. "And so it was," says Florence of Worcester, "that these strangers settled there as loyal men to the King; and he placed English among them to teach them the English language, and they are now English, and the plague of Dyved and South Wales on account of their deceit and lies, in which they exceed any settlers in any other part of the island of Britain."

Two other settlements of Flemings were made in Norfolk and Suffolk—one by Henry I., the other under the direction of Edward III.—and this made of East Anglia for centuries the great cloth-weaving district of England. "Worsted" or "Lindsey-wolsey," "Kerseymere," and "Bocking," derive their names from the several villages that became flourishing weaving centres in Eastern England.

Many Hollanders were also invited over to assist in the

INTRODUCTORY

dyking, draining, and embanking, of the low watery lands in Cambridgeshire and Lincolnshire and in Holderness, and settled there.

During the persecution of Alva a great flight of harassed Flemings came over the sea, and many settled in Spitalfields and Clerkenwell, others in Devon and Cornwall, and in Yorkshire, near the wolds and moors where were the sheep-runs.

When Richmond came over and landed in Milford Haven, he was accompanied by a considerable body of recruits from Brittany—

> "A sort of vagabonds, rascals and runaways,
> A scum of Bretagnes, and base lackey peasants,
> Whom their o'ercloyed country vomits forth,
> To desperate ventures."
> *King Richard III.*, V. III.

After Bosworth these soldiers of fortune had to be rewarded for their services, and the cheapest way of so doing was to dispossess the adherents of Richard, and install in their places those who had come over with Henry.

It was principally at this time that the name of *Britten* or *Le Breton* as a surname came among us, and to the same period we owe some of the *Morleys* (from *Morlaix*), though others had arrived earlier with the Conqueror. The name *Lempole* also came in, a corruption of *Lamballe*, *Kimber* of *Quimper*, and *Pimple* of *Paimpol*.[1] During the reign of Elizabeth many Germans arrived to show the English better methods of mining and smelting of ores, and some went, as already intimated, to Yorkshire, but most to Devon and Cornwall, the stannary counties. It is stated that many, if not most, of the technical terms employed in tin-mining in Cornwall are German. Thus we meet with Mullers, Wagners, Bomgartners, and Aikebaums.

After the Revocation of the Edict of Nantes in 1685, a stream of fugitive Huguenots flowed into England. Some-

[1] But there was an earlier settler from Paimpol, for in 1360 Stephen de Penpel, or Pempel, was Archdeacon of Exeter.

INTRODUCTORY

thing like 70,000 are said to have settled in the United Kingdom. The crypt of Canterbury Cathedral was surrendered to them for their religious meetings. Till the end of the eighteenth century, in some parish churches in Essex, Divine service was held in French for their convenience.

In London they settled about Soho and St. Giles; 2,576 went over to Ireland. In Essex at the present day remain many of their descendants bearing French names, as *Pertwee* for *Pertuis*, *Cockrell* for *Coquerell*; *Melonie*, a coal-merchant at Colchester; and *Deval*, a plumber there.

Many settled in Plymouth. Such names still found there as *Gruyelien* and *Lamoureux* (a seed-merchant) are easily identified, but others have undergone some amount of anglicizing. Thus, *Cherri* has become *Cherry*, *Parc* is *Park*, *Benoit* is *Benoi*; *Tardieu*, *Tardew*; *Viall* has become *Vile*, *Condé* is *Cundy*, *Guillard* is *Jillard*; *Jourdain*, *Jordan*.[1] I knew a schoolmistress who wrote her name *Blampy*. She came from Dittisham, on the Dart, where, as I had studied the parish registers, I knew that her ancestor was a Huguenot refugee named Blancpied. Some of the same family migrated to America, where the name has become *Blompay*.

In 1709 a multitude—8,844 poor wretches—arrived from the Bavarian Palatinate, where their homes, farms, crops, even churches, had been wasted and utterly destroyed by order of Louis XIV. A great camp for them was established at Hampstead, and Queen Anne and the noble ladies and gentlemen and the citizens of London visited and relieved the unfortunates. The able-bodied men were drafted into the army, married, and founded families that thenceforth bore German names; some were sent to Ireland, others deported to Yorkshire and other parts of England.

The accession to the throne of William of Orange was an inducement to a number of Netherlanders to come over and feather their nests at our expense. Much bitter feeling was aroused by the favour that William accorded to his countrymen. To him we owe the Bentincks, Keppels, the Vansittarts, and that soldier of fortune from Germany, Schomberg.

[1] But there were earlier and English Jordans.

INTRODUCTORY

So also, with the promotion to the English throne of the Hanoverian dynasty, the natural result was a swarming over of North Germans.

And what can be said of the inflow of representatives of all nationalities since the French Revolution? We have Swedes and Poles naturalized among us—so much so that in the clergy list may be found the names of Swedes and Poles who have become incumbents to English livings. Swiss have found homes here as well, as clockmakers and opticians, as cooks and confectioners.

Germans have arrived in shoals to escape compulsory military service. We have but to look at the names over the shops in Oxford Street to see how these foreigners are elbowing out our native tradesmen. The Italians have monopolized the restaurants, and the old English chop-house exists no longer.

In the mercantile offices the foreigner proves a useful clerk, and in nine cases out of ten remains, and his family becomes entirely English: only the name proclaims whence he came. The English commercial traveller is also being displaced by the foreigner. German Jews are naturalized, many become Christians or drop their Mosaic peculiarities, and they all contribute names to the general stock, not only *Levi, Samuel, Nathan,* and *Cohen,* but also *Goschen, Holzapfel, Cassel, Wolf, Rothschild*;[1] also Spanish and Portuguese Jews, as *Montefiore* and *Lopes.*

[1] The Rothschild family was from Frankfort, where Mayer Anselm Rothschild was a small money-lender, born 1743. The Landgraves of Hesse-Cassel disposed of their male subjects to England as mercenaries, and Amschel (Anselm) acted as intermediary. In 1775 as many as 12,800 Hessians were thus sold to the British Government to be sent to fight in America, and the number was afterwards swelled to 19,400, or one-twentieth part of the entire population of Hesse-Cassel. Huzars were despatched to patrol the frontiers and drive back the wretched peasants who attempted to escape. The subsidies passed through the hands of Amschel, and a good deal of English gold adhered to his fingers (Vehse, "Geschichte d. deutschen Höfe," vol. xxvii., pp. 174-6, 226). J. Scherr, in "Der rothe Quartal," says, after mentioning the fortune amassed: "To think that one family should have acquired such vast, almost wicked, wealth out of blood-money, when those fathers of their

INTRODUCTORY

It is not possible to fix a date when surnames became hereditary. There are surnames given that were personal, and such there have ever been, but these ceased to be used with the decease of the bearer. But *when*—at what date—a to-name was transmitted to a man's posterity cannot be said with any confidence. Hereditary surnames stole into use by slow degrees and imperceptibly. They began with the assumption of territorial designation by the Normans at the Conquest, as shall be shown in another chapter, but did not become general among the middle classes till the fifteenth century.

Of surnames in Germany it has been said: " Family names did not come into general employ until late in the Middle Ages. First of all, the nobility in the twelfth century called themselves after their ancestral seats, as Conrad von Wettin, Rudolf von Habsburg; then among the citizens they were adopted in the fourteenth century, but did not become general till the sixteenth century."

What is true of German surnames is true also of such as we find in England, only that the acquisition of family names with us came in somewhat earlier than in Germany.

Mr. Bardsley says of nicknames and such other to-names as were given in Anglo-Saxon and early Norman times: " They were but expressions of popular feeling to individual persons by means of which that individuality was increased, and passed away with the lives of their owners. The son, in due course of time, got a sobriquet of his own, by which he

---

people, Charles I., William VIII., Frederick II., and William IX., sold their subjects by thousands and tens of thousands to various war-loving potentates, and *en gros* to the English during the War of Emancipation in America ! This family treasure, to which more curses clung than to the Nibelungen-hort, came in the Napoleonic age to be further swollen by old Amschel, the founder of the Rothschild dynasty ; and he knew so well how to turn money over that his son became, so to speak, the grand-master of European jobbery." But, after all, the real iniquity lay, not with the Rothschilds, but with the Landgraves who trafficked in their subjects, and not much less with the British Government which entered into and encouraged such a scandalous negotiation.

INTRODUCTORY

was familiarly known; but that, too, was but personal and temporary. It was no more hereditary than had been his father's before him, and even, so far as himself was concerned, might be again changed, according to the humour or caprice of his neighbours and acquaintances. And this went on for several more centuries; only, as population increased, these sobriquets became more and more common.

"In the eleventh and twelfth centuries, however, a change took place. By a silent and unpremeditated movement over the whole of the more populated and civilized European societies, nomenclature began to assume a solid, lasting basis. It was the result, in fact, of an insensibly growing necessity. Population was on the increase, commerce was spreading, and society was fast becoming corporate; with all this arose difficulties of individualization. It was impossible, without some further distinction, to maintain a current identity. Hence, what had been but an occasional and irregular custom became a fixed and general practice—the distinguishing sobriquet, not, as I say, of premeditation, but by a silent compact, became part and parcel of a man's property, and passed on with his other possessions to his direct descendants."[1]

There were, however, instances, few and far between, in which a nickname extended to children beyond the father to whom first applied, and that before the Conquest. Mr. Lower quotes from a document among the Cottonian MSS. in the British Museum that, though bearing no date, is certainly earlier than 1066. It states that

"Hwitta Hatte was a keeper of bees at Haethnfelda, and Tate Hatte, his daughter, was the mother of Wulsige, the shooter; and Lulle Hatte, the sister of Wulsige, Helstan had for wife in Wealadune. Wifus and Dunne and Seolce were born in Haethnfelda. Duding Hatte, the son of Wifus, is settled at Wealadene; and Ceolmund Hatte, the son of Dunne, is also settled there; and Aetheleah Hatte, the son of Seolce, is also there; and Tate Hatte, the sister of Cenwald, Moeg hath for his wife at Weligan; also Ealdelm, the

[1] Bardsley, "English Surnames." London, 1889.

INTRODUCTORY

son of Herethrythe, married the daughter of Tate. Werlaff Hatte, the father of Werstan, was the rightful owner of Haethnfelda."

Here we have four generations of Hattes, and the females keep their names of Hatte; but apparently these all derive it from Heathfield, which is Hattes-field, being owned by Werlaff Hatte. It is quite possible that those who drifted away from Haethnfield ceased to bear the to-name. The document is curious, as it shows that before the Conquest the tendency to assume surnames had already spasmodically manifested itself; but we have no authority to say that it had done more than manifest itself.

In the great confusion of names, the alteration, the modification, the corruption, they have undergone, it is not easy for every man to discover whence he came, how he got his name, to what race he pertains. Yet every man must desire to "look to the rock whence he is hewn, and to the hole of the pit whence he is digged." It is hoped that this book may serve him in some fashion to discover his origin.

But continually we hear men make the most incredible assertions relative to their families and the family name, unconscious that documentary evidence could demolish what was assuredly put forward. I can find space for two instances only.

Some fifty years ago there lived an old gentleman of the name of *Gill* in a country town. He was a pompous man who wore two waistcoats, a high cravat, and a beaver curled up at the sides, after the fashion of the Count d'Orsay. What filled him with pride was the conviction—the absolute conviction—that the blood of Kings circulated in his veins. The sole foundation for this belief was that his surname was Gill, and that once upon a time there had been a Norwegian King of the name of Harald Gill.

Now, in the first place, Harald Gill reigned from 1130 to 1136, and at that time hereditary surnames were unknown in Scandinavia. In the next place, we know what became of all the race of this King—that it was blotted out in blood.

INTRODUCTORY

In the third place, he was hardly one to be looked back upon as a glory to the family.

Now hear his story: In the year 1129 there arrived in Norway an Irishman named Gillchrist, who presented himself before King Sigurd the Crusader, and declared that he was his half-brother, the son of Magnus Barefeet, who had been killed in battle in Ireland in 1103. He was a tall, lanky fellow, with a long face and neck, and, unlike a Scandinavian, had black eyes and hair. He spoke Norwegian but brokenly. He pretended that King Magnus had had an intrigue with an Irish girl, and it was said that in the battle in which he fell the King had sung this stave:

> "In Dublin town my hopes reside,
> No more are Norway's maids my cheer.
> Them I'll not see till autumn-tide,
> I love my Irish wench so dear."

Gillchrist brought his mother with him, but no other evidence to establish his assertion. King Sigurd was subject to fits of insanity, and, against the advice of his Council, accepted the claim, and made Gillchrist, or Harald, as he now called himself, swear that he would not contest the kingdom, after his death, with Magnus, his son and sole male issue. Harald took the required oath, and broke it so soon as the King was dead.

Norway at the time was not a compact nationality, and a strong hostility existed between the men of the North and those of the South. The Northerners, or Drontheimers, at once accepted Harald as their King, whilst those of the South proclaimed Magnus so soon as Sigurd was no more. Harald succeeded in getting Magnus into his hands, whereupon he blinded him, cut off one of his feet, and otherwise mutilated him.

Harald Gill, or Gillchrist, "was one of the most unworthy Kings that ever disgraced the throne of Norway," says the historian Boyesen. He left behind him but one legitimate son, Ingi, who was deformed, hunchbacked, and with a withered leg. He died without issue. But Harald left three bastard sons and as many baseborn daughters. Not one

INTRODUCTORY

of the brood inherited the name of Gill. One of them was called Sigurd Mund, from his ugly mouth, and he left issue by his mistresses. His eldest son was born of a slave-girl when he himself was aged but fifteen. A more disreputable set than the spawn of Harald Gill can hardly be conceived. They fought and killed each other, and of those that remained, King Magnus Erlingsson, or, rather, his father Erling, set to work to exterminate them root and branch. But when he supposed that not one of Gill's race remained, there suddenly started up a new claimant, Swerrir, from the Faroe Isles, who pretended that he was the bastard of Sigurd Mund by his cook, who was the wife of a combmaker named Uni, though Swerrir had been born after Uni had married her. The faction of the Drontheimers was quite ready to admit his claim, though totally unsubstantiated by any evidence, and in a battle fought in 1184 Magnus Erlingsson was killed. Now, Swerrir did have sons by the daughter of Roe, the Bishop of the Faroe Isles, but it is very doubtful whether he were married to her, and we know what became of his sons and grandsons. But Swerrir himself, by his own showing, was the illegitimate son of a bastard of Harald Gill, who was himself, as he pretended, an illegitimate son of King Magnus Barefeet.[1] But that was not the end of the farcical tragedy. A man turned up—a little fellow with an ugly face, named Eric—who also pretended to be the son of Sigurd Mouth, on no other grounds than that when in Palestine he had prayed that, should he be a King's son, he might be able to wade or swim across Jordan with a lighted candle in his hand. He does not seem to have known who was his mother. But his son died without issue. All the sons, or pretended sons, and grandsons of Harald Gill bore nicknames, but not one called himself Gill.

Harald's original name was Gillchrist—that is to say, the servant of Christ. It was customary among the Irish and Scots to call themselves servants of Christ or of some saint,

---

[1] The male line, but only through another bastard, came totally to an end with Hakon Longlegs in 1319.

INTRODUCTORY

and some of the noblest in the land were Gillmichael, Gillpatrick Gillbridget, etc. But the name was unknown in Norway before the arrival of Harald, and it perished there with him. So much for this claim put forward to give a false gloss to a name in itself ancient.

Now, *Gill* was a highly honourable name, taken by some of the men of highest rank in Scotland, Cornwall, and Ireland, coupling with it the name of Saint; but it was not Norwegian.

Now for another instance. In the *Western Morning News* for June 10, 1909, is an account of the millenary service of the anniversary of the foundation of the See of Crediton, and also in memory of the martyrdom of Wynfrith (St. Boniface), who was born in Crediton in 680. The newspaper says: " At yesterday's service conspicuous places were occupied by the Rev. A. Winnifrith (Rector of Mariansleigh) and Rev. D. P. Winnifrith (Rector of Igham), father and son, who claim to be descendants of the great St. Boniface."

Now, neither the father nor any brothers of St. Boniface bore the name of Wynfrith; nor, of course, being a monk and an Archbishop, did he himself leave issue. Moreover, hereditary family names did not come into existence in England—at all events, among the English people—till some 500 years after the death of Wynfrith of Crediton.

I give these two instances of the mistakes into which people may fall by making claims as to the antiquity and origin of their names, without having investigated whether any basis exists on which they could be established.

From the moment we come into the world we have, as our very own, our names and our shadows. The latter attend us only when the sun shines, but the former cling to us night and day. We are sensitive about our names: we resent their being misspelt or mispronounced; we fire up at any disparaging remark passed upon them. But otherwise we do not concern ourselves about them. We do not ask when these names came into existence, what their signification is, and what is their history. And yet they deserve more consideration than has been accorded to them; they are heirlooms

INTRODUCTORY

of the past—heirlooms to be kept unblemished, to be passed on without a stain to our children. And they are historical records when rightly read. They inform us to what nation our ancestor belonged, or what was his occupation, what his principal physical or moral characteristics. That man who first had a surname which he transmitted to his children was the Adam of the family. Of all who went before we know nothing; of those who followed we may, perhaps, know nothing till the time of our grandfather; but he, the Name-Father, stands out as *the* family progenitor, and if we desire to know something about him we must question our surname. Our surnames are at the least 300 years old, many from 500 to 600 years old. Language changes—it is in constant flux; but the name, after it has been adopted as a hereditary surname and fixed in registers, is petrified. Spelling was tentative and capricious, and Smith, for instance, was, when enregistered, rung through all changes of Smeeth, Smythe, Smeyt, Smyth, etc.; and Faber, the blacksmith, became Fever, Feures, Ferron, Fieron, etc. Because of the arbitrary manner in which names were enrolled, so many are to us unintelligible at the present day.

This year (1909) I have had difficulties relative to applicants for old-age pensions, because the same person had his surname spelled in one way when baptized, in another way when married, and in a third when he made application. The arbitrary way in which the owners of some of the best of our family names treat them as to pronunciation shows what confusion and mistakes must have been made in registration. *Mainwaring* is pronounced Mannering, *Leveson-Gower* becomes Lewson-Gore, *Marjoribanks* is Marchbanks, *Cholmondeley* is Chumley. It was largely due to such mispronunciation, or to caprice, that so many apparently vulgar and opprobrious nicknames are to be found among us. Originally they were not nicknames at all, as we shall presently see.

CHAPTER II

THE TATTOO AND TRIBAL NAME

THE flight of the hermit from the society of his fellow-men to bury himself in the desert, the bitterness expressed by Timon when he said:

> "Be abhorred
> All feasts, societies and throngs of men!
> His semblable, yea, himself, Timon disdains"

—these are products of an exhausted, dying civilization. The primitive man finds his pleasure, his *ratio vivendi*, in association. He cannot think outside his community. He cannot understand the possibility of man living as a unit, not as a digit in a sum. The most extreme condemnation that could be passed on a Norseman was to proclaim him an outcast, a "wolf"[1] who might not lie under the same roof with, nor speak with, a fellow-man. As one outside the commonwealth, every man's hand was against him. He might be killed with impunity. And the horror with which excommunication was regarded by a man in the Middle Ages was due, not to dread of deprivation of the Sacraments, so much as to dissociation from fellow-men who might not house and converse with him. When the Popes excommunicated whole peoples it lost its force, and sectaries were willing cheerily to excommunicate themselves, for they went forth from the Church in bodies. When Innocent III. excommunicated King Sverrir of Norway, and laid the land under an interdict, it was

---
[1] So also to be proclaimed a "wolf's-head" in England. *Cant. Pilgrims*: "The Coke's Tale."

THE TATTOO AND TRIBAL NAME

generally disregarded, and no one was a penny the worse, though the ban lasted from 1194 to 1202.[1] Everywhere and at all times do we come upon men living in community, meshes in one net, their habitations clustered together as cells in a honeycomb, living in communal houses, as the Bornean Dyaks, where each house constitutes a village, or as the North American cliff-dwellers. The family was unquestionably the egg out of which the tribe was hatched, and out of the tribe, but long after, grew the nation. But the tribe itself in time ramified into subdivisions or septs.

The original idea certainly was that all members of a tribe were of one blood, and it was on this account that such strict rules existed against intermarriage between the members. But in process of time this ceased to be strictly true, as by ·adoption individuals pertaining to one tribe might be taken into another, and a clan which was reduced in numbers through war or plague was glad to recuperate by this means.

So homogeneous was a tribe, that a crime committed by one member of it was resented against the whole; and when a murder had been committed outside it, retaliation was made, not necessarily on the murderer, but on any innocent and innocuous member of the murderer's tribe. We have excellent opportunity for seeing this in operation in the early history of Iceland, where families were established in their several homesteads, but had not as yet multiplied sufficiently to constitute clans; or in Borneo, where this system of vendetta prevails to the present day.

From a very early period—indeed, from the very time when a tribe was formed—it became essential to place some mark upon each member, so that he might be recognized by friend and foe as belonging to it. This is the signification of all the mutilations and disfigurements that are found among men in a primitive state of civilization. It continued even under later conditions. Circumcision among the Jews

---

[1] Remarkably enough, from the moment that the ban was fulminated Providence blessed Sverrir, and his fortunes assumed a favourable turn. He was one of the best Kings Norway ever had.

THE TATTOO AND TRIBAL NAME

was the placing a mark upon the Beni Israel, whereby they might be distinguished from the Gentile nations around. And circumcision has the same significance among the Mohammedans—only that with them it is the badge, not of uniqueness in blood, but of oneness in faith.

Among the ancient Irish, the Druids wore a particular tonsure, indicative of their pertaining to the sacred, in contradistinction to the secular tribe. The Christian missionaries adopted another kind of tonsure. They shaved the head from ear to ear in front, and the native Irish called them "adze-heads" because this gave to their faces the shape of the weapon we commonly call a "celt."

The Normans who followed William the Bastard to England, to distinguish themselves from the Anglo-Saxons, shaved the backs of their heads from ear to ear, as we may see them depicted in the Bayeux Tapestry.

The Romanist tonsure of the priest and the monk has the same significance—the indication by an outward mark that those so disfigured belong to a sacred caste.

Many savage races flatten the head, pierce the cartilage of the nose and insert rings, knock out one or more of the teeth or file them to sharp points, draw forth the nether lip, pierce it, and insert a stick; or else tattoo the face, or face and body together. All these disfigurements had originally, and have still, the object of marking a man or woman as a member of a particular tribe.

When a female marries out of her tribe, then she is required to have additional flourishes tattooed upon her; and anyone acquainted with native ways can read upon her body the history of her life—that she was born into one tribe, but was taken by marriage into another.

On the Congo, says Frobenius, every group, even every village, bears, so to say, visibly on its head its own coat of arms. Nor is this custom confined to the region of the Congo, but prevails beyond Africa over a great part of the world, especially in the region of the Pacific Ocean and the lands bordering on it.

When Julius Cæsar first landed in Britain, he noted that

THE TATTOO AND TRIBAL NAME

the natives were dyed with woad. What he saw was the painting or tattooing that indicated the distinctions of tribes ranged against him.

Long after tattooing had ceased to prevail in Europe, down to our own times, every village distinguished itself, in France, Germany, and elsewhere, from every other by some peculiarity of costume. Costume is now rapidly disappearing, but fifty years ago it prevailed. In 1847, when my father drove through France from St. Malo to Pau, I sketched the head-dresses of the women. Not only was there a difference between those of the different provinces, but there was distinction between those in the several villages. In the National Museum at Munich is a hall given up to the costumes worn by men and women alike in the kingdom. There is, or were, precisely the same differences there. At the present day, in the market at Quimper in Brittany, one may distinguish at a glance a Bigauden from any other peasantess by the hair tightly drawn back from the face, and collected in a black box-cap at the back of the head. The Bigauden is believed to be of a different race from the Breton, and to have Mongolian characteristics. She proclaims the difference by her coiffure.

The author already quoted tells the story of a young French trader who in 1895 started for the Congo, and reached Lake Leopold, where he did so good a business that he resolved on establishing a permanent station there. "But scarcely was the axe applied to the first tree, when one hand of the village chief's was laid on the woodman's shoulder, while the other indicated with unmistakable emphasis that the business must proceed no further. So a palaver was held, and the gentle Mongols insisted that the trader must become a member of the tribe, without which he might not settle. He was rejoiced. He nodded his assent, and through his interpreter asked how this was to be done. 'You must receive the tribal scars,' was the reply. He pulled a long face, but there was no help for it. On all sides, right and left, ivory and rubber were to be had in abundance, and all at the cost of a few gashes.

THE TATTOO AND TRIBAL NAME

"Next morning the *ganga*—that is, the priest of the tribe—introduced himself. On a leather cloth he spread out all sorts of little objects—a couple of horns, black ashes, red dyes, a few small iron implements, and four little wooden figures tied up in a bundle.

"The white brother of the tribe was first manipulated on the temples, a black mixture was rubbed in, and his head scarred with various red lines. Even that did not suffice. Inflammation set in with the wounds, which festered. . . . After four weeks the *ganga* presented himself again. The scorings were repeated. Again he fell ill, lost all patience, and in a few days returned to Europe. The affair had a sad ending. The poor fellow never recovered, and died in the hands of a surgeon, trying to get the hateful disfigurements removed from his temples."[1]

That in time men should revolt against the tortures and mutilations to which they were subjected, in order to earmark them as members of their tribe, may well be supposed. The tartan, the costume, the various modifications of the plaiting of the hair, are substitutes, in the interests of humanity, for the bodily disfigurements. But another substitute was found in the registration of the tribesmen.

In all probability, among the Celts generally, and among the Irish and Welsh certainly, the bard was instituted as the genealogist of the tribe. It was his obligation, for which he was liberally paid, to know and recite the pedigree and position and achievements of every individual of the tribe.

The man who founded a family had a personal name, and imposed that name on his descendants. The sons of Adam were Adamim. But as families multiplied, and became detached more or less from the parent stock, the head of each branch became in turn an ancestor, giving his name to the sept. Yet, as in the subclans of the Highlands of Scotland, the original filiation was never wholly forgotten.

In Genesis we read: "Now these are the generations of the sons of Noah: Shem, Ham, and Japheth; and unto them were sons born after the flood. The sons of Japheth:

[1] Frobenius, "The Childhood of Man." London, 1908.

THE TATTOO AND TRIBAL NAME

Gomer and Magog, and Madai and Javan, and Tubal and Meshech and Tiras. And the sons of Javan: Elishah and Tarshish, Kittim and Dodanim. By these were the isles of the Gentiles divided in their lands: every one after his tongue, after their families, in their nations."

The sacred writer goes on in like manner to give the sons and grandsons of Ham and of Shem. He clearly notes that the tribes and races of whom he had knowledge claimed or were accorded descent from certain named ancestors, but they did not all take the name of the remotest forefather, but of that one which formed the radiating sept.

This fissiparous formation of tribes may go on for a long time, but it must come to an end eventually, so far as retention of relation with the parent stock and with the collateral branches goes; and then in the general welter and confusion of relations the idea of the nation rises to the surface.

Among the Norsemen, the Royal Family was that of the Ynglings, deriving from a mythical ancestor, Ingvi. The Saxon and Angle Kings all traced back to heroic ancestors, and the Saxon Chronicle is careful to record the pedigrees. The Danish Royal Family was that of the Skjöldungs, descended from an ancestor Skjold, of whom this story is told: One day a skiff arrived on the coast of the Baltic with a little boy asleep within it on a shield. He was reared among the people, and became their King. Because he slept on a shield he was called Skjold, and because he was found in a boat he was fabled to be the son of Skiff. Simeon of Durham, in his history of St. Cuthbert, calls Halfdan and his brother, the two Danish Kings of Northumbria, Scaldingi —*i.e.*, Skjöldungs.

But the royal Danish race of this stock expired in the male line with the extinction of the family of Canute the Great, and the crown passed to the son of an Earl Ulf whom Canute had murdered, and who had married his sister. Thenceforth the Danish royal race was entitled the Ulfungs. But among the Northmen there were as well the Björnings, sons of the Bear; Hundings, sons of a dog; Arnungs, issue of an eagle; Nifflungs, children of the mist.

THE TATTOO AND TRIBAL NAME

But no member bore the name Björning, Skjöldung, Hunding, Arnung, etc., as a surname; only the family generally was so designated. It was a tribal name, but it did not adhere as yet to the personal name.

In the Scandinavian stock, the tribal formation had broken down or been dissolved, and descent from the heroic ancestor was attributed to the Royal Family alone. The dissolution of the tribe was largely due to the conformation of the land, which threw people together about the fjords, and forced them to adopt a territorial rather than a tribal organization.

The ancient social organization of the Romans was tribal. The tribe, or rather house, was called a *gens*, and the idea was that all members of a gens were of one blood. The most ancient gentes were all patrician—the Ramni, Titii, and Luceri. But as they died out other gentes were formed. After the reign of Servius Tullius arose plebeian gentes. In some cases in the same gens existed at the same time patrician and plebeian *familiæ*. Such was the case with the gentes Claudia, Cornelia, and Junia. This arose through a plebeian family being elevated into being patrician, whilst the others remained in their former position. Or else a patrician by a marriage out of his order might found a family that became plebeian. Each gens had particular rights. There existed mutual protection; property could not be passed by bequest or sale out of the tribe; and each gens had its own sanctuary and a common burial-place. Every Roman had three names —one personal, one designating the family to which he belonged, and one indicated his gens.

The title of "gentleman" originally signified one belonging to a gens, or tribe, in contradistinction to the rabble without, who pertained to none.

Among the Celts it was much the same as among the Romans. In the Highlands of Scotland, theoretically all Campbells, Ogilvies, Camerons, Farquhars, were regarded as of one blood, when they bore the same clan name. But, as we shall see in the sequel, this was theoretical only. The Irish had the *Fine*, consisting in the first place of the children, brethren, and other relatives, of the *Flath*, or chieftain; but

THE TATTOO AND TRIBAL NAME

it actually comprised as well all who were under his protection and paid him rents. Each of the smaller clans comprised in a great clan gradually assumed a distinctive surname, though they often continued to be regarded, and to regard themselves as included, under the great clan name. The clan names of O'Brian, O'Neill, O'Donovan, O'Sullivan, O'Donnell, like the Greek Homerids in Chaios, the Codrids, the Butids, the Roman Æmilii, Julii, or Fabii, were originally family organizations, swelled later on by adoption from without into the clan.

Like the Roman gentes, the Irish tribes had their tribal cemeteries. Indeed, those mysterious people, who strewed so many lands with their megalithic monuments, had unquestionably a tribal organization — also as certainly tribal names, for their great dolmens and sepulchral chambers were clan mausoleums, and it was only on the dissolution of the tribal formation that the small kistvaen, containing but a single interment, came into use. It is interesting to note that the old clan feeling survives among us relative to our dead. Families like to have their mausoleums and vaults, in which may be gathered together all of the same blood and name.

Sir Henry Maine says: "It would be a very simple explanation of the origin of society if we could base a general conclusion on the hint furnished us by Scripture, that communities began to exist wherever a family held together instead of separating at the death of its patriarchal chieftain. In most of the Greek States and in Rome there long remained the vestiges of an ascending series of groups out of which the State was first constituted. The family, house, and tribe, of the Romans may be taken as the type of them, and they are so described to us that we can scarcely help conceiving them as a system of concentric circles which have gradually expanded from the same point. The elementary group is the family, connected by common subjection to the highest male ascendant. The aggregation of families forms the gens or house. The aggregation of tribes constitutes the commonwealth."[1]

[1] Maine, "Ancient Law," p. 128. London, 1885.

THE TATTOO AND TRIBAL NAME

All in the tribe had one name; but with the division of the tribe into the gens, house, or clan, a new name was taken from the new founder. The original idea was that first the tribe, then the clan or gens, constituted men of one blood. But this ceased to be true when adoption took place, and this took place on a large scale; nevertheless, those adopted assumed the tribal or clan name. Not all the Fabii were of Fabian blood, nor all the O'Brians descendants of Brian, nor all the Camerons of the original crooked-nosed ancestor (Cam-rhon). "The family," says Maine, "is the type of an archaic society in all its modifications which it was capable of meaning; but the family here spoken of is not exactly the family as understood by a modern. In order to reach the ancient conception, we must give to our modern ideas an important extension and an important limitation. We must look on the family as constantly enlarged by the absorption of strangers within its circle, and we must try to regard the fiction of adoption as so closely simulating the reality of kinship that neither law nor opinion makes the slightest difference between a real and an adoptive connection."[1]

We shall see, in the chapter on Scottish and Irish Names, that the adoption of a clan name in a vast number of cases implies no blood relationship whatever.

Tribal organization was a stage in the development of mankind, useful and beneficial for a time, but for a time only, after which it became obstructive to the formation of the greater and nobler conception of nationality.

Tribal organization must inevitably come to an end in time, with the multiplication of families, and instead of asking how it came to an end, the question to be asked is: How did it manage to continue so long as it did in Wales and Scotland? And the answer in both cases is :—Constant wars with the English, with each other, and with the Lowlanders, kept the tribal organization from falling to pieces.

With the extinction of tribal differentiation through the melting of all the members of the several septs into one

[1] Maine, "Ancient Law," p. 133.

THE TATTOO AND TRIBAL NAME

race, the tribal name falls away or adheres to the King alone, and each member of the race is left with his personal name only; and this is how we find our forefathers in England—Celtic, Anglo-Saxon or Danish—with singular names, or personal names, to which were attached descriptive appellations that perished with the bearer, because such designations were not applicable to his sons.

The sequence in the formation of hereditary nomenclature was this:

1. The tribe was at first distinguished by bodily mutilations.

2. Mutilations were abandoned for costume, differentiating tribes.

3. The tribal name fell away, and the personal name alone was left.

4. Personal names were found to be insufficient for differentiating man from man.

5. Consequent introduction of descriptive appellations. These were personal, and expired with the bearer.

6. Finally surnames become hereditary.

CHAPTER III

SIRE-NAMES

A TIME was when, by a sudden cataclysm, the climate of Northern Asia was changed. One day it was temperate if not tropical; then came a wave of glacial cold, and the temperature of Siberia was altered for ever. At once, in one day, all the mammoths that had browsed on the luxuriant vegetation fell, and were congealed and embedded in ice, that preserved them—flesh, skin, and hair, even the undigested food in their paunches—revealing what was the vegetation once found on what are now the frozen tundras that grow nothing but grey moss.

We do not know when this event took place; we know only that it did take place, because these frozen monsters strew the lands that fringe the Polar Circle.

In like fashion, at some time, we know not precisely when, but certainly not simultaneously, all the Toms, Jacks, Wills, Peters, and Harrys, in England, went down and were frozen so far as their names were concerned. If the original Tom could be exhumed from a block of frozen rubble, what a rush would be made from all quarters of the English-speaking globe—of the Tomsons, Thompsons, Thomassons, Thoms, and Tomkins—to have a look at the ancestor from whom they derive! He would be an object of greater interest than the red-haired, mummified, primeval Egyptian in the glass case in the British Museum. But actually all the Tomsons, Thompsons, Thomassons, Thoms, and Tomkins, do not descend from an unique Tom. There was no sole Tom

SIRE-NAMES

among men, the Adam from whose loins issued all these families that bear his name, as the rivers that watered the Garden of Eden issued from a single fount. There were Toms many dotted over the counties of England, who spawned in all directions about the same period, when the blast of fashion swept over the country and fixed them for all time as ancestors, bequeathing their name to generations yet unborn.

There was an ancestral Tom, of course, to every family of Tomson, Thompson, Thomasson, Thoms, and Tomkins, but not the same Tom to all. It would be highly instructive to be able to dig each out and study him scientifically. One may conjecture that he was a Tom of Titanic stature, of superhuman beauty, or of prodigious intellect, so that all his issue were eager to arrogate to themselves his name, and to insure that it should be known to all the world that they had sprung from him. Some, overcome with modesty, feeling their unworthiness to be ranked even as his sons, measuring their littleness against his greatness, were content to call themselves, and to be called, Tomkins or Tomlins, with a diminutive ending.

But in all probability the ancestral Tom was not more than a shrewd, worthy man, perhaps broader in beam, stronger in grip, louder in voice, more potent in swallowing tankards of ale, or could draw a straighter furrow, than any other ploughman in the hamlet; and his sons desired that his mantle might rest on them all, just as, in Memling's painting, that of St. Ursula envelops the 11,000 virgins that bear her company. The fashion or the need of having a to-name determined the adoption.

Among the Hebrews there were no family names. Joshua was the son of Nun, Caleb the son of Jephunneh, David the son of Jesse, Isaiah the son of Amos. Not till the reign of Joseph II., Emperor, were the Jews in Germany constrained to adopt surnames.

In the twelfth century was drawn up the Domesday Book of Iceland, recording the land-taking of all the early settlers, with their pedigrees. Not a single family name occurs, and to this day there does not exist a family name in the island

SIRE-NAMES

pertaining to a native. Every man is known by his personal designation, and as the son of his father.

When I returned from Iceland in 1861, on the boat with me was Eric Magnusson. He became a teacher of the Scandinavian languages and literature in Oxford, and there he was known as Mr. Magnusson. But his son, in Iceland, would not be Magnusson, but Eric's son; only if he remained in England would he be called Magnusson.

Among the Angles, Saxons, and Norsemen, the system of nomenclature was the same, and among ourselves the surnames Johnson, Thomson, Dickson, Wilson, and the like, are mainly Northumbrian in origin—that is to say, proceed from families in the land north of the Humber up to the Tweed; for this was largely colonized from Denmark, and patronymics clung to usage among them more than among the Anglo-Saxons. "A Cumberland deed of 1397 mentions Richard Thomson, showing the true patronymic as still used in Iceland. . . . Many more examples might be given from Yorkshire and Cumberland. It has been thought that the termination *son* is a mark of Scandinavian origin, and, without pressing this too far, it may be said that such surnames are more common in the old Danelaw than elsewhere."[1]

Among the Picts the descent was through the mother. Almost certainly the matriarchate indicates a low moral condition, such as did not exist among the Germanic and Scandinavian peoples.

The Welsh were very late in adopting patronymics as hereditary surnames. Some of the principal landowners did so in the reign of Henry VIII. by the King's desire, but the commonalty did not follow their example till much later. Every man among them was known by his Christian name, followed by *ap* and that of his father.

Cheese has thus been described as

"Adam's own cousin by its birth,
Ap Curd, ap Milk, ap Cow, ap Grass, ap Earth."

---

[1] Collingwood, "Scandinavian Britain," 1909.

SIRE-NAMES

M. A. Lower tells the following story: "An Englishman, riding one dark night among the mountains, heard a cry of distress proceeding from a man who had fallen into a ravine near the highway, and, on listening more attentively, he heard the words, 'Help, master, help!' in a voice truly Cambrian. 'Help! What are you?' inquired the traveller. 'Jenkin-ap-Griffith-ap-Robin-ap-William-ap-Rees-ap-Evan,' was the response. 'Lazy fellows that ye be,' replied the Englishman, setting spurs to his horse, 'to lie rolling in that hole, half a dozen of ye! Why, in the name of common sense, don't ye help one another out?'"

In 1387 Ladislas Jagellon, King of Poland and Duke of Lithuania, required all his subjects to be baptized. The men were divided for the purpose into two companies; those in the first were named Peter, those in the second Paul. In like manner the women were ranged in two batches; all in the first were christened under the name of Catherine, all in the second under that of Margaret. Conceive the bewilderment in a village when there were, let us say, a hundred Peters and as many Pauls! How difficult—nay, how impossible—it would have been in it to establish a case of breach of promise of marriage, when the gay defaulter could dive in and out among the Catherines and Margarets, and perplex a Judge's mind past drawing a conclusion of guilt! It would be absolutely, imperiously necessary for all the Peters and Pauls to assume each a surname for the purpose of identification. Indeed, it would be necessary for the Prince to insist upon it, otherwise what evasion and subterfuge would be resorted to in order to escape taxation or shirk military duty!

To the present day, in the western hills of Yorkshire, the people know themselves, and are known among their comrades, by their descent. A man is John a' Jake's a' Hal's, and a woman is Mary a' Tom's a' Bill's. Should there have been a moral slip, it is not forgotten; it is duly represented as Joe a' Tom's a' Katie's. The people employ their surnames for registration alone, and, were it not for being enrolled at school, most children would be ignorant of the fact that they

SIRE-NAMES

possessed a surname. Indeed, it would seem that the people themselves a few generations ago had none, and arbitrarily assumed any that entered their heads when it came to the matter of a marriage or a christening. At Hebden Bridge nearly everyone called himself Greenwood.

Masses of rock, angular and rugged, that have fallen into a torrent, by the time that they have reached the plain have lost their asperities, and have been converted into smooth and rounded pebbles.

Names also, since their first adoption, have been abraded almost past recognition in rolling down the stream of time, before they became fixed in registers and legal documents.

1. A sire-name is simple enough when it is plain Thomson, Tompson, Johnson, Jackson, Wilson, and the like. But even here there has been some loss, for the original form was Thomas-his-son, John-his-son, William-his-son. The pronoun has been elided, and even the 's of the genitive case in some cases, as Williamson.

2. A further abbreviation took place when the *son* fell away, and the name remained as Thoms, Johns, Jacks, or Wills. Here the mark of the genitive case remained. But where the employment of the final s was uneuphonious, because the paternal name ended in that letter, and a duplication of it would be intolerable to the ear, it was dropped. Thus we have Francis, Denys, James, Charles, Nicholas, in place of Franciss, Deniss, Jamess, Charless, Nicholass.

3. A termination expressive of sonship or descent, in use among the Anglo-Saxons and Scandinavians, was *ing*. In the pedigree of the West Saxon Kings it is used systematically. Edgar is Edmunding, Edmund is Edwarding, Edward is Alfreding, Alfred is Alfwolding, and so on. But *ing* was also broadly applied, much as O' in Irish and "the son of" in Scripture, to signify descent from an ancestor more remote than an immediate parent. Moreover, we cannot assure ourselves that all names that end in *ing* are patronymics, for the same termination is employed in a variety of ways, as shall be shown in another chapter.

SIRE-NAMES

4. *Ap*, as already stated, signifies "the son of" in Welsh. It is a contraction of *Mab*. This has gone through corruption, in being anglicized, as Prodger for Ap Roger, Bowen for Ap Owen, Beaven for Ap Ewan.

5. *Mac* or *Mc* in Scotland stands for "the son of," and is the Gaelic form of the Brythonic *Map*. It is applied to clansmen, although not necessarily blood relations of the chief. *McAlister* is the son of Alexander, *MacCheyne* or *MacShane* is the son of John, *Macgrath* or *Macreath* is the Weaver's son, *Macdermot* is the son of Diarmidh, *MacPherson* is the Parson's son.

6. *O'* has much the same significance among the Irish as has *Mac*. But it is employed as grandfather, or some remoter progenitor. It was said:

"Per Mac atque O, tu veros cognoscis Hibernos.
His duobus demptis, nullus Hibernus adest."

That may be rendered:

"By Mac and O you the Irishman may always know.
Take both away and no Irishman remains."

7. Another word for "son" is the Norman-French *Fitz*, for *fils*. When Henry I. desired to marry the wealthy heiress of the Baron FitzHamon to his illegitimate son, Robert of Gloucester, she scornfully replied:

"It were to me a mighty shame
To have a lord withouten his two name."

Thereupon Henry gave him the sur or sire name of Fitzroy.

The Duke of Berwick was named *FitzJames* as being the illegitimate son of James II. The Duke of Grafton is *Fitzroy*, as descended from a bastard of Charles II. by Nell Gwynn.

But *Fitz* by no means originally indicated bastardy. We find in the Roll of Battle Abbey and in Domesday a considerable number of Normans who were known only as Fitz this or that, and these did not acquire an hereditary surname till a long time after. Godric de Clairfait, supposed to have been the son of Ketilbern or Chatelber, named in Domesday, lived in Yorkshire during the reign of Henry I. His son

SIRE-NAMES

called himself William FitzGodric, and William's son designated himself William FitzWilliam. Next came a Thomas FitzWilliam, and then a William FitzThomas, and so on till the latter part of the fourteenth century, when a Sir John called himself FitzWilliam, and settled that this name should be hereditary.

Some—I may say almost all—personal names have gone through sad corruption. I need here only instance Batt for Bartholomew, Taffy for David, Kitt for Christopher, Bill for William.

These corrupted personal names have been taken up into the composition of family names.

Herodotus informs us that in Scythia existed a people addicted to eating their parents. When a father became venerable he was set to climb a tree, and made to hang on to a branch. The children then shook the trunk, and if the parent clung successfully he was pronounced to be not fully ripe. If, however, he dropped, his offspring considered him to be in prime condition, and devoured him with avidity. It was regarded as the highest compliment that could be paid to him, to be devoured, for it showed an appreciation of his qualities, mental, moral, and physical, in which his children desired to participate, and that could only be acquired in the manner described. This is no fable of the Father of History.

On the same principle all cannibal races devour their enemies. The most heroic and able-bodied foe is esteemed the choicest morsel. Lunholtz says of the Queenslanders of Australia that they are cannibals. "The most delicate portion is the fat about the kidneys. By eating this they believe that they acquire a portion of the strength of the person slain, and, so far as I could understand, this was even more true of the kidneys themselves; for, according to a widespread Australian belief, the kidneys are the centre of life."

In South Guinea the natives devour by preference the brain of some highly respected member of their own tribe, in order to acquire his admirable qualities. Indeed, the

SIRE-NAMES

more gifted in every way a man is, the more eagerly are eyes fixed on him, and mouths water to enjoy him as a meal. The custom assumes an even more repulsive form when the deceased man's relatives consume the maggots bred out of his decaying body. To them these maggots appear to be the life of the dead man escaping from his carcass in another form, and by this means they are able to possess themselves of his estimable qualities in a concentrated extract.

With this practice is closely associated the horrible custom of pressing out and swallowing the moisture of the mouldering corpse. This custom is by no means rare among the natives of the East Indian Archipelago, of Western Africa, and of North-Eastern Brazil. Among the Indians of North-West America exists a class of *hametses*, or medicine-men, held in high esteem. To become one of the number requires long preparation—as long as four years. Part of the ceremony of investiture consists in biting pieces of flesh out of living members of the tribe. Jacobson says: "The hamets's highest privilege consists in his right to feed on the corpses of his dead associates, since his mere partaking of these meals raises him in the opinion of his fellow-tribesmen to the highest pinnacle of worth and holiness. In the deep recesses of the forest the hametses gather together for their cannibal banquet, which no outsider may approach, and at which they produce a body from either one of the wooden boxes suspended to the trees, or from one of the raised wooden platforms where it has been dried by the action of the wind Then they soften this mummified corpse in water, after which they bite off and swallow large pieces of this loathsome fare. When the bodies are old enough—that is, belong to persons who have been dead at least one or two years—such food appears to be not unwholesome. On the other hand, it has repeatedly happened that hametses have died of blood-poisoning."

A less revolting method of acquiring the virtues and abilities of the deceased is practised in one part of New Guinea. A redoubted chief who has fallen is placed in a bed of chalk and left to decay therein, and the chalk imbibes

SIRE-NAMES

the moisture that distils from the body. When thoroughly saturated, the chalk is used by the natives to rub into their foreheads, under the impression that in this way the soul of the departed warrior will pass into their own brain-pans.

An Icelandic saga relates a story of one Bodvar at the Court of Rolf Krake. He there saw a poor timid boy who was brutally ill-treated by the King's bodyguard. He took compassion on him, and gave him to drink of the blood of a redoubted enemy. Thereby the frightened lad was transformed into a daring warrior.

Gilbert's ballad, " The Yarn of the *Nancy Bell*," may be recalled. I give some verses to relieve a subject that is gruesome and unsavoury :

> "'Twas on the shores that round our coast
> From Deal to Ramsgate span,
> That I found alone on a piece of stone
> An elderly naval man."

And this man ever murmured:

> "' Oh, I am a cook and a captain bold,
> And the mate of the *Nancy* brig,
> And a bo'sun tight, and a midshipmite,
> And the crew of the captain's gig.'
>
> "' Oh, elderly man, it's little I know
> Of the duties of men of the sea;
> But I'll eat my head if I understand
> However you can be
>
> "' At once a cook and a captain bold,
> And the mate of the *Nancy* brig,
> And a bo'sun tight, and a midshipmite,
> And the crew of the captain's gig.'"

The elderly man explains that the good ship *Nancy Bell* sailed to the Indian Sea, but ran on a reef and was wrecked. Whereupon the ten survivors escaped in a boat :

> "' For a month we'd neither wittles nor drink,
> Till a-hungry we did feel;
> So we drawed a lot, and accordin' shot
> The captain for our meal.'"

SIRE-NAMES

Next to be eaten were the mate and the midshipman.

> "'And then we murdered the bo'sun tight,
> And he much resembled pig;
> Then we wittled free, did the cook and me,
> On the crew of the captain's gig.'"

Then all left were the elderly man and the cook, who contended amicably as to which was to eat the other.

> "Says he: 'Dear James, to murder me
> Were a foolish thing to do;
> For don't you see that you can't cook me,
> While I can, and will, cook you.'"

So he filled a copper and put in the necessary ingredients.

> "'And he stirred it round and round and round,
> And he sniffed at the foaming froth;
> When I ups with his heels and smothers his squeals
> In the scum of the boiling broth.

> "'And I eat that cook in a week or two,
> And, as I eating be
> The last of his chops, why I almost drops,
> For a wessel in sight I see.

> "'And I never larf, and I never smile,
> And I never lark nor play;
> But sit and croak, and a single joke
> I have, which is to say:

> 'Oh, I am a cook and a captain bold,
> And the mate of the *Nancy* brig,
> And a bo'sun tight, and a midshipmite,
> And the crew of the captain's gig.'"

What is Gilbert's nonsense is to the unsophisticated man sheer common sense. He desires to sum in himself the personal beauty of A, the success in *affaires de cœur* of B, the eloquence in a pow-wow of C, the heroism in war of D, and the acquisitiveness in scalps or skulls of E; and accordingly he eats A, B, C, D, and E, fondly supposing that he has thereby concentrated all their abilities and luck and good looks in himself. On the Congo, if a native has his hair cut, he eats what has been shorn, lest another man, possessing

SIRE-NAMES

himself of it and consuming it, should absorb therewith his power.

Among primitive peoples a man's name is regarded as of the highest importance; it not merely belongs to him, but it is to some extent inseparable from him. He who gets hold of his name acquires a powerful but undefined control over the man himself. So strongly is this felt that the name is kept concealed from enemies; it is never uttered. He is spoken of by a nickname; he is alluded to in an oblique manner. His true name is kept from all but his nearest of kin. Just as a savage is afraid of having his portrait taken, lest by this means the artist should obtain control over him, so does he shrink from allowing any person to get hold of his real name.

The medieval witch made a figure of wax, called over it the name of a person she sought to injure, and then stabbed it with needles, inflicting thereby on the person in whose name the figure was moulded the most excruciating pains. Into the Cursing Well of St. Elian, in North Wales, till the end of the eighteenth century, were dropped pieces of lead inscribed with the names of such individuals as the envious and malignant sought to destroy; and so strong was the conviction that by so doing sickness and death were produced, that those who believed that their names had been so plunged would have recourse to the keeper of the well, and bribe him to draw their names out.

In the folk-tale of Rumpelstiltskin we have preserved the universal belief that, if a person's name became known, his power was broken.

By incantation with the name of a demon, the necromancer obtained control over that devil, and was able to convert him into a veritable lackey. By invocation of a saint by name, that saint is almost compelled to listen to and answer the prayer put up.

We have seen how costume and the tartan took the place of disfigurement and tattoo. In like manner the use of a man's name took the place of eating him. By the application to another of the name of an ancestor or of a hero, that

SIRE-NAMES

other became a possessor of the qualities of him whose name he bore. But this is not all. Among many primitive peoples exists the belief in reincarnation. After death the soul escapes to the spirit-world, where for a while it leads a flighty and vacuous existence, and then returns to earth into a fruit, a herb, or a fungus.

Should a man eat of any one of these in which is lodged the spirit of the departed, the spirit lies latent in him till his next son is born, when it is reincarnate in the child. Should a beast devour the disguised soul, there is still hope for it if that beast be a wild-pig or a deer; for should a hunter kill it and eat the flesh, he absorbs into his system the ancient soul, which will come to new birth in his next offspring. But should the spirit in its vegetable envelope perish uneaten, the soul within it is extinguished for ever.

The system is open to objections, as savage men readily perceived. For either by this means all the brilliant qualities of an ancestor might be totally lost to the family, or else pass into the possession of a warrior of a hostile tribe, who had chanced to consume the imprisoned spirit. And no perspicuity would avail a man to distinguish the dear lineaments or admired moral qualities of a parent when hidden in a banana or a potato. He accordingly puzzled his brains to discover a remedy. This he found by securing the name of the deceased and applying it to his son or grandson. By laying hold of either the name or the shadow of a man, that man was secured soul and body by the captor, as certainly as you master a monkey by laying hold of his tail, or a cat by clinging to the scruff of his neck. The shadow was of a nature too elusive to be caught; moreover, that of a full-grown man would hardly accommodate itself to a new-born infant. But with the name it was otherwise, and by imposing that of a heroic ancestor on a child the child became his reincarnation, and acquired all his qualities as surely as if that ancestor had been distilled into its feeding-bottle.

The name of the father was not given to a son unless it were posthumous; that was an invariable rule, for naturally enough no parent chose, whilst alive, to transmit his identity

SIRE-NAMES

to his child, and himself thereby fall back into nonentity. The rule was strictly observed among the Scandinavians, even after they had emerged from a condition of belief in the transmigration of souls.

However absurd these convictions and practices may seem to us, they were matters of serious belief and conduct among primitive peoples, and even after our forefathers became Christians traces of them remain.

It will be remembered with what astonishment the relatives of Zachariah and Elizabeth heard that the name of the child was to be John. " They said unto her [Elizabeth], There is none of thy kindred that is called by this name."

One spring night in 1024 a boy was born to Olaf Haraldsson, King of Norway. It was so frail in appearance, and seemed so likely to die, that the priest, Sighvat, hastened to baptize it—without holding communication with the King, who had left strict injunctions not to be disturbed in his sleep. Beating about for a name, the thought of Charlemagne occurred to him, and he christened the child Magnus. This name had not been previously employed in Scandinavia. Next day Olaf heard of the event, and was furious. He asked Sighvat how he had dared to christen the boy without consulting him, and to give him such an outlandish name. The priest told him his reason, that he had called the infant after the greatest of all Emperors. Then Olaf was pleased, for he thought that the luck in war, and genius, and spirit, of the great Charlemagne would follow the name and adhere to his son.

This feeling, in a modified form, exists among us still. When John Jobson calls his son Percy, he trusts that some of the radiance of the great Northumbrian house will surround the boy, and that any flashes of petulance he may exhibit will be attributed to a spiritual filiation from Hotspur.

We like to name a child after some honoured member of the family long ago passed to the majority, with a hope that he may resemble him. And I have heard it often remarked, as something more than a coincidence, that a resemblance in features or in character does go along with the name. In

SIRE-NAMES

my own family I called one of my daughters Diana Amelia, after my grandmother, and she, and she alone among my fourteen children, resembled her, to a remarkable degree, in face. I named a son William Drake, after my grandfather's grandfather, whose portrait hangs in our dining-room. And it has been repeatedly noticed how curiously my son resembles his namesake of the eighteenth century. I was visiting a friend, and saw in his hall a portrait, as I supposed, of his wife. I remarked to him what an excellent likeness it was. He replied laughingly: "That is the picture of her great-great-grandmother, and, curiously enough, she bears the same Christian name. Moreover, none of her sisters in the slightest degree resemble the old lady."

One of my daughters, named Margaret, was so called after the daughter of the before-mentioned William Drake Gould. One night, at a ball in North Devon, my daughter was dancing with a gentleman whom she had not previously met, when he said abruptly: "How like you are to your great-great-grandmother!"

"Why," said my daughter, "did you ever meet her? I think you can be hardly old enough for that."

"No," he replied, "but I have her portrait in my house, and you really look to me as though you were she who had stepped out of the frame to dance with me this evening."

Of course these are coincidences, and coincidences only; but such coincidences may have occurred in other families, and have helped to confirm the supposition that the giving a name to a child conveys to that child a something—a likeness in face or in character to the individual after whom it is called.

Among Roman Catholics the name of a saint is conferred on an infant, and it is devoutly held that thenceforth the saint takes particular care of his or her namesake, is its patron, protector, and advocate. When a Pope, on his elevation to the chair of St. Peter, adopts a name, it is that of a predecessor whose policy he purposes following, and whose spirit he trusts will rest upon him. It was so with the present Pope, Pius X., who desired with the name to

SIRE-NAMES

tread in the footsteps of that most obscurantist and retrogressive of all Popes, Pius IX.

The princely family of Reuss has long laid great stress on the name Henry. The first so called died in the year 1162. Henry II. had three sons, every one named Henry. Without a break the line of Henrys has continued to the present day. Henry XVI. had three sons; each was a Henry. Of one branch of the family, Henry LV. died without issue in 1636. Henry XLII. of another line had three sons; each was a Henry. Of the junior Reuss line, Henry LXXIII. died in 1855; of the elder line, Henry LXIX. was born in 1792; of another branch Henry LXXIV. was born in 1856. In fact, in this family, in all its branches, every son is baptized Henry. Since 1162 there have been in the Reuss family over 168 Henrys, and not a single son bearing another Christian name. Surely it must be held that fortune and continuance in the Reuss family depend on its male representatives being every one a Henry.

The idea that lay at the root of taking the name of a grandfather or of a more remote ancestor was long forgotten when patronymics became hereditary, but a custom survives the reason why adopted. The first step after the eating of a grandparent had become an antiquated custom was the assumption of the grandfather's name. This was when personal names were single. If not that of a grandfather, then that of an heroic ancestor, who became thereby reincarnate in the child, or, if not actually reincarnate, contributed with his name some of his qualities to the child.

That some names are fortunate, others ill-omened—"fausta nomina," as Tacitus calls the former—has always been held. After the murder of Prince Arthur by King John, for long no Arthurs occur among English Christian names.

"'Now, my dear brother,' said Mr. Shandy, 'had my child arrived safe into the world, unmartyred in that precious part of him—fanciful and extravagant as I may appear to the world in my opinion of Christian names and of that magic bias which good or bad names irresistibly impress upon our characters and conducts—Heaven is witness that

SIRE-NAMES

in the warmest transports of my wishes for the prosperity of my child I never once wished to crown his head with more glory and honour than what George or Edward would have spread around it. But, alas! as the greatest evil has befallen him—I must counteract and undo it with the greatest good. He shall be christened *Trismegistus*, brother.' 'I wish it may answer,' replied my uncle Toby, rising up."[1]

The practice of reproducing a favourite name in a family lasted for many generations after the idea of reincarnation had been abandoned. The father's or the grandfather's name was given to the child out of affection to the former possessor, and perhaps for no other reason; but it continued to be given. In my own family there has been an almost unbroken chain of Edwards from the beginning of the seventeenth century.

It is quite possible that, when the patronymic of Thomson, for instance, was adopted as hereditary, it was not that those who assumed it were the actual sons of Thomas, but that they regarded Thomas as the prevailing and dominant name in their family. They may have been sons of a John, son of Thomas, but had acquired a poor opinion of the abilities and character of their parent. He may have outlived his vigour, and the infirmities of temper or body may have become vexatious to his offspring, and as their estimation of their father went down, that of Thomas, their grandfather, went up; and when it came to the adoption of a patronymic as a fixture, they elected to be known, and their posterity to be known, as Thomsons instead of Johnsons.

I will now subjoin a list, not by any means exhaustive, of the Christian names of men that have been adopted in the formation of patronymics, many of them in a so contracted and corrupted form as at first glance to be unrecognizable:

ADAM; whence come *Adams, Adamson, Adye, Adcock, Addyman* (servant of Adam), *Addison, Adkins, Atkinson*.

AGILWARD; whence come *Aylward, Allardson, Alardice, Alward*.

[1] "Tristram Shandy," 1760, iv., p. 8.

SIRE-NAMES

AILBRED; whence come *Aubrey, Aubrison, Brison* (if not from Brice).

ALAN; whence come *Alanson, Hallet* (or from Hal—Henry), *Alkin* (when not from Elias), Allen.

ALDRED; whence comes *Alderson.*

ALEXANDER; whence come *Saunderson, Saunders, Alkey, Sandercock, McAlister, Palister* (ap Alister).

ANDREW; whence come *Anderson, Anson, Andrews, Henderson, Henson, Anderton.*

ANTHONY; whence come *Tonson, Tennison* (or from Dennis), *Townson, Tonkins, Toney, Tonks.*

ANSELM; whence come *Ansell* (or from Ancelot, contraction of Lancelot).

ARCHIBALD; whence come *Archison, Aicheson, Balderson, Archbutt.*

ARTHUR; whence come *Atty, McArthur, Barth* (ap Arthur), but not always.

BALDWIN; whence come *Balderson* (or from Archibald), *Bawson, Body, Budd, Baldock, Bodkin, Bawcock, Bawkin, Bawden.*

BARNABAS; whence come *Burnaby, Barnby, Abby;* but *Barnby* is also a place-name.

BARTHOLOMEW; whence come *Bartlett, Letts, Letson, Batts, Bates, Battey, Batson, Bettison, Badcock, Bartle, Tolley, Tolson, Bartley.*

BENEDICT; whence come *Bennett, Benson, Bennie, Benn, Bennetson, Benison.*

BENJAMIN; whence come, perhaps, some of the above; but Benjamin was never as favourite a name as Benedict.

BERNARD; whence come *Bernardson, Burnard, Barnes,* possibly.

BRICE; whence come *Bryson, Bryce,* but generally for Ap Rice.

CÆSAR; whence come *Keysar, Cayzer.*

CHARLES; whence come *Charley, Caroll, O'Caroll* (or from Cearbhoil), *Kelson* (but Kelson may come from Nicholson).

CHRISTOPHER; whence come *Christopherson, Christison, Christie, Kitts, Kitson, Keates, Kitto.*

SIRE-NAMES

CLEMENT; whence come *Clements, Clemo, Clemson, Climpson, Clymo.*

CONSTANTINE; whence come *Custance, Cust, Custerson, Custison, Cossentine.*

CRISPIN; whence come *Cripps, Crisp, Crespin.*

CUTHBERT; whence come *Cuthbertson, Cutbeard, Cutts, Hubbard, Cobbet, Cobett, Crewdson* (with an intrusive *r*).

DAVID; whence come *Davidson, Dayson, Davis, Davies, Davey, Dawe, Dawkins, Dawes, Davidge, Duffy, Dakins, Davitt, Dawson, Dawkes, Dowson.*

DANIEL; whence come *Dancet, Dance, Danson, Tancock.*

DENNIS; whence come *Dennison, Tennyson* (or from Anthony's son), *Denson, Dyson, Denny, Dyatt, Dyett.*

DIGORY; whence come *Digges, Diggins, Dickens* (when not from Dick), *Digginson, Dickenson, Dickory, Diggman.*

DODA (old Saxon); whence come *Dodds, Dodson, Dodd.*

DONALD; whence come *Donaldson, Donkin.*

EDWARD; whence come *Edwardes, Edkins, Edes, Beddoe* (ap Edward), *Eddison.*

EDMUND; whence come *Edmunds, Edmundson, Emson, Empson.*

EDWIN; whence come *Winson, Winston.*

ELIAS; whence come *Ellis, Ellison, Elliot, Elliotson, Ellet, Elkins, Ellicock, Elliott, Eales, Eeles.*

EUSTACE; whence come *Stace, Stacey.*

FRANCIS; whence come *Franks, Franson.*

FULK; whence come *Fookes, Fawkes, Vaux* (when not from De Vaux), *Faucett, Fawson, Vokes, Foulkes,* sometimes *Fox.*

GABRIEL; whence come *Gabb, Gabell, Gabelson, Gable.*

GEOFREY; whence come *Jeffson, Jefferson, Jeffs, Jeffries, Jepson, Jefcock, Goff, Guthrie.*

GEORGE; whence come *Georges, Jorris,* perhaps *Jury, Jorrock.*

GERARD; whence come *Garrod, Garrett, Garrick, Jarred, Jerold, Jarratt.*

GILBERT; whence come *Gilbertson, Gibson, Gibbs, Gibbings, Gibbon, Gilbard, Gilpin* (from Gibb-kin).

SIRE-NAMES

GILES; whence come *Gilson, Gillot, Gillett, Gilcock, Jelly, Jellicock.*

GODBERT; whence come *Gotobed, Gobbett,* perhaps, or from Godbald.

GODARD (GOTHARD); whence comes *Goddard.*

GODBER; whence comes *Goodyear.*

GODESCHALK; whence come *Goodchild, Godshall.*

GODFREY; whence come *Godkin, Goad, Freyson.*

GODRICK; whence come *Goodrich, Godrich, Goodridge.*

GODWIN[1]; whence come *Goodwin, Godden, Godding, Godon.*

GREGORY; whence come *Gregson, Greyson, Gregg, Griggs, Gresson.*

GUTHLAC; whence come *Goodlake, Goodluck.*

HALBERT; whence come *Hobbie* (see "The Black Dwarf"), *Hobbs, Hobson.*

HAMON or AYMON; whence come *Hamond, Hampson, Hammett, Hammick,* also as diminutive *Hamlyn, Hamley.*

HENRY; whence come *Harrison, Harris, Hawson, Hawkins, Halse, Hawes, Hallet, Halket, Hacket, Allcock, Parry, Harriman* (servant of Harry), *Hall.*

HILARY; whence come *Larkins, Hilson.*

HUBERT; whence comes *Hubbard.*

HUGH; whence come *Hughes, Hewson, Pugh, Hutchins, Huggins, Hodgkins, Hoskinson, Higgins, Hickes, Hickson, Higginson, Hewett, Howett, Hudson, Higman.*

ISAAC; whence come *Isaacson,* and possibly *Hicks, Higgs, Higgins.* However, Langland writes of "Hikke, the hackneyman, and Hugh, the nedlere."

IVO and IVAR; whence come *Ivison, Ivers, MacIver.*

JAMES; whence come *Jameson, Jimson, Jeames, Jacox, Jacks, Jaques, Jackson, Jacobs, Jacobson, Jimpson, Cobb.*

JOB; whence come *Jobson, Jope, Jopling* (unless from Jublains), *Jupp.*

---

[1] Many of our surnames beginning with "Good" come from the Anglo-Saxon name beginning with "God." *Goodchild* is Godeschild (the shield of God), or else a Godchild; *Goodbody* is God's bothie or habitation; *Gattacre* is really God's acre; *Goodfellow* is God's fellow or friend.

SIRE-NAMES

JOEL; whence come *Joule, Jowle, Yole* (a Norman form was Judual), *Jewel.*

JOHN; whence come *Johnson, Jonson, Jenkins, Evans, Heavens, Jennings, Hanson, Hancock, Bevan, Hawkinson, Ians, Jevons, Joynes.*

JORDAN; whence come *Judd, Judson, Juxon* (or else from Jude), *Judkin, Jukes.*

JOSEPH; whence come *Josephs, Joskin, Jose, Jephson, Jessop* (Giuseppe).

JUDE; whence come *Judd, Judson.* See above under "Jordan."

JULIAN; whence come *Jolland, Jillson, Golland, Jule, Gilson.*

KENNETH; whence come *Kennedy* and *McKenzie.*

LAMBERT; whence come *Lampson, Lambkin, Lambett* (whence *Labett*), *Lampert.*

LAURENCE; whence come *Larkin, Lawes, Law, Laurie, Ranely, Lawson.*

LUKE; whence come *Lukis, Lukin, Luxon, Lukitt, Locock.*

LEVI; whence come *Levison, Lawson, Lewson, Leeson, Lewis,* as if for Louis.

MAGNUS; whence comes *Manson.*

MARK; whence come *Marks, Marson, Markin, Marcock, Marcheson, Marcet.*

MATTHEW; whence come *Matheson, Mathews, Matson, Maddison, Mahew* (French Maheu), *May,* for *Maheu, Matkin, Makin.*

MAURICE; whence come *Morris, Morrison, Mawson, Moxon, Morson, Morse.*

MICHAEL; whence come *Mitchell, Mitcheson, Kilson.*

MILO; whence come *Miles, Milson, Millet, Milsom* ("som" for "son").

NICHOLAS; whence come *Nichols, Nicholson, Nixon, Coles, Collis, Collison, Collins, Colson, Collin, Collett, Close, Clowes, Glascock.*

NIGEL; whence come *Neale, Neilson, Nelson, O'Neil, McNeal, Nihill.*

OLIVER; whence come *Nollikins, Knollys, Knowles.*

SIRE-NAMES

OSBALD, OSBERT, OSBORN, OSMUND, all have their modern representatives in surnames.

OWEN ; whence comes *Bowen.*

PATRICK ; whence come *Patrickson, Padson, Pattison, Gilpatrick, Kilpatrick, Patterson, Patton, Patey, Petherick, Pethick.* But these two last from PETROC.

PAUL ; whence come *Paull, Paulson, Powlson, Pawson, Porson, Paulett, Powlett, Palk* (for Paulkin).

PETER ; whence come *Peterson, Peters, Pierson, Pierce, Perks, Perkins, Purkis, Parkinson, Parr, Parsons, Perrin, Perrot, Pether, Peer.*[1]

PHILIP; whence come *Phillips, Philipson, Phipson, Phipps, Lipson, Lipton, Filson, Philpott, Phillpots, Philkin, Phippen.*

RALPH ; whence come *Rawlins, Rawlinson, Rowe, Rapson, Rawson, Raffson, Rawes, Rolfe, Rawkins, Rawle, Rolle, Roley.*

RANDOLF ; whence come *Randals, Ranson, Rankin, Randall.*

REGINALD ; whence come *Reynolds, Reynell, Rennell, Rennie, Renson.*

REGINHARD (REYNARD); whence come *Reynard, Reynardson, Reyner, Reynerson.*

RICHARD ; whence come *Richards, Richardson, Dicks, Dixie, Dickson, Dixon, Dickens* (when not from Digory), *Dickenson, Hitchens, Hitchcock, Pritchard* (ap Richard), *Rickards, Ricketts, Rickson.*

ROBERT: whence come *Robbins, Robertson, Robson, Dobbs, Dobson, Dobie, Hobbs, Hobson, Hopkins, Roberts, Robartes, Hopkinson, Probert* (ap Robert), *Probyn* (ap Robin), *Hobbins, Hobbes.*

ROGER; whence come *Rogers, Rogerson, Hodge, Hodges, Hodgson, Hodgkins, Hosking, Hoskinson, Hodgman, Dodge, Prodger, Dodson, Dudgeon.*

ROLAND and ROLLO ; whence come *Rowlandson, Rollson, Rowlett, Rolle, Rawlins, Rawlinson.*

RUDOLF ; whence come *Rudall, Ruddle, Rolf.*

SAMSON ; whence come *Sampson, Sansom, Samms.*

SAMUEL ; whence come *Samuelson, Samwell, Smollett.*

[1] In the *Guardian,* No. 82, p. 1713, is a memoir of William Peer, the actor, who died of a broken heart because he was growing fat.

SIRE-NAMES

SEBRIGHT (for Sigbert); whence comes *Seabright.*
SERLO; whence come *Searle, Serell, Sarell, Serlson.*
SIBALD; whence come *Sibbald, Sibbaldson, Sibbson.*
SIMON; whence come *Simonds, Symonds, Simmens, Sims, Symes, Simson, Simpkin, Simkinson, Simcoe, Simcox.*
SIWARD and SIGGEIR; whence come *Seaward, Seward, Sayer, Seager, Secker, Sears, Sugar, Siggers, Syer.*
SOLOMON; whence come *Salman, Salmon, Sammonds.*
STEPHEN; whence come *Stephens, Stevens, Stephenson, Stevenson, Stimson, Stibbs, Stebbing, Stepkin, Stiff.*
SWEYN; whence come *Swaine, Swanson, Swinson, Swaynson.*
THEOBALD; whence come *Tibbald, Tibbs, Tippet, Tipkin, Tebbets.*
THEODORIC; whence come *Theed, Terry.*
THOMAS; whence come *Thoms, Toms, Thompson, Tompson, Tomson, Tomlyn, Tomlinson, Tomkin, Tomkinson, Thompsett, Tombling, Tapson, Tapling.*
THOROLD; whence come *Thoroldson, Tyrell, Terrell.*
THURGOD; whence come *Thoroughgood, Toogood, Tuggett.*
THURKELL; whence come *Thurrel, Thurkill;* in some cases *Killson.*
TIMOTHY; whence come *Timms, Timbs, Timson, Timmins, Timcock.*
TOBIT; whence come *Tubbes, Betson, Beatson, Tobyn, Tobey* (changed to *Sobey*).
WALERAN; whence comes *Walrond.*
WALTER; whence come *Walters, Watts, Watson, Watkins, Vautier, Goodyear* (from French Gautier), *Waterson, Watkinson.*
WARIN (for Guarin); whence come *Warren, Waring, Warison, Warson.*
WILLIAM; whence come *Williams, Williamson, Wilson, Wills, Wilkins, Wylie, Willett, Gillott, Wellings, Bill, Bilson.*
WUNEBALD; whence comes *Wimbold.*

To this list of patronymics must be added one of metronymics. These naturally lead us to suspect that such as bore their mothers' names, and not those of their fathers, were

SIRE-NAMES

baseborn; and although, no doubt, this is so in a good number of cases, yet it is not invariably so. Sweyn, King of Denmark, was called Estrithson, after his mother, who was the sister of Canute the Great, though married to Earl Ulf, because it was through her that he obtained his right to the throne. In a good many instances the metronymic name was taken in like manner, because the mother was of higher birth than the father, and through her the son inherited some land. Henry II. was entitled FitzEmpress because through her he had his claim to the throne of England. The mother, again, may have been a widow, and the son born after the death of his father. It seems hardly credible that a man should accept and transmit to his descendants a name proclaiming his bastardy, unless it were unavoidable. It is true that among the Normans no idea of disgrace attached to bastardy, but surnames were not assumed by the generality of the people till long after the Conquest, when opinion on this matter had become more healthy.

Again, it is often a mistake to assume that the name proclaims illegitimacy because it derives, apparently, from a female, for many personal names had a male as well as a female form, as Julian. Only in the eighteenth century did the name become Juliana in the feminine. *Gilson* may well be the son of a male Julian. There was a Jocosus as well as a Jocosa, a Joyeux as well as a Joyeuse, to furnish the family name of *Joyce*. *Letson* and *Letts* are not necessarily descended from Læticia or Lettice, as shall be shown presently. Nor are *Nelsons* the illegitimate sons of a Nelly, but the legitimate offspring of Nigel.

Mr. Bardsley gives a long list of metronymics, which, if accepted, point to a state of demoralization in England, at the time when surnames were assumed, that is truly appalling; not only so, but to the indifference English people showed to being proclaimed bastards, and to handing on such a name to the end of time, to children yet unborn. I do not, however, believe that there was such a condition of affairs as would be implied were we to accept Mr. Bardsley's list. I will give some of what he calls metronymics, and shall, I

SIRE-NAMES

trust, be able to show that in a good many cases he has misinterpreted them :

Allison, son of Alice. I would say, of Alexander.
Amelot, Amye, Aimes, son of Amy. Why not of Amias ?
Anson, son of Anne. I suppose same as Hanson, son of John, or may be of Anthony. But *Annott* may indicate bastardy.
Aplin, son of Apolonia. It is the same as *Ablin,* from *Abel.*
Ansty, Anstice, from Anastasia. Anastasius was a man's name.
Aveling, son of Evelina. But it may stand for Abeling, diminutive of Abel.
Avis, Avison, son of Avicia.
Awdrey and *Audrey,* son of Ethelreda. But why may not the name of St. Ethelreda have been assumed by some resident in the Isle of Ely, out of devotion to the saint ?
Babb and *Barbe,* for Barbara. Possibly enough, rather from St. Barbe, a Norman place-name.
Beaton, Bettison, Betts, Betson, Beatie, etc., the illegitimate issue of a Beatrice. *Beaton* is from Bethune ; so *Beatie* and *Betts* and *Betson* are mere softenings of Batt and Batson, for Bartholomew.
Bell, Bellot, Bellison, Izod, Ibbott, Ebbott, Bibby, Ibsen, Empson, Epps, Isbel, Libby, Nibbs, Knibb, are all supposed to represent the offspring of Isabella or Isolt, its diminutive. *Bell* and *Bellot* may more probably come from the shop or tavern sign.
Cass, the son of Cassandra. It is another form of *Case.*
Catlin, from Catherine, a North Country form.
Cecil, the illegitimate son of Cicely. Probably a place-name—Chessel, in Essex.
Claridge, son of Clarice.
Custance, Cosens, Custeson, sons of Constance. It is true that Chaucer uses Custance and Constance as forms of the same name, but *Custance* actually stands for Coûtance.
Deuce, son of Dionisia. The name, which is common in Yorkshire, is also spelled Dewis, and means son of Dewi or David.

SIRE-NAMES

Dowse and *Dowson*, from Dulcitia. Probably same as *Dewis* and *Dawson*.

Dye, Dyson, Dyot, Dight, all from Dionisia, just as rightly derive from Dennis or Dionis.

Eames, Emmott, Imeson, Empson, from a mother Emma. *Eames* is a maternal uncle; *Empson*, a cousin through the mother's uncle.

Ede, Eden, Eade, Eddison, Etty, from a feminine name Eade. But why not from Edward, contracted to Eddy? There is also a place-name Ide, pronounced Ede, near Exeter.

Elwes, the son of Heloise. Quite as likely, son of Aldwy.

Eves, Eave, Eveson, Evett, sons of Eve. Why not of Ivo?

Florance, Florry, and *Flurry*, sons of Florence. Florence was a man's as well as a woman's Christian name, as for instance in the famous Geste of Florence and Blanchefleur. Moreover, these names most probably were given to Florentine merchants, settlers in England.

Gallon, derived from Julian, a man's as well as a woman's name. So also *Gilott, Gillow, Gillson*, cannot be accepted as the brood of a Juliana.

Gossett, Jose, Goss, are assumed to derive from Joyce. Jose may be from Joseph. *Goss* means a goose, and *Gossett* a little goose.

Grundy, from Gundreda. But Gundred may have been a male form.

Helling, from Ellen. Very doubtful.

Idson, Ide, sons of Ida. As already said, *Ide* is a place-name, and *Idson* is a corruption of Judson.

Izzard Mr. Bardsley derives from Ysolt. As a fact, it comes from Les Essards, in Normandy.

Jillot, Gellot, Gilson, Jowett, Joll, are supposed to be derived from Juliet and Juliana; but, as above said, Julian is not exclusively a female name, and *Joll* was a name in Cornwall before the Conquest, and before the introduction into England of Juliana and Juliet.

Letts, Letson, come from Letitia. But Letson is a corrup-

SIRE-NAMES

tion of Ledsham, near Pontefract; and Letts, as already said, is from Bartlett.

Mabb, Mabley, Maberley, Mabbot, Mapleson, are the sons of Mabel. *Maberley* is the same as Moberley, a parish in Cheshire.

Maddison is not the son of Maude, but of Matthew, and is the same as *Mattheson*.

Maggs, Margeson, Margetson, Poggson, are the sons of Margaret.

Mallinson, Mallison, Marriott, Maryatt, Mayson, Moxon, Moggs, all signify the sons of Mary. As to *Marriott* and *Maryatt*, it is possible enough that they are place-names— Merriott in Somersetshire. *May*, moreover, comes from Maheu, the French for Matthew.

Maude and *Mawson*, from Matilda. More likely from the English name Maldred or from Morris. Maude is also Le Maudit (see Battle Abbey Roll).

Parnell and *Pernell* come from Petronella, and the word was used to describe a light-charactered wench.

Sisson, from Cicely. Very doubtful.

Tagg, Taggett, from Agnes. *Tegg*, however, is from Teague, and *Tagg*, is its diminutive.

Tillett and *Tillotson*, from Matilda.

It will be seen that, although apparently a good number of names appear to be metronymics, it is quite possible that they may be so in appearance only. *Son* is an easy alteration from *ston* as the end of a name. I possess a manor that was called in Domesday Waddleston; it is now called and spelled Warson. I should be most reluctant to suppose, unless constrained by evidence so to do, that all the apparent metronymics are actually the unblushing acceptance by English people of names proclaiming the taint of bastardy. Some unfortunates could not escape. When the Act of 1538 was passed, rendering registration compulsory in country parishes, doubtless there were "love-children" whose origin was so well known that they could not escape having their names recorded as fatherless. But we may well be

SIRE-NAMES

mistaken if we rush to the conclusion that all these names are reminiscent of a scandal. No man, as I have said, would register his surname if he thought it smacked of that.

There was another reason above those already mentioned that may have led to the use of a name derived from a female. Among the Northern people—and the Normans, though Frenchified and Christian, had their ancestral beliefs and superstitions uneradicated—there existed a conviction that men without hair on their faces changed sex every ninth day. That which caused the burning of the worthy Njall his wife and sons, in their house, was the taunt of a certain Skarpedin, who threw a pair of breeches at a certain Flossi and bade him wear them, as he was a woman every ninth day. This was an insult that could be expunged only with blood or fire. In the Gullathing laws is one condemning to outlawry any man who charged another with change of sex, or with having given birth to a child. When Thorvald the Wide-travelled went round Iceland with a German missionary Bishop named Frederick, preaching the Gospel, the smooth face and long petticoats, and perhaps the portly paunch of the prelate, gave rise to bitter jests. A local poet sang:

> "Nine bairns born
> The Bishop hath,
> And of all and eke
> Is Thorvald father."

This was more than Thorvald could endure, and he hewed down the scald with his battle-axe.

It is quite possible that some beardless father of a family may have been nicknamed Little Mary (Marriott) or the Girl (Piggot). Gilbert Folliott may have been designated Filliot from his shaven and effeminate face, and he preferred to be known as Folliot (the Little Fool) to Filliot (the Little Girl).

Curiously enough, relationships have formed surnames—a thing not easy of explanation. *Neames* signifies uncle (the Old English is "neme"[1]), and *Neaves* is nephew. "Neve,

---

[1] Neames was the name of one of the knights in the popular romance of "The Four Sons of Aymon."

SIRE-NAMES

sony's sone, neptis," says the " Promptuarium Parvulorum."
Eame is in A.S. a maternal uncle, hence *Eames*. Cousins
we have many, also *Brothers* and *Freres*, as surnames; but
these latter may be due to the bearers at first having been
friars who had quitted their convents. *Nevins* stands for
Nevinson, the great-nephew. *Beaufrere*, becoming *Beaufere*,
and then *Buffer*, gave a surname, as also its equivalent *Fairbrother*; but *Mauf* was the Old English for a brother-in-law,
and this remains in the rare surname *Whatmough*—i.e., Wat's
brother-in-law. *Maeg* was a sister-in-law, and just possibly
may have originated some of our *Meeks*. Sometimes we
have "son" attached to a trade-name. That is explicable
enough. When a man had to be enregistered who had no
surname, nor his father either, it was simple enough to enroll
him as *Clerkson* or *Cookson*, *Smithson*, or *Ritson* (for wright's
son); or, again, *Saggerson*, as the son of the sagar, or sawyer.
Why Sackerson should have been a name applied to a bear
is not apparent (" Merry Wives," I. I.), but possibly it was
due to the up-and-down movements of Bruin.

Christian names when adopted as surnames underwent
alteration. Alban is transformed into *Allbone*, the German
Albrecht into *Allbright;* Wulferic became *Woolridge*, the
name of a little blacksmith from whom I derived many
traditional ballads—a man so small that one could hardly
imagine him descended from a sturdy Saxon stock. The
Norse Arnkettil in Yorkshire became *Arkle*, and then settled
down to *Artle*, which was the name of the cook at Horbury
Vicarage some thirty years ago. Baldwin has become
Bawden, and Alberic *Aubrey*. A sire-name may be so altered
as to look like a place-name. An example in point is *Baynham*.
As it happens, we know its pedigree. The Heralds' Visitation
of Gloucestershire of 1623 tells us that Robert ap Einion had
a son Robert, who changed ap Einion into Baynham, and
settled at Chorewell, in the Forest of Dean. *Bedward* is not
a to-name that looks back to a Lord of a Bedchamber to a
King, but derives from Ap-Edward.

A great change took place in English Christian names
after the Conquest. Before that, those borne by men and

SIRE-NAMES

women were of very ancient character, formed out of the Anglo-Saxon or Scandinavian tongues. But after that event came in names of saints and such as were Norman.

For the history of nomenclature Domesday is of especial value, for it gives us both Anglo-Saxon names at a period before *to-names* had begun to become hereditary, and also Norman names when on their way to become surnames. It shows us many of our invaders who were known only as sons of such and such a father, precisely as were Saxon thegns; and others who had Christian names, and nothing else. Others, again, had nicknames, and many men were designated after their castles in Normandy. Previous to the Conquest, Scriptural and saintly names were rarely employed by the Anglo-Saxons, but with the advent of the Normans they came in with a flood. "The great mass of our Old English names," says Freeman, "were gradually driven out. The change began at once. The Norman names became the fashion. The Englishman's child was held at the font by a Norman gossip. The Englishman who was on friendly terms with his Norman lord or his Norman neighbour—nay, the Englishman who simply thought it fine to call his children after the reigning King or Queen—now cast aside his own name and the names of his parents to give his sons and daughters names after the new foreign pattern. The child of Godric and Godgifu was no longer Godwine and Eadgyth, but William and Matilda. . . . In every list of names throughout the eleventh and twelfth centuries we find the habit spreading. The name of the father is English; the name of the son is Norman. This is a point of far more importance than anything in the mere history of nomenclature. It helps to disguise one side of the fusion between Norman and English. Many a man who bears a Norman name—many a Richard or Gilbert whose parentage does not happen to be recorded—must have been as good an Englishman as if he had been called Ealdred or Aethelbert.

"When this fashion set in, it took root. The Norman names gradually spread themselves through all classes, till

SIRE-NAMES

even a villain was more commonly called by a Norman name than by an English name. The great mass of English names went out of use, a few only excepted, which were favoured by accidental circumstances."

We see something of the same thing taking place at the present day, when labourers' sons and the children of colliers are christened Percy, Vane, Vere, Granville, and are given half the aristocratic names in the peerage.

The romances of chivalry exercised a great influence on nomenclature, at first only on members of the Norman-French families, but mediately on the English. The fable of King Arthur and the Round Table was vastly popular, and supplied us with our *Launcelots, Tristans, Percivals,* and some of our *Kayes*. The following fanciful pedigree of the romances relative to Ogier the Dane, Godfrey de Bouillon, and the Four Sons of Aymon, will show how these names were taken up, and eventually became surnames. These I have italicized.

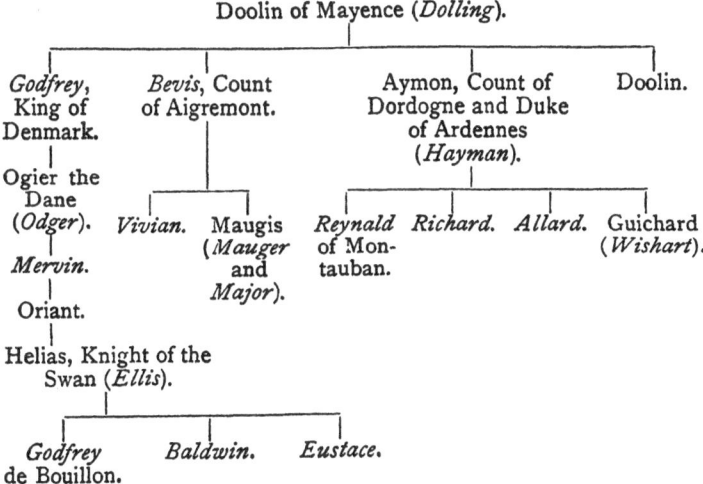

All these names, with the exception of Oriant, were taken up. Not only so, but also that of *Bayard* (*Baird*), the name of the horse that was ridden by the Four Sons of Aymon.

SIRE-NAMES

The story of the Four Sons of Aymon is now forgotten, although at one time most popular; and, indeed, it is a touching tale. The Four Sons of Aymon were at feud with Charlemagne, and all four rode on the back of their great horse Bayard. At last, through the intercession of their mother, the great King agreed to receive the Four Sons of Aymon into favour again, on condition that they surrendered to him their horse Bayard. This was agreed to, and Reynald gave up the steed to Charlemagne, who had two millstones attached to Bayard's neck, and the horse was then precipitated into the water. Bayard managed to disengage himself from the load, and rose to the surface, saw his master Reynald, and swam to him and laid his head on his shoulder. When the King saw this he demanded the horse again, and Reynald gave it up. Charles the Great now had a millstone attached to each foot of the horse and two to its neck, and again it was cast into the water. But once more Bayard managed to free himself, and swam up to Reynald and looked at him piteously, as much as to say: "Why have you done this to me, your true friend?" Reynald caressed the poor beast, and trusted that the Emperor now would waive his determination to have it destroyed. But Charles once more insisted, and against the will of his brothers, who to save the faithful beast would have renewed their feud with the Emperor, he gave Bayard up for the third time, but as he parted with it he said: "Oh, old friend, how hardly am I repaying all your trusty service to us brothers!" Then Charlemagne had millstones attached as before, and he bade Reynald turn his head away, and not look at the horse, should it again reach the surface. Again was Bayard flung into the river; again the horse rose and turned its eyes towards its master. But Reynald had his head directed elsewhere, and when Bayard could not meet his master's eyes it sank to rise no more.

The surname Bayard occurs repeatedly in English records from 1273 down. It has even travelled to America with our colonists. It does not come from the knight *sans peur et sans reproche*, who died in 1524, as it occurs many

SIRE-NAMES

centuries earlier. Bayard undoubtedly means "the bay-coloured." But it was the romance that gave the name its popularity.

To the romances are also due such female names as Gwenever, that remains to this day in Cornwall as Jenefer; and Iseult, that became in English mouths Isolt; also Ellaine, that became Ellen. *Firebrace* is a surname derived from the romance of Fierabras. A family of *Amadys* appears in the Heralds' Visitation of Devon in 1620. The pedigree does not go back before the reign of Henry VIII. The family of Amadys was one of merchants at Plymouth, never of much consideration nor of landed estate. When the Adam of the family, William, was pricked to serve Henry VIII. in arms, he cast about for a surname, and thought he could not do better than assume that of the famous champion, Amadys of Gaul. The names of *Miles* and *Ames*, or *Amye*, doubtless derived from the romance of the story of Milles and Amys, *les nobles et vaillants chevaliers*. Perhaps also some of our *Mills* may hence derive. When William rode to the battle in which the destinies of England were determined, Wace informs us:

> "Taillifer qui moult bien chantait
> Sur un cheval qui tost alloit,
> Devant eus alloit chantant
> De l'Allemaigne et de Rollant,
> Et d'Olivet et de Vassaux,
> Qui moururent à Rainchevaux."

From that day the famous song of Roland was dear to the hearts of the Norman French, and gave occasion to the spread of the names of *Oliver* and *Roland*, and so to their being adopted as surnames. Not all *Courteneys* are lineal descendants of the grand William de Courtney, Duke of Aquitaine. Even the female name of the patient Grizzel was assumed, and became a family appellation as *Griselle*. Although the surname *Turpin*—it is borne by a carrier of Plymouth, and was made famous by a highwayman—derives from Thorfinn, yet it is so but mediately as a family name. It owes its introduction to the popularity of the fictitious

SIRE-NAMES

Turpin, Archbishop of Rheims, who was the reputed author of the romantic "History of Charlemagne." *Waring* as a surname comes from Guerin de Montglave, another famous hero of romance. In the Hundred Rolls of 1273 are two entries—John le Ape, of Oxfordshire, and Alured Ape, of Norfolk. I do not suppose that the name of *Ape* was given or assumed out of anything simian in the appearance or conduct of John and Alured, but was due to the romance of Milles and Amys, above mentioned. Milles and Amys went on pilgrimage to Jerusalem, and the former left his two children in their cradle to the guardianship of a trusty ape. Lubiane, the wife of Amys, resolved on their destruction, and had them thrown into the sea. The ape swam after them till two angels carried them off. The ape floundered about disconsolate, and was picked up by a merchant vessel. On landing he searched everywhere for the lost children, subsisting the while on herbs and water, although habitually addicted to the pleasures of the table. Finding his search in vain, he proceeded to Clermont, the paternal inheritance of his wards, where he was received with acclamations by the populace; but he declined the honours of an entertainment, as he felt his spirits depressed on account of the loss of the children. Meanwhile Lubiane had set out for the Court of Charlemagne to obtain a grant of the county of Clermont, on pretence that the race of Milles was extinct. The ape got wind of this, had a letter composed, narrating how matters really stood, and hastened to Paris with it. But, on account of the badness of the roads and want of relays, he did not reach the Court of the Emperor till some days after Lubiane. He made his first appearance at Court in his travelling dress during a great festival, and signalized his arrival by assaulting the Countess and rending her garments. He then respectfully presented the letter to Charlemagne, who ordered that the case should be decided by single combat. Lubiane readily procured a champion, and the ape met him in the lists and defeated him. Lubiane's champion was obliged to confess himself defeated, in order to avoid being torn piecemeal. According to the

SIRE-NAMES

established custom, he was hanged, and Lubiane was burnt alive.

The story of the faithful ape was so popular that it was represented in painting on the walls of the great hall of the Hôtel de Ville in Paris, and, according to Monmerqué, was a favourite subject for tapestry hangings. Now, as the horse of the Sons of Aymon furnished a surname, it is quite possible that the ape of Milles did so as well, as a symbol of fidelity. At the present day the novels so assiduously read furnish numerous Christian names, and the romances and ballads that were the delight of our medieval forefathers in like manner supplied both Christian names and surnames. We must figure to ourselves our ancestors called on, perhaps suddenly, to give their surnames. They had none, and, being constrained at a push to call themselves something, laid hold of the name of the *preux chevalier*, or even the ape, whose exploits they had just heard sung by a strolling jongleur, or which were familiar to them through the hangings of their tapestried chamber. Such, I can have little doubt, was the origin of some of these. But besides the introduction of Biblical, saintly, and romantic names, through fashion or imitation of the Normans, surnames began to become general. As they were beginning to be assumed by the conquerors, they began to be assumed also by the conquered. Among these latter the process was slow. It took something like 500 years to become general. It worked downward from the Norman Baron to the English serf.

I will again quote Mr. Freeman:

" Besides this change in personal nomenclature, this introduction of a new set of Christian names, the Norman Conquest also brought with it the novelty of family nomenclature—that is to say, the use of hereditary surnames. . . . Among many men of the same name within the same *gens*, one needs to be distinguished from another by some epithet marking him out from his namesake. He may be marked out from them by the name of his father, by the name of his calling, or by some peculiarity of person or manner. The distinctive epithet may be sportive or serious; it may be

SIRE-NAMES

given in contempt or in reverence. In all these cases its nature is essentially the same. In all cases it is in strictness a *surname*. Surnames of this kind are common in all times and places; they were as common in England before the Conquest as anywhere else. . . . Beside the patronymics, the local surnames, the surnames descriptive of the bearer's person, there are others which are not so intelligible—surnames which are mere pet-names or nicknames, whether given in scorn or affection, or in caprice.

" But in England before the Conquest there is no ascertained case of a strictly hereditary surname. A surname cannot be looked on as strictly hereditary till it has ceased to be personally descriptive. The line is drawn when the surname of the father passes to the son as a matter of course, though it may no longer be really applicable to him. In the older state of things we may be sure that Wulfred the Black was really a swarthy man; that Sired, Ælfred's son, was really the son of an Ælfred; that Godred at Fecham really lived at Fecham. When hereditary surnames are established, the surname of Black may be borne by a pale man, that of Ælfred's son by one whose father was not named Ælfred, that of Fecham by one who neither lived at Fecham nor owned any land there. If the Norman Conquest had never happened, it is almost certain that we should have found for ourselves a system of hereditary surnames. Still, as a matter of fact, the use of hereditary surnames begins in England with the Norman Conquest, and it may be set down as one of its results.

"At the time of the invasion of England, the practice of hereditary surnames seems still to have been a novelty in Normandy, but a novelty which was fast taking root. Numbers of the great Norman Barons already bore surnames, sometimes territorial, sometimes patronymic, of which the former class easily became hereditary.

" But the patronymic surname did not so readily become hereditary as the local surname. When a man takes his surname from the actual place of possession or residence, it is very hard to say at what particular point the personal

SIRE-NAMES

description passes into hereditary surname. The stages are therefore more easily marked in names of the other class. When Thomas, the son of John, the son of Richard, calls himself, not FitzJohn or Johnson, but FitzRichard or Richardson, the change is a rather violent one. But when, on the other hand, a Norman who bore the name of his birthplace or possessions in Normandy—Robert of Bruce or William of Percy—found himself the possessor of far greater estates in England than in Normandy, when his main interests were no longer Norman, but English, the surname ceased to be really descriptive. It became a mere arbitrary hereditary surname. It no longer suggested the original Norman holding; it remained in use even if the Norman holding passed away from the family. When a Bruce or a Percy had lost his original connection with the place Bruce or Percy, when the name no longer suggested a thought of the place, Bruce and Percy became strict surnames in the modern sense. There is nothing like this in England before the Norman Conquest; the change is strictly one of the results of that event. And the like process would take place with those landowners, whether of Norman or of English birth, who took their surnames from places in England. With them, too, the local description gradually passed into the hereditary surname."[1]

This is a long quotation, but it is too important, as bearing on the subject of English nomenclature, not to be given. Moreover, the authority of Mr. Freeman is so great that I am glad to invoke it to show that the practice of using hereditary surnames in England began with the latter half of the eleventh century, and that there was nothing of the sort before in England.

[1] "Norman Conquest," vol. v., p. 563 *et seq.*

CHAPTER IV

TOTEMISM AND NAMES

SOME of the most delightful of nursery tales are those that relate to transformation of Princes into beasts, and their release through woman's love, as The Frog Prince, and Beauty and the Beast; or the reverse, where the woman is transformed, as The White Cat.

Similar stories abound in folklore everywhere. A damsel finds a serpent lying stark with cold on the house doorstep, and takes it within. It pleads to lie outside her chamber door; she allows this. Then it asks to be admitted to her bed; she again consents, whereupon it is transformed into a beautiful youth.

In a cave lives a monster like an overgrown toad. It can be released on one condition only—that a fair maid shall kiss it on the lips. A peasant girl does so, and it at once becomes a nobleman and marries her.

The Greeks also had their metamorphoses. Zeus, for the love he bore to Europa, became a bull; for the sake of Leda, a swan.

The following tale is told by the Bosjemen of South Africa. A girl dreamed that a baboon came to carry her off and make her his wife. Alarmed at the prospect, she fled to a certain Owanciguacha, who lived in the river as a water-snake, but at night came ashore, divested himself of his skin, became human, and slept on a mat. The damsel obtained a magic herb, and watched hidden among the reeds till Owanciguacha emerged from the water and retired to his mat, whereupon she obtained possession of the cast skin,

TOTEMISM AND NAMES

burnt it, and thrust the herb into the sleeper's mouth, whereupon he remained a man, made her his wife, and through her became the ancestor of a tribe.[1]

The Scandinavians have a tale that the Valkyrie are maidens who fly about in the form of swans, but occasionally lay aside their feather dresses to bathe, and appear as women. A man once observed them alight, concealed himself, and got possession of one of the swan robes. When the Valkyrie left the water, all reassumed their bird-forms save one, and he secured her, made her his wife and mother of his children. But one day she opened a chest and found in it her feather dress. She at once put it on and flew away, never again to return. The descendants of this man and the swan wife would be denominated Alptings.

In Aurora Island in the Pacific the natives tell a similar tale. Once some women came down from heaven to earth to bathe, and before entering the water divested themselves of their wings. A certain Quat saw them, and stole one of the pinions. When the maidens came out of the water, all flew away save one, who could not, because her wing was stolen.

Quat took her home with him and married her, and she became the mother of his children. He had concealed the wing under a post of the house, under ground. Quat's mother proved unkind to the wife, and she leaned against the post and wept, till her tears made a hole in the soil and disclosed the wing. Thereupon she put it on and flew away, deserting her husband and children for ever.[2]

Here is another tale from Celebes. Utahagi, with six other nymphs, her sisters, flew down from heaven to bathe in a pool. At that time a man named Kasimbaha was there among the reeds, and saw them. He stole one of their feather dresses. By this means Kasimbaha secured possession of that one, Utahagi, whose dress he had obtained. He made her his wife, and she bore him a son whom he named Tambaga. Utahagi had a white hair on her head, and she warned her husband on no account to pluck it out. Disregarding her caution, he did so, and she at once fled back to

[1] Frobenius, "The Childhood of Man," p. 118. [2] *Ibid.*, p. 305.

TOTEMISM AND NAMES

heaven, and no more returned to earth. But her son Tambaga remained, and became the ancestor of a tribe.[1]

Now, how comes it that peoples divided by vast tracts of ocean, and who have no racial affinities, should possess similar, even identical, stories? The reason is that among these peoples there are tribes that regard themselves as descended from swans, have the swan as their totem, and have excogitated myths to explain the origin of the totem and tribal name.

The following story is found in an Icelandic saga, and is also given in brief by Norman-English writers as the origin of the family of Earl Ulf, who married the sister of Canute the Great, and by her became the ancestor of the Royal Family of Denmark, the Ulfungs. But he himself was a Björning, a Bear's son.

Björn was the son of King Ring of the Uplands in Norway. A jealous stepmother transformed him into a bear, and bade him ravage his father's flocks and herds. Björn loved a small bonder's daughter named Bera,[2] and he carried her off to his den among the rocks, and when the sun set he reverted to the form of a man. One night he told Bera that his mind presaged trouble or death, and he bade her, in the event of his being killed on the morrow, on no account to allow herself to be induced to taste his roast flesh. It fell out as he foresaw. Next day King Ring's hunters killed him, and at night his roasted flesh was served in the hall. The wicked Queen endeavoured to induce Bera to eat of it, but she refused. She clenched her teeth, yet by force the Queen succeeded in thrusting a small portion between her lips. Soon after Bera gave birth to three sons, and, because some of the bear's flesh had been in her mouth, two of them were deformed, and the third, Bodvar, could change himself at pleasure into the form of a bear. He married the daughter of Hrolf Krake, King of Leidre, or Denmark, and, in the great battle in which Hrolf fell, Bodvar fought at one time in the shape of a bear, at another in human form.

[1] Frobenius, "The Childhood of Man," p. 312.
[2] *Bera* means "bear" as well as *björn*.

TOTEMISM AND NAMES

Now, one interesting point in this tale is that in which Bera is reluctantly obliged to admit some of the flesh of the bear into her mouth.

One of the murderers of Thomas à Becket was Sir Reginald FitzUrse. The family was descended from *Ursus*, the Bear, who in the time of William the Conqueror held lands in Wiltshire, of the Abbey of Glastonbury. There can exist little doubt that this Bear descended from the stock of the Björnings, of which the story has just been told. So also did the *Orsini* of Italy. One legend of their origin is that they derive from the son of a Gothic chieftain named Aldvin, who was suckled by a bear. Another story is that Aldvin was of a Saxon family, Lords of Ballenstedt and Ascania in the Hartz Mountains, and that he was a younger son. Albert, the Bear of the Ascanian house, was born in 1100, and became Margrave of Brandenburg, and ancestor of the present Emperor of Germany. The Ballenstedt arms are a black bear hugging a chessboard. The possible origin of this is that Earl Ulf, the Bear's son, was playing chess one day with King Canute. After they had played together awhile, the King made a false move, at which the Earl took a knight from the King; but Canute set the piece again upon the board, and bade the Earl make another move. Ulf, being incensed, threw the chessboard on the floor with all the men, and stalked away. The King shouted after him: "Run away, Ulf the Timorous!" whereat the Earl replied: "Thou wouldst have run away in a certain battle had not I come to thine aid."

Next morning Canute sent his Chamberlain to kill Ulf. The man found him in the church, and there ran him through with his sword whilst he was engaged in prayer. The early pedigree of Albert the Bear is not to be found, but it is conceivable that he may have derived from Earl Ulf's second son Björn (the Bear). Ulf was killed in 1028, and the story of the chessboard may have given rise to the representation on the arms of the Ballenstedt family, now represented by the Duke of Anhalt.

But to return to that point of the story that concerns

TOTEMISM AND NAMES

Bera having partaken of a particle of the flesh of the bear. The persistence of the Queen to force her to eat, and the struggle of the young wife not to receive the food, stamp the story as one of a totem-taboo.

Among primitive people everywhere, wheresoever totemism exists, there the partaking of the flesh of the beast, bird, or fish, from which the tribe derives, is strictly forbidden. In totemistic families the people look upon it as the worst of crimes to taste of the flesh of the animal whose name they bear. We do not know the story of the origin of the Chatti —the modern Hessians—but certainly they looked to a cat as their progenitor; and the Count of Katzenellenbogen had doubtless a legend concerning a cat to account for his remarkable name.

One of the oldest of the Highland clans was the Clan Chattan—Children of the Cat—and the younger clans bore animals on their banners. The Clan Alpine had a boar as its totem.

The Picts—the name is a Latin rendering of Cruithni, the painted or tattooed men—certainly had symbolic animals figured on their bodies. Cæsar speaks of the Britons as dyed with woad, but Solinus is more explicit. He says that they were figured over with forms of divers animals—in fact, distinguishing tattooes marking off the several tribes, each tribe having had an animal ancestor.

In all likelihood Romulus and Remus, in the earliest form of the story, were the actual offspring of the wolf, and it was a rationalizing of the myth to make them to have been merely suckled by her.

One of the greatest families in Norway—one that came to the front and played a conspicuous part in its history—was that of the Arnungs, or Eaglings.

It was related of its origin that the ancestor was found in an eagle's nest wrapped in silk. None knew whence it came, whether laid there by human hands or hatched out of an eagle's egg.[1]

[1] The Stanley family pretended to a similar derivation. Its crest is an oak-tree supporting a nest containing a swaddled babe, above which is an

TOTEMISM AND NAMES

This ancestor was named Finnvid, the Foundling, and his son was Thorarin (Thor's Eagle), and his grandson Arnvid (Eaglewood), the father of Earl Arnmod (Eaglemood). Arnmod's son was again Arne, who had sons Arnbjörn and Arne, so that the family clung to the eagle ancestry, perpetuating the name of Arne from generation to generation. One of Arne's granddaughters married Malcolm Caenmore, King of Scotland, and so brought the eagle blood into that race.

We can hardly doubt that in the primitive form of the legend the ancestor of the Arnungs was actually an eagle, and that Finnvid was hatched out of her egg. But the story was modified to suit the views of a later and more sceptical generation.

We do not know for certain, but we may suspect, that Hengist and Horsa, if not the symbols of the Saxon tribes, looked to an equine ancestor. The white horse of the Saxons was their totem, and it is open to question whether Hengist and Horsa really existed. Hengist means a stallion, and it is supposed that the leaders were merely representatives of families deriving traditionally from totemistic horses.

Our present Royal Family is that of the *Guelfs*. And, indeed, the Guelfs were widely represented on princely and electoral thrones in Germany. The story of the origin of the race is this: A certain Countess of Querfurt bore at a birth nine sons. Ashamed of this, she committed them to her maid to drown. As the servant was on her way to the river with the infants in a basket, she met the Count, who asked her what she bore. She replied: " Only some whelps to be drowned." " I want a young whelp," said he, and opened the basket; and so the truth came out. He had them secretly brought up, and did not reveal that they were his sons till they were of age. Thence came all the branches of the *Guelf* family.

---

eagle. King Alfred found the child, reared it, and named it Nesting. The story is in the "Vita Stæ. Wulfhildæ" in Capgrave, "Nova Legenda Angliæ."

TOTEMISM AND NAMES

The same story is told of Isenhardt of Altorp and his wife Irmentrude, sister-in-law of Charlemagne. Thence came the Swabian Counts of Zollen, who bore on their shield, quartered black and white, a dog's head.

The Hund family also derives from one of nine whelps, and in commemoration of this have as their crest nine pinks, representing the nine sons, and on their arms a hound.

One of the Hunds of Wenckenheim it was who carried off Luther when he was returning from Worms, and conveyed him to the Wartburg. From the Guelfs also came the Princes of Scala at Verona. They changed their name to Scala or Scaliger, but retained on their arms two dogs, in commemoration of their origin.

Another noble family, again, was that of Ruden, that has the same tale told of its origin, but with this difference: In this case the ancestor of the family scoffed at a beggar woman because she had three rosy-cheeked boys born at a birth. Incensed at his mockery, she prayed that he might be the father of four times as many boys, that they might have the appetites of dogs, and reduce him to mendicancy. In process of time he did have twelve sons, who were so voracious that they were called *Ruden*—that is to say, dogs —and they ate their father out of house and home, so that he was driven to beg his daily bread. The Ruden wear on their crest and in their arms a dog's head.

Everyone, through the opera of "Lohengrin," has been made familiar with the mythical origin of the Dukes of Cleves. In the story a mysterious knight arrives at the castle, drawn up the Rhine in a boat by a swan. He fights for the heiress, and marries her. She is forbidden to ask the name of her deliverer, yet one day puts to him the fatal question, whereupon the boat and swan reappear, and he leaves to go, none know whither. Thenceforth the swan remained the badge of the House of Cleves; and our taverns that bear the swan as their sign date from the arrival of Anne of Cleves in England to be the wife of Henry VIII., and testify to a certain amount of sympathy for her, entertained in the country at the time.

TOTEMISM AND NAMES

Judging from the name, we may conjecture that the Merewings, the royal Frank family, derived from a mythical merow or merman.

The Lusignans certainly took their name from a half-fish ancestress, Melusina. A gallant knight passing a spring surprised and captured a transcendently beautiful nymph, and induced her to become his wife. She consented on one condition only—that on every Saturday she should be allowed to retire to her bathroom and remain there for a whole day invisible. She became a mother, and ancestress of a splendid race that wore the crowns of Jerusalem and Cyprus. One day, overcome by curiosity, the husband peered through a chink in the bathroom door, and saw, to his dismay, his wife transformed from the waist downwards into a fish. Somewhat later, in some domestic tiff, he sneered at her as a merow, whereupon, with a cry, she fled out of the window.

But whenever ill-luck is to befall a Lusignan, or a death to occur, Melusina is to be seen hovering about the castle wailing and wringing her hands. It was due to this mythical origin that the mermaid formed the crest of every Lusignan, waved on their banner, and creaked on the vanes of the castle towers. Here again we have a totem story.

There are indications that in an early state of development the Romans derived their families from animal ancestors. They had their Asinian, Aquillian, Porcian, Caninian gentes, and often fantastic stories were invented to account for these names. The Tremellian family obtained the title of *Scropha*, or Sow, according to the tale, in a peculiarly discreditable manner, as we should think, but by an exhibition of justifiable cleverness, as was considered at the time. A sow having strayed from a neighbour's yard into that of the Tremellii, the servants of the latter killed her. The master caused the carcass to be placed in his wife's bed, and when the neighbour came to claim his strayed sow, the Tremellian gentleman swore by all that was holy that there was no sow on his premises save that lying in the bed, and his neighbour concluded that the allusion was to the lady herself.

TOTEMISM AND NAMES

One of the Fabian families was named after a buzzard—*Buteo*—and the fable was invented, to account for it, that a bird of this species had lighted on the vessel of a Fabian when he was on a voyage.

Corvinus was the name of another Roman family, so called after a crow. The name of *Cæsar* was from an elephant.

The children of Israel were in tribes, and each had its banner: the lion of the tribe of Judah, the ass of Issachar, the wolf of Benjamin, the serpent of Dan.

The name of *Lovell* is still current among us. It signifies a young wolf. A story is told as to its origin. Count Ascelin de Perceval obtained it on account of his violent temper. " By ill-usage and torture," says Sir Francis Palgrave, " he compelled his liege lord (William de Breteuil) to grant him his daughter Isabel, with £3,000 of Dreux currency. During three months Breteuil was kept in duress, ironed, chained, plagued, and starved, without yielding, till at length the livres and the lady were extorted by an ingenious mode of torture. In the depth of winter Ascelin fastened him to the grating at the bleak top of a tower, unclothed save by a poor thin shirt; he was thus exposed to the biting, whistling winds, while water was poured upon him abundantly and continually, till he was sheeted with ice. This anguish Breteuil could not resist; he consented to the terms proposed, endowed Isabel in the church porch, and gave her away."

Ascelin appears in Domesday as Gouel, intended for Lovel or Louvel. His son William inherited his father's ferocity of character, and with it his name of Young Wolf. But there is some reason for suspecting that the family considered itself to be descended from a wolf—to be Ulfings.

In fact, we may generally take it for granted that, where at an early period families bear animal names, they were held to descend from a bestial ancestor.

The sons of Lodbrog, who harried the coasts of England in the ninth century, brought with them from Denmark a raven banner, embroidered by their sisters. It had this virtue, that before the battle it spread and flapped its wings.

TOTEMISM AND NAMES

Now, this raven banner had its significance. The Lodbrog sons were the descendants, not the actual sons, of one Ragnar Lodbrog, who died about the year 794. He left no legitimate issue. His posterity, the royal race of Sweden and Denmark, descended from a concubine named Kraka, "the Crow." Either the family substituted a raven for a crow, or, what is more probable, the English chroniclers mistook a crow for a raven. But this seems to show that the descendants of Lodbrog looked to an ancestral crow as the source of the family. Moreover, Ragnar's death-song (not that of the first, but the second Ragnar) is called "The Song of the Crow." We may suspect that the story of Kraka is really a réchauffé of an earlier tale in which the ancestress was represented as an actual crow.

The *Corbyns* and the *Corbetts* (Corbeaux) came over to England with the Conqueror, and, we may suspect, were of the Lodbrog stock, descendants of Kraka, as the younger Ragnar thrust up the Seine and took Paris in 845, and his son Björn ravaged in Normandy and other parts of France in 843 and 857, and another son, Sigurd, and a nephew, Guthrod, were there also in 891; so that it is far from unlikely that they left some descendants behind them in Normandy.

There were other Norman families that bore the names of animals. Indeed, Hugh, who was created Earl of Chester, went by the name of Lupus, the Wolf. There was among the Conqueror's attendants an Asinus, *l'Ane*, and we can hardly conceive of a noble family accepting such an appellation unless there was some story to dignify it. The *De Moels* bore mules on their arms and as their crest. The *Oliphants* were named, like the Cæsars, after an elephant.

Le Grize was a swine, with a swine's head as crest. *Griis* is a pig in Danish to this day. *Le Goz* was a goose. *De la Vache* was another animal name, and *Thoreau* was another. Although the *Lyons* are supposed to have derived their name from the Forest of Lyon in Normandy, we cannot be confident that they did not impose their name upon their hunting-ground, and fable a descent from the king

TOTEMISM AND NAMES

of the beasts, that figured on their helms and shields and banners.

Mr. Bardsley gives a list of beast, bird, and fish names of individuals found in the Hundred Rolls, Post-Mortem Inquisitions, and other medieval documents. His idea is that these names were accorded by neighbours, descriptive or expressive of the moral or physical character of the individual. If so, then they were mere nicknames that would die out with those who bore them. This was no doubt the case with some such names, not necessarily bestial, that are recorded in the Hundred Rolls and elsewhere. Some are names that no man with any self-respect would carry, and certainly his sons would repudiate their transmission. Such are " Milksop," " Drinkedregges," " Sourale," " Sparewater," " Pinsemaille," " Pickcheese." Those who drew up the registers were not always particular to take the name by which a man himself chose to be known, and accepted any that his neighbours gave him. This may possibly enough account for such nicknames as " Rat," " Mouse," " Calf," " Smelt," " Shark," " Whale," that have found their way in. But in some cases the names exhibit a misapprehension. " Whale " was probably Welsh; " Hawke " may stand for Hawker; " Kite " may have been written for Kitt—Christopher. " Otter " may not have anything to do with the animal, and represent Othere, of which the German form is Otto or Otho. " Palfrey " stands for le Balafré, the scarred; and " Salmon " is a shortening of Solomon.

But where an animal name is handed down from generation to generation it stands otherwise; in that case the name cannot be a mere nickname, applied to one member of a family and carried forward for no reason whatever to later generations. There must have been a significance in the name—a significance accepted by the family.

There are several explanations of the acceptance by a family of a hereditary plant or animal name. Either

(1) That name indicated its mythical origin;
(2) It was due to some incident in the family history, the memory of which it desired to perpetuate;

TOTEMISM AND NAMES

(3) It represented the arms of the master under whom the bearer had served; or

(4) It was derived from a sign over a shop or a tavern where the family had long been.

1. I have said enough about the totems of noble families; but it is quite possible that, among those who had belonged to the manor or been among the retainers of a great family, there may have been an impression that they pertained to it in blood, and had a right to the same totem. This took a peculiar form after the tribal organization came to an end. Among the Scandinavians it was a common thing to say of a man that he was not "einhamr"—*i.e.*, not one-shaped. It was supposed that he could at will change into some other form—not any form, but one particular shape—in which he could range the country: a bear, a wolf, a fox, an eagle, a dolphin, or, with a woman, a swan, a she-wolf, a hare, or a cat.

In the *Manchester Directory* for 1861 appeared the name *Hell-cat*, and the name occurs in Northumbria in the Middle Ages. The name was accepted without compunction by the family, because it supposed that some, at all events, among the womenkind were able to change shape into cats at night. The conviction that this transformation was possible remained rooted in the minds of men throughout the Middle Ages, and gave rise to the many stories of werewolves and of human bears, and of witches running about in the shape of hares and bitches and vixens.

Indeed, the belief is not extinct at the present day in the East of Europe, and is only so in comparatively recent times in France and Germany.

Accordingly, a family that at a remote period believed that it was descended from a totemistic beast or bird or reptile or fish, at a later period held that some among its members possessed the faculty, at will, of transformation into the beast, bird, fish, or reptile, whose name it bare; and it was proud to retain this name, as giving to it a distinction above others in the same village, and one that imposed on the neighbours a certain respect and awe.

2. It is also possible enough that some incident connected

TOTEMISM AND NAMES

with an animal of some sort may have become a hereditary family story, and so may have given occasion to the perpetuation of the name. And this would apply to other objects as well as animals.

In the twelfth century a Mansfeld was in the Battle of Wolfshitze, fought in 1115, and was almost the only one on his side who escaped with his life; he was taken prisoner by the Emperor Lothair. Angry at his lot, which he regarded as dishonourable, he exclaimed, "I'm like a fly-away goose," and he ever after bore the name of *Gans* (Goose), and transmitted it to his posterity, that bears the name to the present day.

Now, if these things happened and gave names to historic families, why may not events of moment in domestic annals have been the occasion of fixing names on families not in the highest ranks?

3. Many an old retainer or man-at-arms of a noble or gentle family, who had marched under its banner, followed its crest, borne its cognizance on his surcoat, married and settled down on a little farm of his master, when past service; and his old surcoat, with the lion, or the bear, or the fox, the badger or the hart, was hung up over his mantelshelf, and was pointed to with great pride by the ancient trooper. If he wanted a surname, what better could he take than that of the cognizance he had so bravely borne for many a year on the fields of Guyenne or Normandy?

> "This day is call'd the feast of Crispian:
> He that outlives this day, and comes safe home,
> Will stand a tip-toe when this day is nam'd,
> And rouse him at the name of Crispian.
> He that shall see this day, and live old age,
> Will yearly on the vigil feast his neighbours,
> And say, "To-morrow is Saint Crispian:"
> Then will he strip his sleeve and show his scars. . . .
> Old men forget; yea, all shall be forgot,
> But he'll remember with advantages
> What feats he did that day. . . .
> This story shall the good man teach his son;
> And Crispin Crispian shall ne'er go by,

TOTEMISM AND NAMES

> From this day to the ending of the world,
> But we in it shall be remembered;
> We few, we happy few, we band of brothers;
> For he to-day that sheds his blood with me
> Shall be my brother; be he ne'er so vile,
> This day shall gentle his condition."

And what surname would the soldier adopt, when his position was made gentle, but one from the banner under which he had fought?

Moreover, every serving-man bore on his arm the badge of the house where he served; and we may well suppose that, when retiring to his cottage after years spent in his master's hall, at his master's table, or running as a page in early days by his master's horse, he would be proud to name himself after the badge in silver that had so long and so honourably adorned his arm.

4. We come now to the signs that were suspended in the streets above shops, and such as swung before alehouses. In the Hundred Rolls are entries "at Roebuck," "at the Cock," "de Whitehorse," etc., indicative of signs.

A good many of our families, though not the majority of them, draw their descent from the class of tradesmen who adopted signs for their shops. Houses were not numbered, and were distinguished by some device that swung in the street. Taverns, moreover, have retained their signs. These usually followed the heraldry of the noble or gentle families that held the manor. In former days it was not always possible for the mansion to receive all the retinue of a visitor, and they were sent to the manor inn, placed under the arms of the lord.

Camden, in his "Remaines," says: "Many names that seem unfitting for men, as bruitish beasts, etc., come from the very signs of the houses where they inhabited; for I have heard of them which say they spake of knowledge, that some of late time dwelling at the signe of the Dolphin, Bull, White Horse, Racket, Peacock, etc., were commonly called Thomas at the Dolphin, Will at the Bull, George at the White Horse, Robin at the Racket, which names, as

TOTEMISM AND NAMES

many others of like sort, with omitting *at*, became afterwards hereditary to their children."

Pasquin, in his "Nightcap," published in 1612, gives the following lines, that show how in the seventeenth century persons were individualized by their shop signs:

> "First there is Master Peter at the *Bell*,
> A Linendraper and a wealthy man.
> Then Master Thomas that doth stockings sell,
> And George the Grocer at the *Frying Pan*.
> And Master Timothie, the Woollendraper,
> And Master Saloman, the Leatherscraper.
> And Frank the Goldsmith at the *Rose*,
> And Master Philip with the fiery nose.
> And Master Miles, the mercer at the *Harrow*,
> And Master Nicke, the Silkman at the *Plow*.
> And Master Giles, the Salter at the *Sparrow*,
> And Master Dike, the Vintner at the *Cow*.
> And Harry Haberdasher at the *Horne*.
> And Oliver, the Dyer, at the *Thorne*.
> And Bernard, Barber-surgeon, at the *Fiddle*,
> And Moses, Merchant-tailor, at the *Needle*."

One can see that in a very short time those occupying such shops would acquire the name either of their trade or of the sign under which it was conducted. Peter would be known either as *Dyer* or as *Bell*, Frank as *Goldsmith* or as *Rose*, Miles as *Mercer* or as *Harrow*. And, indeed, every one of the above signs, excepting only the Frying-pan, has become subsequently a surname.

In the *Spectator*, No. 28, 1711, is this: "Our streets are filled with blue Boars, black Swans, and red Lions; not to mention flying Pigs, and Hogs in Armour, with many other Creatures more extraordinary than any in the Desarts of Africk. . . . The Bell and the Neat's-Tongue, the Dog and the Gridiron, the Fox and Goose, may suppose to have met, but what has the Fox and the Seven Stars to do together? And when did the Lamb and the Dolphin ever meet, except upon a signpost? As for the Cat and Fiddle, there is a conceit in it; and therefore I do not intend that anything I have here said should affect it. I must, however, observe to you upon this subject, that it is usual for a young Trades-

TOTEMISM AND NAMES

man, at his first setting up, to add to his own Sign that of the Master whom he served; as the Husband after Marriage gives a place to his Mistress's Arms in his own Coat. This I take to have given Rise to many of those Absurdities which are committed over our Heads; and, as I am informed, first occasioned the three Nuns and a Hare, which we see so frequently joined together. I would therefore establish certain Rules, for the determining how far one Tradesman may give the Sign of another, and in what Cases he may be allowed to quarter it with his own: I would enjoin every Shop to make use of a sign which bears some Affinity to the Wares in which it deals. What can be more inconsistent than to see a Taylor at the Lion? A Cook should not live at the Boot, nor a Shoemaker at the roasted Pig; and yet, for want of this Regulation, I have seen a Goat set up before the Door of a Perfumer, and the French King's Head at a Sword-Cutler's."[1]

It must be remembered that the same family, perhaps for several generations, carried on the same trade under the same sign, so that the family became as identified with its sign as a gentle race was with its heraldic crest or coat. Not only so, but it acquired a respect for and love of the weather-beaten sign that had swung over the shop from year to year, under father and grandfather and great-grandfather, and which was a symbol as well of honesty and just dealing.

The following is a list of some of the shop signs that have contributed names to English nomenclature—not, of course, complete, for a complete list, if obtainable, would occupy too much space.

BADGER. The Old English name is *Brock*, and both occur as surnames. The brock was a cognizance of the De Brooke family, and so may have been a tavern sign.

BEE. This occurs but rarely as a surname, yet the busy bee must assuredly have served as a sign. The bee was perhaps obscured by the hive. *A beille* is the French for a bee, whence the names *Able* and *Abeillard*, condensed into *Ballard*.

BULL is a common name, and was a tavern sign and also

[1] There is another paper on Signs in the *Tatler*, No. 18, 1709.

TOTEMISM AND NAMES

a shop sign. It occurs in the Hundred Rolls and in Postmortem Inquisitions. Other cognate names are *Steer, Calf, Stot*, or *Bullock*. *Calf* is a rare surname. *Veale* occurs in the Hundred Rolls as Le Veale, but represents Le Viel, the old man.

CAT. Although a sign, the name of *Catt* probably comes from the Low Countries. A Christopher Catt kept a coffee-house at which assembled a club of wits in Queen Anne's time. The members resolved to be painted by Sir Godfrey Kneller, all of a size, three-quarter length, and this originated the designation of "kit-cat" for the dimension of canvas. There was a famous designer of emblems named Catt, whose book is now much sought after.

CRANE, a shop sign.

DOG. The *Talbot* was a heraldic cognizance. The name *Kenn* is perhaps from *Chien*.

DRAKE, a dragon. The drake *gules* was the cognizance of the ancient family of *Drake* of Ashe, near Axminster. In this instance it is probable that the armorial bearing was occasioned by the name, and that some legend lay behind the name. Sir Francis Drake, the navigator, assumed the arms, though he could establish no relationship, and a contest of words ensued in the presence of Queen Elizabeth between Sir Bernard Drake of Ashe and the sailor.

"Well," said the Queen, "I will settle the dispute. Sir Francis shall bear on his coat a ship carrying reversed on its flag the wyvern *gules*."

Eventually, unwilling to mortify so worthy a man as Sir Bernard, she granted to Sir Francis an entirely different coat.

DOVE, as a sacred symbol, was certain to appear on a signboard. *Dove* was the name of the great clothier of Exeter, commemorated by Delony in his prose romance of "Tom of Reading," *circa* 1590. Of this Dove the jingle ran:

> "Welcome to town, Tom Dove, Tom Dove,
>   The merriest man alive;
> Thy company we do love, love, love:
>   God grant thee well to thrive."

Pigeon also is a surname; *Columb* as well. *Columbarium*

TOTEMISM AND NAMES

became contracted to Culverhouse, a pigeonry, and thence came the surname *Claverhouse*.

DUCK. Shovellers and other water-birds appear on so many coats of arms, and are vulgarly all called ducks, that we might be sure to find *Duck* as a surname. I have seen it spelled in registers *Doke*, and the surname *Duke* is actually a substitution for *Duck*. The name appears variously spelled in the Hundred Rolls and elsewhere.

Among some of the ducks that appear on coats of arms are coots, the bearing of the *Coode* family. But this name does not come from the bird, but from the Celtic for a wood, *coet*, it being a Cornish family.

EAGLE. The king of the birds, we know was a sign. The two-headed eagle was an armorial bearing; it was the symbol of the Habsburg Emperors. When the Archduke John was shooting in Tyrol, he one day brought down an eagle. On contemplating it he expressed his astonishment. "Why," he exclaimed, "it has one head only!" Gilbert de la Hegle appears in the Hundred Rolls; so also does Custance le Egle. But the usual name for an eagle was an *erne*. "Eagle" was from the French—an imported word.

FALCON. This is still an inn sign. The bird was variously described from the sign as a *Kite* and a *Hawk*, a Sparrow-hawk or *Sparke*, and a *Glede*. This last name is found in *Gledhill* and *Gledstone*.

FINCH, probably the sign of a birdseller, or *Burder*. The training and sale of bullfinches was the occupation of a special tradesman, also called a *Fincher*. The story is told of a certain damsel, that she once dreamed of finding a nest containing seven young finches, which in course of time was realized by her becoming the wife of a Mr. Finch and mother of seven children. From one of these nestlings is descended the present Earl of Winchelsea, who is a *Finch*. Probably, however, *Finch* is but a contraction of *Fincher*.

FISH, the sign hanging over a fishmonger's shop.[1] The

---

[1] But in the register of Bishop Stafford of Exeter, 1395-1419, the same man, Edward Fysch, is called elsewhere Edward Fyshacre, showing how names got clipped.

TOTEMISM AND NAMES

name is found in early records as *Fyshe* or *Fyske*. A good many fish have contributed surnames. *Dolphin* is from a sign or an heraldic cognizance. A Dolphin is named in Domesday. *Herring* is not uncommon.

> " Of all the fish in the sea that swim,
> There is none better than Herring the King."

Codd, *Mackerel*, *Whiting*, *Keeling*, *Crabbe*, *Chubb*, *Tench*, *Pike*, and *Spratt*, are names, but we cannot be at all sure that they originally were used in the sense of fish-names. A *Codner* was a cordwainer, and *Codd* may be but the shortening of this name. *Whiting* may be, and probably is, a whitinger or whitster. *Crabbe* is probably after the crab-tree. *Chubb* is probably a contraction of Cuthbert or of Job. *Pike* is a pikeman, and *Spratt* is St. Privat, or St. Pratt, a French place-name.

FOWL is either the sign of a poulterer, or a contraction of *Fowler*, or stands for the Welsh *foel* (bald).

FOX. The Fox and Grapes and the Fox and Hounds are common tavern signs. But *Fox* is also a corruption of *Fawkes*, itself a rendering in the vernacular of *Folko* or *Foulques*, a Norman name. We have also the name *Tod* (a male fox), *Renaud* or *Renard* or *Reynard*; but these latter are alterations of the Norman name that came from Reginhard, and had nothing to do with foxes.

GOAT. An entry in the Parliamentary writs, "John att Gote," points to the sign of the Goat hanging over his shop. Under the French form, *Chèvre*, we get the name *Chivers*. *Kidd* is not from a kid, but from Christopher, that became *Kitt*, and then *Kidd*.

GOOSE, a very likely sign for a shop where feathers and down were sold for beds and pillows. We have the name among us under the old form of *Goss*. *Gosling* is not the young of a goose in nomenclature, but Gauscelin or Joscelyn.

GULL. I doubt if it ever were a sign. The surname is from Goelo, a district in Brittany whence followers came who attended William the Conqueror. The name is also found as *Gully*.

TOTEMISM AND NAMES

HART, as certainly a sign as it was a crest. There were *Buck* and *Stag*, *Doe* and *Roe*; but *Buck* may stand for buckmaster, *Stag* in the West of England means a cock, and *Roe* may be a Danish name or a corruption of Ralph. *Hart* is the name from a sign, or from a knightly crest that has found much favour in England.

HERON, or *Herne*, and *Hernshaw* (a young heron), are names that occur, and we can well imagine the Heron as a sign. Tihel de Heroun came over with the Conqueror, and is supposed to have taken his name from a place; but undoubtedly he would take a heron as his cognizance.

HOG was a family name, as *Hogg*. A man so called was being tried before Judge Bacon on a capital charge. He pleaded to be dealt with mercifully on account of the relationship implied by his name. "No, my friend," said the Chief Justice, "not till you are hanged." Richard III. assumed as his symbol the boar, and inns with this sign date from his reign. It was said:

"The Rat, the Cat, and Lovel the Dog,
Rule all England under the Hog."

The Rat was Radcliffe, and the Cat was Catesby. Other names for a hog are, as already given, *Gryse*, also *Galt*; both have contributed to our nomenclature. *Sug* was a sow, and comes into the name *Sugden*. *Pig* is also a surname; Christopher *Pigg* was Lord Mayor of Lyme Regis in 1742. The name *Piggott*, or little pig, came in with the Conquest; it occurs several times in Domesday; but the derivation is probably from *pigge*, a little girl.

HORSE. The White Horse figured as a sign, and there is an entry "Walter de Whitehorse" in the Calendar of Patent Rolls in the Tower. There were also the *Colt*, the *Palfrey*, and the *Charger*. But the horse has not contributed much to our nomenclature directly, except under the French form, *Cheval*, which in English became *Capel*. Chaucer uses the word—"and gave him caples to his cart." A quarryman on Dartmoor, from whom I took down many folk airs, was named *Nankivell*—*i.e.*, the Valley of the Horse (Cornish).

TOTEMISM AND NAMES

His mates called him "Old Capel." From *Capel* (Caballus) comes the surname *Cable*.

HOWLET, an owl. Hence, possibly, the name *Hollet*, then *Hollick*.

JAY and POPINJAY certainly would be signs. Walter le Jay occurs among Inquisitiones Post-Mortem. The popinjay was a stuffed bird adorned with ribbons, that served as a mark for shooters with bow and crossbow. From its gay colours it gave a title to the parrot. The name occurs in Norfolk as a to-name in 1371. Among the privy purse expenses of Elizabeth of York, 1502, is the entry: "To a servant of William ap Howell for bringing of a popynjay to the Queene to Windesore xiiis. iiii*d*." Hence the names *Popjoy* and *Popgay*, also *Jaye*.

LAMB. The Lamb and Flag was a Church alehouse sign—a symbol of the Resurrection. A brother-in-law of John Wesley bore the name of *Whitelamb*.

LARK or LAVROCK. Hamo Larke appears in the Hundred Rolls. *Larkins* does not come from the lark, but is a diminutive of Laurence.

LION, that figures—blue, red, gold, and green—on so many signs, has certainly contributed some lion surnames.

LUCE, the Old English name for a pike, but also for a lily (the *fleur de luce*), has given a name to the Lucy family at Guy's Cliff and to others elsewhere. The wife of one of my farmers was a *Luce*. Shakespeare got into trouble with Squire Luce, or Lucy, J.P., for poaching, and he revenged himself on him by drawing him as Justice Shallow:

"*Slender*. A dozen white luces in their coat.
Shallow. It is an old coat."

Actually, the Lucy family bore as arms three pikes naiant; but as *Lily* and *Lilley* it exists as a surname, taken from the sign for the Annunciation.

PARROT. Of this as a surname we cannot be sure that it is not a form of *Pierrot*.

PARTRIDGE is not, as a surname, from a bird, but is a corruption of Patrick. The transitive form of the name is *Partrick*.

TOTEMISM AND NAMES

PEACOCK, a sign of an inn or of a shop. There was an Icelander, Olaf, who was nicknamed Pá, or the Peacock, because he dressed gaily, but the name died with him; and so, if given in England to a man for his gay attire, it would expire with him. But it would remain to a family that carried on business for several generations at the sign of the Peacock. But some *Peacocks* may derive from Peter the Cook.

PYE or MAGPIE, an inn sign; probably a shop sign as well.

RAM. The entry "Thomas atte Ram" among the muniments in the London Guildhall shows that the Ram was a sign.

RAVEN, again a sign, the armorial bearing of the Corbetts. But *Rafn*, the Old Norse for a raven, remained in Northumbria as a personal name till late.

ROOK, also a sign; hence the surname *Rooke*.

SWAN. This bird naturally, from its beauty, commended itself as a sign, and was also used as a crest.

WOLF has been already dealt with. As Lupus, Louve, it has undergone a strange alteration into *Love*.

WOODPECKER, commonly called in the country the Woodwall—*i.e.*, Woodcall. This has furnished surnames—*Woodwall, Woodwale,* and *Hoodwall.*

WOODCOCK appears as a surname, not likely to be taken from a sign. It is a corruption of Woodcott.

The sign of the *Angel* was by no means infrequent, and it has contributed a name to our family nomenclature. The *Lily* for the symbol of the Annunciation has been already alluded to. Various symbols of saints have also served as signs, as the *Cross Keys* for St. Peter, and this has given us the name.

Key and *Keyes* are names: Key was a sign of a locksmith, but Keyes refers to those of St. Peter. The *Cross* and the *Crucifix* have also given us surnames. So also the *Leg*[1] (a

---

[1] The name of the Earl of Dartmouth's family, *Legge*, may be a corruption of Liége.

TOTEMISM AND NAMES

Golden Leg having been a sign); so also a *Foot*, for a hosier and a shoemaker. The red *Hand* for a glover has likewise furnished us with many Hands. The *Head* as well, either as the sign of a hatter or as an armorial bearing, has given us not only Heads, but also Têtes, as *Tait* and *Tate*, unless this name comes from the Norse *Teitr*. *Morshead* is from the swaying sign of the Blackamore's Head. In some cases, though not in all, *Chalice* may derive from the sign of the gold cup with a serpent issuing from it, the symbol of John the Divine; but it also represents the Christian name Calixtus. Beauflower, now *Boutflower*, and corrupted to *Buffler*, represents the sign of the Beaupot with flower-bunch in it. Our *Flowers*, however, are a corruption of *Floyers*. There is a shop at Plymouth under the two names of *Dainty* and *Dilly*—the former from the French *denté*, and the latter name comes, perhaps, from the sign of the Daffy-down-dilly. The *Rose* was the usual badge of a goldsmith. The surname *Nation* may be a mutilation of Carnation, and the sign of the *Planta genista* originated the surname of *Broom*. The bunch of *Savory*, the token of the shop of a herbalist, probably gave its name to a family of some note in Devon, one of whom was an inventor of the steam-engine—unless Savory be a corruption of St. Ebrard. *Lavender* as a surname does not come from the herb, but signifies a washerman. The *Primrose* remains as a surname; it is that of Lord Rosebery, whose remote ancestor chose

> "Pale primroses
> That die unmarried, ere they can behold
> Bright Phœbus in his strength,"

by a happy inspiration, as the sign of his shop.

Some of the many *Kings* who are found among us derive their name from the King's Head or the Three Kings that swung over the ancestral shop. So also our *Greens* look back to the Green Man, or Jack-in-the-Green, of May Day, a common and popular sign. The name of *Savage*, also, refers to the sign of the *Wild Man*, which has contributed a name in that form, oftenest shortened into *Wilde* or *Wylde*. The

TOTEMISM AND NAMES

Barber's Pole probably gave its appellation to the family of *De-la-Pole*, that rose from an ignoble stock rapidly into power and pride. *Snake* is a rare surname, but it exists. William and Robert Snake were ancient Provosts of Bristol. The name comes from the sign of the rod of Æsculapius with the intertwined serpents, that indicated the shop of the apothecary. *Pepper* comes from the peppercorn, that betokened the place where the spicer had his counter; but *Onion* is the Welsh Einion, and *Garlick* in some cases from the German Gerlach, but may be in others from the sign of the garlick-seller. The *Bell*, the *Hammer*, the *Harrow*, the *Image*, the *Plough*, the *Rainbow*, the *Gauntlet*, the *Shield*, the *Buckler*, and many more signs, have contributed to English nomenclature.

It seems strange at first sight that the sign of the *Sun* should not have contributed names to families, as the Blazing Orb or the Rising Sun was a common sign. But the reason was that *Son* and *Sun* were interchangeable, and *son* entered in composition into so many names. Edward of York says:

"Henceforward will I bear
Upon my target three fair-shining suns.
Richard. Nay, bear three daughters: by your
  leave I speak it,
You love the breeder better than the male."
Henry VI., Part III., II. 1.

The *Moon* occurs, but it is a corruption, at least in Devonshire, of *Mohun*.

Starre, for Star, we do possess, as also the German importation of *Stern* or *Sterne*, the surname of the famous Laurence, author of "Tristram Shandy."

The little town of Sterzing, on the Brenner Pass, was once far more flourishing than it is at present, owing to the silvermines in the neighbourhood, once extensively worked, but now fallen into decay. It consists of one long street of medieval houses, with a gateway at each end. Every house has its sign—the Bear, the Lion, the Swan, the Stork, the Golden Sun, the Star of the Magi, the Crown, the Spurs, the

TOTEMISM AND NAMES

Pine, the Talbot, and the Eagle, all in lively colours and blazing with goldleaf. One can form a judgment from this street, with the projecting elaborate and delicate ironwork supports and the depending painted boards, what must have been the picturesque aspect of an English town thoroughfare in medieval days, even in those of Elizabeth.

Macaulay, in his account of London in the reign of Charles II., says: "The houses were not numbered. There would, indeed, have been little advantage in numbering them; for of the coachmen, chairmen, porters, and errand boys, of London, a very small proportion could read. It was necessary to use marks which the most ignorant could understand. The shops were therefore distinguished by painted signs, which gave a gay and grotesque aspect to the streets. The walk from Charing Cross to Whitechapel lay through an endless succession of Saracen's Heads, Royal Oaks, Blue Boars, and Golden Lambs, which disappeared when they were no longer required for the common people."

They disappeared indeed as signs, but remained in family nomenclature.

CHAPTER V

THE CASTLE AND THE MANOR

THE Conquest and resettlement of England by William the Bastard caused as great a change in the social condition as did the Revolution in France, but in an inverse manner.

Previously the land had been in the possession of freeholders—thegns and haulds and smaller men—with their well-defined rights to so much acreage, pasture, common, and vert. The Crown appointed the Sheriff, but the minor officers were elected by the people, and were responsible to them for the proper discharge of their duties. But after the Conquest all this was changed. The land throughout England was claimed as the property of the Crown, to be distributed among foreign favourites under feudal tenure.

"There can be little doubt," says Freeman, "that it was to the great transfer of lands from Englishmen to strangers that the Norman Conquest of England owes its distinguishing character. This was the cause, more than any one cause, which made the Norman Conquest so thorough and lasting if we look at it from one point of view, so transitory if we look at it from another.... William's foreign knights and men-at-arms were changed into English landowners, holding the soil of England according to English law. He had his garrisons in every corner of the land, but his garrison was formed of the chief lords of the soil and the chief tenants who held under them."[1]

After the coronation of William no man could hold an acre by an ante-Norman title. All were obliged to obtain a

---

[1] "Norman Conquest," vol. iv., p. 54.

THE CASTLE AND THE MANOR

regrant from the King, and it was exceptional that a thegn of the time of King Edward should retain his possessions under King William. Dispossessed, he must sink to be a tenant-farmer or a villein. The freeholder of his allodial land had become extinct, and a network of officials was cast over England, holding the people involved in its toils.

Some of the Barons held a great number of manors. They could not reside on them all, and were constrained to place subtenants in them. Many of these were men of foreign race—Normans, Bretons, Flemings; but some were native Englishmen. These latter could not, however, reckon on permanency of tenure, for they were always liable to be displaced, to make way for a superannuated dependent of the lord, for whom a home had to be found, that his place might be filled by one younger and more active.

We read in the Buckinghamshire Domesday: "Ailric holds four hides of William Fitzansculf [the new Norman lord] . . . the same held it in the time of King Edward; and he now holds it at farm of William under heavy circumstances and miserably."

This case was not unique. Thus: "Leofwin holds of the Earl Bure in Herefordshire. This land the same Leofwin held of King Edward, and he could sell it. Now he holds it as farm of the Earl." These passages illustrate the remark of Bracton that there were before the Conquest freemen who held their lands by free service, but who, after they had been ousted by more powerful men, took back the same tenements to be held in villeinage. Some who were fortunate secured the freehold of a scrap of their former estate.

The ordinary arrangement in every manor was this: It was divided into two parts. One portion was the great home-farm about the seigneurial manor-house, held distinct from that of the tenants. The rest of the manor, called the tenantry part, was divided into small copyholdings, of about nearly equal value, and enjoying equal rights of commonage. There was, however, a constant pressure brought to bear upon the tenantry to reduce their privileges, and the functionaries of the lord were on the alert to pare down their rights.

THE CASTLE AND THE MANOR

Here is a list of the ten largest holders of land after the Conquest:

1. The King held as many as - - 1,422 manors.
2. The Earl of Mortaine held - - 793 ,,
3. Alan, Earl of Brittany, held - - 442 ,,
4. Odo, Bishop of Bayeux, held - 439 ,,
5. Gosfrid, Bishop of Coûtance, held 280 ,,
6. Roger de Busle held - - - 174 ,,
7. Ilbert de Laci held - - - 164 ,,
8. William Peverel held - - - 162 ,,
9. Robert de Stradford held - - 150 ,,
10. Roger de Laci held - - - 116 ,,

As may well be conceived, the great Barons must have employed numerous officials, not only about their own persons, but in supervision of their many and scattered estates; and thus there arose a whole class of functionaries, who had to be maintained out of the land, so that the unfortunate under-tenants and copyholders were oppressed with the burden, not only of the King's taxes, but also of rent to the overlord, and dues for the support of the swarm of officials.

The Norman Conquest introduced into England Bumbledom and Flunkeyism.

Every great owner of manors must have his baíliff, his steward, his reves, his rangers, his foresters, beside the many officials about his person. And these latter were men of consideration, who had to be well paid, naturally at the cost of the tenants.

Charles the Great had instituted the order of Ministrales. About his sacred person were grouped functionaries who were hereditary servers at his table—butlers, shoers of his horses, dispensers of the provisions in his household. His Court was "crowded with officers of every rank; some of the most eminent of them exercised functions about the royal person which would have been thought fit only for slaves in the palace of Augustus or Antonine. To carry his banner or his lance, lead his array, to be his marshal, or constable, or sewer, or carver; to do, in fact, such services,

THE CASTLE AND THE MANOR

trivial or otherwise, as his lord might have done for himself in proper person, had it so pleased him—this was the position coveted by youths of birth and distinction at such a period as this."

From the Court of the Emperor the system descended to that of Dukes and Earls. William the Conqueror had his Marshal and his Despenser. And these offices were by no means sinecures, as may be gathered from the story of the transfer of that of High Steward to the Conqueror from William FitzOsbern to Eudo de Rie. At dinner one day FitzOsbern with his own hands had placed before the King a crane that was but half roasted; whereat William raised his fist to strike him in the face, but Eudo warded off the blow. FitzOsbern, very angry, asked to be relieved of his function, and it was given to Eudo.

The *Stuarts* were the hereditary Stewards of the Crown of Scotland. The *Marshalls*, whom the Conqueror elevated to become Earls of Pembroke, were his stable-keepers, and saw to the curry-combing of his horses, and the pitchforking out every day of their dung to the heap. The *Despensers* were royal officials placed in charge of the buttery, or "spence," where the store of meat and bread was kept; such was the origin of the family of *Spencer*, Duke of Marlborough. The ancestor of the *Grosvenors*, Dukes of Westminster, was the chief huntsman of the Duke of Normandy.

The modest Le Boteler was the proto-parent of the family of *Butler*. James Butler, Duke of Ormond, derived in lineal descent from a grave individual, bottle in hand, who stood behind some Prince, or perhaps only petty squire, and said deferentially, in the corresponding terms of the day : " Port or sherry, sir ?" Earl Ferrers, who shot his valet for showing lack of proper respect, might with advantage have looked back to the founder of his family in a leather apron, shoeing the Bastard's horse before the Battle of Hastings.

The *Chamberlaynes* derive also from the race of Ministrales, of whom Boyet and Malvolio are the types, pacing backward, making legs, kissing the hand, cap lowered, an eternal

THE CASTLE AND THE MANOR

smile on the face, proud of their chain of office, that was also a badge of servitude. Lord *Napier* of Magdala derives his descent from the functionary in charge of the napery, sheets, pillow-cases, table-linen—the man with a towel over his arm, like the modern *garçon* or *kellner*, ready to wipe his master's fingers after he had washed them in the ewer, having finished tearing his food with his hands. And consider the family motto, implying that the race was with "na-na-peer"! What dexterity in wiping gravied fingers and a dirty mouth it must have displayed, or in ironing and folding bed-linen, that it could boast of having no equal!

The Earl of Morley is a *Parker*, and the office of the parker was to see to the palings of the seigneurial park, lest they should rot and allow the deer to break forth—the same office as that held by the *Pallisers*.

After all, it may be thought that the more honourable ancestry is that of a freeborn, honest, independent yeoman, rather than that of one of the flunkeys who capered attendance on the great.

The official life of feudal times has left its existing record in our family nomenclature. It is a record that will never be effaced, and it is one that tells its own tale.

The higher feudatories in England, as elsewhere, imitated the example set them by the Court of the Kings, and the lower Barons followed suit as a matter of course, and were copied eventually by every manorial lord or squire as far as his means allowed. Consequently, household officers sprang up on all sides thick as toadstools.

But the names pertaining to these offices did not become hereditary unless the offices themselves became hereditary, and then adhered solely to the tenant of the office, and not to all his sons, and to none of his brothers.

The hereditary principle became such a recognized institution in feudal Europe that the son of a chamberlain or forester might expect as his due to enter upon his father's functions when that father died or retired, and his lord would recognize the claim as just and admissible.

Suppose that John the Chamberlain had three sons—Tom,

THE CASTLE AND THE MANOR

Dick, and Harry. Tom, as the eldest, remained with his father, and acquired aptitude in all the functions of a chamberlain. But Dickon would have to suit himself with a situation elsewhere, and would be accommodated, let us say, with that of forester, whilst his brother Harry would be happy to enter on that of bailiff. Then the two younger sons of John Chamberlain would be Dickon the Forester and Harry the Bailie. Tom Chamberlain in turn would be the father of Robert, Gregory, and Walter. Robert would succeed to the office and title of Chamberlain; but Gregory, may be, would migrate to a town and become a mercer; and Walter, having a capacity that way, would become a cook. Neither would carry away with him the title of Chamberlain. No man steps into his father's shoes unless they fit him.

Only after a particular office had been held for several generations in lineal descent, till the period when surnames became general, would the title of the bearer of the office be applied to all his family, although not exercising his functions, and so become a hereditary surname.

In feudal tenure there was a graduated scale from the highest to the lowest functionary, but below him a line was drawn that was for some time difficult to pass. From the lord down to the lowest official, all were of foreign blood; their home was in the castle or the manorial hall, and their language was French. But below the line of feudatories and retainers were the villeins, boors, cotters, coliberts, socmen, and churls. The only intervening class was that of the Vavasours, suspended, like Mahomet's coffin, between the heaven of the Norman castle and the earth of the villein hamlet.

In this chapter we will deal only with the official class, and that, moreover, which belongs mainly to the land, and not to the town.

In the next we will step out of the castle into the village, from the chatter of French tongues to the grave speech of the English farmer and peasant in the field. It will be

THE CASTLE AND THE MANOR

seen that both have contributed to the formation of English surnames.

ACHATOUR, the purveyor of the castle or hall, purchasing the necessary food, and handing it over to the steward. Hence our surnames of *Cator, Chater, Astor,* and *Caterer.* Chaucer remarks of the manciple who was so "nise in buying of victuals" that of him "Achatour mighten take example." Among Oxford University accounts for 1459 mention is made of the "catours."

ARMIGER, the esquire who carried the knight's shield. Robert Shallow Esquire, Slender says, is "a gentleman born, who writes himself *armigero* in any bill, warrant, quittance, or obligation *armigero.*" "*Shallow.* Ay, that I do, and have done any time these three hundred years." We retain the word as a family name in *Armiger.*

ASSAYER, a taster, to assure the lord at table that the food and drink had not been poisoned. The word is used as well for a tester of metals. The names *Sayer, Sayers, Saer,* come hence.

ASTRINGER, the functionary entrusted with the charge of the goshawk, or "oster." "The gentle Astringer" is introduced in "All's Well that Ends Well." As a surname we have *Stringer* and *Austringer.*

AVENER, the official whose charge it was to supply hay—avoine—for the stables. Hence comes *Venners.*

BAILIFF, the same as reve or steward. Wicklyffe, in Luke xvi. 2, has, "Yelde rekenying of thi Baylye, for thou myght not now be baylyf," where in the Authorized Version we have this officer rendered "steward."

BEDALL. The official is mentioned in Domesday Book. He was the functionary who executed processes in the courts of the manor, or in a forest, or any other court. The surname remains as *Beadell, Beadle, Beadall,* and contracted to *Biddle,* also *Bedell.*

BERNER. The berner was a special houndsman who stood with fresh relays of dogs, ready to unleash them if the chase grew long and the hounds out showed signs of being

THE CASTLE AND THE MANOR

spent. In the Parliamentary Rolls he is termed a "yeoman-berner."

BERWARD or BEARWARD. Some nobles kept bears for the amusement of having them baited. The man who baited them was the *Bateman;* he in charge of the brutes was the *Bearward* or *Bearman*, often spelled *Borman*. In the household expenses of the Earl of Northumberland in 1511 is "6s. 8d. to the Kings and Queenes Barward, if they have one, when they come to the Earl." In the Parliamentary Rolls mention is made of the "Beremaster of the Forest of Peake."

Bears were taken about from town to town, to be baited for public amusement. Bear-baiting was not forbidden by Act of Parliament till 1835. Slender says: "Be there bears in the town?" "*Anne.* I think there are, sir. I heard them talked of." Surnames of *Barman* and *Berman* remain; also *Bates* for the Bater's-man.

BLOWER or HORNBLOWER, the man who at a chase called the dogs together. Both forms remain, but *Blower* is often contracted to *Blore* and *Blow;* also the surname *Horniman*.

BOWER and BOWERS, an indoor servant, attendant on the ladies. Also *Bowerman* and *Burman*.

BUCKMASTER, an officer of the chase; shortened to *Buck*.

CARVER, the servant who carved the meat. Same as *Dresser*.

CASTELLAN, the keeper of a castle. As a surname, contracted to *Castle*.

CELLARER. The name remains as a surname in the form of *Sellars*, unless this be from the salt-makers.

CHAMBERLAIN, one of the most intimate servants in a seigneurial house, and one who had charge of the accounts. The surname from the office is sometimes shortened to *Chambers*.

CHANCELLOR, keeper of records.

CLAVINGER, the keeper of the keys; also a mace-bearer. As a surname, *Cleaver* and *Claver*.

CONSTABLE. The office ranged from one very high, as that of a Constable of France, to the constable of a village.

THE CASTLE AND THE MANOR

In "The Man of Law's Tale" Chaucer speaks of the Constable of the Castle.

COOK or LE COQ, a very important functionary. His name enters into numerous combinations, as *Badcock* (Bartholomew le coq), *Wilcox* (Will le coq), *Hancock* (John le coq). Mr. Lower and Mr. Bardsley think "cock" is a diminutive only. But it is always found after a Christian name that is already in the diminutive, and I consider that it means "the cook." Beside the French termination le Coq, whence *Coxe*, we have the English surname *Cooke*. But that *cock* and *cox* so frequently end names indicates that the Norman lords did not trust to having Englishmen in their kitchen to prepare their food. The name is sometimes spelled *Cooke*. We have also the names *Cookson*, *Cookman*, and *Cokeman*. The entry "Robert. fil. Coci" in the Hundred Rolls shows that some Cooks' sons were so designated whose fathers had no recognized surnames. Also *Kitchen* and *Kitchener*.

DEERMAN, a warder to look after the wild animals in a park.

DESPENSER, the officer in charge of the victuals in the buttery. Hence the surnames *Spenser* and *Spencer*. "Adam, that was the Spencer" ("The Coke's Tale" in the "Canterbury Pilgrims").

DRESSER, the official who dressed the table for a meal, described in the "Promptuarium Parvulorum." Our word "dresser," for a side-table on which the meat is placed and cut up, comes hence.

ENGINEER, the officer in charge of catapults and other engines of war. The Hundred Rolls give William le Engynur and Wallis le Ginnur. Hence come our surnames *Ginners*, *Jenners*, and *Ginns*.

ESKRIMIGER, attendant on a knight or a noble to instruct the youths in the art of employing their weapons. Such a mock-fight was a skrimmage. The word comes from the French *eskrimer*, to fence. Hence the fencing-master has furnished us with the surnames *Skrimiger* and *Skrimshire*.

ESQUIRE. The place of shield-bearer and attendant on a noble or knight was much sought after by the sons of men

THE CASTLE AND THE MANOR

in good position, as it was an admirable apprenticeship for war. By the time of Henry VI. the word was adopted by the heirs of gentle houses. From it come our *Squires*, *Squeers* of Dotheboys Hall, and *Swiers*. These names were acquired by such as did not proceed to knighthood.

ESPIGURNEL, the official in charge of the lord's seal. Hence the surname *Spurnell*.

FALCONER. In Domesday four tenants-in-chief are given the title of Falconers. Until the reign of King John it was unlawful for any but those of the highest rank to keep hawks. By a statute passed in the reign of Edward IV., anyone who found a strayed falcon was bound to bring it to the Sheriff of the county, who made thereupon proclamation for the owner to claim it. If the finder concealed the bird, he was liable to two years' imprisonment. We have the surnames *Falconer, Falkner, Faulconer, Fauconer,* and *Faukner*.

FEUTERER or VAULTRIER was the man who unleashed the hounds. The surnames of *Future* and *Futurer* come from this functionary.

FORESTER, a very important officer charged with the supervision of the royal forests. There were, of course, many under-foresters. From these officers, when the offices became hereditary, came the surnames of *Forester, Forster, Foster*.

FORSET (Old Norse *forseti*, a judge) has given surname to *Forset, Fawcett*. The title was used only in Northumbria, and the office was changed and lost its Scandinavian designation after the complete reduction of the North by William. It occurs in Domesday.

GARDENER. The name is French; we may conclude, therefore, that the Anglo-Saxons had no gardens, only orchards. The surname is often spelled *Gardiner* and *Gardner*, also *Jardine*.

GAOLER, a French name, showing that no Englishman could be trusted by a Norman with the keys of the prison. The surnames from the office are *Gayler, Gale,* and *Jelly*, perhaps.

GRANGER, one who occupied the grange of the lord,

THE CASTLE AND THE MANOR

secular or ecclesiastical, in which the corn "grain" was stored.

GRIEVE, the Gerefa or Reeve, the manorial bailiff. The "Boke of Curtasye" says:

> "Grayvis and baylys and parkers
> Shall come to accountes every yere
> Byfore the auditours of the lorde."

As a surname the title is still with us, either as *Grieves* or *Greaves* or *Greeves*. We have also *Grierson*, the son of the Grieve.

GUNNER, the officer in charge of the guns. Our surname contracted to *Gunn*. In Northumbria, however, from Old Norse *Gunnar*.

HARBORER, the functionary who had charge of the guests to see them properly disposed of; or an officer who preceded his lord when he progressed looking out for lodgings for the night for him and his retinue. In the "Canterbury Tales" we have:

> "The fame anon throughout the town is borne,
> Here Alla King shall come on pilgrimage,
> By harbergeours that wenten him before."

The modern German is *herberger*. The several Coldharbours found in England express that there were comfortless shelters for travellers. The surname *Arbour* or *Arber* comes from this officer.

HARAUD, the herald. In the metrical romance of "Torrent of Portygale," *circa* 1435, spelled Haraud. Everyone in London knows *Harrod's* Stores, but not one in a thousand has any idea that the ancestor was a herald in tabard, and held in high honour; unless, indeed, the name be from Harrold, near Bedford.

HARPER. Most large castles had in them the harper. The surname remains.

HARTMAN, the officer who looked after the harts in the chase. The surname from it may be *Hardman*,[1] and sometimes only *Hart*.

---
[1] But *Hardman* may be the serving-man of *Hardy*.

THE CASTLE AND THE MANOR

HASTLER, the turnspit. From *hasta*, a spear, to which the spit bore some resemblance. Surnames: *Hasler, Haseler, Haysler.*

HAUBERGER and HAUMER, those entrusted with the habergeon and the hawlm, or helmet. The latter has supplied the surname *Homer.*

The FURBISHER or FROBISHER kept the armour polished.

HENCHMAN, a messenger. Surnames: *Hinksman, Hinchman.*

HIND, the man who looked after his master's affairs in the home-farm. Hence the surnames *Hynde* and *Hyne.*

HOARDER, the English name for the cellarer. From it we have the surnames *Horder, Horden, Hoadener, Herder.*

HOBBLER was a tenant holding his tenure on the obligation of coming out on a hobby, or farm-horse, when called upon by his lord. An ordinance of Edward III. speaks of men-at-arms, hobblers, and archers.

HUNTSMAN. As *Hunter* the name of the office remains a surname. Shortened also to *Hunt.*

KNIGHT by no means invariably means one who has received knighthood. A knight is a *knecht*, a servant. The surname *Midnight*, perhaps, means the mead-cniht, the man who poured out the mead.

JACKMAN, a man-at-arms in a coat of mail or jacket, and wearing jack-boots.

MARSHALL, originally the horse-groom. He rose into consideration and became a regulator of ceremonies. The "Boke of Curtasye" says:

> "In halle marshalle alle men shalle sette
> After their degree, withouten lett."

MESSENGER, a servant much needed when there was no post. Every great house had to keep its messenger. As a surname, sometimes *Massenger*. But the Old English word was *Sandiman* or *Sandman.*

MILLER. The mill belonged to the lord of the manor, and the tenants were not allowed to grind their corn at any other. Hence *Milner* and *Milward* (Anglo-Saxon for a miller), *Millman.*

THE CASTLE AND THE MANOR

NAPPER, the servant who attended to the napery. Hence *Napier*, and perhaps *Knapper*.

PAGE; of this PAGET is the diminutive.

PALFREYMAN, the keeper of the ladies' palfreys.

PANTLER, the servant in charge of the pantry.

PARKER, the official in charge of the deer-park. Hence *Parkman*, *Parkes*.

PENNIGER, the man who bore his lord's banner. Some of the *Pennys* we meet with may take their name from Penniger. Pfeniger is still a surname in Germany. In Scotland the corresponding officer was called *Bannerman*.

PIKEMAN. From him, by contraction, comes the name *Pyke*.

PORTER, the gatekeeper. The family of *Porter* of Saltash is one of hereditary gatekeepers of Trematon Castle. The English of Porter is *Durward*.

POTTINGER, the gardener of potherbs for the kitchen.

POYNDER, a bailiff.

PRICKMAN, the man whose duty it was to look after the prickets. *Cf.* "Love's Labour Lost," IV. II. Also *Prickett*; but *Prickard* is Ap Richard.

PROCURATOR, an attorney. Hence *Procter*, *Procktor*.

RANGER, a keeper.

REVE, from Gerefa. There were reeves of various kinds, looking after the manorial rights: Woodkeepers, whence the surnames *Woodward* and *Woodrow*; fenreeves, to look after the rights to turbary; hythereeves, taking harbour dues; portreeves, in coast towns.

RIDER. The Barons maintained German mercenaries as horsemen. These were the *Reiter*, or, as the English called them, *Reuters*. They soon, however, changed Reuter into *Rider* and *Ryder*. An old song begins:

"Rutterkyn is come into oure towne
In a cloke withoute cote or gowne,
Save a ragged hood to cover his crowne
Like a rutter hoyda."

All our *Ryders* may with confidence look back to a German or Brabant origin, when the ancestor came over "withoute

THE CASTLE AND THE MANOR

cote or gowne" to take the King's or some Earl's or Baron's money as a mercenary, but saw a pretty English wench, married, and settled down among his wife's people.

RYMER, a reciter of poems and ballads.

SCRIVENER. In the castle or hall the illiterate noble or Lord of the Manor was obliged to employ a writer, to put down his accounts, arrange contracts in writing with his tenants, and do for him his general correspondence. As a surname we have both *Scrivener* and *Scribner*.

SENESCHAL. In Latin *Dapifer*, and so found in Domesday. The *schalk* that we have here and in *Marshall*, and in the old word for a porter, *Gateschall*, from which the surname *Gattishill*, is the Anglo-Saxon *schalk*, a servant. In German *Schalk* now means a rogue. In an old poem we have:

"Then the *schalkes* sharply shift their horses,
To show them seemly in their sheen weeds."

From this word *schalk* comes the surname *Chalk*.

SEWER is simply a server, a waiter. The "Boke of Servynge" says: "The server must serve, and from the borde convey all manner of pottages, metes, and sauces." As a surname it has become *Sour* and *Shower*.

SEIGNEUR, a lord, has become the surname *Senior*.

SHERIFF, a royal officer in the county, and only inserted here because the great noble was often nominated to be a Sheriff. Probably the surname *Sheriff* comes from some Sheriff's officer.

SQUILLER, one who washed up the escuelles, porringers, and bowls. Hence our words "scullery" and "scullion." Robert of Brunne says:

"And the squyler of the kitchen
Piers, that hath woned [dwelt] here yn."

The "Promptuarium Parvulorum" defines "Swyllare: Dysche—weschowr." Hence the surname *Quiller*.

STABLER, an ostler.

STALLER, much the same.

STEWARD. Hence *Stewart* and *Stuart*.

TODMAN, the man employed to destroy foxes (tods), as

THE CASTLE AND THE MANOR

keeping down the game. *Todhunter* and *Tadman*, for *Todman*, are still surnames among us.

TROTTER, a running footman.

USHER, from the French *huissier*. The "Boke of Curtasye" says:

"Usher before the dore
In outer chamber lies on the floor."

The learned Archbishop of Armagh spelled his name *Ussher*. In Scotland the name is *Wischart*.[1] In England, *Hazard*. There is, however, a place-name *Ushaw* in Durham.

VENOUR, the hunter; whence *Fenner*.

VEUTER, one who tracks deer by the fuite; hence the surname *Future*.

VYLER, the player on the viols; hence *Fyler*.

WARDEN or GUARD, a keeper. *Warden, Warde, Garde*, and *Garden* for Warden.

WAGEOUR, a hired soldier. Surname, *Wager*.

WARDROPER, the keeper of the wardrobe.

WARRENER, the official in charge of the warren. Contracted to *Warne*.

[1] Unless from Guiscard; but Guiscard itself is Huissier, with the common Norman-French ending *ard*.

CHAPTER VI

THE VILLAGE

IN 1085-86 the great inquest was made into the tenure of land in England, and into the amount of land that was taxable. Commissioners were sent into the shires, who took evidence on oath from the Sheriffs, the parish priests, the reeves, and the men generally, French and English alike, in every lordship. They were to report who had held the land in the time of Edward the Confessor, and who held it then; also as to how many lived on it, what was their quality and what was the value of the soil, and whether there was any prospect of the value being raised.

The Chronicle says: "He sent over all England, into every shire, his men to find out how many hundred hides were in the shire, and what the King himself had of land and cattle in the land. Also what rights he ought to have in the twelve months in the shire. Also he let enquire how much land his Archbishops had, and his Bishops, and his Abbots, and his Earls, and though I tell it at more length, what and how much every man had that was a land-holder in England, in land or in cattle, and how much fee it was worth. So very narrowly did he let the investigation be carried out, that there was not a single hide, nor a yard of land, not so much as—it is a shame to tell it, and he thought it no shame to do it—not an ox nor a cow, nor a swine, was left that was not set in his writ. And all the writs were brought to him."

The taking of this inquisition roused great dissatisfaction that broke out in tumults, and some blood was shed.

THE VILLAGE

Hitherto the land-holders, with a little shuffling and some bribing, had been able to assess their lands lower than their actual value. This would now be impossible, and they looked to the hard hand of the tax-gatherer coming down on them, and remorselessly squeezing out the due for every acre, whether in cultivation or fallow. From Domesday we learn what were the several classes among the English who were now under the heel of the Norman.

The old THEGNS were no longer great men; they had to bow their necks under the yoke, and see their land taken from them and their influence and authority gone. Some, luckily, remained on as tenants on the land where they had been freeholders, and in remembrance of the past still called themselves Thegns or Theins, and continued to be so called. Hence it comes that we have the surname of *Thynne*.

The FREEMEN, freeholders, held their land after the Conquest no longer as freemen, but subject to military service, and were taxable. Their representatives later were the yeomen. They have contributed to our nomenclature the names *Freeman* and *Free*. *Freebody* signified a freeholder of a little wooden cot. *Fry* as a surname comes thence as well.

RADMEN were socmen, possessed of a greater amount of freedom than others. Hence the surname *Redman*.

SOCMEN, inferior landowners who held their lands in the soc, or franchise, of a great lord. Hence *Suckerman, Suckman*.

FRANKLYN was much the same as the Freeman. From Chaucer's account, he would seem to have been a householder in a comfortable position, a well-to-do yeoman:

" Withouten bake-mete never was his house,
Of fish and flesh, and that so plenteous.
It snowed in his hous of mete and drinke
Of all deinties that men coud thinke.
After the sondry seasons of the yere
So changed he his mete and his soupere."

As a surname the appellation occurs frequently in the Hundred Rolls and Inquisitiones Post-Mortem, as *Franklyn, Franckon*, for *Franch-homme*, or simply as *Franks*. Our *Francombs* and *Frankhams* have the same origin.

THE VILLAGE

BONDER. The old Norse bonder was the man in highest position under the Earl. He was the freeholder, responsible to none save the Earl. It was because Harald Fairhair resolved on introducing the feudal tenure of land into Norway that a great exodus of the Bonders took place, and they migrated to and colonized Iceland and the Faroe Isles. In parts of England the name of Bonder seems to have been used in place of Franklyn and Freeman—notably in Northumbria and East Anglia—that were occupied by Danes and Northmen. Hence the surname *Bond*. And yet sometimes the word was employed for the serf:

> "Of all men in lande
> Most toileth the bonde."

In Domesday, Freemen, Franklyns, and Bonders, are all included under the heading *Liberi*.

BURS or GEBURS were workmen giving a certain number of days' work in the fields, and a small money payment to the Lord of the Manor. In return, a Bur received two men—villeins—as his labourers, and one cow, seven acres of tillage land, and his house full furnished. As a surname we have *Burr*.

BORDARS, a poor but numerous class, tenants of lands which their lord kept expressly for the maintenance of his table, the rental being paid in kind. Hence the old English law-books speak of board-service and board-land. We still have a reminiscence of this class in the surname *Boardman* and *Boarder*.

COTTARS and COTTRELS, also COTMENS, COSCETS. The cottar could hold nothing of his own, nor acquire anything without the consent of his lord. The Cottrel was in no better position. Shakespeare employs the word *coystril*, a corruption of *cottrel*, as descriptive of a very poor peasant. Hence our *Cotterels, Cottrels, Cotmans, Cottars, Coatmans,* and *Coates*. The *coscet* was a cottar paying a small rent for a very small piece of land. *Guscot* is the coscet's cottage.

VILLEINS were men in the servitude of the Lord of the Manor, who held the folkland, by which they supported

THE VILLAGE

themselves and their families. They stood somewhat higher than the serfs. They were also designated as *knaves*. The odium attaching to a class so low has stood in the way of the name passing into our family nomenclature, at all events in its Norman-French form. But it remains as *Churl* for *Ceorl*. The constellation of the Great Bear is commonly called Charles's Wain, and in this instance Charles stands for Ceorl. In the Edda of Sæmund the churl is represented by no means as a villein or thrall, but as a freeman. In Anglo-Saxon the ceorl is almost, if not quite, indistinguishable from the serf. In the Edda the churl is represented, indeed, as the offspring of different parents from the noble and from the thrall, but he occupies the position of the free bonder.[1] *Carl* signified a man generally. Charles is rarely found as a Christian name in England before the time of Charles I. The surnames *Charles*, *Charley*, and *Caroll*, from the Latin form *Carolus*, remain with us—the last in the United States.

CENSORS are named in Domesday. They were villeins who paid a *censum*, a kind of relief, by which they redeemed their estates. Being in a transitional state, they have left no trace in our nomenclature.

SERF, the poor wretch who owned nothing of his own but his wife and his children, is only recognizable in family names as *Server*, *Sewer*. *Servant* became *Sergeant*, and rose to be an official.

THRALL was given the surname *Thrale*.

AKERMAN occurs repeatedly in the Hundred Rolls, and seems to mean a ploughman.

MAN, in Latin *homo*, occurs in almost every page of the

[1] The parents of Jarl, the noble, were named Father and Mother. "Light was his hair, bright his cheeks, his eyes piercing as a young serpent's." Those of Churl were Afi and Amma. "He grew up and well throve; learned to tame oxen, and make a plough, houses to build, and barns to construct, and make carts, and drive the plough." The parents of Thrall are Ai and Edda. "Of his hands the skin was shrivelled, the knuckles knotty, and the fingers thick. A hideous countenance he had, a bowed back, and protruding heels."—*Rig-mal*. The three classes are the noble, the free farmer, and the serf.

THE VILLAGE

Domesday Survey, and included every kind of feudatory tenant. One of his most important privileges was that his person and case could be tried only in the court of his lord, to whom he was bound by submission. Hence the word *homage*. A *Newman* was a man who came into the jurisdiction of the lord from some other manor. Also described as a *Newcomen*. The surname of *Man* would be puzzling if we did not know its origin as a term designating a particular class.

COLIBERTS were tenants of a middle class who do not seem to have had an enduring tenure in England.

Such were the classes on the land. Now let us turn to the occupations. But before proceeding any farther in this division it will be as well to explain the entry of ANGLI—*i.e.*, ENGLISH—in Domesday, which would be as inexplicable as *Man* did we not know its origin. These Angli or Anglici were certain English subtenants on the Welsh frontier. At the time of taking the Survey, those of Shrewsbury paid the whole of the local geld for the support of the State. Probably at that time the majority of the inhabitants were of Welsh origin, and those of Saxon were distinguished as *English*.

ASHBURNER, the man employed on the production of potash. Till soap was invented, ashes were employed as a detergent. Also *Ashman*.

BADGER, properly a Bagger. " Up to the seventeenth century an ordinary term for one who had a special licence to purchase corn from farmers at the provincial markets and fairs, and then dispose of it again elsewhere, without the penalties of engrossing " (Bardsley).

BARKER, the man who barks for the tanner; *Barkis* is "at the Bark-house."

BERCHER or BERGER, a shepherd. A Norman-French name little used, yet surviving as a surname.

BEEMASTER. Occurs in Domesday as *Apium Custos*. An important man before the introduction of sugar, as honey was employed not only for the making of honey-cakes, but also in the brewing of metheglin or hydromel, and the wax was

THE VILLAGE

needed for candles. We have the Beemaster contributing to nomenclature in *Beamster* and *Honeyman*, or simply as *Honey*.

BEECHER, a spademan; from the Norman-French *bêche*.

BOLTER, the bolter of flour, a servant of the miller. Surname *Boult*.

BULLMAN, the bull-herdsman. Hence *Pullman;* also in some cases *Buller*.

BUSHER, the man employed to cut down and clear away bushes or undergrowth for the accommodation of the hunter, and also to serve the ashburner. Hence the name *Bush*.

BUZICARL, a seaman. The name occurs in Domesday, and was the title of a noble in Northumbria, as head of the fleet of merchant vessels; but as a surname I know it only in France as *Buscarlet*.

CALFHERD, now turned into the surname of *Calvert*.

CARPENTER, in country and town alike. In Domesday *Carpentarius*.

CARTER comes to us in many forms as a surname—*e.g.*, *Carter, Cartman*.

CARTWRIGHT, the maker of carts.

CARTERET, a small carter—*i.e.*, not a little man in size, but one who drove a small cart. But *Carteret* is also a Norman place-name.

CATCHPOLE, a village as well as a town officer; an under-sergeant who obtained his name from catching his victim by the head by means of a long wooden forceps that nipped by the throat the delinquent who was wanted. The name was borne by Margaret Catchpole, the horse-thief who was sentenced to be hanged at Ipswich, but was transported, in 1841. We have the name also as *Catchpool*. In "Piers Plowman's Vision" we are told, of the two thieves crucified on Calvary, that—

"A Catchpole came forth
And cracked both their legges."

CHALKER, the marl-digger or chalk-quarryman, who provided the chalk-marl for the fields, or the chalk for the lime-burner, or the clunch for the carver or sculptor. The

THE VILLAGE

chaucer, or shoemaker, will be dealt with in the list of town tradesmen.

CHURCHWARDEN. This officer, from the function being discharged from generation to generation in one family, became finally a surname, and survives as *Churchward*, also corrupted to *Churchyard*.

CLAYER or CLAYMAN, the marl-digger. To this day, in the Fens of Cambridge, the fields are dressed by digging down below the vegetable mould to the greasy marl beneath, and this is spread as manure over the soil. But the clayer also dug the clay for kneading with straw for the building of cob-walls. As a surname, *Claye*.

COCKER, an owner of fighting-cocks; also *Cockman*. The author of the "Townley Mysteries" puts him in bad company:

> "These dysars [dicers] and these hullars,
> These cokkers and these bullars [bull-wards],
> And all purse cuttars,
> Be well ware of these men."

Our name of *Cockerel* may come from *Cotterel*, and not signify a petty cockfighter; but a *Coker* and *Coaker* refer to the man who supplied entertainment by keeping a cockpit.

COLTHERD, the herdsman in charge of the colts; now, as a surname, *Colthard*.

COWHERD, the herdsman of the cows; hence *Coward*.

CRAMER or CREAMER, a huckster; hence *Cranmer*.

CRUDE, a wheelbarrow; hence, probably, *Cruden* for *Crudener*.

DIGGER, DITCHER, and DYKER, all much the same—the man who attended to the dykes. The surname *Digges* may come from this or from Digory; but *Dykes* is certainly hence, as also *Ditcher*.

DEYMAN or DAYMAN, a day-labourer; as surname often *Daye*. A *deie* (Old Norse *deigja*) is a dairy-woman; so in 'Promptuarium Parvulorum"; see also "Love's Labour Lost," I. II.

DYKEWARD, the man appointed on the East Coast to

THE VILLAGE

watch the embankments. As a surname it has become *Duckworth*.

DRIVER, the driftman; on moors the man employed to sweep together colts and horses and cattle and sheep sent out on the commons, to a centre where the owners may claim them, and such as have no right to send their beasts on the commons are fined. He has still his function on Dartmoor, and a drift there is a lively scene. No notice is given beforehand, except to the moormen or drivers. Horns are blown, and horses employed to drive the beasts.

DUDMAN, a man who sold coarse, common cloth garments, generally second-hand and patched. The name remains as *Dodman* and *Deadman*. A schoolmaster of the latter name was at Stowford in Devon; he fell down the Lydford Waterfall rocks, 70 feet, but was not killed. It was reported of him that he went down a dead man, and came up at the bottom a live man. The contraction of *Dodds* remains.

EWART or EWEHERD. As surname also *Youart*. John Eweherd, 1379, Yorkshire Poll-Tax.

FANNER, the winnower of corn. Also, among tin-miners, the fanner tossed the pounded stone into the air, fanning it, and the wind blew away the light dust and left the tin ore on his fanning shovel. The surnames *Fenner* and *Vanner* may derive hence.

FARMER remains on the land, and has contributed to our nomenclature. Also *Fermor*.

FARRAR and FARRIER, the man who shoes horses. *Fearon* is a smith; also *Ferrier*.

FINCHER, the bird-catcher who provided finches that were in great favour with our forefathers as cage-birds. The surnames *Fincher* and *Finch* remain.

FOWLER is a common surname, and explains its origin. This is sometimes contracted to *Fowles* and *Fowle*; also as *Vowler*.

GATEHERD is probably only *Goatherd*. It has contributed the surnames *Gatherd* and *Gateard*; and GOATHERD has given us *Goddart* and *Goatman*; but *Goddart* may, and probably does, in most cases derive through the German *Gothardt*.

GELDER, the gelder of hogs, etc.; hence *Geldart*.

THE VILLAGE

GOOSEHERD, the man who takes charge of the geese of a village. The office is still general in Germany, but is now given to a girl. "Barfüssle" is the story by Auerbach of a little goose-girl. The surname from it is *Gozzard*.

GRAVER, a digger of graves—*i.e.*, fall-pits for catching wild beasts; also of ditches. So Gravesend is at the end of a long dyke. The surnames hence are *Graves* and *Greaves*. A greave is also a woodland avenue, graved out of the forest. *Hargreave* is a trapper of hares by pitfalls.

HACKMAN is a hatchetman, a chopper of wood for the hearth or the furnace. The designation remains as a surname.

HAYMAN[1] or HAYWARD was the village official whose duty it was to guard the cattle that grazed on the village common, that they did not trespass on the ground where was the grass grown for hay during the winter. Until hedges became common, the hayward had to keep a sharp lookout on the cattle committed to his charge. In "Piers Plowman" we have:

> "I have a horne and be a *Hayward*,
> And liggen out at nyghtes,
> And kepe my corne and my croft
> From pykers and theves."

In an old song descriptive of summer and autumn it is said that "The hayward bloweth merry his horne." For his services it would seem that he was not only paid a few pence, but was also given by the parish a cottage and a croft. The surname now sometimes *Heyman;* also as *Haybiddel* (*i.e.*, hay-beadle) and *Hayter*.

HERDMAN. His duties much the same as those of the hayman; hence *Hurd, Heard, Hird, Hardman*.

HAWKER, or HUCKSTER, much the same as an itinerant pedlar. *Huxter, Hawkes*.

HEDGER and HEDGEMAN, he who made up the hedges.

HEWER, a woodcutter. But a *hewer* on the coast is a man who is stationed on the cliffs, to give notice when a shoal

---

[1] But some Haymans may be from Aymon.

THE VILLAGE

of pilchards or herrings is in sight. From the Norman-French *hué*.

HOGGARD or HOGWARD (whence the surname *Hogarth*), the village hog-keeper. The artist's name was originally Hoggart; he altered the spelling.

HONEYMAN. See BEEMASTER.

HUSBAND, the man who cultivated the portion of soil which derived from him the name of husband-land, a measure known in the Merse and Lothian. Hence the surname *Younghusband*—*i.e.*, (John) Young the Husband (land-holder).

KIDDER and KIDNER, the man who wove kitts, or rush baskets. A butterkitt was one of those in which butter was carried to market. Our word "junket" comes from the curd being sold wrapped up, as it still is in France, in rushes (*jonc*). A kidder was also a huckster. Hence the surname *Kidd* when not a contraction of Christopher.

KILNER, a lime-burner.

MADER or MATHER, a mower. On August 16, 1417, was served a writ to the Sheriff of Lancashire to arrest Mathew le Madder, husbandman. Cotton *Mather* must have descended from a mower.

NUTTARD, probably NEATHERD.

OYSELER, a professional bird-catcher; hence *Whistler* and *Oseler*.

PADMAN, PEDLAR, PEDDAR, all mean the same as *Packman*, of whom Autolycus is the type. *Packman* has been corrupted into *Paxman*. The packman was, however, a superior pedlar, as he had a horse, or even more than one, that carried his packs.

PEARMAN, PERRIMAN, PERRIER, are the names of growers of pears for making perry.

PIGMAN, the village pig-driver; whence the surname *Pickman*, when not a pikeman. He was also a LARDER, a fattener of pigs on acorns and beechnuts; also a PORKER, hence our surname *Porcher*. How speedily the servitors began to rise from the lowest rank may be seen by a monument, in Upton Pyne Church, of Edmund Larder in armour. The date is 1520, and yet—certainly but a few centuries

THE VILLAGE

before, even if so much as a few, his ancestor was a fattener of pigs. Also the surname *Lardner*.

PLOUGHMAN, hence *Plower* and *Plows*.

RUSHMAN, the collector and strewer of rushes on the church floor and the floor of halls; hence the surname *Rush*.

SAWYER, also *Sagar* and *Sayer*.

SHEPHERD, spelled as a surname also *Shephard* and *Sheppard*.

SLATER or SCLATER gives also *Slatter* as a surname.

STALLARD is, properly, the man who let out stalls at a fair or market.

STEADMAN or STEDMAN, a farmer occupying a homestead.

STODDART, the keeper of the village stots, or bullocks.

STUBBARD, the keeper of the parish bull. The old word for a bull was a *stubb*. Hence the surname *Stobbart*.

SWINEHERD explains itself.

TABORER or TABERNER, the village player on the tabor, or small drum, at dances, etc. The surname remained also as *Tabor*.

TAVERNER, the innkeeper; also found, but much more rarely, as *Innman*.

THRESHER, also TASKER, the flailman.

THACKER, the thatcher; also *Reader* and *Reeder*.

TILER or TYLER, the tile-maker; also *Tilewright*.

TILLY, a common labourer. In full he was called eordtilie, earth-tiller. So in Lagamon's "Brut," *circa* 1275, and in the "Ancren Riwle," *circa* 1225. Thence the surname *Tilly*, when not a place-name.

TRANTER, the man who peddles and hawks from place to place. The name remains as *Trant*.

WAGGONER, usually WAINMAN; hence *Wenman*.

WOODMAN, WOODREVE, as a surname *Woodrow*, *Woodward*, *Woodyer*.

WRIGHT, either a *wainwright* or a *wheelwright*—the former synonymous with a Cartwright.

YEATMAN, the man in charge of the heifers.

WYEMAN, probably the man who had charge of the two-year-old heifers.

THE VILLAGE

WYSEMAN was the name given to the juggler or conjurer at markets or fairs. Often contracted to *Wyse* and *Wise*. But probably Cardinal Wiseman derived his name from some individual of good counsel, and not from a showman by profession. Sometimes, no doubt, the wiseman was the male witch, as the wisewoman was the female dealer in the lighter forms of soothsaying and charming away of ills. The wiseman and wisewoman emphatically protested against having any dealings with the Evil One. There are such exercising their profession as white-witches still in Devonshire, and deriving a revenue from it.

CHAPTER VII

THE TOWN : TRADE-NAMES

SHOULD any man desire to acquire a conception of what the trade guilds were in medieval Europe, he should attend one of the great Church festivals at Ghent, Bruges, or Malines. There he would see the masters of each trade in their several guilds, marching in procession, each confraternity preceded by a banner and by a wonderfully carved and gilt pole surmounted by a figure of the patron saint of the trade—Crispin for the shoemakers, Blaize for the woolcombers, Barbara for the armourers, and so on—between two flickering tapers.

Almost every guild has its own band, each its chapel in the great church, its guildhall, its special coffer, and its particular charities. In each hall hangs suspended an elaborately wrought symbol of the trade, surmounted by a wreath. The crown is expressive of the high esteem in which the trade is held by the workers : it considers itself ennobled by its toil; it holds that it merits its coronet as truly as does any Baron or Earl.

Our London City guilds have lost most of their significance, but it is not so in Belgium. It was not so in Germany till a comparatively recent date.

In Munich the insignia, the coffers, and the banners, even the painted candles, of the guilds, are collected in the National Museum in one chamber. They are no more required, for the old guilds, if not disbanded, have lost their purpose. Among the relics there gathered is a coach-wheel, the *meister-stück* of a wright named Gnettmann, of Lechhausen-near-Augsburg, who on July 20, 1709, made the wheel and trundled it up to Munich, thirty-eight miles, all in one day.

THE TOWN : TRADE-NAMES

Formerly the masters in each guild met in the council-hall to consider the cost of the raw material, to determine the price to be put on the manufactured goods; also to test the quality of what had been worked up. They decided the number of apprentices each master was justified in employing, and what was the remuneration each should receive. The masters likewise required of an apprentice a test production before he could be admitted into the confraternity of masters, and it put a stamp guaranteeing the quality of every piece of goods turned out by a member, just as still, with us, the Goldsmiths' Company places its stamp, guaranteeing the quality of silver and gold plate. Any master whose work was bad, who sold vamped goods, or sold at a price higher than that determined by the guild as just, was evicted from the company, as among us a dishonest lawyer is struck off the roll. Our Apothecaries' Company still maintains a right to license men to act in the trade. Every member of a guild who fell sick or met with an accident was provided for out of the common chest. There was no climbing over the wall into any trade; it could be entered only through the door of worthy apprenticeship.

Moreover, in order that the trade might not get into a groove and not progress with the times, the apprentices were required to go out into the world—to travel for three years—so as to observe what was done elsewhere, enlarge their minds, and gain experience. Every apprentice thus sent forth carried with him a certificate from the master whom he had served. But that was not all. A certificate might be stolen and fraudulently employed. As a guarantee against this, every town had its *Wahrzeichen*, certain peculiar tokens: a horseshoe nailed against the city gate; a cock carved on the keystone of the bridge; a St. Christopher of gigantic size painted on the wall of a tower; a face under a clock that rolled its eyes and lolled its tongue at the stroke of the hour; a fountain surmounted by a stork with a baby in its beak; and so on, infinitely varied. When a wandering apprentice presented his written credentials, the master, before receiving him, catechized him on the particular tokens of the town

THE TOWN : TRADE-NAMES

whence he came, and if he could answer correctly to these questions he was given work.

The young fellows, *arme Reisender* or *wandernde Burschen*, were, not so many years ago, familiar objects in Germany. I can recall them, when I was a boy, on all the roads, staff in hand, in light blouses girded about the waist with a leather belt, singing cheerily, with dusty feet and sweat-bedewed brows. They were always poor, and were allowed free admission to show-places. They were kindly received into houses when they solicited food and a shake-down, and they were almost invariably as well-conducted as they were light-hearted. Now one sees them no more; universal military service has put an end to the *Wanderjahre*. Most, if not all, of these youths were the sons of master tradesmen. They had but a single ambition—to qualify themselves for the trade, so that in course of time they also might become masters.

These men were as proud of the Golden Boot, the Yellow Saddle, the Blacksmith's Pincers, as any knight could be of the Green Dragon, the Fireballs, or the Talbot, on his shield.

A point that I desire to impress upon the reader is the high esteem in which every member of a trade held his particular trade. But there is another point to be borne in mind—that the several trades were to a large extent in the hands of particular families. In former days, except for the wild-bloods who elected a profession of arms and attached themselves to knights, and the tame-spirited who chose servitude in a gentleman's family, the sons of, say, the village smith became in their turn smiths, and the sons of a tailor grew up to sit cross-legged and ply the needle; consequently the name of the trade carried on for some generations by a certain family adhered to it. Verstegan says : " It is not to be doubted but that their ancestors have gotten them [these trade-names] by using trades, and the children of such parents being contented to take them upon them, after-coming posterity could hardly avoid them."

Mr. M. A. Lower says : " There was much greater propriety

THE TOWN : TRADE-NAMES

in making the names of occupations stationary family names than appeared at first sight; for the same trade was often pursued for many generations by the descendants of the individual who in the first instance used it. Sometimes a particular trade is retained by most of the male branches of a family even for centuries. Thus, the family of Oxley, in Sussex, were nearly all smiths or iron-founders during the long period of 280 years. Most of the Ades of the same county have been farmers for a still longer period. The trade of weaving has been carried on by another Sussex family, named Webb (weaver), as far back as the traditions of the family extend, and it is not improbable that the business has been exercised by them ever since the first assumption of the term as a surname by some fabricator of cloth in the thirteenth or fourteenth century." Harry the Smith's sons—John, Joe, and Phil—all swung the hammer and wore the leathern apron; all were Smiths. But Harry may have had a son Ralph, who, wearied of plying the bellows, went off to the wars, and he would be called Ralph Smithson, instead of Ralph Smith.

To the present day, in many of our villages, a man is spoken of by his trade, as Millard, Carpenter, Mason, Cobbler, with the Christian name attached and the surname ignored, as John Millard, Joe Carpenter, Mason Bill, and Cobbler Dick.

I give a list of the principal trades pursued in a town during the period when surnames were becoming hereditary, and which contributed to their formation.

A good many of these trades are now obsolete, and we have to look into the books of old writers to discover of what nature they were. One point strikes the student in so doing, and that is, the differentiation of the trades. There would seem in the Middle Ages to have been no Jack-of-all-trades, who could turn his hand to anything. Trade was too serious to be treated with levity.

"Four distinct classes of artisans were engaged on the structure of the arrow, and, as we might expect, all are familiar names of to-day. John le Arowsmyth we may set

THE TOWN : TRADE-NAMES

first. He confined himself to the manufacture of the arrow-head. Thus we find the following statement made in an Act passed in 1405: 'Item, because the Arrowsmyths do make many faulty heads for arrows and quarrels, it is ordained and established that all heads of arrows and quarrels, after this time to be made, shall be well boiled or braised, and hardened at the points with steel.' 'Clement le Settere' or 'Alexander le Settere' was busied in affixing these to the shaft, and 'John le Tippere' or 'William le Tippere' in pointing them off. Nor is this all; there is yet the feather, the origin of such medieval folk as 'Robert le Flecher' or 'Ada le Flecher' (Bardsley). The fletcher, or fledger, in fact, was he who gave wings to the arrow. Mr. Bardsley might have added a fifth trade—that of the shafter.

The dressing of a man in a good cloth suit demanded the co-operation of many and various workers.

In the first place, when a farmer had wool to sell, the *Packer* was sent for, to fasten it up in bales of a determined size and weight. These were then consigned to the *Stapler*, who classed or sorted the wool. One fleece will frequently contain half a dozen qualities or sorts. The greater part would be wool adapted for combing, but the bellies and shorter portions would be thrown out for carding. After the sorting, the wool goes to the manufacturer. When in his hands it is thoroughly scoured and dried. The combing portion is committed to the *Comber*, and on leaving him is ready for the *Spinner*, who in turn passes the spun wool, or worsted, to the *Warper*, to be made into suitable lengths, and the required number of threads wide for the fabric desired to be produced. The warp is then ready for the *Weaver* or *Webber* or *Webster*, who has it put into his loom on a beam, from whence it is passed through the slay or harness to receive the weft.

The short wool is taken from the sorter to the willay, a machine which thoroughly shakes it, getting out all the dust, and it is then oiled and given to the *Carder*, who combs it. It leaves his hands in the form of a rope, and passes to the *Mule-spinner*, who brings it to the exact size required, and

THE TOWN: TRADE-NAMES

at the same time winds it on a bobbin, which fits into the shuttle of the weaver, who is supplied with the weft for his cloth. On being cut out of the loom, the cloth is first burled, which is a process for ridding it of imperfections, and this burling is done by the *Fuller*, who washes it with soap and places it in the stocks, where it is hammered till it shrinks to the required length and width. This was formerly done by trampling on the cloth with the feet; the treading up and down on it was done by the *Walker*.

But fuller and walker were often synonymous terms, as the same man often fulled and walked the same piece of cloth. This process made the serges get both narrower and thicker. The cloth then passed to the *Dyer*, and from him went to the *Tenter*, who stretched it to the width required. A *Lister* was a comber.

In the case of linen-weaving, the *Whitster* was the man who saw to the bleaching.

Another name for a fuller was a *Tucker*, and fulling-mills often went by the name of "tucking-mills." The *Tozer* or *Towzer* was he who brought up the nap by going over it with teazles.

But the cloth on reaching the *Tailor*, or, as the English called him, the *Shaper*, went through the hands of the *Cutter*. Then it was taken up by the *Seamer* and run together. *Seamer* is the Anglo-Saxon word for a tailor. The name was displaced by the French *tailleur*, as the "inn" has now become an "hotel." In the fashionable French *tailor's* shop the English seamer fell into a subordinate position.

But even when fitted and adjusted the garment was not complete. The *Trimmer* had to be called in to supply the ornamental laces, and the *Pointer* to furnish the fashionable points without which no gentleman's dress was complete.

LIST OF TRADES FURNISHING SURNAMES.

ADAM, a gaoler ("Comedy of Errors," IV. III.).

ANCERER or ANCELER, from the vessel in which provisions were weighed before they could be sold in the market. The

THE TOWN: TRADE-NAMES

surname *Ansell* may derive hence, if not from Anselm. But also anceler is a handle-maker.

APOTHECARY, now found as *Pothicary*. A *pottinger* was another name for the apothecary, and this has become a surname.[1]

ARBALASTER, a man who works a catapult for hurling stones in time of war. Now found as *Alabaster* or *Ballister*.

ARCHER, a bowman. Every town, every village, had its archer. And the *Butts* were outside the town for common practice. The Butts as well as the Archer have provided family names.

ARKWRIGHT, the chest-maker, maker of those coffers that were intended to preserve linen and tapestries, curtains, etc. Such as were made of cypress wood were called sprucechests.

ARMOURER, an important man. The name has been shortened into *Armour* as a surname.

ARROWSMITH, the maker of arrow-heads.

BAKER. The feminine form is *Bagster* or *Baxter*. The French *Boulanger* furnished the surnames *Bullinger* and *Pullinger*. We hear of French bread being consumed in England during the Middle Ages. The French word *Fournier* has also furnished the surname *Furner*.

BALANCER. The ancerer and the balancer were both scalemakers. The manufacturer of such is mentioned in "Cocke Lorelle's Bote":

> "Arowe-heders, maltemen and cornemongers,
> *Balancers*, tynne-casters and skryvenors."

BANISTER, the keeper of a bath; from the French *bain*.

BARBER. Till the year 1745 every surgeon was a member of the Barbers' Company. The surname of *Surgeon* is not often met with, but that of *Barber* is very common. Mr. Camden Hotten, in his book on "Signboards," quotes these lines:

> "His pole with pewter basons hung,
> Black, rotten teeth in order strung,

---

[1] The pottinger was originally the man who grew pot-herbs and medicinal herbs as well; then the town herbalist.

THE TOWN : TRADE-NAMES

> Rang'd cups that in the window stood,
> Lined with red rags to look like blood,
> Did well his threefold trade explain,
> Who shaved, drew teeth, and breathed a vein."

From the barber we get *Barbour* and *Barbor*.

BEADMAKER, who made paternosters. The word has been compressed into *Bedmaker*.

BEATER, woollen-beater, engaged on one of the processes in the manufacture of cloth.

BELLMAN, the crier.

BELLSETTER. The "Promptuarium Parvulorum" gives *Bellezeter* as the then usual name for the bell-caster. It got corrupted to *Belleyeter*, and then to *Billiter*.

BIDDER, one sent out to summon to a wedding or a church-ale. In Germany, among the peasantry, the bidder is still a person of office and importance.

BENCHER, a banker.

BIGGER, a builder.

BILLMAN, he who carries a bill or pike, as official attendant on a Sheriff or constable.

BINDER of books. In the York pageant of 1415 the Parchmenters and Bookbinders marched together.

BLACKSMITH. This trade has constituted the surnames *Black* and *Smith*, *Smyth*, *Smeyt*, *Smijth*, as well as *Faber*, *Fabricius*, *Ferrier*, *Ferrers*, *Fervour*, *Fearon*.

BLACKSTER, a bleacher of linen. Also *Blacker*. Hence we have the names *Blaxter*, *Blackister*, *Blake*, for Blaker. The same as the Whitster. Anglo-Saxon *blac* is white, but *blaec* is black.

BLADEMAKER or BLADESMITH, the same as our modern cutler. As a surname it has been condensed into *Blades* and *Blaydes*.

BLOCKER, he who made blocks for hats. From the block came the slang "bloke" and "blockhead."

BLOOMER, a man who runs iron into moulds.

BLOWER, the man employed to work the bellows in a furnace or smelting-house; often corrupted into *Blore* or *Blow*. The architect of the first name and the musician of

THE TOWN : TRADE-NAMES

the second must each have descended from a very humble ancestor. But some *Blowers* are *Hornblowers*.

BOTELLER, a leather-bottle-maker. The name has been absorbed by that of *Butler*.

BOUCHER is the French *boucher;* we have it in the form of *Botcher* as well as *Bouchier*. *Labouchere* is no other than the female butcher.

BOURDER, a jester. Hence *Burder*. But a byrder was a catcher of finches.

BOWYER, the bowmaker. As a surname we have it in *Bower* and *Boyer*.

BOWDLER, a puddler in iron.

BOWLER, a maker of wooden bowls. Also *Bolister*.

BRACEGIRDLER, a maker of braces. " Brace " is from the French *brayles*. Sir John Mandeville, in his " Travels," speaks of a breek-girdle. The name is found still as *Brayler*.

BRAZIER, BREWER, or BREWSTER. It was not till the close of the fifteenth century that the hop was introduced into England by the Flemings.

> " Hops, Reformation, baize and beer,
> Came to England all in one year."

Previously ale had been brewed with other ingredients, as wormwood. Mead, or metheglin, was largely drunk. Hence *Browse* — *i.e.*, at the brewhouse. *Chamier* is from the medieval Latin *cambarius*, a brewer.

BRIDGEMAN and BRIDGER, toll-taker at bridges.

BROWKER or BROGGER, he who transacted business between ourselves and the Dutch in the shipping off of wool, and the introduction of cloth from Flemish manufacturers. James I. speaks of the broker as one who went " betweene Merchant Englishe and Merchant Strangers, and Tradesmen in the contrivinge, makinge and concluding Bargaines and Contractes to be made betweene them concerning their wares and merchandises." They seem not to have borne a high character, for in " King John " the Bastard speaks of the shifty conscience :

> " That sly devil,
> That broker that still breaks the pale of faith."

THE TOWN : TRADE-NAMES

BROWNSMITH, a coppersmith.

BUCKLER, a maker of buckles.

BURELLER, a weaver of a cheap kind of cloth, brown in colour and of everlasting wear, and worn by the poorer classes, who came to be designated as "borel-folk."

The friar in the "Canterbury Tales" thought that it accorded not with one of his faculty to have acquaintance with lazars, beggars, and "such poraile"—*i.e.*, boraile. The surname *Burrell*, is tolerably widespread in England, and is the family name of Lord Gwydyr.

BUTTONER, a maker of buttons. The *er* of the concluding syllable is generally omitted in the surname.

BYRDER, a professional birdcatcher, mainly of finches. The surname *Bird* is merely the abbreviation of *Byrder*. Also *Oseler*. *Osl* is Anglo-Saxon for a blackbird.

CADER, a maker of cades, or casks. Shakespeare represents Jack Cade as a clothier, and his father a bricklayer, showing that the name from the trade exercised by the founder of the family had become hereditary without reference to the trade practised. The cader is also called *Cadman*.

CAIRD, a tinker.

CALLENDER, one who puts a gloss on linen.

CALLMAN, the maker of ladies' calls. In the "Wife of Bath's Tale," the wife appeals to the Queen's attendants :

> "Let see, which is the proudest of them all,
> That weareth or a kerchief or a calle."

Sir John Call, Bart., the distinguished engineer in India, the son of a Cornish farmer, derived his name from an ancestor who made ladies' headgear.

CALTHROPER or CALCRAFTMAN was the maker of calthrops —irons with four spikes, so made that, whichever way they fell, one point always stood upwards. They were used in war, thrown into breaches or placed on bridges, to annoy an enemy's horse. A similar instrument with three iron spikes was used in hunting the wolf. As a surname, *Calthrop*. But *Calcraft* is probably Calves-croft.

THE TOWN : TRADE-NAMES

CAPPER, the maker of caps. Also the French *Chapeller*. Like so many other trade-names when adopted as a surname, the last syllable has been dropped, and the name has become *Chapell*. But *Capper* remains.

CARDER or CARDMAKER, maker of cards for weaving. Christopher Sly said of himself: "By birth a pedlar, by education a cardmaker."

CARPENTER needs no explanation.

CARTWRIGHT, maker of carts.

CATER, a confectioner, maker of cates.

> "Though my cates be mean, take them in good part;
> Better cheer may you have, but not with better heart."
> *Comedy of Errors*, III. 1.

CHALLICER, a maker of drinking vessels out of metal; hence the names *Challis* and *Challys*, unless named from Calais.

CHALONER, an importer or manufacturer of chalons—woollen coverlets originally introduced from Chalons-sur-Marne. In the "Reve's Tale" we are told of the miller, that

> "In his owen chambre he made a bedde
> With shetes, and with *chalons* fair yspredde."

Surname *Chawner*.

CHANDLER, candle-maker.

CHANTER, cantor, a singer in church; hence the surnames *Chanter* and *Caunter*.

CHAPMAN, a travelling merchant. Cheap-Jack takes his name from the word, so does Cheapside. Copenhagen is the chapman's haven.

CHAUCER, from *chausseur*, a shoemaker.

CHEESEMAN, dealer in cheese. Also called a *Fromisher*, from the French *fromage*.

CLERK, one who could read, and plead the benefit of the clergy. Hence *Clark* and *Clarke*.

COBBLER, a mender of boots and shoes.

CODNER, a cordwainer.

COFFERER has two meanings—a *coiffeur*, or hairdresser, and a maker of coffers, boxes, or chests.

THE TOWN : TRADE-NAMES

COGGER, a skipper in a small boat; whence our word "coxswain" (coggs-swain). The expression "an old codger" is hence derived. But a *cogger* is also a cheat by loading dice, and is so employed by Shakespeare.

COVERER, the maker of *cuves*, tubs and vats.

COLLIER. Although originally a charcoal-burner, the name came to be used for the dealer in the town in charcoal and in sea-coal.

COMBER, maker of combs. This has become a surname, as *Comper, Kemster, Kimber, Kemble*.

CONDER, a partner in a fishing-boat.

COOK enters into many combinations, as in Norman-French *Le Coq, Badcock* (Bartholomew the Cook), *Hancock* (John the Cook), *Wilcox* (William le Coq), etc.

COOPER, a maker of vats and barrels.

COSTER, a doorkeeper.

COSTERMONGER, properly Costardmonger, a dealer in apples and other fruit.

COUCHER, a maker of beds. The surname *Couch* comes from hence.

COWLER, a maker of cowls or calls for ladies; the same as a callman.

COWPER or COUPER, a maker of cups. Langland speaks of

"Coupes of clere gold
And coppes of silver."

CROCKER, maker of common earthenware crocks. Wyckliffe in Matt. xv. 7 uses the word. Hence *Crocker* and *Croker*.

CRAMMER or CRANMER (German *kramer*), a packman.

CROWDER, a player on the crowd, or fiddle; hence *Crowther*.

CRYER, the town bellman.

CURRIER, the curer of skins; hence *Curry*.

CUTTER, a cutter of cloth for the tailor. The cutter is still employed by every tailor.

CUTLER, properly Scutler, a shield-maker, from the Latin *scutum*.

DANCER, a morris-dancer.

THE TOWN: TRADE-NAMES

DEMPSTER, a Deemster, Member of Parliament in the Isle of Man and in Scotland. *Deemer, Deamer*, and with intrusive *r*, *Dearmer*.

DOSER, a stuffer of pillows for the back of seats.

DRAPER, from the French *drap*.

DRESSER, a hemp-dresser, but also one who cuts up the meat at a sideboard for the banquet. Chaucer speaks of dressing a heritage—*i.e.*, of dividing it among the heirs ("The Coke's Tale").

DUBBER. In the "Liber Albus" we have a Peter le Dubbour, whose trade was to furbish up old clothes. But a *Dauber* was the decorator of walls. In "Cocke Lorelle's Bote" we have

"Tylers, bryckeleyers, hardehewers;
Paris-plasterers, *daubers* and lymeborners."

DYER or DISTER, also *Dexter, Dwyer*.

FABER, a smith.

FARRIER, also *Ferrier* and *Farrar*, a shoer of horses.

FARMAN, a ferryman.

FARADAY, a travelling merchant.

FELLMONGER, a seller of skins. Remains as a surname as *Fell*.

FLANNER, maker of pancakes.

FLAXMAN, dealer in flax.

FLESHER, a butcher, or *flesh-hewer*.

FLETCHER, an arrowsmith; French *flèche*.

FLOYER, one who skins beasts for the tanyard. Surname *Flower*.

FORCER, a maker of small caskets delicately carved, for the keeping of jewellery.

FRIEZEMAKER, contracted as a surname to *Frieze;* unless a Frieslander.

FRUITERER, a greengrocer.

FULLER, already described.

FURRIER, also as PELTER.

FUSTER or FEWSTER was the joiner employed on the wooden fabric of a saddle. It is derived from the Old French

THE TOWN : TRADE-NAMES

fust, wood. Sir Jenner Fust's ancestor must have been a saddler.

GAGER or GAUGER. "His office was to attend to the King's revenue at the seaports, and with the measurement of all liquids, such as oil, wine, and honey. The tun, the pipe, the tierce, the puncheon, casks and barrels of a specified size—these came under his immediate supervision, and the royal fee was accordingly" (Bardsley). The surname *Gage* comes from this officer.

GAUNTER, a glover. *Gunter*—unless from the German *Gunther*.

GIRDLER, a maker of girdles.

GLAZIER needs no explanation.

GLOVER, same as Gaunter.

GROCER, a rare and late word; properly an engrosser, one who took into his own hands several different branches of trade, as those of the spicer, drug-merchant, pepper-dealer. A statute of Edward III. in 1363 speaks of " Merchauntz money-Grossers," so termed because they " engrossent totes maners de marchandises vendables." The surname *Grosser* exists.

HABERDASHER, a seller of hats and small wares. One was in the party of Canterbury pilgrims.

HAMPERS or HANAPERS, basket-makers.

HARNESS-MAKERS, as a surname contracted to *Harness*.

HELLIER, a slater. "To hell" is to cover in. In the West of England slates are hellens. As a surname, *Hillyard* and *Hellyer*.

HOLDER, an upholsterer, or stuffer of mattresses, beds, and cushions.

HOOKER, a maker of crooks.

HOOPER, a maker of hoops for casks.

HORNER, a maker of cups and other articles out of horn also of children's horn-books and lanterns glazed with horn. In the " Franklin's Tale," descriptive of winter, it is said :

> "James sits by the fire with double berd
> And drinketh of the bugle horn the wine."

This refers to the double use of the bugle. It had a metal

THE TOWN : TRADE-NAMES

plug to stop the mouthpiece, so as, if required, to serve as a drinking horn. In the second part of " Henry VI." we have Thomas Horner, an armourer, showing that the man had drifted into another profession from that which furnished him with his surname.

HOSIER, seller of long stockings, in wool or silk. Surname *Hozier*.

HURRER, seller of a peculiar sort of hairy hat. All kinds of hoods and caps came under his hands, so that he was what we now call a hatter. *Hurell* for Hurreller.

IRONMONGER, usually *Iremonger*. To the present day in the West of England " iron " is pronounced " ire." A band of *ire*, not of iron. Hence the surname *Irons*.

JOINER, a maker of chairs and tables, etc.

JESSMAKER, maker of jesses for hawks; hence the surname *Jesse*.

KISSER, maker of " cuisses " (greaves).

KITCHENER, from *cuisinier*, a French or Norman name for a cook.

KINCH, a worker in the bleaching-fields.

LACER, maker of laces (not lace), the strings of twisted or plaited wool or silk for fastening portions of the dress together.

LANER, a dealer in wool—*lain*.

LARDINER or LARDNER, if not a fattener of hogs, is a dealer in lard and bacon.

LATINER, altered to *Latimer*, an interpreter.

LATONER, a maker of latten, a mixture of lead and tin—in fact, a pewterer.

LAUNDER or LAVENDER, a washerman. We have a trace of the word in "laundress" and in a "launder" that brings water. Hence the surnames *Launder* and *Landor*. Beatrice ap Rice, who washed for the Princess Mary, daughter of Henry VIII., is always set down in the accounts as Mistress Launder. Sir Hugh Evans, in "The Merry Wives of Windsor," calls Mistress Quickly the " dry-nurse, or cook, or laundry, or washer, or wringer," of Dr. Caius.

LAYMAN, lagman or lawyer.

THE TOWN : TRADE-NAMES

LEADBEATER, the maker of leaden vessels and the lead for roofs. The word has been corrupted to *Ledbitter* and *Liberty*.

LEADER, a drawer and carrier of water in a town—properly, a water-leader. The surname of *Loder* is the same as *Leader*.

LEAPER. A "leap" was a sort of basket made of rush. In Wyckliffe's version, Moses is placed in a "leap of segg"—*i.e.*, basket of sedge. So also Matt. viii. 8 : " And thei eeten and weren fulfilled, and thei taken up that that left sevene leepis." Hence the names *Lipman, Leapman, Lipper*. Has nothing to do with "lepper."[1]

LEECH or LEACH, a surgeon, so called because he ministers to the health of the lych, or body.

LIMMER, an artist who decorates manuscripts.

LISTER, engaged in one part of clothweaving.

LOCKSMITH or LOCKIER, hence *Lockyer* and *Locke*.

LYNER, a dealer in linen. The surname remains as *Line* and *Lyne*.

LORIMER, maker of straps, bits, and girths.

LYTEMAN, probably the torch or link bearer. The surname *Lyte* comes from it. Also SPELTMAN, that has become *Spellman* (Anglo-Saxon *speld*, a torch).

MAILER, a maker of mails or leather portmanteaus. Perhaps the surname of *Mellor* may in some instances derive hence.

MALSTER, for *Maltster*.

MARINER. The name of *sailor* is very uncommon ; the usual word descriptive of one who lived on the sea was " mariner "—hence *Marner*.

MASON, also *Waller* and *Walster*.

MAUNDER, a maker of maunds, or hampers, and then a beggar who collected food given to him in a maund.

MAZERER, a turner of mazer bowls in maplewood. " It was the favourite bowl of all classes of society. By the rich it was valued according as it was made from the knotted

---

[1] But the Dutch *loeper*, German *laufer*, is a running footman. *Cf.* Pott, " Personnennamen," p. 632.

THE TOWN : TRADE-NAMES

grain, or chased and rimmed with gold and silver and precious stones " (Bardsley). We are told of Sir Thopas, that

> " They fetched him first the swete win,
> And made eke in a *maselin*,
> And real spicere."

Mazerer was also Mazeliner—hence the name of the famous conjurer, *Maskelyne*.

MERCER, a dealer in silks.

MERCHANT, also *Marchant*, from the French, in place of the English " monger."

MITCHENER, a pastrycook; maker of mitchkin, a cake or small loaf.

MONIER, maker of current coins minted in many towns. Also *Minter*, *Monyer*, and *Money*, if this last do not stand for De Mauney.

MUSTARDER, seller of mustard. As a surname reduced to *Mustard*.

NEEDLER, needlemaker. As surname, *Neelder*. *Aguillier*, a French form, gives *Aguillar* and *Gillard*.

ORFEVER, a goldsmith; hence our modern surnames of *Offerer* and *Offor*, if this last be not a place-name.

OSTLER, hence *Oastler* and *Hostler*; but OSELER, as already said, is a birdcatcher.

PACKER, a woolpacker; also *Pack* as a surname.

PAINTER, often as a surname *Paynter*.

PARCHMENTER, preparer of parchment and vellum.

PARGITER, a plasterer.

PARMINTER, for *parmentier*, a tailor—a French fashionable tailor, doubtless.

PATTENER, maker of pattens. Surname *Patner*.

PELTER, a furrier.

PEPPERER, a seller of pepper; name remains as *Pepper*.

PESSONER, a fishmonger.

PEWTERER, also *Powter*.

PILCHER, a maker of warm garments lined with fur; much the same as a pelter.

PINNER, a pinmaker.

PLASTERER, as a surname *Plaister*.

THE TOWN : TRADE-NAMES

PLATNER, a maker of dishes and plates. Surname *Platt*.

PLAYER, an actor by profession.

PLUMBER remains in surnames as *Plumer* and *Plummer*.

POINTER, one who made "points," tags to dresses by which laces were fastened together—often made of silver. Surname *Poynter*.

POTTER, maker of common pots. The name remains both as *Potter* and *Potts*.

POUCHER, maker of pouches. A poacher is so called because he carries a pouch for the game he secures.

POULTERER. The surname remains as *Poulter* and *Pulter*.

POYSER, a weigher, a scalemaker.

PURSER or BURSER, a pursemaker.

PYEBAKER, shortened into *Pye*.

QUILLER, also *Keeler*, the dresser of quilled ruffs and collars, such as were worn in the reign of Elizabeth. Mr. Quiller-Couch has in his name references to two trades —the starcher who quilled collars, and the coucher who stuffed beds, etc.

QUILTER, the liner of garments and coverlets.

RAFFMAN, also RAFFLER, the dealer in rags and rubbish.

RECORDER, a player on the record, a musical instrument; hence the surname *Corder*.

RIDLER, a maker of sieves and riddles.

ROCKSTER, a maker of rocks or spindles; hence the surname *Rockstro*, and sometimes also *Rock*; also *Rooker* and *Rooke* and *Rookard*. Mr. Bardsley strangely makes of the last a rookward, or keeper of rooks.

ROPER and RAPER, a cordwainer, a ropemaker. *Cordery* is the man at the ropewalk.

RUNCIMAN, a dealer in an inferior kind of horses. The shipman among the Canterbury pilgrims rode upon a "rouncy."

SACKER, a maker of sacks. Archbishop Secker derived, doubtless, from a sackmaker.

SADLER, also SELLER, from the French *sellier*. We have both as surnames.

SALTER, also SALTMAN, a salt-boiler.

THE TOWN : TRADE-NAMES

SAWYER, self-explanatory.

SHIPMAN, a merchant sea-captain. One was among the Canterbury pilgrims: "The hoote somer hadde maad his hew at broun, and certlinly he was a good felawe."

SEALER, a seal-cutter. In some cases may have originated the surname *Seale*.

SEAMER and the feminine SEMPSTER, a maker of seams for the tailor.

SEXTON, also as *Saxton*, for Sacristan.

SHEARMAN, one who shaves or shears worsted and fustians. *Sherman, Shears*.

SHAILER, a maker of ladders (*echelles*). As a surname, *Shayler* and *Sheller*.

SHOEMAKER, curiously enough, rare as a surname. The Old English name (from the French) was *Corser*, but also *Souter = Chausseur*; hence *Chaucer*.

SILKMAN, a mercer. The surname remains as *Silke* and *Sylke*.

SINGER, a professional chanter, a ballad-singer or minstrel. *Sangster*.

SKINNER, one who prepared skins for the tanyard. As a surname, *Skynner*.

SLAYER or SLAYWRIGHT, one who makes slays for weaving.

SLAUGHTERER, the man who kills for the butcher. A late Government School Inspector was Colonel Slaughter.[1]

SLOPER, a maker of slops, a loose upper garment. In the "Chanon Yemannes Tale" it is said that

"His overest sloppe is not worth a mite."

SMITH, a general term. There were Whitesmiths, *i.e.*, Tinmen, Goldsmiths, Brownsmiths, Blacksmiths, Arrowsmiths, Spearsmiths, Nailsmiths, etc.

SOAPER, a soap-boiler. *Soper*.

SOUTER, a shoemaker. The surname *Shutter* is from *Shoester*.

SPICER, from the French *épicier*.

SPILLER, a maker of spills or spindles.

SPINNER. The feminine form is SPINSTER.

[1] There are, however, two villages so named in Gloucestershire.

THE TOWN : TRADE-NAMES

SPOONER, maker of spoons in wood and horn.

SPURRIER, maker of spurs.

STAMPER, the official who put the stamp either on tin or on the nobler metals. It has been corrupted into *Stammer*.

STARCHER, important in Elizabethan times and in that of James I., when yellow starch came in. Perhaps the origin of *Starke* and *Starkie*.

STAPLER, the merchant who bought wool *en gros*. As a surname it exists as *Staples*.

STEYNER, the maker of *steenes*, or stone jars, out of white clay. The surname remains as *Steyner* or *Stayner*.

STRAKER, a twine-spinner.

SUMMONER or SUMNER, one who conveys legal summons. Sumner was an Archbishop of Canterbury. According to Chaucer, the summoner was not a man of high character.

SURGEON, a chirurgeon, was merged in the barber and apothecary. If it ever became a surname, it has been overwhelmed by *Sergeant*.

TAILOR, variously spelled as a surname, in the vain hope to disguise its humble and somewhat despised origin. A *taizler* was the same as a *tozer*, a man who brought up the nap on cloth with teasels, and it is possible that some *Taizlers* may have become *Tayleurs*. The Old English name for a tailor was a *schepper* or *shaper*. Possibly enough some *Sheppards* may derive thence.

TANNER needs no explanation.

TAPISER, a tapestry worker, contracted to *Tapster*, and so goes along with the tavern assistant.

TABURNER, one who played on the tambourine.

TAWER, a skinner or leather-dresser; hence *Tower* and *Tuer*.

TENTOR, one who stretches cloth.

TESTER, same as *Assayer*.

TELLER or TELLWRIGHT, a tentmaker. Old English for a tent was *teld*.

THROWER, a silkwinder; hence *Trower*.

TINNER, a whitesmith—usually *tinker* and *tinkler*. There is an old ballad still sung by the Devonshire peasants of

THE TOWN : TRADE-NAMES

"The Maid and the Box." She was serving in London, but desired to return to see her parents in Falmouth.

> "Her master paid her wages, and
> Her wages were five pound.
> She put the money in a box
> With flowers flourished round.
>
> "She put the money in the box,
> She put in that her clothes;
> She set it all upon her head,
> And nimbly forth she goes.
>
> "She had not walkèd very far,
> The space was scarce a mile,
> Before a *tinkler* she espied
> Was lying at a stile."

The tinkler requires her to set down the box, that he may examine its contents, and to hand him the key. She does this; but as he lays aside his stick and budget, that he may open the box, she

> "Seized the walking-stick
> And struck him sharp a knock.
>
> "She struck the *tinkler* on the head,
> She struck him strokes full three,
> And ne'er a word he spoke or stirred;
> The tinkler—still lay he."

Of her further adventures, and of how she married the Squire, I have not space to tell, the ballad consisting of sixteen double verses. A surname is *Tingler*.

TIREMAN, a maker of ladies' tires, or headgear.

TOLLER (Anglo-Saxon), the official who received the royal tolls at fairs and in harbours. As a surname it remains, also as *Towler;* but possibly the latter may be a corruption of *Toulousier*, an adventurer from Toulouse.

TOZER, or TOWZER, or TAIZLER. See under Tailor.

TRIMMER, the provider of laces for garnishing the dresses of ladies and gentlemen.

TUBMAN or TUBBER, a maker of tubs, a step in the social scale below the cooper; hence the surnames *Tupman* and *Tubbs*.

THE TOWN : TRADE-NAMES

TUCKER, one engaged in part of the process of woolmaking into cloth. Tucking mills were introduced in all wool dis tricts. The name takes the form of *Toker, Tooker,* and *Towker.*

TURNER, spelled as a surname also *Turnour.*[1]

TYLER, tilemaker; sometimes *Tittler.*

VINTNER, sometimes as *Vyner.*

WADMAN, a dealer in woad for dyeing. *Wadster.*

WAINWRIGHT, a maker of carts or waggons. As a surname spelled *Waynwright.*

WALKER. Cloth before the introduction of the roller had to be trodden underfoot. In Wyckliffe's version of the Transfiguration he describes Christ's raiment as shining so as no "fullers or walkers of cloth" could whiten. Langland, in describing the process of cloth manufacture, says:

> "Cloth that cometh fro the wevyng
> Is nought comely to wear
> Till it be fulled under foot,
> Or in fullying stokkes,
> Washen well with water.
> And with taseles craccked
> Y-ton-ked and y-teynted,
> And under tailleurs hands."

WATERER or WATERMAN, a boatman on the Thames.

WAYMAN, a driver of wains.

WAYTE, a watchman (Old French, *guet*); hence the surnames *Wade, Gates, Yates,* and *Wakeman.*

WEAVER, same as *Webber* and *Webster;* sometimes *Webbe.*

WHEELER, a wheelwright.

WHITSTER, a bleacher of linen. Mrs. Ford says: "John and Robin . . . take this basket on your shoulders. That done, trudge with it in all haste, and carry it among the *whitsters* in Datchet mead."

WHIFFLER, a piper.

---

[1] Some Turners pretend that the name derives from some imaginary Tour Noire. In early entries we have always le Tourneur, never de la Tour Noire. There was, however, a "Sire de le Tourneur" at Hastings.

THE TOWN: TRADE-NAMES

WHITTIER, a white Tawier; one who prepares the finer skins for gloves, whitening them. *Wheatman, Wightman.*

WIRER, a wire-drawer.

WOOLER, a wool-monger, a collector of fleeces from farmers and yeomen. Also *Woolner.*

It is remarkable, and admirable as well, to see how many of the descendants of quite humble tradesmen are now represented in the House of Lords.

The Duke of Northumberland is actually no Percy, but a *Smithson*, and must recognize that his ancestor wielded the hammer at the anvil. Little can the nominal ancestor, " his brow wet with honest sweat," have imagined that his descendant would reign in Alnwick Castle.

The viscounty of Strangford is now extinct, but that was held by a Smith disguised as *Smythe;* but Earl Carrington is a *Smith*, though apparently not descended from a blacksmith, but from a goldsmith. The family seems to have pursued this trade and banking and money-lending till the middle of the eighteenth century.

Lord Gwydyr is a *Burrell*, and his ancestor, judging from his name, was a weaver of coarse cloth, such as was sold only to labouring men. The ancestor of Lord Alverstone was a webster or weaver. Lord Ribblesdale's family ancestor—a *Lister*—must have been a wool-worker. That of the Marquess of Headfort, a tailor sitting cross-legged on a table, and no disguise of Tailor into *Tayleur* can obscure the fact. Earl Winterton is a Turner, dignified into *Turnour*, and the ancestor of Lord Castlemaine must have been a John the Cook in some nobleman's or squire's house, for the family name is *Handcock*. Earl *Cowper* derives his family and titular name from a tradesman who made drinking-mugs, and Lord Monkswell from a *collier*, who carried sacks of coals over his shoulder. If *Sturt* comes from the Anglo-Saxon *Steort*, then Baron Alington's family must have come literally from the plough-tail.[1]

[1] There is, however, a place called Stert near Devizes, and entries in the Hundred Rolls, etc., confirm the derivation from a place—William de la Sturte, 1273.

THE TOWN : TRADE-NAMES

As might have been anticipated, many domestic and other servants have climbed up their masters' backs, stepped over their shoulders, and installed themselves in their places.

Baron Forrester and Viscount Massereene derive from salaried attendants who ministered to the pleasures of their masters in the chase. Barons Gardner and Burghclere derive from some worthy working man who, when engaged in the potting-shed or in manuring the soil, had no notion that a descendant would wear a coronet. Lord Bateman deduces, as the name implies, from the bear-warder in some castle, where he fed the brutes that were to be baited for his master's amusement. The Earl of Morley, as a *Parker*, must have had as ancestor one who looked to his lord's park and kept the palings in order; so also the Earl of Macclesfield. The Earl of Harrowby, as a *Ryder*, had as an ancestor some German *reuter*, who sold his sword for his entertainment and some plunder; and Barons Napier and Ettrick and Napier of Magdala derive, as already said, from the official who looked after the linen for bed and table in a noble house. The ancestors of the Earls of Carrick, Glengall, Lanesborough, of the Marquess of Ormonde, of Viscount Mountgarret, and of Baron Dunboyne, were all butlers.

Baron Calthorpe is descended from a maker of balls with spikes, used in war. Earl Summers had as his nominal ancestor a Sompner :

> " A Sompnour was ther with us in that place,
> That hadd a fyr-reed cherubyns face,
> For saweeflem [pimply] he was, with eyghen [eyes]
>   narwe [narrow]
> As hoot he was, and leecherous, as a sparwe [sparrow]."

So Chaucer describes the sompner, or summoner. The ancestor of the Earls of Leicester, judging from the name, was a *Cook*, whose place was not by any means in the House of Lords, but in the kitchen; and that of the Earl of Shaftesbury was a *Cooper*.

Lord Teynham, being a *Roper*, must have drawn his family from one who was a cord-wainer, pacing hourly backwards and dealing out the hemp that was being spun and

THE TOWN : TRADE-NAMES

twisted, a monotonous toil from dawn to sunset, unlightened by a glimpse of the future in which a descendant would wear the six pearls and have as crest a lion rampant bearing a ducal crown.

Baron Newland's ancestor was a hosier, who from behind his counter sold silk stockings to ladies and gents, and worsted stockings to farmers and domestics.

If we chose to look among the Baronets, what a string of trade-names should we find!

There are six *Smiths*, one affecting the spelling *Smyth*, and one *Smythe*; as many *Walkers*; a *Webster*; a *Quilter*; a *Poynder*, a *Poynter*, both having the same meaning, a maker of points to hold the garments together—we use buttons instead:

> "*Fals.* Their points being broken. ·
> *Poins.* Down fell their hose."
> · *King Henry IV.*, Part II., XI. iv.

—a *Runciman*; a *Spicer*; a *Chapman*; a *Tupper*—a hog and ram gelder; a *Naesmyth*—*i.e.*, nailsmith; a *Pender*, or pindar; a *Loder*, or water-carrier. Half a dozen hail from the *Mill*. Two *Jardines* derive from French gardeners. There are *Forsters*, *Fosters*, contractions from Forester; a *Fowler* and a *Falkener*; a *Dyer*; two *Cooks*; four *Coopers*, and one *Couper*; an *Ashman*, who prepared ashes for the soap-boiler; and one *Farmer*.

No pedigree of any of these families goes back to the original Smith or Tailor, Webster or Runciman, Cooper or Miller, but the name is an indelible stamp of a trade origin. Why any man should be ashamed of this I fail to see. The honest tradesman was a far worthier man than the loafer about the Court, and the hotspur who "kills me some six or seven dozen of Scots at a breakfast, washes his hands, and says to his wife: 'Fye upon this quiet life!'" Yet I presume there is some dislike of the fact, for the arms chosen never bear any reference to the trade of the name-founder of the family, and in a good many cases, where there is a trade-name, it is either wriggled out of or smothered by the addition of some more aristocratic and resonant name.

And yet anyone who can be shown to have borne, or his

THE TOWN: TRADE-NAMES

forbears to have borne, a name connected with a trade most certainly did spring from the shop or the factory. There can be no mistake about it. The name may be twisted or tinkered into Smijthe, Tayleure, Cuttlare, or what you will: it makes no difference. The Adam of each wielded a hammer, or patched the knees and seat of old breeches, or fashioned scissors or shield. In Germany no man is esteemed to be *adel*—that is to say, can write himself *armiger*, a gentleman—who has not a *von* before his name, and the old historic families can always be recognized by a territorial name preceded by *von*. We know, without consulting a peerage, that a Von Falkenstein or a Von Rabeneck has a pedigree of over eight descents, and had his seat in former days in a castle Falkenstein or Rabeneck, now in ruins. However, during last century a considerable number of Webers, Dreschlers, Gärtners, and Schmidts were ennobled; but their names remain as permanent testimonies to their *bürger* descent from a weaver, a turner, a gardener, and a smith.

And they have no reason to be other than proud of the fact. Whilst the *Vons* were ravaging the country, and rendering the roads insecure for peaceful traders, the citizens within the walls of the towns were building up the prosperity of their country.

"William the Conqueror divided England among the commanders of his army," writes an American,[1] "and conferred about twenty earldoms. Not one of them exists to-day. Nor do any of the honours conferred by William Rufus, 1087-1100; Henry I, 1100-1135; Stephen, 1135-1154; Henry II., 1154-1189; Richard I., 1189-1199; or John, 1199-1216.

"All the dukedoms created from the institution of Edward III., 1327-1377, down to the commencement of the reign of Charles II., 1649, except Norfolk and Somerset and Cornwall—the title held by the Prince of Wales—have perished. Winchester and Worcester—the latter merged in the dukedom of Beaufort—are the only marquisates older

[1] "England and the English,"*Scribner's Magazine*, February, 1909.

THE TOWN : TRADE-NAMES

than George III. (1760-1820). Of all earldoms conferred by the Normans, Plantagenets, and Tudors, only eleven remain, and six of these are merged in higher honours. The House of Lords to-day does not number a single male descendant of any of the Barons who were chosen to enforce Magna Charta. The House of Lords does not contain a single male descendant of the Peers who fought at Agincourt. There is only one single family in all the realm—Wrottesley —which can boast of a male descendant from the date of the institution of the Garter (1349). In a word, the present House of Lords is conspicuously and predominantly a democratic body, chosen from the successful of the land. Seventy of the Peers were ennobled on account of distinction in the practice of the law alone. The Dukes of Leeds trace back to a cloth-worker; the Earls of Craven to a tailor; the families of Dartmouth, Ducie, Pomfret, Tankerville, Dormer, Romney, Dudley, Fitzwilliam, Cowper, Leigh, Darnley, Hill, Normanby, all sprang from London shops and counting-houses, and that not so very long ago.

"Ashburton, Carrington, Belper, Overstone, Mount-Stephen, Hindlip, Burton, Battersea, Glenesk, Aldenham, Cheylesmore, Lister, Avebury, Burnham, Biddulph, Northcliffe, Nunburnholme, Winterstoke, Rothschild, Brassey, Revelstoke, Strathcona and Mount Royal, Michelham, and others too many to mention, have taken their places among the Peers by force of long purses gained in trade.

"Lord Belper, for example, created in 1856, is the grandson of Jedidiah Strutt, who was the son of a small farmer, and made wonderful ribbed stockings.

> "Wealth, however got, in England makes
> Lords of mechanics, gentlemen of rakes.
> Antiquity and birth are needless here;
> 'Tis impudence and money makes the Peer.
> * * * *
> Great families of yesterday we show,
> And Lords whose parents were the Lord knows who."

In the names given before this quotation I have relied solely on the testimony of the family appellation, and have left on one side altogether such noble families as can be

THE TOWN : TRADE-NAMES

proved by reliable pedigrees to have issued from the commercial class. If we were to add those known historically to have so risen to those known to have risen by the evidence of their names, it would be found that they make up the overwhelming majority of the aristocracy of the land.

The prophet saw in vision the House of Israel as a boiling pot set upon live coals, and sending its scum to the surface. He was thinking of the "smart set" of the time. But England from the middle of the eleventh century has also been set on the coals; but, unlike the House of Israel, it has sent its very best to the top, and often from the very bottom, and has brought down from above that which was worthless, there perhaps to recover and again to mount aloft. I have taken pains to show in the chapter on Battle Abbey Roll, and also in that on French Names, that there has been such a descent. There is nothing stationary in the social caldron —all is in revolution, not violent, but gentle, natural, healthy. And be it further remembered that most of our humble tradesmen of old, those who gave their trade-names to their families, issued originally from the class of manumitted serfs and villeins—men of English blood probably—and then we can see for ourselves how that the down-trampled native of our isle has succeeded in reversing the condition of affairs: he is at the top, and the bearer of the Norman name is nowhere.

Hear again what the American—an outsider—has to say on the subject of our nobility: "William the Conqueror was a bastard, and his mother was the daughter of a humble tanner of Falaise. The mother of the great Queen Elizabeth was the daughter of a plain English gentleman.

"The Englishman would not be what he is, nor would he in the least be transmitting his very valuable Saxon heritage, if he gave up his democratic custom of an aristocracy of power for the feeble Continental custom of an aristocracy of birth. What the one and the other is to-day answers the question as to the relative merits of the two systems without need of discussion. The English, though nowadays many of them do not know it themselves, are the most democratic of all nations."

CHAPTER VIII

PLACE-NAMES

CAMDEN says: "About the year of our Lord 1000 (that we may not minute out the time) surnames began to be taken up in France, and in England about the time of the Conquest, or else a very little before, under King Edward the Confessor, who was all Frenchified. . . . This will seem strange to some Englishmen and Scottishmen, which, like the Arcadians, think their surnames as ancient as the moone, or at the least to reach many an age beyond the Conquest. But they which think it most strange (I speak under correction) I doubt they will hardly finde any surname which descended to posterity before that time; neither have they seene (I feare) any deede or donation before the Conquest, but subsigned with crosses and single names without surnames in this manner: ✠ Ego Eadredus confirmavi. ✠ Ego Sigarius conclusi. ✠ Ego Olfstunus consolidavi, etc."

This is true so far as that there were no hereditary surnames before about 1000; but there were nick, or descriptive, names in use, and appear in charters, but these were personal, and did not descend to the sons.

The Normans who came over with the Conqueror brought with them the names of their estates and castles in Normandy and Brittany, or else some personal name, which they transmitted to their posterity; or they held hereditary offices, as stewards, constables, marshals, from which they took their names and passed them on. Some had personal names, originally Norse, but altered through contact with French.

"Under the feudal system," says Mr. Lower, "the great Barons assumed as surnames the proper names of their

PLACE-NAMES

seigniories; the knights who held under them did the like, and those in turn were imitated by all who possessed a landed estate, however small. Camden remarks that there is not a single village in Normandy that has not surnamed some family in England."

In Britain settlements by the Celtic freeholders took the names of the settlers. *Tre*, or *tref*, the house of, preceded the name of the man who built the house, as Trecarrel, Trevanion, Tremadoc. A church also took the name of its founder, as Llanaelhaiarn, Llancadoc; but in far later times, when place-names were taken up as surnames, then we shall find a Henry de Trecarrel, a John Trevanion, and a David Tremadoc; also the church might give a name to a layman, as in Cornwall, de Lanyon—*i.e.*, the Church of St. John.

The Saxons and Angles also called places after their names. The English Chronicle is, of course, wrong in making Portsmouth derive from a settler named Port; nevertheless, there is abundance of evidence that the new colonists did denominate many places after their own names.

Wright, in his "History of Ludlow," says: "Many of the names of places, of which the meaning seems most difficult to explain, are compounded of those of Anglo-Saxon possessors or cultivators, and the original forms of such words are readily discovered by a reference to Domesday Book. . . . Names of places having *ing* in the middle are generally formed from patronymics, which in Anglo-Saxon had this termination. Thus, a son of Alfred was Ælfreding; his descendants in general were Ælfredings or Ælfredingas. These patronymics are generally compounded with *ham*, *tun*, etc., and whenever we can find the name of a place in pure Saxon documents, we have the patronymic in the genitive case plural. Thus, Birmingham was Beorm-inge-ham, the home or residence of the sons and descendants of Beorm. There are not many names of this form in the neighbourhood of Ludlow; Berrington (Beoringaton) was perhaps the enclosure of the sons or family of Beor, and Culmington that of the family of Culm."

PLACE-NAMES

In Northumbria and East Anglia the Danes had begun to settle from the seventh or beginning of the eighth century. They were of the same stock as the Angles, derived their royal race from the same ancestry, and spoke pretty much the same tongue. The Angles came from the modern Schleswig, and the home of the Danes was the island of Zealand, with the hall of the King and the temple of the national god at Leidre. A continual stream of Danes passed into the North of England. The Kings of Leidre demanded, and indeed exacted, *scatt*, or tribute, from the Northumbrians. At length, in 878, by the peace of Wedmore, the whole of the country north of the Watlingstreet—the great Roman road that ran straight as an arrow from London to Chester—was ceded to the Danes. In the Saga of Egill Skallagrimson we are told that at the time when he was in Northumbria—*i.e.*, in the tenth century—nearly all the inhabitants were Scandinavians on the father's or mother's side, and a very great many on both sides.

The place-names in Yorkshire are largely Scandinavian. Baldersby, Thukleby, Grimsthorpe, Ormskirk, Greeta (Griot-á), the stony river, and a thousand others, point to the continuous occupation by the Danes and Northmen. A hundred and sixty-seven places with names ending in *by* have been reckoned in Yorkshire. In the same county are ninety-four ending in *thorpe;* twenty end in *with*—*i.e.*, wood; there are numerous *royds*, clearings in its woods. Lincolnshire was also peopled with Danes. The conquest of the whole of England by Cnut, or Canute the Great, tended still further to introduce Scandinavian names (personal) into the land, but the grip on it was not sufficiently extended to affect place-names seriously beyond Northumbria and East Anglia. The islands, however, about the coast—haunts of the Vikings—mostly received and retained the names given to them by these Scandinavian pirates, as Lundy (Puffin Isle), Ramsey, Mersea, Anglesey, Brightlingsea (Brithelm's-ey), once all but an island.

Iceland was colonized from Norway between the years 872 and 890 by bonders of ancient pedigree and large posses-

PLACE-NAMES

sions, who had hitherto held their land as allodial ground, and King Harald Fairhair insisted on converting all freeholds into tenures from the crown in feof. Rather than endure this, these men took their movable goods with them, their wives, children, and serfs, and migrated to Iceland, which was then uncolonized.

Happily we have preserved a Landnamabok, or record of the settlement of the island, with the names and genealogies of all the emigrants, and what concerns us now, the names they gave to every place where they planted themselves. As the same procedure took place in England when Jutes, Angles, Saxons, Danes, and Northmen came into our island and settled there, this Landnamabok is to us very instructive, and helps us to elucidate the place-names over a large portion of England, and through the place-names the surnames derived from these places.

In Iceland there has been scarcely any infiltration of foreign blood; consequently, what the first settlers called their new homes retain the names unaltered to the present day. This has not been the case in England, and among us names have been altered and degraded almost past recognition.

We find among the Icelanders that very generally, when a colonist planted himself on the soil and built a house, he called that new home after his own name. It was to record, to the end of time, who had first come there to dwell. But this was not invariably the case; sometimes the settler was less ambitious, and gave to his new quarters a descriptive appellation. But, whether called after his name or descriptive, the name is double, the second portion signifying a *by*, or farm, a holding, a *tun*, town, a *bjarg*, or fortification.

The subject of place-names is too wide to be dealt with here except generally, and would not be touched on at all were it not that so large a proportion of our surnames are taken from places. Nor is there need for dealing with such with anything like completeness, as Mr. Isaac Taylor has investigated the subject, and his books, " Words and Places " and " Names and their Histories," are accessible to all. In the appendix to the latter is a treatise on " English Village

PLACE-NAMES

Names." A few pages may, however, be devoted to place-names as affecting surnames, under Mr. Taylor's guidance, that those persons bearing such may have some understanding as to their significance.

It is necessary to remember that place-names were in ancient times in an oblique case, usually the locative or dative, and in course of time names in this case came to be regarded as undeclinable nouns, or were themselves declined as nominatives. Thus Newton appears in Anglo-Saxon charters as Newantune, which is the dative singular, and the *n* has been retained in Newnton in Wiltshire. Elsewhere it lingers on in Newington, much disguised. Newanham is now Newnham. *Heah* (high) makes *hean* in the dative singular, and remains perceptible as such in Hampstead for Heansted.

The dative plural ends in *um*. Thus *hus*, a house, forms *husum*, "to the houses," and this we have corrupted into Housham in Lincolnshire. Newsham is really New-husum, and Moorsholm is More-husum. Wothersome is Wode-husum, "to or at the Wooden Houses."

The dative plural of *cot* is *cotum*, and gives its name to Coatham, near Redcar in Yorkshire, and Cottam in Derbyshire; whence the surname *Cotton*.

Botl is a building of boards, a log-hut. The plural is *bodlum*, "at the bottles": hence Beadlam. *Hillum*, "at the hills," becomes Hillam; and Wellum, "at the wells," becomes Welham.

Consequently, we cannot always be sure that a place-termination in *ham* has the significance of *hām* (a home) or *hăm* (an enclosure).

The Anglo-Saxon *burh* (a fortified place) in the dative becomes *byrig*. Edinburgh is derived from the nominative case, but Canterbury from the dative; so also Salisbury, Amesbury, Shaftesbury.

The following list of terminations is by no means exhaustive, but will be found useful:[1]

---

[1] A.S.=Anglo-Saxon; C.=Celtic; O.E.=Old English; Gk.=Greek; O.N.=Old Norse; G.=German; D.=Danish; Lat.=Latin.

PLACE-NAMES

ACRE always meant the cornland, ploughed or sown. It enters into many combinations: *Goodacre, Oldacre, Longacre, Whitacre.* Whitaker is a chalky field, or else one in which spar is turned up. In Devonshire such spar is called Whitacre stone.

ANGLE, a corner. Atten-Angle has given us *Nangle.* John de Angulo, 1273 (Hundred Rolls).

BARROW (A.S. *bearw*), a wooded hill fit for pasturing swine: Mapleborough, Barrow-in-Furness. The dative plural is *bearwe.* In Devonshire it is the origin of many Beres. But "barrow" is also employed as a cairn or mound of stone, as Eylesbarrow, the Eagles' Cairn (A.S. *beorh*, a hill).

BECK (A.S. *bec*), a brook; the German *bach.* "Beck" is still in common use in the North of England, as Kirkbeck, Holbeck. "*Beckett*" is a small beck. Gilbert-a-Becket took his name from Bec in Normandy, named from "bec" or brook hard by the monastery.

BENT is an Old English name for a high pasture or shelving piece of moorland; thence the names *Broadbent* and *Bentley.*

> "Downward on an hil under a bent
> Ther stood the tempul of Marz armypotent."
> *Canterbury Pilgrims:* "Knight's Tale."

BERE or BEARE. See above, under "Barrow."

BOLD, a built house, one of stone, when bothies were in general use, and halls of timber: *Newbold.*

BOCLE (O.E.), a hill swelling out; hence the names *Bickley, Bickle, Buckle* (G. *büchel*).

BOTH (A.S.), a booth or wooden house. Also Celtic *bodd*, a settlement, as Bodmin, the monastic settlement; *Freebody,* and other names ending in *bod* and *body.*

BOTTLE (A.S. *botl*), a diminutive of *both.* In the Highlands a bothie is so used; in German we have *Wolfen-büttel.* It occurs in *Harbottle* (the highly-situated bottle), *Newbottle. Bolton* is the *tun* containing a bottle; *Bothwell* and *Claypole,* the bottle in the clay.

BOTTOM (A.S. *botn*), the head of a valley. We have it in

PLACE-NAMES

composition as *Sidebottom, Ramsbottom* (the bottom where ramson or garlic grows), *Winterbottom* (the winding head of the valley). In Lancashire "hichin" is the mountain-ash, whence the name *Higginbottom; Shufflebotham* for Sheeppen-bottom. Also *Bottome.*

BRIGG, a bridge: *Philbrick,* where it is altered into *brick; Trowbridge, Bridgwater, Bristol,* for Brigg-Stowe.

BURG (A.S. *burh,* in O.N. *bjorg,* D. *borg,* G. *burg*), a fortified place; closely akin to *berg,* a mountain. It enters into many combinations, both in singular and dative, as Edinburgh, Newborough, Canterbury, Aldermanbury, and Carrisbrugh, corrupted to Carisbrooke.

BERRY, a further corruption of *burh:* Roseberry; found in the West of England at Berry Head, Berry Pomeroy Castle, and as a surname *Berry.*

BREND, a steep declivity.

BROOK, originally a morass, then a stream, a very common name. It occurs over and over again in the Hundred Rolls, as Alice de la Broke, Andrew ate Broke, Peter ad le Broke, Matilda ad Broke, Sarra de Broke, Reginald behind Broke, Richard apud Broke, Reginald del Broke (Bardsley). It would be absurd to suppose that all these Brooks belonged to one family. It was purely a designation of place where some humble individuals dwelt who had no surname as yet. Often we have *Brooks.*

BUTTS. Near every town and village were the butts, where archery was practised. He who lived by it was "atten Butts." Some butts had special designation; hence the surname *Sowerbutt.* Dr. Butts was physician to Henry VIII.

BY (O.N. *baer, byr;* D. *by,* a farm), originally a single house, then came to be employed of a group of houses. Enters into numerous combinations, as *Maltby* (Malthouse), *Enderby* (Andrew's house); sometimes contracted into *bee,* as Aislabee.

CAR (C. *caer*), a camp: Caer Caradoc, Carlisle, Carmarthen, Carhayes.

CAR (O.N.), moorland: Redcar.

PLACE-NAMES

CARN (C.), a pile of stones, sometimes over a dead man: Carnbrea, Carnmarth, *Carnaby* (the farm by the Carn).

CASTER, CHESTER (Lat. *castrum*), as Lancaster, Chester, Exeter (Exanceaster), Chester-le-Street (the castrum on the Roman road).

CLIFF, CLEAVE (A.S. *clif*): Clifton, Topcliff, Rowcliff; in Devon, Cleave, as Clovelly (Cleave-ley), and Lustleigh and Tavy Cleaves. Surnames *Cleave, Clive, Cliffe*.

CLOSE, an enclosure.

CLOUGH, a glen, used in the North; hence *Clowes*.

COMBE (C. *cwm*), a lateral valley; very general in the West of England, Sussex, and Cumberland. A poet of the latter county says:

"There's Cumwitten, Cumwhinton, Cumranton,
Cumranger, Cumrew, Cumcatch,
And many mair Cums in the County,
But nin wi' Gumdurock can match."

Coombe is a surname, also *Westcoombe, Sutcombe*, etc.

COP (G. *kopf*), a head. In Wicklyffe's version of Luke iv. 29 we have: "And thei . . . ledden him to the *coppe* of the hill on which their cytee was bilded to cast him down." Hence the surnames *Cope, Copps, Copley, Copeland, Cobbe, Cobley*, etc.

COT (A.S.), a thatched cottage, with mud walls. Draycott is the dry cottage. Woodmancott explains itself. Coatham and Cotton are from the dative plural. A *Cotterel* in Domesday signifies a small cottage. In the North of England Cot assumes the form of *Coate*. Cot as a suffix sometimes becomes "cock," just as "apricot" becomes "apricox."

CRAG (C. *cryg*), a rock, lengthened in the North into *Craig*. In the Old Scottish metrical version of Ps. cxxxvii., the verse "Blessed shall he be that taketh thy children and throweth them against the stones" is rendered:

" How blessed shall that horseman be,
That, riding on his naggie,
Shall take thy bairns within his airms,
And cast them 'gainst the craggie."

The surnames *Craike, Crayke*, derive hence.

PLACE-NAMES

CRICK (A.S. *cric*), a creek; not usual as a suffix, but found as *Creech, Evercreech, Cricklade*.

CROFT (A.S.), a small enclosure; hence the surnames *Croft, Holcroft, Crofton. Bancroft* is a beancroft. *Haycroft*, one hedged about. In the West of England corrupted to Crap, *Lillicrap*, the little croft.

DALE (O.N. *dalr*): Swaledale, Nithsdale, Borowdale. But Dalton does not signify the *tun* in the dale, but the tun divided in two by a brook. In one of the Robin Hood ballads we have:

> "'By the faith of my body,' then said the young man,
> ' My name it is Allan a Dale.' "

Dale is often " dall "; *Tindall* stands for Tyne-dale. Udall is the yew-dale. Sometimes Dale is corrupted into " dow " or " daw," as *Lindow* or *Lindaw*.

DEN or DEANE (A.S. *dene*), a wooded valley in which cattle might find covert and pasture. Hence the Forest of Dean, Ar-den, Rottingdean, Tenterden, Surrenden, Hazledene, Hawarden, Willesden, Brogden (the badger's den), Roden (that of the roe). Hoxton is really Hogsden. We have the surnames *Deane, Oxenden, Sugden* (a sow-den), *Dearden, Denman* (one living in a deane); also *Denyer*, that has the same significance.

DINGLE, a depth of wood. In an Old English homily in the 13th century it is used of the sea-bottom. Surname *Dingley*.

DUN (C.), a fortress, but also a hill: Dunmere, Furzedon, Hambledon. Surname *Dunn*.

ECCLES (Gr.), a church: Egloskerry, Egloshayle, Eccles in Norfolk and Lancashire, Ecclesfield in Yorkshire, and Eccleston. All as prefixes. *Eccles* was the name of a musical composer of Purcell's time, and only second to him.

EDGE, the brow of a hill, as Edgehill, Audley Edge. In names, for euphony, an *l* is sometimes introduced, as *Cumberledge, Depledge;* but it is possible enough that " ledge " may have been used as shelf on a hill.

END. "A certain number of names . . . have arisen from a somewhat peculiar colloquial use of the term 'end'

ACE-NAMES

in vogue with our Saxon forefathers. The mode of its employment is still common in Lancashire and Yorkshire. The poorer classes still speak of a neighbour as dwelling at 'the street end'; they never by any chance use the fuller phrase, 'the end of the street.' Chaucer uses it as a familiar mode of expression. The Friar, in the preface to his story, says slightingly:

> "'A Sompnour is a rener up and down
> With mandements for furnication,
> And is beaten at every towne end.'

Numerous contributions occur in the Hundred Rolls as names: John ate-Bruge-end, Walter-at-Townshende, Margaret ate Laneande, Thomas atte Greavesende, etc." (Bardsley).

Much dispute has occurred as to the meaning of the rubric directing the Priest at the Communion Service to stand "at the North side of the Table." This has been taken as a direction that he should be like Cheevy Slyme, "Always round the corner, sir." Had the Reformers meant this, they would have used the word *end*. An altar has a middle and two sides as well as two ends. We have the surnames *Townend, Townshend, Townsend*, etc.

EY (O.N.), an island, sometimes a peninsula: Bardsey, Ely, Battersey, Mersea, Ramsey, Lundy. The A.S. *ig* (in the dative *ige*), a watery place, has the same signification. Sheppey in A.S. is Sheapig; Ramsey, Ramsige; Hinksey is Hingestesige (Hengest's island).

FELL (O.N. *fjall*), a mountain: Scarfell.

FIELD is properly a clearing, where trees have been felled. This enters into numerous compositions, as *Somerfield*, the field of the Somerlid, or Viking; *Suffield*, the south field; *Haverfield*, the field of oats.

FLEET (O.N. *fljot*), a tidal estuary. The Norse, and the A.S. *fliot*, signify alike a place where ships can float. Swinefleet, near Goole, and Adlingfleet, a few miles lower down at the old mouth of the Don, are inlets which sheltered the ships of Sweyn and Edgar Etheling when their host

PLACE-NAMES

marched inland and took York. *Fleetwood* is a surname; *Amphlet* is "atten Fleet."

FORD (C. *fordd*; A.S. *ford*), a way; only in a secondary sense signifies a ford across a river. The numerous places whose names end in "ford" often show how common fords were, and how scarce were bridges. Several fords are named after the river through which the ford lay. There are fifteen Stamfords, Stanfords or Stainforths where were stepping-stones. Coggleford was paved with cobbles. Staplefords were protected by piles driven into the bed of the stream. Twenty-two Sandfords or Samfords indicate sandy bottoms. Stratfords point to fords on old Roman roads. It must not, however, be lost sight of that a good many places ending in "ford" are on no river at all, or on tiny brooks, that could be stepped across. Such places take their names from the use of the word "ford" as a highway. In the West of England "ford" is often altered into *ver*—Vitiver is the Whiteford, or white-paved highway leading across Dartmoor and above the head of the Webburn. Rediver is the Redford, also where is no stream.

Ford may also be a modernization of the O.N. *varðr*, a place of protection and defence. And it is not possible in many cases, without local knowledge, to determine whether "ford" stands for road, ford over a river, or place of defence.

FORTH (O.N. *fjord*), an arm of the sea; also *Firth*.

FYRTH (A.S.), a forest, a retired glen where is to be found peace (*frid*); and this use of the word seems to have extended farther. In the "Noble Art of Venerie" it is said: "There is difference between the fryth and the fell. By fells are understood the mountain, valleys and pastures, with corne and such like; the frythes betoken the springs and coppyses." And in the "Boke of S. Alban's" we have—

"Wheresoever ye fall by frythe or by fell,
My dere chylde, take heed how Tristram doth you tell."

In the Craven dialect the word "frith" is still used to describe a tract enclosed by the hills, usually for a plantation. Thus we have the place-names: Chápel-le-Frith; Frith in

PLACE-NAMES

the parish of Forest, Durham; Fritham in the New Forest; and Frithelstock (a stockade in a frith) in Devonshire. *Frith* is still employed as a surname.

GARTH (A.S.), an enclosed place; hence garden, yard.

GATE may mean a road, as Bishopsgate; but also a barrier. Sometimes corrupted to *yat:* Ramsgate, Margate, Westgate; surnames *Gates* and *Yates, Yeatman* (the gatekeeper).

GILL (O.N.), a ravine: Pickersgill, Fothergill.

GLYN (C.), a glen, also *Lynn:* Glyncotty, Lynmouth. Used also as a surname.

GOOLE, a canal.

GORE, a ravine or narrow strip of land, usually three-cornered: *Gorell* (dim.), *Gorham*.

GOTT, a watercourse—equivalent to *Goyt* and *Gut.*

GRANGE is given elsewhere; hence *Granger* and *Grange.*

GRAVE (A.S. *graef*), a ditch; also a pit for catching wild beasts: Stonegrave, Palgrave (a wood-lined pit). Falsgrave is the A.S. Wallesgrave. Waldegrave is a pitfall in a wood, or a woodsreeve. We have the surnames *Greaves* and *Graves.*

GROVE (A.S. *graf*): Broomsgrove, Boxgrove, Nutgrove. As a surname, *Groves.*

HATCH and HACKET, a gate or bar thrown across a gap. A gate turned, but a hatch consisted of bars that had to be removed. Many indications of hatches remain in Cornwall and Devon—notched blocks of stone, in which the bars rested. The name *Balhatchet* signifies the hatchet giving access to a *bal*, or mine. The surnames of *Hatch, Hatcher, Hatchman*, are still here. *Hatchard* in another form. Hatch was originally "atte Hatch." In the Hundred Rolls we have De la Hatche.

HAL and HALE signify a corner.

HALL and HEAL (A.S.), a slope. Tichenhall is Ticenhealh, the slope of the goat. Holton in Somerset is Healhton —in A.S., the tun on a slope. *Heale* is a name of a place and a surname in Devon. Rushall in Yorkshire is the rushy slope. Willenhall is the slope of Willan. Hales signifies the slopes. Willingale Spain was Uulingehala, a hill-slope on which a soldier of fortune from Spain named Henry de

PLACE-NAMES

Ispania settled. But it had an earlier settler called Willa, whose family was that of the Willings. Hall, however, is the *aula* of a manor as well, and has given its name to families, but probably not so often as the slope; for the family in the *aula* would be well known as manorial owners, and have their names, whereas the humble cotter on the hillside would be a William on Healh or Richard Hall.

HAM (A.S.) has two significations—with the *a* long it signifies home; with the *a* short it signifies a field enclosed. Burnham is the enclosure by the brook. Birmingham, on the other hand, was the home of the Beormings. Farnham is the field of ferns. Cheltenham is the enclosure on the Chelt. When *ham* is associated with a personal name, then it signifies the "home of." As we have already seen, it sometimes disguises the dative plural in *um*. Singularly enough, the Americans have reverted to the ending. Thus they have *Barnum* for Barnham. *Ham* is a common surname in Devon, and the rich, fertile land below Dartmoor to the sea is called the "South Hams." Hampshire is the shire of enclosures.

HANGER is a hill-slope in the West of England, but the A.S. is *hangra*, a meadow: Halshanger in Devon, Birchanger in Essex, Clayhanger in three counties, Ostenhanger in Kent, Goldhanger in Essex; also Ongar in Essex, called Angra in Domesday.

HAUGH, pronounced *Haff*, is low-lying level ground by the side of a river.

HAY, a hedge to an enclosure; often a small park. Chaucer in "Troilus" has—

> "But right so as these holtes and these hayes,
> That have in winter dead beene and dry,
> Revesten them in greene when May is;
> When every lusty beast lusteth to pley."

From this simple root we have the surnames *Hay, Hayes, Haigh*, and *Hawis* and *Hawes*, and in combination *Haywood, Haworth, Haughton*. As a termination it gets reduced to *ay*, sometimes *ey*—*Fotheringay; Halley*, the enclosure on the hillside.

PLACE-NAMES

HEAD, the upper end, becomes sometimes *ett*: *Aikinhead*, *Birkenhead*, *Blackett* for Blackhead, and *Beckett*, either the brook-head or the little brook.

HEATH explains itself. In *Hebburn* we have it in combination—a heath-burn.

HERNE, any nook or corner that has been taken possession of by a squatter. Chaucer speaks of

"Lurking in hearnes and in lanes blind."

HEUGH, pronounced *Heuhh*, is a crag, a cliff. This word or "haugh" is liable to attract to it the *s* from the end of the foregoing word. Thus Earnshaw is Ernsheugh, the Eagles' Cliff.

HOE (A.S. *hoh*), high ground: Langenhoe, Wyvenhoe, the Hoe, Plymouth. But it is difficult to say whether *haugr*, a cairn, may not have originated some of the heughs and hoes; sometimes changed to "enough," as *Goodenough* is Goodenheugh.

HYTHE (A.S. *hyd*), a haven, a wharf; hence the surname *Hyde*.

HOLM (O.N.), a flat island. Duels were called "holmgöngir," because fought on islands. Flat Holme and Steep Holme in the Bristol Channel; *Holmes* as surname.

HOLT is the same as the German *Holz*, a wood or copse: Bergholt in Essex. *Holt* is a surname in Yorkshire. Becomes "shot" in composition occasionally, as *Aldershot*, *Sparshot*.

HOPE (O.N. *hop*), an opening, a small bay; also a gap in the hills or in a forest. "In Yarrow, almost every farmhouse is sheltered in a recess or hollow of the hills, and the names in 'hope' are correspondingly numerous—as, for instance, Kirkhope, Dryhope, Whitehope, etc.—more than twenty in all. In Upper Weardale, Durham, we find another cluster of these names, such as Stanhope, Burnhope, Westenhope, Wellhope, Harthope, Swinehope, Rockhope, and Rollehope, the meaning of which is most transparent." Also Glossop and Heslop in Derbyshire, Worksop in Notts, and to the same source may be attributed *Hopton*. *Hartopp* is a surname, as is *Hope*. So also *Blenkinsop* and *Widdop*. It is also

PLACE-NAMES

corrupted into *ship*. *Nettleship* is the nettle-overgrown opening in the woods.

HOUSE (A.S. and O.N.), often contracted into *us*, as *Aldus* (the old house), *Malthus* (the malt-house), *Loftus* (the house with a loft). The tavern sign Bear and Bachus is a corruption of Beer and Bakehouse. Surnames *Woodhouse, House*, etc.

HUISH (A.S. *hiwise*), a hide of land.

HURST (A.S.), a wood, very common in Sussex: *Brocklehurst*, a badger's wood; *Hazelhurst*, one of hazel-trees; *Dewhurst*, one of deer; *Lindhurst*, one of linden-trees, all used as surnames. Stonyhurst, Hurstpierpoint, are place-names. *Hurst*, alone, exists as a surname.

INCH or INCE (C. *ynys*), an island. In Cornwall occurs the surname *Enys*. Hence also the surname *Ince*.

ING (O.N. *eng*), a meadow by a river. It is difficult always to say whether the ending refers to a personal name or to a field. But in such cases as Ermington, Dartington, there can exist no doubt that these were *tuns* on the *ings* of the Rivers Erm and Dart.

KELD (A.S. *celd*), a source of water. Hallkeld in Yorkshire is the Holy Spring; Bapchild, near Sittingbourne, occurs in A.S. as Baccancilde, the source of a beck. Kildwick in Yorkshire is the village by the source: this has been corrupted into the surname *Killick*. The Anglo-Saxon is cognate with the German *quelle*, and Weldale, in Yorkshire, in Domesday appears as Queldale.

KNAPP (A.S. *cnaep*), a hill-top; hence our names *Knapman, Knopps, Knapton*.

KNOLL (A.S. *cnoll*), a small round hill; hence *Knowles, Knowlers, Knowlman*, and *Knollys*, when not from Oliver.

LADE (O.N.), a barn, but in A.S. a path: *Ladbrook, Lade, Lathe, Laight*.

LANE. On the Hundred Rolls are numerous entries such as these: Cecilia in the Lane, Emma a la Lane, John de la Lane, Philippa atte Lane, Thomas super Lane; so that, although a Norman family of L'Ane came over with the Conqueror, we cannot set down all the *Lanes* as his descendants.

PLACE-NAMES

The author of a favourite hymn, "There's a Friend for little children above the bright blue sky," was a Mr. *Midlane*.

LAUND, a grassy sward in a forest. From the O.N. *lund*, that signified a sacred grove. Chaucer says of Theseus:

> "To the *Launde* he rideth ful right;
> There was the harte wont to have his flight."

Hence our surnames *Laund, Lands, Lowndes;* also the name *Lund*.

LAW (A.S. *hlewe*), a hill: Bassetlaw in the North, Harlow in Essex, Oswaldslaw in Worcestershire, Cotteslow in Bucks, Bucklaw in Cheshire. But *low* is also employed of a grave-mound.

LEET, LAKE (A.S.), a lead or channel for water made artificially; hence the surname *Lake*.

LEE, LEGH, LEIGH, LEY, LEA (A.S. *leah*, m.), a fallow pasturage, but *leah*, f., signifies a rough woodland pasture. Local names being usually in the dative, *lea* for *leah* (m.) is nominally the source of the suffix *ley*. This word enters into endless compositions, as *Stanley, Calverley, Wesley, Hadleigh, Berkley, Leyton*, etc. It is found as a surname in all forms. There is a saying in reference to the extension of the name:

> "As many Lees
> As there be fleas."

Low. See above under *Law*.

LYNCH (A.S. *hlinc*, a hill, a boundary); perhaps the same origin as the Northern *links*.

MERE (A.S.), a sheet of water: Wittleseamere, Dosmare in Cornwall. Merton is a tun by a mere. Mere is, however, also employed as a boundary, so that Merton might also mean the *tun* on a boundary.

MOOR, a name that explains itself, and gives surnames as *Moore* and *More, Muir, Blackmore, Delamore, Morton, Morley, Moorhayes*. *Paramore* is an enclosure on the moor (O.E. *parren*, to enclose).

MOUNTAIN is found as a surname, probably brought in by the French emigrants. Also *Mount*.

PLACE-NAMES

ORE (A.S. *ofer* and *ora*), the shore of the sea or the bank of a river (the German *ufer*): Pershore, Edensore. Esher is Ase-ore, the ash-tree bank. *Wardour*, that gives a title to Lord Arundel, is Weard-ora. The same word enters into the formation of *Windsor*.

OVER (A.S. *ofer*), as above. An old poem, quoted by Halliwell, says:

> "She comes out of Sexlonde,
> And 'rived here at Dovere
> That stands upon the see's overe."

It denotes the flat lands that lie along low coasts. *Over, Overman*, as surnames.

NANT (C.), a valley: *Pennant*, the head of the valley; *Nankivel*, the valley of the horse.

PEN (C.), the head: Pendennis, the castle on the headland; Penycomebequick, the village at the head of the combe; Penigent, the white head.

PITT, a sawpit, coalpit, or pitfall. Woolpit in Suffolk is the wolfpit. Fallapit in Devon, the ancient seat of the Fortescues, derives its names from a falling-into pit—*i.e.*, a pitfall for wild beasts. Mr. Lower tells the following story of a foundling christened Moses, and surnamed Pitt because found in a marl-pit. "Nobody likes you," said this crabbed piece of humanity to a neighbour with whom he was at strife. "Nor you," replied the other. "Not even your mother, who abandoned you."

PLATT, low-lying ground. Now we speak of a garden plot—actually plat. This word remains in surnames.

POL (A.S. *pol*; C. *pwll*), a pool.

> "Pol, Tre and Pen
> Are the names of Cornishmen."

Polwheel, Poldue (black pool).

RAYNE, a boundary: *Raine, Raynes*—*i.e.*, one living at the bounds.

RIDGE or RIGG (A.S.), generally applied to an old Roman road: *Ridgeway; Aldridge, Aldrich*—the name At Ridg or At Rigg has become *Trigg* or *Triggs; Beveridge, Kimmeridge, Ashridge*.

PLACE-NAMES

Ros (C. *rhos*), a heath : *Roskelly, Penrose, Rosedue*.

Royd (O.N.), a clearing in a wood; German *rode*, as Gernerode, or *Reute*. Much used in Yorkshire: *Kebroyd, Holroyd, Akenoyd* (oak clearing), *Ormrod* (the clearing made by Orme); the Yorkshire family of *Rhodes*.[1]

Rye (A.S., *hrycg*), a ridge or bank of sand and pebbles.

Rye (A.S. *rith*), a mountain stream. Shottery, Leatherhead, is A.S. *Chilla-rith*, the stream from the source.

Rupell, a coppice : Philip atte Ruple, in Somersetshire, *temp.* Edward I.

Seale, Sel, Sele (O.N. *sel;* A.S. *seale*), a residence or hall : Seal in Worcestershire, Zeal in Devon, Seale in Surrey, Selworthy; surnames *Selborne, Selby, Seale*, perhaps *Seeley; Ingersoll, Plimsoll*. Inger is the Norse Ingvar, a settler who called the seal or sel after himself.

Scale (O.N. *skali*), a wooden house: Winterscales in Yorkshire. Surname *Scales*.

Shelf (A.S. *scylfe*), a ridge of land, a shelf: Raskelf in Yorkshire, a raw shelf above a morass. The saying is:

> " Raskelf without a steeple,
> Rascally church and rascally people."

Bashall in Yorkshire is Bascelf in Domesday.

Shaw (O.N. *skog*) is—(1) A small wood or coppice; (2) a flat at the foot of a hill; (3) a boggy place by a river: Ellershaw, Painshaw; but see what is said under *Heugh*, corrupted into *shot*, as Aldershot.

---

[1] The following passage from the Icelandic Kjalnessinga Saga illustrates what took place in the North of England, where the woods covered hill and dale : " All the Kjalness was overgrown with wood, so that it had to be cleared [royded], and men cleared [royded] for farms and ways. Soon much was cleared [royded] to the hills from Hof. There Helgi and Andrith cleared [royded] in spring. And when they came to the holt, then said Helgi : ' Here, Arnoth, will I give you land, and you shall erect a farmhouse [boer].' "—" Islendinga Sögur," 1847, ii., p. 400. The surname *Ruddiman* may not be descriptive of a florid countenance, but indicate a man who royded woodland, cutting down trees and stubbing up their roots. Mr. *Rudyard* Kipling takes his first name from a garth that has been so cleared. The Yorkshire Ridings designate the clearings effected.

PLACE-NAM

SIDE, employed for a mountain, as Great Wernside, Akenside, Garside.

SLADE (A.S. *slæd*), a steep of greensward between two woods or between two breadths of townland : Waterslade in Somersetshire, Slaidburn, Slaithwait, and Sledmere. *Slade* is a not uncommon Northern surname; also *Greenslade*, *Whiteslade*.

SKROGG, brushwood. The word occurs in the "Morte d'Arthur." Hence the surname *Scroggs*. A village in Dumfries is so called.

SLEIGH or SLEY (O.N. *slethr*), level land. The surname *Slee* may come from it. *Sleeman* is the occupant of a holding on the Sley.

STAPLE, a market: *Barnstaple*, *Huxtable*.

SHORE and SANDS have furnished names to those dwelling by the sea.

SOLE, a pond, a Kentish term : Peter atte Sole, Co. Kent, 1273 (Hundred Rolls). Surname *Soley*.

STEAD (A.S.), a home : Hampstead, Ringstead, Greenstead, Felsted, *Wellstead*. *Stedman* is a farmer; *Westhead* is the western stead.

STREET, the paved highway.

SYKE, a stagnant piece of water that soaks away and has no flow in it. *Sykes* is a surname.

STOKE, STOWE (A.S.), a stockade : Tavistock, Basingstoke, Stokesley, Stocton, Felixstowe, Bristowe (now Bristol) —the stockade at the bridge.

THORPE (A.S.; D. *torp*; G. *dorf*), a hamlet: Sibthorpe is Sigbert's village; Langthorpe, Kettlethorpe. *Thorpe* is a common surname in the Danish districts of Yorkshire and Lincolnshire. In "The Clerke's Tale" we are told :

> "Naught far fro thir palace honourable,
> There stood a *thorpe* of sight delitable,
> In which the poor folk of the village
> Hadden their bestes and their harborage."

Hence the surnames *Thrupp*, *Winthrop* or *Winterthorp*, *Gawthorp*, *Calthrop*, etc. *Kirkup* stands for Kirkthorp.

PLACE-NAMES

THWAITE, the O.N. *thveit*, signifies an outlying paddock. Thwaites are mostly found in Cumberland, mainly on high ground, and seem to denote clearings. The compounds are numerous: *Brathwaite* (the broad thwaite), *Thwaites*, *Applethwaite*, *Crossthwaite*, *Micklethwaite*, *Longthwaite*, etc. *Lilywhite* is probably a corruption of Littlethwaite.

TOFT (D.), an enclosed field near a farmhouse. The name is found in Iceland—Toptavellir, the fields in the plains. As an ending corrupted to *toe*, as *Shillitoe* or *Sillitoe*.

TOWN. See *Tun*.

TRAVERSE, a cross-roads; hence *Travers* and *Travis*.[1]

TREE (A.S. *treow*). Places are called after some peculiarly old and perhaps sacred tree. Thus we have Tiptree, Heavitree, Wavertree, Pichtree, Harptree, Plymtree. Till within the memory of old men in many places in Devon, there were "dancing trees" in villages, peculiarly cut at the head, on the top of which a platform was erected, upon which, on the occasion of the village revel, dancing took place, and about which the elders of the parish assembled to converse. This was a survival of religious homage paid to the sacred tree. In some names the *treow* has gone through corruption. Austey in Warwickshire was in Anglo-Saxon *Adulfstreow*, Eadulf's tree. Tree in an abraded form is found in Coventry, Oswestry perhaps—but in this probably the Welsh *tref* is to be found. Sometimes "tree" becomes *der*, as in Mappowder, the maple-tree; Langtree is the long tree. In Ireland, Kildare is the church of the oak. The Celtic *tre* or *tref*, "the homestead of," precedes the name of the owner, and rarely occurs as a suffix, as *Trelawney, Trefry*.

TUN (O.N.), the enclosure about a farm, enters into many combinations, as *ton* and *town*. Brighton is Brighthelmston, Wolverhampton is Wolfardes-home-field. Chaucer says:

> "Then saw I but a large field,
> As farre as ever I might see,
> Without *toune*, house or tree."

---

[1] But there is a Trévières in Normandy.

PLACE-NAMES

And Wyckliffe in his Bible, for "one went to his farm, another to his merchandise," has "one into his toune," and in the story of the Prodigal Son the citizen "sente him into his toun to feed swyn." In Iceland the *tun* is the field about the house, enclosed and manured. In Scotland it still has this meaning, and it had the same in Devonshire.

TYE is a piece of common pasture. Surnames *Tye, Tighe.* Hugh de la Tye and Peter at Tye are met with; hence *Attye.*

WADE or WATH, a ford.

WELL, a spring or source, enters into many combinations: Cholwell; Pinwell, from the custom of dropping pins into it; Halwell, the Holy Well; Loddiswell, Our Lady's Well; Greenwell; Kettlewell, and its equivalent, Wherwell (A.S. *hvor*, a ewer); Cromwell, the crooked well; Gulwell, St. Wolvella's well. In Devonshire a well is in the vernacular a *willis.*

WICK, WYKE, WEEK (Lat. *vicus*), a settlement: Warwick, Greenwich, Berwick, Germansweek, Week St. Mary, Hardwick, Norwich, and many others. The surnames *Weeks, Wykes, Quick,* are from this.

WHISTLE (O.N. *kvisl*), a small side-stream joining another: *Birdwhistle, Entwhistle.*

WITH (O.N. *viði*), a wood: *Beckwith, Skipwith.*

WOLD, high open ground; but WEALD, cognate with the German *wald*, is forest-land: Cotswold, Easingwold, The Weald of Sussex.

WOOD becomes sometimes in combination Hood, sometimes Good, as *Thoroughgood* is Thorolf's-wood.

WORTH, WORTHY (O.N. *varðr*), a fortified enclosure or a small estate, as Beaworthy, Wolfardisworthy; also *Hepworth, Wigglesworth,* Tamworth. *Charlesworth* is the churl's worth; it was looked upon as something insolent and out of place that a churl should fortify his hovel. *Wordsworth* is a reduplication—a worth within a worth.

WRAY, a corner set apart, as *Thackeray*, the place apart for storing thatch; also *Wroe.*

WYCH and WYKE (O.N. *vik*), a bay of the sea, or even a

PLACE-NAMES

tidal river. Thus Sandwich, Ipswich, and Droitwich (because of its salt springs).

YAT, for *Gate*, a still common pronunciation; hence the surname *Yates*. *Byatt* stands for By-yat, and *Woodyat* for Wood-gate.

In " The Clerke's Tale " we are told that Griselda went

"With glad chere to the *yate*."

And Piers Plowman says that our Lord came into the upper chamber through

" Both dore and yates
To Peter and to the Apostles."

In the " Townley Mysteries " we have both forms. Jacob in his vision is represented as saying:

" And now is there none other gate,
But Godes howse and heven's yate."

Those persons who took their names from places, prefixed to the place-name *at*, *by*, or *of*, that in documents are rendered in Latin or French *ad*, *de*, or *apud*, *a la*, *de la*, *del*.

In the " Coventry Mysteries " we hear mention made of

"Tom Tynker and Bettys Belle,
Peyrs Potter and Watt *at the Well*."

And Piers Plowman represents Covetousness as saying:

" For some Tyme I served
Symme *atte Style*
And was his prentice."

Atten, really the plural form, got attached to the substantive, as *Attenborough*; and then the *Atte* drops away, but leaves the *n* attached to the thing or place which is described. Thus *Nokes* is Atten-oaks, Atten-ey becomes *Nye*, and Atten-ash *Nash*. But more common is the retention of *At*. This gives us such names as *Atwell*, *Atwood*, *Athill*, *Ethridge* for At-ridge, *Atterbury*, *Atley* for At-lea, *Atworth*; sometimes reduced to *t*, and Atwell becomes *Twells*, and Atwyche is reduced to *Twigge*.[1]

[1] Some of the many surnames formed with the prefix *Atten* or *At* are *Abdey*, at the Abbey; *Agate*, at the Gate; *Amphlet*, at the Tidal Fleet, or

PLACE-NAMES

By remains as *Bygrove, Bywood, Byfield, Byden.*[1]
Of was once common. Clim of the Clough was a famous archer; he soon became Clim Clough. Or else *Of* slid into A. The site of a man's cot was indicated by *Under* or *Over*, or *Upper, Middle,* and *Lower* or *Nether*. Thus we get the names *Underhill, Underwood, Overbury, Overton, Uppcott, Upton, Upwood, Middleton, Medlicott, Middlemas, Netherton. Lowermoor* changed to *Levermore*.

But I shall have more to say on this subject in another chapter.

The colour of wood, moor, lea, and well, etc., has given us the names *Blackwood, Blackmore, Blakely, Blackwell, Blackburn, Blackall, Blackstone;* also *Whitwood, Whitmore, Whitby, Whitwell, Whitburn, Whitstone;* also *Redcliff, Redhill, Rugby, Radmore, Greenhill* and *Greenwell, Greenwood* and *Greendon,* contracted to *Grindon*.

Size comparative is also marked, as *Micklethwaite* and *Littleton;* also relative age, as *Aldborough* and *Oldcastle, Newton* and *Newcastle*.

The points of the compass also enter into composition of place-names. But of these, also, something shall be said farther on. As England has been a place of refuge for all sorts of people, good and bad, who could not get on happily in their own country; or else of peoples who came to oust the natives and take the land to themselves; or, again, of mercenaries who arrived to serve our great Barons and Earls, and settled down on the land; or else of merchants from abroad, who planted themselves to make money among

---

River; *Atford, Achurch,* and *Atkirk; Atock,* at the Oak; *Atfend,* at the Fen; *Atfield, Attwood, Attwater, Attwell, Atwick, Atworth, Attley, Atthill, Attridge, Attmore; Armitage,* at the Hermitage. Besides these, *At* is to be understood in many names, as *Ackroyd,* at the Oak-clearing; *Ackland, Appleyard, Ashe, Barnes, Barr; Birkett,* at the Birchwoodhead; *Browse,* at the Brewhouse; *Backhouse,* at the Bakehouse; *Hatch,* at the Wicket; *Hawes,* at the Hawe; and many more.

[1] *By* remains as well in *Byford; Bidlake,* by the Lake or Leet; *Byatt,* by the Gate; *Byass,* by the House—*i.e.,* the Great House; *Barkiss,* at or by the Barkhouse; *Bythesea, Bywater; Biffen,* by the Fen; and it remains understood in many names as does *At.*

PLACE-NAMES

us, such persons came to be designated by their nationality, probably as having no surnames of their own, or as having them unpronounceable by English mouths. Foreign merchants arrived in large numbers, and opened their shops in nearly every town. French, Flemings, Germans, English, jostled each other in the streets and knelt together in the same churches. It was not as at an earlier period, when, as in Exeter and at Colchester, there were two towns side by side, the one occupied by the native population, the other by the conquerors. The French especially began to form a permanent element in the population of the town, and the fusion of races began to take effect at an early time, becoming more rapid and thorough during the reign of the Plantagenet Kings.

Throughout the country the haggling at market and fair must have been carried on in English that was rapidly becoming spiced with foreign words. In the country places as well the French and Brabant soldiery mingled with the people, flirted with the pretty fair-haired, fresh-complexioned English girls, necessarily in broken English. Every Christmas, with its message of peace and goodwill, the Yule festival, with boar's head bedecked with holly and rosemary, the mummers and rapier-dancers, tended to bring together the native and the foreigner, and to make the latter forget much of his French tongue, and the former to acquire many foreign words. And with this the outlandish soldier and merchant came to feel very much at home in England, and, settling there, their children retained no smack of their alien origin, save the permanent surname only, indicative of whence they came.

The following is a list of the principal surnames, more of these will be given in another chapter:

ALMAIN, ALMAYNE, DALMAIN, from Allemagne (Germany). We have also as surnames from this source *Lalleman*, perhaps *Dolman*.

BEAMISH is Boemish, Bohemian.

BRIDGES, often from Bruges. *Briggs* occasionally; also *Burgess*.

PLACE-NAMES

BULLEN, from Boulogne.
BRABANT, BRABAZON, from Brabant.
BRAME, from Bremen.
BRETT, BRETON, BRITTON, from Brittany.
BURGOYNE, BURGAN, from Burgundy.
CANDY, from Crete or Candia.
CHAMPNEY, from Champagne.
CHILDERS may perhaps come from Gueldres.
CORNISH, CORNWALLIS, from Cornweales, Cornwall; acquired after the West Welsh were suffered to creep back over the Tamar, beyond which Athelstan had banned them.
CULLEN, from Cologne.
DANES, DENMAN, DENNIS, from Denmark. In deeds and Hundred Rolls we have So-and-so described as Le Danois.
DOUCH, for Dutch. Skelton, in his "Parrot," says that besides "French, Lattyn, Ebrew,

"With Douch, with Spanysh, my tong can agree."

Hence the surnames *Dowch*, and perhaps also *Douce*, when not from the French.
EASTERLING, corrupted into *Stradling*, a native of one of the Hanseatic towns. The pure coinage introduced by these in the reign of Richard I. gave rise to the expression Easterling or Sterling money. Hence our names *Easterman, Oysterman*, and *Easte*.
ESPAGNOL has become *Aspinall*.
ENGLISH, in Scotch *Inglis*, a designation acquired, as already explained, in Shewsbury and on the Welsh border, also in Scotland.
FLEMING. In Cornwall the French pronunciation of Flamand has produced *Flamank* as a surname.
FRENCH needs no explanation.
GALE is Gael, an Irish Scott.
GANT, GAUNT, GENT, a man of Ghent.
GASCOIGNE and GASKIN, from Gascony.
GERMAINE, from Germany, corrupted to *Jarman;* but some Germains may derive from the name of the saint.

PLACE-NAMES

GOTT, a native of Gothland, when not from a watercourse, or from Gautr.
HANSARD, from one of the Hanseatic towns.
HANWAY, HANNAH, from Hainault.
HOLLAND explains itself.
HOLSTEINER became *Stayner* and *Holst*.
JANWAY, from Genoa. An old poem, alluding to Brabant as a general mart, says:

> "Englysshe and French, Lumbardes, Jannoyes,
> Cathalones, theder they take their wayes."

The Genoese coin was called a "jane," and hence may perhaps come our surnames *Jayne* and *Jane*, but also from Jean, John. Hall, in his Chronicles, speaking of the Duke of Clarence ravaging the French coast in the reign of Henry IV., says: "In his retournying he encountred with two great Carickes of Jeane laden with rych merchandise."

LEGGE, a merchant from Liége.
LOREYN, LORING, from Loraine.
LUBBARD, a Lombard.
LUBBOCK, a merchant of Lubeck.
MAYNE, from the province of Maine.
NORMAN and NORREYS, a Northman; but *Norris* is sometimes *la nourrice*, the nurse.
PAVEY, from Pavia.
PICKARD, from Pickardy.
POITEVIN, changed to *Portwine* and *Peto*, from Poitou.
POLAND, POLLOCK, a native of Poland.

> "He smote the sledded Polack on the ice."
> *Hamlet.*

POINTZ is from Pontoise.
PROVINCE, from Provence.
PRUSS, from Prussia; now *Prust*, also *Prosser*.
RUSS, a Russian, possibly in some cases has become *Rush* and *Rouse*.
SARSON, a Saracen. Skelton addresses one thus:

> "I say, ye solem Sarson, all blake is your ble."

But the surname may come from the sign of the Saracen's Head. It is probable enough that some Saracen captives

PLACE-NAMES

may have been brought to England, but I am much more disposed to consider the surname as derived from the tavern sign.

VENESS, a Venetian. There is a pretty English folk-song found on broadsides, but still sung by our peasantry, that plays on the interchangeableness of *Venus* and *Veness*.[1]

Such names as *Scott, Spain, Welsh, Wallis, Wight,* need no elucidation. I have not included in the above list the Norman place-names, or many that are French, because these will be dealt with later on.

In the heart of Dartmoor lives, and has lived since the earliest records of the Duchy of Cornwall allow us to trace the family, one of the name of *French*. There can exist but little doubt that the founder of that family was a Frenchman. How came he into those inhospitable, treeless wilds? Probably he was brought there by one of the Earls of Cornwall to act as inspector of the tin-smelting at King's Oven, where the tin was run out of the ore and stamped, and the blocks counted for the revenue of the Earls, afterwards Dukes, of Cornwall. And it is near the King's Oven that the French family is still to be found, hale and vigorous, though the oven itself has been destroyed.

I can remember a long-established firm of drapers named *Flamank*, an instance, probably, of the continuation in one family of the trade of the first Fleming who settled as a clothier in Cornwall.

There are names that strike one as peculiarly grotesque, which are reducible to place-names. Such is that of *Toplady*, the author of the hymn "Rock of Ages." It is a compound name, made up of "toft" and "lade," and signifies the barnfield. Our *Wagstaffe* and *Bickerstaffe* have had nothing to do with staves, so far as to give them their

---

[1] " She was named the Virgin Dove,
    With a lading all of love,
And she signall'd that for Venus [Venice] she was bound.
    But a pilot who should steer,
    She required—for sore her fear,
Lest without one she should chance to run aground.'

PLACE-NAMES

names. *Staff* is a corruption of *steth*, or *stead*, a farm, and these[1] are Cumberland place-names.

Goodbody and *Truebody* derive from a *bothy*, a wooden house or shanty. *Sealy, Silly, Silliman*, imply no idiocy. The names come either from the Scilly Isles, or from a " sell," or hall.

Surnames ending in *love* have nothing amatory in their origin, but derive from some " lowe," hill or tumulus. It is very unjust to hold that all *Lemans* derive from a light wench, when the true derivation is from Le Mans in Normandy.

Tothill has been derived from a *totiller*, a whisperer of secrets, but it is obviously a place-name; and *Drinkwater* does not necessarily imply that the man who gave that name to his descendants was conspicuously temperate, but that he lived by a place where the river or stream was contracted to a *dring*.[2] The surname of *Welcome* is not descriptive of hospitality, but derives from the village of Well-combe in Devon, where the holy well that gives its water to flow down the combe is still the main supply of the village.

There are names of counties borne by families that have migrated from one to another, as *Essex, Devonshire, Yorkshire*, etc., and very often a surname is none other than the name of the township, village, or hamlet, where a family resided or from which it had moved away to some other locality.

Some place-names get corrupted when they become surnames, as Adnam for Addingham, Swetnam for Swettenham, Debnam for Debenham, Putnam for Puttenham. But, indeed, such contractions are common everywhere where a place-name is long; as Lanson for Launceston, Daintry for Daventry, Brumigem for Birmingham, Brighton for Brightelmston, Kirton for Crediton, and even Lunnon for London.

The name *Affleck* is really Auchinleck. Sir Edmund Affleck, created Baronet in 1782, was sixth in descent from Sir John Auchinleck.

---

[1] Falstaff, however, is an alteration of Fastolf.
[2] So we have the name *Dringwell* and the surname *Thring*. The German is *dringen*, and we have " to throng."

PLACE-NAMES

Vowels get altered or permuted. Thus Annesley, a place in Nottinghamshire, as a surname has become *Ainsley*. Beaumont has been changed to *Beeman* and *Beamont*. Alchorne in Sussex gave its name to a family that has modified it to *Oldcorn*. Consonants get altered and aspirates dropped out or added. Ampthill has become *Antill*. Names whose suffix is *cliff* are liable to lose the *c*, as *Antliffe* for Arncliff, *Cudliffe* for Cutcliff. Broomhall has become *Brammel*, and then has degenerated to *Bramble*. Broomhill, an estate near Bude, has given a name to *Brimmel*, a photographer in Launceston. Sometimes a letter is intruded, as *Broadripp*, from Bawdrip, near Bridgwater. One of the most curious alterations is Bon-enfant, that has become *Bullivant*. It is a change that we might well question had we not documentary evidence to prove it. This is not, however, a place-name, but it illustrates the manner in which *l* and *n* get permuted.

In 1619 Sir Robert Mansell erected some glassworks at Newcastle, and brought to them foreign workmen. Among these was one named Teswicke. The surname has spread with surprising rapidity, and has assumed the form of *Tyzack*.

Burghill in Herefordshire gives as a surname *Berrill* and *Beryll*. There can be little doubt about it, as Robert de Berhulle appears in the reign of Edward I. Godalming has become *Godliman*.

In dealing with surnames we must be careful to look through the old rolls and lists and registers, and note what was the prefix to a name at the period when surnames were in the process of formation. Where we find a *de* before a name, we may be quite sure that that name belongs to a place, although we may not be able at once to find the locality on the map, not knowing in which county to look for it. But when the name is preceded by *le*, then we know for certain that it indicates a trade or profession, or is descriptive.

When we find in the Court Rolls of Edward III. Henry del Mosse, and in a Yorkshire poll-tax of 1379 Robert de

PLACE-NAMES

Mos, we know that these men took their surnames from some moss or moor; but otherwise we may assume that Moss is a contraction for Moses, adopted by those of Jewish lineage.[1] If we find a Thomas de Motlawe in 1379, we know that there must be somewhere, though we cannot put our finger on the spot, a place called Motlawe or Motley; but if we come across a Gilbert le Motley, we know that he was a jester. In the first year of Edward III. we notice an entry of Robert de Mutone among the Post-Mortem Inquisitions, and we know that there was a place called Muton, whence Robert came; but when in the same Inquisitions we light on Philip le Mutton, we know that he was called after a sheep.

We might have confidently assumed that the *Allansons* were descended from an Allan, but in some cases the name stands for Alençon. We meet with a John de Alençon in the reign of Richard I., a Robert de Alenson in 1220, and Hubert de Alezon was Sheriff of Norfolk in the reign of Henry III.

[1] Mosse fil. Jacobi, the Jew (Hundred Rolls, 1273).

CHAPTER IX

ANGLO-SAXON NAMES: DOMESDAY

A SENSE of sadness steals over the mind as we note the disappearance of the spring flowers, and the appearance in their room of the monotonous summer blooms, mostly yellow, and none with the charm of those that gladdened heart and eye in May. There is a banality in their forms and colours. And it is with some feeling akin to this that we observe how after the Conquest the rich and varied crop of Anglo-Saxon names disappears, and makes way for Toms and Dicks and Harrys in wearisome iteration. I have already quoted Mr. Freeman on this theme; I will now quote Mr. Bardsley:

"Throughout all the records and rolls of the twelfth and thirteenth centuries we find, with but the rarest exceptions, all our personal names are Norman. The Saxon seems to have become wellnigh extinct. There might have been a war of extermination against them. In an unbroken succession we meet with such names as John or Richard, Robert and Henry, Thomas and Ralph, Geoffrey and Jordan, Stephen and Martin, Joscelyn and Almaric, Benedict and Laurence, Reginald and Gilbert, Roger and Walter, Eustace and Baldwin, Francis and Maurice—no Harold even, saving in very isolated cases. It is the same with female names. While Mabel and Matilda, Mirabella and Avelina, Amabilla and Idonia, Sibilla and Ida, Letitia and Agnes, Petronilla or Parnel and Lucy, Alicia and Avice, Alienara and Anora, Dowsabelle, Clarice and Muriel, Martha and Rosamund, Felicia and Adelina, Julia and Blanche, Isolda

ANGLO-SAXON NAMES

and Amelia or Emelia, Beatrix and Euphemia, Annabel and Theophania, Constance and Joanna abound, Ethelreda, Edith, and Ermentrude are of the rarest occurrence, and are the only names which may breathe to us of purely Saxon times. In the case of several, however, a special effort was made later on, when the policy of allaying the jealous feeling of the popular class was resorted to. For a considerable time the royal and baronial families had, in their pride, sought names for their children from the Norman category mainly. After the lapse of a century, however, finding the Saxon spirit still chafed and uneasy under a foreign thrall, several names of a popular character were introduced into the royal nursery. Thus it was with Edward and Edmund. The former of these appellations was represented by Edward I., the latter by his brother Edmund, Earl of Lancaster."[1]

It was not all at once throughout Europe that the old names were abandoned and a fresh series adopted, either from the calendar or from those employed by the ruling caste.

In 991, at Rheims, assembled Bishops and Archbishops in council: Guido de Soissons, Adalbero of Laon, Herveius of Beauvais, Godesmann of Amiens, Radbod of Noyon, Odo of Senlis, Archbishop Adalbert of Bourges, Walter of Autun, Bruno of Langres, Milo of Macon, Archbishop Siguin of Sens, with his suffragans, Arnulf of Orleans and Hubert of Auxerre. Among these thirteen Bishops there is not to be found one who does not bear a Teutonic name. Guido is Wido and Herveius is Heriwig, both latinized—that is all.

But now mark the difference. At Christmas, 1171, Henry Courthose, son of Henry II., held his Court at Bayeux. It occurred to two Williams, the Seneschal of Brittany and the Governor of Normandy, to exclude from the outer hall every guest who was not named William, and they were able to admit 117 knights of that name, and this was in addition to the Williams who sat at table with the young King. This showed how popular a single name had become,

[1] "English Surnames," pp. 18, 19.

ANGLO-SAXON NAMES

and how men had got to follow a cut-and-dried system and abandon the creative name period.

To give anything like a complete list of Anglo-Saxon names would take up too much space,[1] but I will give in the Appendix a list of the tenants in the time of Edward the Confessor—not, indeed, complete, for some have to be omitted in order to keep it within reasonable limits—but sufficient to afford an idea of what Anglo-Saxon nomenclature was; and it is of interest to us, as in it we are able to trace the germs of a good many of our modern surnames.

But it must be borne in mind, in examining the list, that the scribes were not English, but were Normans, following a phonetic and arbitrary, and by no means an etymological, rule. The *Sbern* repeatedly entered shows that they did not catch the letter *o* with which the name began, as *Osbern*, because lightly sounded. *Biga* occurring as a name several times is not a name at all, but signifies a cart, and describes the man as a carrier. The *Cocus* is a cook; a *Croc* indicates the man as a hunchback. Among the Normans we have a Radulf de Curva Spina.

Some other entries as names are not personal names at all, as the numerous *Bonds*, but descriptive of their tenure of land as freeholders. *Gamel* and *Gamelcarle* describe old men as such, without giving any personal name. The numerous *Blacks* and *Whites* are descriptive of appearance.

Felaga, found in Essex, signifies a companion, a fellow, and the numerous *Dons* are Domini (Masters). So-and-so was known to those who appeared before the Commissioners as Masters; they were spoken of as Masters. If they had any personal names, such were not known to those who gave evidence. Certain of the names that will be noticed in the list are recognizable at the present day as surnames. But, as already said, it is hard to account for this, as such an interval exists between Domesday and the taking of hereditary surnames by the middle—and still more by the lower—classes of the English people, unless we accept the theory that

[1] A complete list is given by Dr. Barber in "British Surnames"; another list is in W. De Gray Birch's "Domesday Book," S.P.C.K., 1887.

ANGLO-SAXON NAMES

these came from place-names, with the termination allowed to slip out, such as denoted residence at the place, as Thorlogaboe would give Thorlogsby and then *Thurlock*. In Cornwall, at the time of Edward the Confessor, was an under-tenant named Jaul, and *Joll* is a family name in the county to this day. Aluric may possibly remain, altered into *Aldrich*, though this latter more probably derives from residence beside an old ridgeway, or road. Alward continues among us as *Aylward*. Ardgrip is found several centuries later in Parliamentary writs as *Hardgripe*. Aseloc is a mistake for *Havelock*. Baco we have in many *Bacons*[1], and Bar as *Bear*, variously spelt: perhaps it stood for *Beere*. Bill is still present, and Boda as *Body*, and Bou as *Bow*, Brodo as *Brodie*, Cava as *Cave*. Celcott was the ancestor of the *Chilcotts*, Clac of the *Clacks*, Couta of the *Coutts*, Doda of the *Dodds*, Don of the *Donnes* maybe. Epy may have given his surname to Uriah *Heep*; Felaga certainly has to *Fellowes*. Gamel is still represented in Yorkshire. Gos was the name now *Goss*. Gribol had his representatives in my time in a grocer at Tavistock named *Gribble*. Jalf was the forbear of the *Jelfs*. Juin or Juing, which was the Norman scribe's rendering of the reverse of Gamel, was the *Young* of his day. Kee is now *Kaye*. Lewin carries his name unaltered from the time of Edward the Confessor to that of Edward VII. It is the French way of writing Leofwin. *Finns* and *Phinns* are here still, so are the *Rocks*, and the *Salmons*, from Salomon, and the *Osborns* and the *Seawards*, for Syward. Snellinc in Domesday was the nominal ancestor of the *Snellings* of to-day, Ster or Stere of the *Steeres*, Thorlog of the *Thurlows*, Wadelo of the *Waddiloves*, Whelp of the *Helps*. Tor, who was in Yorkshire before the days of the Conquest, is there still as *Torre*. Tovi, found in Hampshire, has his representative now in *Toovy*, also in *Dovey*. Col and Cole have supplied us with plenty of *Coles*. Ulward gives us *Willard*, and Cruk is the ancestor of many *Crookes*.

[1] But this is a Norman, not a Saxon, name. Edward the Confessor drew many Normans to his Court, and gave them land in England.

ANGLO-SAXON NAMES

Among those whose names are given in Domesday is a *Brand* among under-tenants, and a Brand now furnishes us with his extract of beef. A *Radmore* was in Devon before William showed his face in England, and I knew a coachman of that name in Devon a couple of years ago. The Bolle found in Hampshire is the father of the name of the present family of *Bowles*, and Dolfin of Derbyshire of the modern *Dolphins*.

Now, it is quite true, as Mr. Bardsley says, that Christian names after the Conquest were no longer Saxon, but Norman. Yet there must have been a clinging by men of English blood to the old names borne by their forefathers, and, although they might no longer give them at the font to their little ones, and they no more appear in registers and deeds, yet possibly they were preserved as pet names or used as Christian names, treasured as family relics, some to come forth and be assumed when the time arrived when the assumption of hereditary family names became customary. With what tenacity Northern people held to a nomenclature to which they were familiar may be gathered from the Dane Guthrum, who was baptized in England in 878 by the name of Athelstan. He received that name at the font, and speedily shed it; he was never after known by other than his old pagan designation of the Divine Serpent. Another instance may be taken from the occasion of a revolt of the Swedes against their King Eric, in 1018, when they elected his son Jacob to be their King in his father's room, but absolutely refused to allow him to bear his baptismal name, and insisted on his calling himself, and being called, Oenund. That the English people were quite as unwilling to abandon wholly a class of names endeared to them by tradition, and to adopt others that pertained to the Latin races and to the Hebrews, we can well believe. They had their children baptized with a Norman or ecclesiastical name, but in the depths of their hearts, in the treasure-house of their memories, lay the old name of the dear ancestor who was evicted from his hall, and robbed of his acres, and degraded from being a Thegn or a Hauld to being a tenant-farmer. I remember once a

ANGLO-SAXON NAMES

small lodging-house keeper in Shepherd's Bush showing me a miniature of her grandfather, who had been a naval Lieutenant. He was a gentleman, she said, and had married a real lady. But misfortune had fallen on their offspring, and now his descendant had her meals in the kitchen with the servant down the area; but every day she looked at the miniature of the grandfather "who was a gentleman," and showed it to every visitor with a flutter of colour in her cheek. And so with the dispossessed Anglo-Saxons. They stored in their memories the names of the freeholders who were driven out, but whose ancestors for many generations had been freeholders before them. And by degrees, as time went on, the name was produced, and when the Anglo-Norman lord flourished his name, taken from a poky little castle in Normandy, where now he owned not a chair to sit on, the tenant-farmer held up his head, and said: "And I, too, have a name—and a name to be proud of—the name of the last Childe, or Wake, or Hauld, or Bonder, or Thegn, who had none above him but the King."

And I suppose that this is the explanation of the fact that a certain number of Saxon names do remain amidst us as hereditary surnames; and prouder should those be who bear them than such as flourish the names of the Norman conquerors, for these last are representatives of a violated right, and the former represent the victims of outrage and robbery. But, in addition to personal names adopted as family names, we have among us such as represent conditions of life and tenure of land among the Anglo-Saxons that came to an end with the Conquest.

An honoured name among us is that of *Childe*—that of the great banker.

The title of Childe was held by the eldest sons of Thegns, and represented them as heirs to their father's honours and possessions. Then came the Conquest, and the Childes of 1066 were smitten out of their rights, and lost all their expectations—glad, indeed, if suffered to build a cottage on some untilled portion of what was once their ancestral domain. The old Thegn had died, either on the field of

ANGLO-SAXON NAMES

Senlac or of a broken heart at seeing the ruin of his family. Generation followed generation, and his descendants looked on the hall that had been theirs, on the lands that had belonged to them, on the serfs that had once done their bidding, and they called themselves either after the dispossessed Thegn or the Childe who had reared the new habitation, and begun to break up the moorland accorded to him by the Norman intruder. Thus we have our *Thynnes*[1] and *Childes;* thus also our *Bonds*. The Haulds, also freeholders, have given us *Olds* and *Holds*; and the Lagman, who of old sat in the Witenagemot, has left his titular name to the *Layman* of to-day.[2] There is, I take it, something pathetic in this picture of a family looking back to, and clinging to, the memory of its ancient dignities, of which it had been despoiled.

[1] The Thynnes of Longleat have, however, a different origin, according to the story, true or false—probably the latter.
[2] The Lagman was one with a knowledge of the laws, but in the reign of Swerrir of Norway (1182-1202) Lagman became a title equivalent to Judge, Justiciary.

CHAPTER X

SCANDINAVIAN NAMES: THE " LIBER VITÆ "

THE "Book of Life" of Durham Minster is of exceptional value for the study of the development of surnames. It is a catalogue that was kept from the ninth century, of benefactors to the Church of Durham, ending only with the Reformation and Dissolution.

A writer in 1672 on " The Ancient Rites and Monuments of the Monastical and Cathedral Church of Durham " thus describes the book: " There did lie on the High Altar an excellent fine book, very richly covered with gold and silver, containing the names of all the benefactors towards St. Cuthbert's Church, from the very original foundation thereof, the very letters of the book being, for the most part, all gilt ; as is apparent in the said book to this day. The laying that book on the High Altar did show how highly they esteemed their founders and benefactors, and the quotidian remembrance thus had of them in the time of Mass and divine service. And thus did appear, not only their gratitude, but also a most divine and charitable affection to the souls of their benefactors, as well dead as living; which book is still extant, declaring the said use in the inscriptions thereof."

The volume is described on the title as the " Liber Vitæ " of the Church of Durham. The fact of the benefactors' names being recorded in the book was coupled with the hope and the prayer that the same might at the last find

SCANDINAVIAN NAMES

a place in the "Book of Life," in which are recorded those who shall be entitled to eternal salvation.[1]

The manuscript itself is one of peculiar interest, from the manner in which it is written. From the commencement, at folio 12 to folio 42 it is executed in alternate lines of gold and silver, written in a handwriting of peculiar elegance, the precise age of which it is not easy to decide, but which may probably be referred to the ninth century. From that period downwards to the Dissolution it is continued in various hands, each less elegant than that which preceded it. When the volume was commenced, it was so prepared as to admit the names of benefactors being arranged according to rank; but at a subsequent period, as unoccupied parchment grew scarcer in the volume, the scribes from time to time took advantage of any blank spaces that might occur, and entered there the names of those benefactors who were far more recent. Hence the list is not chronologically sequent, and to read it aright demands that these additions should be distinguished from the text of the earlier writer. This, however, can be done, because the style of writing in the different centuries varied considerably.

The earlier names are almost all either Angle or Scandinavian, with a sprinkling of Celtic. A recent student has examined the list, and has sought to discriminate between those that are Anglo-Saxon, those that are Danish, and such as are Norwegian. Those which are Celtic can at once be detected, but it is very doubtful whether it is possible so nicely to separate such as are Norse from such as are Danish.

After the Norman Conquest occur occasional Norman names, and these become more frequent as time goes on. These latter are the sole that can be called surnames till a much later period. In the earlier centuries the names are single and simple, and with great rarity does a man bear a Biblical name or one derived from the calendar of the Church. Even monks and clergy clung to the old names, so easily

[1] "Liber Vitæ Ecclesiæ Dunelmensis" (Surtees Society publication), 1841.

SCANDINAVIAN NAMES

and so richly formed out of the native tongue, and shrank from the banality of turning to the calendar for the nomenclature of their children. Here, for instance, is the list of the anchorites in priest's orders:

Œdillwald, Vermund, Baldhelm, Peligeld, Wigbert, Hæmgils, Eadwald, Herebert, Boisil, Herefrid, Æthwin, Eadhelm, Balthere, Tilwin, Fronka, Aldbert, Echha, Tilfrith, Alhæth, Augustinus, Bilfrith, Hadured, Wilthegn, Garwulf (*i.e.*, Werewolf), Cuthred, Wulfsig, Hadumund, Wigbert. But a single saintly name amongst them—Augustinus.[1]

Among the Abbots in priest's orders are given sixty-seven names; one alone among them is Scriptural—Elias; none from the calendar.

If this were so among monks and clergy, it may well be supposed that the laity clung to their traditional vernacular names.

On folio 24*b* we have sixty-three pure Angle or Scandinavian names, and then come these: Osbert son of William, Matthild, Robert and Hugo, Isabel, Thomas, Emma, John, Ulard, Cecilia, John, Richard, Alice, Walter, Robert, Nicolas, Thomas. We know at once that these belong to a later period; in fact, they are an insertion of the thirteenth century.

Observe that among all these even then there is no trace of a surname.

When in the list of benefactors of the twelfth century we find that Biblical and French Christian names are creeping in and displacing those that are more ancient and vernacular, then also we see that the germs of surnames appear. Here is the list of assistant monks (*fol.* 52):

Wido, Robert, three Williams, Henry of Addington, Galfrid, William Benignus and Eva his wife (this a monk!), Edward, John, Adam, Henry, Robert, Richard, Margaret (how comes she *en cette galère?*), Sweyn, Olaf, Hedbald, William de Grenville, Walter Carvi, Patric of Paxton and Patric of Hoveden, Richard, Gamel (priest of Coldingham), Walter of Querendon, Robert the Provost, Brother Ælward, Thomas of Bishopton, Albert of Mandeville, Robert of Bollesdon, Ulkill, Colban, Hyun, Henry the Sewer, Adam, Alfin, Richard Gur', Gilebert Halsard, William the Pistor, Augustine, Hugh, Roger, David, Stephen the Medicine Man, etc.

---

[1] I have slightly modernized the spelling of the names.

SCANDINAVIAN NAMES

We have three Williams, entered one after the other, without any distinction. We have also several Roberts. Clearly, it was expedient to give them distinguishing names, either nicknames or surnames.

On folio 53 are 193 names, and the writing is of the thirteenth century, with some exceptions, to be noted presently, that are of the fifteenth. Among all these there are forty-three described as "of" such and such a place, but some of these are only "Priors of," and two are "de Brus"—*i.e.*, de Breos or Bruce. There are some entered as sons of So-and-so, but there is no indication that such was a surname. But there are a few surnames—Roger Muref, William Walais (*i.e.*, Wallace), Roger Pauper (Poor), Hugh Bard, Robert Watkynson, Bartholomew Peck, Master John Abegeis, William, Earl Marshall, and Alexander and Gilbert Marshall, Roger Gernet of Hawton and Roger Kernet of Burch, William Tredweuge, Alan, Matilda, Henry and John Colstan, William Faber (the smith), William Halywell, and William Warcworth. In this same list in which the family of Colstan appears, with a distinct surname attaching to each member, occur three Johns without anything to particularize them, one after the other. Fourteen genuine surnames among 193 individuals without.

Let us next take folio 56, which is of the thirteenth and fourteenth centuries. Here we progress somewhat. We get these: Thomas Henknoll, Hugh Muchante (is this a misprint for "merchante"?), William Rodum, Robert Butt, Thomas the Ditcher ("fossor"), Thomas Keylgarn, Thomas Launcel, Henry Lovechild (*i.e.*, bastard), Thomas Daylle, Robert Johnson, Richard Atkynson, Robert Hughalt, Gilbert Hansard, Osbert Giffard, William Deu, Ulkill the Fuller, Geoffrey Picot, John Cutler, John Billerby, and John Thirlwath. These three last are additions of the fifteenth century. Now here we have Johnson and Atkynson become surnames, distinct from the entries of "filius." In this series the number of references to places whence the benefactors came is largely increased, but there still remains a residue of Johns and Henries, of Nicolases and Williams, without individualization.

SCANDINAVIAN NAMES

When, however, we arrive at the fifteenth century, the number of surnames has vastly increased. Here is a scrap of that period in the register: John Blyet and his wife, William and his wife Margaret Blyet, Francis Foster, John Blythe, Robert Bluett, Robert Rousse, Bryan Teller, Thomas Fenwyke, Robert Ballard.

In a hand of the thirteenth or, more probably, the fourteenth century appears the entry: " William Chepe, cocus de Coldingham;" a wise cook, to enter the kitchen already provided with a surname, and so escape being called Wilcox.

Here are more entries of the fifteenth century: "John Palfreyman, Arstulf Hillerby, Thomas Westmoreland, William Parlour, William Smith and Alice his wife, Thomas Elwyke, John Euke, Thomas Warwick, Thomas Schele, Joanna Brown and Master, William Browne and Antony Browne, Bernard Bailey." Surnames were becoming common in the fifteenth century, at least among persons of some substance, so as to be regarded as liberal benefactors to the Church of Durham.

And now let us turn to the end of the book, to the list of names that preceded the Dissolution, and we shall find that everyone has a surname. I will not give this list here, because too lengthy.

What took place in Durham took place all over England, but the Durham practice was somewhat behind that of the South and the Midlands, and York was probably not much more in advance than Durham.

What the " Liber Vitæ " teaches us is that men were specialized by the place whence they came, irrespective of the fact that they were not landholders there, or else they were distinguished by being described as being the sons of such and such fathers. The adhesion of a place-name did not take place so as to constitute a family name till the fifteenth century, except among the Barons and families of Norman descent. Patronymics such as *Johnson, Thomson, Atkinson,* came in very sporadically in the fourteenth century, and became permanent only in the fifteenth. Not till this latter century does *Smith* appear as a family name; for

SCANDINAVIAN NAMES

although we have seen *Faber* given earlier, this is descriptive of the trade pursued by the bearer, and was not a surname.

In the fourteenth century the *de* and *of* before the place-name had not fallen away. When it did, then the name of the locality attached itself permanently to the man and his posterity.

One feature of the lists in the " Liber Vitæ " must not be overlooked—the extreme scarcity of names descriptive of personal appearance and indicative of natural defects, and of vulgar nicknames. This leads one to suspect that, when such names occur in the secular lists, as the Hundred Rolls, Feet of Fines, etc., they were inscribed without the consent of those so designated, for the convenience of identification and without regard to the feelings of the men so described. But also it leads to the conviction that, where such designations were accepted, they bore a very different signification to what they bear on the surface. If this were not the case, such names would have been repudiated as an outrage.

Some domestic officials are entered in the book as donors, a "butelair," a sewer, and a dapifer, but singularly few tradesmen—a merchant, a smith, a taverner, a fuller, and that is about all. The tradesmen of Durham seem to have buttoned up their pockets, or else the smallness of their donations did not entitle them to commendation in the Book of Life.

On the flyleaf of a tenth-century manuscript book of the Gospels in the library of York Minster is a list of the "festermen" at the election of Archbishop Ælfric of York, 1023. It has been published by Dr. Jon Stefanson ("Saga-book of the Viking Club," 1908). The names are mostly Norse and Danish.

I give in the Appendix a list of Scandinavian names that may be recognized as surnames at the present day. Those that have come to us in a circuitous way through the Normans have been excluded. Some surnames may come from the Anglo-Saxon or from the Norse and Danish, and, as happens in other cases, some names now not uncommon among us may have a double derivation—in Northumbria

SCANDINAVIAN NAMES

from a Norse origin, in other parts of England from another quite different. Thus, *Eagle* may be derived from a tavern sign, or, when encountered in East Anglia, from Egill. *Atlay* when met with in the North of England may derive from Atli, elsewhere from Atte-legh.

A name that occurs still, and which has a romantic or mythical origin, is that of *Wayland*, sometimes reduced to *Welland*. Wayland Smith's Cave, a dolmen near Lambourne, has been utilized by Sir Walter Scott in his "Woodstock"; but he made a mistake in treating of Wayland the Smith as a man living in this dolmen in the seventeenth century. The story of Wayland, or Viglund, is found in the Elder Edda, and is one of the most ancient monuments of Scandinavian poetry. The Edda was put together in the eleventh century by Sœmund to preserve these ancient poems from loss, as, being redolent with paganism, they were falling into disrepute and oblivion.

There was a King in Sweden named Nidud, who had two sons, and a daughter whose name was Bödvild. There was at the time a famous smith named Velund, who excelled all other smiths. King Nidud ordered him to be seized and hamstrung, and a gold ring that Velund had fashioned to be given to his daughter. Then he placed Velund on a small island, and set him to make all kinds of precious things. No one was suffered to go near the island save the King alone.

Velund knew that Bödvild wore the gold ring stolen from him, and both on this account and on that of his being lamed he resolved on revenge.

One day the two Princes secretly visited the isle and asked to be shown the gold necklaces and rings that Velund made. The smith took the occasion to kill both. He cut off their heads, cleared the skulls of flesh and set them in silver as drinking-bowls, and sent them to Nidud, who received them without the least suspicion that they were the heads of his sons.

Some time after Bödvild broke her ring, and, without telling her father or mother, privily went to the smithy to have it mended. Velund seized on the occasion to outrage her.

SCANDINAVIAN NAMES

After that he laboured to fashion for himself a pair of wings, and when these were perfected he flew away; but before quitting the place for ever he flew to where he could communicate with the King and Queen, and to them he shouted how he had avenged himself.

The story was well known to the Anglo-Saxons, and a fragment of an Anglo-Saxon poem exists containing the lamentations of Bödvild. The old poem of Beowulf also alludes to Velund. Higelac boasts that the best of his armour had been fashioned by Weland. King Alfred also mentions the famous smith in his paraphrase of Boëtius: "Where are now the bones of Weland, that was the most famous of goldsmiths?" In the metrical romance of King Horn is another allusion. Of swords brought to Horn is one "the make of Miming: of all swordes it is king, and Weland it wrought." Even Geoffrey of Monmouth, in a poem of the twelfth century, mentions the smith Guieland, who made cups richly sculptured.

Wayland or Welland was, accordingly, one well remembered in England in early days, and we cannot be surprised that he gave his name to two villages and to a river. It is from one or other of these villages that the families of Welland and Wayland take their name.

Thomas de Weylaund appears in Suffolk in 1273, and William de Welond in Gloucestershire in the same year.

That these villages should derive from some well I think improbable, for no village was without a well of some kind. More likely each was a stead or tun of a Velund.

CHAPTER XI

THE ROLL OF BATTLE ABBEY

ON the morrow of the Battle of Hastings, William, Duke of Normandy, summoned to him a clerk who had enrolled the names of all those who had accompanied him to England, and bade him read it aloud, that he might learn who had fallen and who were still alive. After that he bade Odo, Bishop of Bayeux, sing Mass for the souls of such as were dead.

Later, William founded Battle Abbey on the site, not only as a memorial of his victory, but to serve as a chantry for the slain, and the names of his companions-in-arms enshrined in this bede-roll were to be read out in church on special occasions, and notably on the day of commemoration of the battle—the Feast of St. Calixtus.

This roll was accordingly preserved in the abbey. It was on parchment, and bore a Latin superscription that may be thus translated: " This place is named Battle, on account of a battle fought here, in which the English were defeated and left dead upon the field. They fell on the festival of Calixtus, Christ's martyr. In the year 1066 the English fell, when a comet appeared."

In 1538 the abbey was dissolved, and it, with its lands, was granted by Henry VIII. to Sir Anthony Browne, Master of Horse to the King. He commenced building a manor-house there out of the stones of the abbey, which was completed by his son, Viscount Montague, but was seldom occupied by his descendants, who preferred to it their noble residence at Cowdray, in the same county.

THE ROLL OF BATTLE ABBEY

The story goes that, as Sir Anthony Browne was pulling down the abbey for the erection of his mansion, one of the dispossessed monks approached, and pronounced a solemn curse on him and his family, that it should perish by water and by fire.

The eighth Viscount Montague was drowned in the Rhine in September, 1793, when only twenty-four years of age. He was on a boating expedition with his friend, Mr. Sedley Burdett, and made a foolhardy attempt to shoot the rapids at Laufenburg. They had been cautioned of the danger of the venture, and entreated not to risk it, but in vain. At the last moment, as they were stepping into the boat, Lord Montague's servant clutched his collar, saying: "My lord, the curse of water!" But he wrenched himself away and sprang out of his reach. The boat capsized in the rapids, and the two gentlemen, with their dog, were seen swimming gallantly through the surges, till all disappeared.

At that same time, on the night of September 24, 1793, Cowdray House, with its magnificent collection of paintings, tapestry, carvings, and furniture, was burnt to the ground.

By flood and fire the family of Sir Anthony, in the male line, had come to an end, and Cowdray and Battle passed to the sister of the last Viscount, who married Stephen Poyntz, of Midgeham in Berkshire, in 1794, and by him had two sons and three daughters. In the summer of 1813 Mr. and Mrs. Poyntz were staying with the children at Bognor, and two Misses Parry were on a visit to them. One fine day Mr. Poyntz took out his sons and the Misses Parry on a boating expedition, but Mrs. Poyntz, who had a superstitious dread of the water, refused to be one of the party.

As evening drew on Mrs. Poyntz seated herself at a window to watch their return. They were close to shore, when a sudden squall struck the sail and upset the boat, and the wretched mother saw her two sons drowned before her eyes. For some time they clung to their father's coat, who had managed to lay hold of the capsized boat; but their strength failed them, and they dropped back into the sea. This took place on July 7, 1815. Mr. Poyntz was saved, but the two Misses Parry were drowned.

THE ROLL OF BATTLE ABBEY

It is not known for certain what became of the Battle Abbey Roll, but in all probability it was taken by Sir Anthony Browne to Cowdray, and perished by fire when that house was burnt. Consequently we have not the original roll to refer to for the list of those who came over with the Conqueror.

But, before the Dissolution, Leland the antiquary visited Battle, and made a very careful copy of the roll. So careful was he that he noted the gaps left in it, and the dots that were marked between the lines in the gaps. The names were not arranged alphabetically, but were strung together in rude rhymes, and were 495 in 257 lines, each line containing two names, with the solitary exception of one that contains three, and those on each line begin with the same initial letter. Some names are duplicated.

The list as given by Leland is unquestionably the best, if not the only authentic, copy that exists of the famous Battle Abbey Roll. It is published in his "Collectanea," vol. i., p. 206.

Holinshed, in his "Chronicle," 1577, gives another, but this does not pretend to be an exact transcript, as he arranges the names alphabetically. Moreover, he gives as many as 629 names, 134 more than were transcribed by Leland, so that he cannot have copied from the original roll, but from some faked copy of it.

But the original roll that Leland transcribed was not faultless. It also had been "faked," and the gaps left in the roll were left so as to be filled in with the names of such families as were disposed to pay a price for insertion. Had we the original roll, we should be able to detect the insertions by the handwriting; but as it is, we can do so only by what we know of families that rose to the surface at a later period, and by striking out such as are not named in Domesday or in the "Roman de Rou," by Wace.

Dugdale detected the interpolations. He wrote: "Such hath been the subtilty of some Monks of old, that finding it acceptable unto most to be reputed descendants to those who were Companions with Duke William in that memorable

THE ROLL OF BATTLE ABBEY

Expedition, whereby he became Conqueror of this Realm, as that, to gratify them (but not without their own advantage), they inserted their Names into that ancient Catalogue."

Camden also speaks of these interpolations : " Whosoever considers well shall find them always to be forged, and those names inserted which the time in every age favoured, and were never mentioned in that authenticated record."

Sir Egerton Brydges stigmatizes the roll as an imposture, because of "the insertion of families who did not come to England till a subsequent period, and of surnames which were not adopted for some ages after the Conquest, of which the greater part of the list is composed. If the Roll of Battle Abbey had been genuine, it must have received confirmation from that authentic record of the reign of Henry II., the 'Liber Niger Sacarii,' but no two registers can less agree." This, however, is an overstatement.

Freeman speaks of the roll as "a source of falsehood" and " a transparent fiction." Mr. Ferguson endeavoured to restore the credit in a measure in his "Surnames as a Science," but with little success. The author of "The Norman People" conjectured from the spelling of the names that it had been compiled in the reign of Edward I., but some of the spelling is of a still later date.

We cannot doubt that there was such a roll at Battle, but at first it was a roll containing only the names of the dead, whose obits had to be observed, and who had to be prayed for by name. But in process of time other names were added, successively, as paid for.

It contains such obvious interpolations as Audley, Gray, Hastings, Hawley, Howard, Gower, and Berry.

There are in the lists of Leland and of Holinshed several duplications—Blundel, Avenell, Barry, Bernevile, De la Laund, FitzAleyn, FitzRobert, Filiot, Morley, Peverel, Pikard, Vernon; but these may be explained and justified when two of the same family came with the Conqueror, or, in the cases of FitzAleyne and FitzRobert, there may have been two quite unrelated personages, sons of Robert and Aleyne. Filiot is a nickname, and means the same as "sonny," that might be applied to any youngster.

THE ROLL OF BATTLE ABBEY

In some cases the interpolations are very obvious, as in the line "Soucheville, Coudray et Colleville." It is the sole line in which are three names. Moreover, almost invariably the purpose was to tack together in pairs names beginning with the same letter. There had been gaps left to be filled in as folk paid for insertion, as before mentioned, and these had to be thrust in anywhere.

The list is remarkable for omissions. If we compare it with that of Wace we notice this. Leland, moreover, does not give us Arundell, Bagott, Berners, Lutterel, Marmion, Montgomery, Mainwaring, Marny, and many others.

But it must be remembered that names were in a condition of flux. Thus, Roger de Montgomerie, who came over with the Conqueror, had five sons—Robert de Belesmes, Hugh le Preux (Earl of Shrewsbury), Roger de Poitou, Philip le Clerk, and Arnulph Carew, the holder of Carew Castle in Pembrokeshire, and supposed ancestor of the Carews. A son was not justified in assuming the place-name borne by his father during his father's life, and whilst his father lived he was called after some other castle or manor belonging to his parent. Moreover, only the eldest son succeeded to the parental territorial name. This has, of course, led to considerable confusion.

Then, again, the spelling of names was not fixed; it was very arbitrary till several centuries later, and the Battle Abbey Roll, from which copies were made, was certainly not that originally drawn up, but a transcript with additions, and the copyist made blunders. In the original, two names beginning with the same letter were inscribed in the same line; but the transcriber copied "Constable et Tally" for "Constable et Cally," "Graunson et Tracy" for "Graunson et Gracy."

The letter u is often interchanged with n, and w with m, and the long s with l, and the short s with r. The copyist has occasionally inverted the order of the letters.

To the errors of the copyist we must also add those of the printer. And consequently the identification of those named is not always easy, and is occasionally conjectural.

THE ROLL OF BATTLE ABBEY

Properly, the study of the families that are represented in the roll and in Domesday and in Wace demand a much more profound and searching investigation than has been given to the subject, and much apocryphal matter has to be winnowed out. I do not pretend to have done more in the following list than give the result of such researches as have been already made.

Still there remains this objection—that Leland did not specify the list he gives as having been transcribed by him from the Roll of Battle Abbey. It is, however, certain that he visited Battle Abbey previous to its sequestration, for he gives a catalogue of the books contained in the library. He was, moreover, so accurate and painstaking a student that it is hardly possible to conceive that he should have omitted to transcribe so valuable a record as the roll.

Leland also gives another list, " Un role de ceux queux veignent en Angleterre avesque roy William le Conquerour," containing eighty names, but this is simply a transcript from the list in the " Roman de Rou."

There were other lists of those who accompanied the Conqueror, but none are to be trusted. In itself the Roll of Battle Abbey is discredited, and we must go to genuine documents for the list of those who really came over with William, and were enfeoffed by him in England in reward for their services. We do not lack these. There is, above all, the Domesday Book, and then Wace's metrical chronicle, the " Roman de Rou."

That after the Conquest many needy adventurers trooped over to England, tendering their services to William, to Rufus, and to Henry Beauclerk, we need not doubt, and the " Liber Niger Sacarii" gives us a trustworthy list of all the Normans and French settled in England in the reign of Henry II.

But as the Roll of Battle Abbey is so often appealed to as an authority for the antiquity of a family, it will be well to look at the names that occur in it.

The Duchess of Cleveland in 1889 published in three volumes " The Battle Abbey Roll; with Some Account of

THE ROLL OF BATTLE ABBEY

the Norman Lineages." The book must have had considerable labour expended on it. But it is not critical. The Duchess takes Holinshed's list as a basis for work, one of the most adulterated of all copies, and she lays some stress on the almost worthless " Dives Roll," as she calls it—a list drawn up by M. Leopold Delisle for the purpose of glorifying the French Norman gentry, and of no authority whatever.

The roll has been illustrated by Planché,[1] by the author of " The Norman People," and by Sir Bernard Burke.

Wace was born in Jersey about the year 1100. " His traditions of the Conquest, though not put into writing till after the middle of the twelfth century, practically date from his early years—the years of his boyhood at Caen. He indulges in no rhetorical embellishments; in the historical parts of his greatest work he refuses to set down anything for which he has not authority; and when his authorities differ, he frequently gives two alternative versions " (D.N.B.).

Wace names about 115 nobles, but, curiously enough, omits Richard d'Evreux and his son William, and he makes a few slips in the Christian names.

He does not profess to have recorded all who attended William to Hastings. He says:

> " Ne sai nomer toz les barons,
> Ne de tos dire les sornoms,
> De Normandie e de Bretagne,
> Que li duc ont en sa campagne."

The best edition of Wace's " Roman de Rou " is that by Andreson, Heilbronn, 1879. The list begins about the line 8,440, and ends 8,728.

Wace's list can be in part substantiated by Ordericus Vitalis and William of Poitiers—who was chaplain to the Conqueror on his expedition to England, by William de Jumièges, in whose work lib. vii. is by Robert de Torignie, and by others.

[1] "Companions of the Conqueror," London, 1874; "The Norman People," London, 1874; Sir Bernard Burke, "The Roll of Battle Abbey,' London, 1848.

THE ROLL OF BATTLE ABBEY

It is worth observing how loosely territorial surnames hung on the bearers.

Stephen d'Aumale was the son of Odo de Champagne and Adelaide, sister of the Conqueror.

Roger de Beaumont is the same as Roger de Vielles. He was the son of Humphrey de Vielles.

Richard de Bienfaite is the same as Richard d'Orbec. His brother was Baldwin de Meulles, and they were the sons of Gislbert de Brionne.

Walter Giffard de Longueville was the son of Osbert de Bolbec.

Again, Nicolas de Bacqueville married a niece of the Duchess Gunnor, and their son is held to have been that William Malet who appears prominently in the history of the Conqueror. Baldwin le Sap and Baldwin de Meulles is one and the same person.

Robert de Mortain and Odo, Bishop of Bayeux, were sons of Herluin de Couteville, who married Arletta, the cast-off mistress of Duke Robert, and therefore half-brothers of the Conqueror.

Roger de Mortemer was the son of Hugh Aimeric de Thouars.

All this shows how very unformed was the nomenclature in Normandy at the time of the Conquest. It was beginning to be fixed, but beginning only.

The following is the list of names in Leland's copy of the roll, with a few included that pertained to representatives who were at Hastings unquestionably, but who were not included in the roll, possibly enough, because the fee was not forthcoming, as later in the case of Heralds' Visitations, from which families of undoubted antiquity and with right to bear arms were excluded, because they did not care to pay for insertion.

ADRYELLE, not identifiable.

AIGUILLON — in Leland, Aungeloun; an interpolation. From Aguilon in Guienne. The name came in with the Hundred Years' War.

THE ROLL OF BATTLE ABBEY

AIMERIS, a personal name, Amauri, now *Emery* and *Amory* and *Amery*.

AINCOURT—in Leland, Deyncourt; from a fief in the Norman Vezin. Walter d'Aincourt held sixty manors, mainly in Lincolnshire (Domesday). In 1835 a Lincolnshire gentleman named Tennyson assumed the arms and name of *D'Eyncourt*, as descended in a zigzag fashion through a succession of spindles from Lady Anne Leke, daughter of the first Earl of Scarsdale, Baron D'Eyncourt.

AMAY—in Leland, Damay. Not in Domesday, nor found before the end of the twelfth century. An interpolation. Now *Dames*.

ANGEVIN. Two brothers appear in Domesday as estated in Essex and Norfolk. But the name is not a surname; it is descriptive of the province whence they came. The descendants of the second brother called themselves *Thorpe*.

AQUINEY—in Leland, Dakeny. From Acquigny, near Louviers. Not in Domesday; does not occur in England earlier than the thirteenth century. The origin of the names *Dakins, Dakeyne*. But *Dakin* may be Davidkin.

ARCY — in Leland, Darcy. From Arci in Normandy. Norman d'Arci held thirty-three manors in Lincoln from the Conqueror (Domesday). The name remained as *Darcy*.

ARGENTAN — in Leland, Argenteyn. From a castle in Berry. David d'Argentun held lands in Cambridgeshire and Bedfordshire (Domesday). Modern surname, *Argent*.

ARUNDELL, not in Leland. In Domesday, Roger Arundell held a barony of twenty-eight manors. Name not taken from Arundel in Sussex.

AUBIGNY or DE ALBINI, appears in !Domesday as holding a great barony in the counties of Buckingham, Leicester, Bedford, and Warwick. Now *Albany* and *Daubeny*. Aubigny is near Periers, in the Cotentin.

AUDEL—an interpolation. It is *Audley*, the name of a manor in Staffordshire. In Domesday, Aldidelege.

AUMALE—in Leland, Aumerill. This became in England *Albemarle*. From Aumale, on the River Bresle, at the point where it divides Normandy from Picardy. The Sire d'Aumale

THE ROLL OF BATTLE ABBEY

fought at the Conqueror's side. He married William's sister, Adeliza.

AUNAY, not in Leland — which is strange, as the Sire d'Alneto was certainly at Hastings. He was one of the five knights who challenged Harold to come forth. The name is from Aunou-le-Faucon, near Argenton. The name *Dawnay* is that of Viscount Downe.

AVENEL, occurs twice in Leland. The name is also in Wace. The Avenels were Lords of Les Biards, in the arrondissement of Mortain.

AVESNES—in Leland, Aveneries. From a place of that name in Normandy.

AVRANCHES—in Leland, Davrenches. The family bore the surname of Le Gotz, Goes, or Goz. Richard Le Gotz married Emma, daughter of Arletta the washerwoman, mother of the Conqueror. His son Lupus went over with William, and was created Earl of Chester.

BALADON—in Leland, Bealun. From a place of the name in Normandy. Three of the Baladons came over with the Conqueror. One was given large estates in Cornwall and Wales. The name survives as *Bayldon*.

BALDWIN, twice in Leland — as Baudewyn and Baudyn. Baldwin the Sheriff was largely rewarded by the Conqueror for his assistance. The name is personal.

BALIOL—in Leland, Bailoff. Perhaps from Bailleul, near Argenton.

BANISTER, from Banastree—now Beneter, near Estampes. Robert Banastre, who came over with William, held Prestatyn in Flintshire under Robert de Ruelent.

BARBE D'OR, probably the Hugo Barbatus of Domesday. A descriptive name and not a surname.

BARDOLF, a personal name.

BARNEVALE, from a castle near Carteret. The family settled in the Scottish Lowlands and in Ireland.

BARRY, in Leland as Barry and Barray. From de Barre, in the Cotentin, possibly. But probably an interpolation, named later from Barrey Isle, near Cardiff. But perhaps a mistake for *Barrett*, which is a name found in Domesday.

THE ROLL OF BATTLE ABBEY

BASSET, an interpolation. Ordericus Vitalis says of Ralph Basset, Justiciary under Henry I.: "He was issued from an ignoble stock, and was accorded great power over both nobles and citizens." The Justiciary, in fact, made the family, and the insertion in the Battle Roll was paid for. There is no evidence that the Bassets of Cornwall derive from the Justiciary, but that there was such descent is most probable.

BAVENT, from a place of that name on the Dive, near Varaville. Bavent held a knight's fee, under William d'Albini, in Norfolk.

BASKERVILLE. Martels de Basqueville was in the Battle of Hastings, yet the name does not occur in Domesday. Possibly he may have fallen in the battle. "At the beginning of the thirteenth century there were Baskervilles in Herefordshire, Nottinghamshire, and Shropshire; in Warwickshire, Norfolk, Buckinghamshire, Wiltshire, and possibly other counties" (Eyton, "Shropshire."). The most eminent branch was that of Eardesley. One single branch is now represented in the male line, and that has changed its name to *Glegg*. There are two others, but through the spindle, who have assumed the name of Baskerville. It is not uncommon among the peasantry of Devon.

BASTARD, not in Leland. Robert the Bastard was an illegitimate son of the Conqueror, and received from his father a barony in Devonshire. The family is still represented there.

BAYEUX, in Leland, Baius. Backwell-Bayouse in Somerset takes the name from this family. The name has been corrupted into *Beyouse*, *Bayes*, and *Bewes*, if not for Bevis.

BEACHAMP. In Domesday, Belchamp held a large barony in Hertfordshire, Buckinghamshire, and Bedfordshire. Not a single male representative remains of this historic house. Earl Beauchamp's family name is now Lygon, but that is an assumption for Pyndar.

BEAUFORD, de Bello Fago. The name comes from Beaufer, near Pont l'Évêque. In Leland, corrupted to Bifford. Robert le Sire de Belfore is in Wace's list.

THE ROLL OF BATTLE ABBEY

William de Beaufoi held many manors in Norfolk (Domesday). But *Byford* may stand for By-the-Ford.

BEAUMONT. Roger de Vielles was also called de Beaumont. He was lord of Belmont-le-Rogier. He furnished the Conqueror with sixty vessels, and fought at Hastings, as did also his son. He received a great barony of ninety manors in Warwickshire, Leicestershire, Wiltshire, and Northamptonshire.

BECARD, not found earlier than 1202; probably an interpolation.

BELLEW, from Belleau or Bella Aqua in Normandy. Not in Domesday or in Wace. First heard of in the twelfth century. An interpolation. *Pellow* and *Pellew* are corruptions.

BELVILLE, from a place of that name, near Dieppe. Jean de Belleville took part in the Third Crusade. This old Norman house is now represented by the Marquis de Belleville. Nicholas de Belville held lands in Devon (Testa de Nevill), and the family is still represented there as *Belfield*.

BERNEVILLE, in Domesday, Berneville; a Baron. It is difficult, if not impossible, to distinguish Berneville from Barneville. Some *Barnfields* derive hence.

BENNY, from Beaunai, a fief in Normandy.

BERTIN, not in Domesday or Wace. Not heard of till the second half of the twelfth century. An interpolation.

BERTRAM, the Hunchback, is mentioned by Wace. "A younger branch, from whom came the Mitfords, formed establishments, though not of much account, in England, and it is probably descended from William (younger brother of the Crookback), or from another William who stands in Domesday as a small holder in Hampshire" (I. Taylor). Nothing can really be concluded as to the connection of the Mitfords with the Bertram of the Conquest, as Bertram is a personal name and not a surname.

BEVERS. Hugh de Beverde was an under-tenant in Suffolk (Domesday), but the name meant is almost certainly *Bouvery*, from La Beuvière, near Bethune. Drogo de la Boveres was married to a cousin of the Conqueror, and

THE ROLL OF BATTLE ABBEY

received the whole of Holderness, eighty-seven manors, and twenty-four in Lincolnshire.

BIARD, a seigneurie of the Avenells.

BIGOT or WIGOT. "He served the Duke in his house as one of his Seneschals, which office he held in fee. He had with him a large troop, and was a noble vassal. He was small of body, but very brave and bold, and assailed the English with great gallantry." Robert Bigot was apparently the first of his name; his father was Roger. But Wace says: "L'anceste Hue le Bigot qui avait terre à Maletot." It has been said that he took his nickname from the oath he had frequently in his mouth, "By God!" but it is possible that he was a Bigaud, of the neighbourhood of Quimper. He held 117 manors in Suffolk, besides other lands in Norfolk and Essex (Domesday).

BIRON, from Beuron, near Mantes. Erneis de Buron appears in Domesday as a great landholder in Yorkshire. Ancestor of the *Byrons*.

BLUETT. This family gave its name to Brineville-la-Bluette in Normandy. The Bluetts long resided in Devonshire.

BLEYN, or DE BLOIN, held five manors in Cornwall (Domesday). Name now, *Blaine* and *Bloyne*.

BLOUNT or BLUNT, descriptive, le Blond, the fair-haired. Two named in Domesday, sons of the Sieur de Guisnes.

BLONDELL came to England with the Conqueror. The name is descriptive and diminutive—"the little fair-haired fellow." The family was long estated in Lancashire, but, being Roman Catholic, was cruelly oppressed and robbed in the reign of Elizabeth. *Blundell*, a merchant, founded a school at Tiverton.

BODIN, in Leland, Biden; held a large estate in Yorkshire (Domesday).

BOHUN, in Leland, Boown. Two villages near Carentan are St. Georges and St. Andre-de-Bohun. Humphrey de Bohun received the Manor of Talesford in Norfolk (Domesday). The Bohuns acquired the earldoms of Hereford, Essex, and Northampton. The name is still extant as *Bone* and *Boone*.

THE ROLL OF BATTLE ABBEY

Bois or Du Bois. There were five families that bore the name. *Boys* is still found as a surname.

Benett, a personal name.

Bonville, from the castle of Bonneville in Normandy. Leland gives Bondeville. The family became great. Sir William was created Lord Bonville in 1466. " He and his house perished in the Wars of the Roses. Within the space of less that two months the last male heirs were swept away. His son and grandson were killed in the Battle of Wakefield, 1460, on the last day of the year, and his own grey head fell on the scaffold in the ensuing February. One little great-granddaughter, a child of two years old, remained as representative of the family. She married Thomas Grey, Marquess of Dorset, and was the great-grandmother of Lady Jane Grey."

Boskerville, from Boscherville, between Pont-Audemer and Honfleur. Not in Domesday or Wace, but probably came over with the Conqueror, as the name occurs early in the twelfth century.

Boteler. The name is entered thrice in Domesday. It by no means follows that every *Butler* is a descendant of Hugo Pincernus, who came over with the Conqueror, as every nobleman, as well as William I., kept his butler.

Bournaville, in Leland, Bromevile. William de Bournaville held lands in Norfolk and Suffolk (Domesday).

Boutevilain. He was at Hastings. He is named by Wace.

Boyville, from Beuville, near Caen. Two of the name occur in Domesday, in Herefordshire and Suffolk. Hence *Bevill*.

Brabazon, in Leland, Brabasoun; a Brabant family. Jacques Brabançon followed the Conqueror, and was given lands at Betchworth, in Surrey; but the family reached distinction in Ireland, where it is still represented.

Bracy. William de Braceio appears in a charter of 1080 as holding Wistaton in Cheshire. The name became *Brescie*. Lord Brassey might suppose that he derives from the Sieur de Braçy. Possibly Samson and Sally Brass may have done the same.

Braund. William Brant was an under-tenant in Norfolk

THE ROLL OF BATTLE ABBEY

(Domesday). No evidence that Brand or Braund was not a Saxon.

BRAY does not occur in Domesday, but the men of Bray marched with the Conqueror. They came from Bray, near Evreux. No Sieur de Bray is mentioned. Bray is not uncommon as a surname in Cornwall, possibly descendants of some of these "men of Bray."

BRETTEVILLE is given twice by Leland. It stands for Breteville, a barony near Caen. Gilbert de Bretteville was a Domesday Baron, holding lands in Hampshire, Wiltshire, Oxfordshire, and Berkshire.

BREBŒUF, in Leland, Baybot; appears in Domesday as holding Watringbury, in Kent.

BRETON. No less than nine Bretons appear in Domesday. Not a surname, but a designation of sundry Breton adventurers who followed Alan Fergeant. The name is still found, also as *Brett*.

BRIANCON—in Leland, Briansoun. None from Briançon in Dauphiny can have been with William at the Conquest, and the name does not occur in England till 1189. Possibly the roll may have meant the son of de Brionne.

BRICOURT or BRIENCOURT. The name does not occur in England till the reign of Henry II. Wace mentions "those of Briencourt."

BRIONNE, in Leland, Brian. Baldum de Brionne was Viscount of Devon in the Conqueror's time, and Wido de Brionne acquired a seigneury in Wales. Hence the *Bryans* and *Briants* in England.

BROWNE, in Leland, Boroun; in interpolation.

BROY. From Broyes, in the Pays de Brie. Apparently the same as Bardolf, who is said to have been grandson of Renart, Sieur de Broyes.

BRUYS. Leland gives his name twice—once, as we suppose, for *Braosse*, and the other for *Brix*. William de Braosse was one of the most powerful Barons following the Conqueror, and was by him richly rewarded.

BRUYS for Brix or Bruce. Named from the castle of Bruys, now Brix, near Cherbourg. Robert de Bruys held a

THE ROLL OF BATTLE ABBEY

barony of ninety-four manors in Yorkshire (Domesday). He was the ancestor of the Scottish *Bruces*.

BURDON, a name found shortly after the Conquest, in Durham. But "burdon" signifies a pilgrim's staff, and there may have been many Burdons throughout the county.

BURGH. Serlo de Burgh came over with the Conqueror, but left no issue. His nephew succeeded. An apocryphal pedigree of the de Burghs appeared in the eighteenth century, giving the family an imperial Carlovingian descent. It has not a shadow of foundation. The family has become *Burke* in Ireland.

Some surprising omissions—as *Bec, Belvoir,* and *Bagott;* but these two last come in under *Todeni,* as we shall see later on. There are some—not many, and perhaps not of much importance—named by Wace that do not occur in Leland's copy of the roll.

CAILLEY. This is printed in the old edition of Leland " Constable et Tally," where the second name should begin with C. We may, I think, equate this with Quilly or Cuilly, near Falaise, a part of the possessions of the Burdetts. In fact, Robert Bordett, or Burdett, who came to England at the Conquest, was Sieur de Cailly. The surname in time degenerated into *Cully*.

CAMEVILLE or CAMPVILLE. From a place near Coûtance. Richard de Camville, surnamed Poignant (the fighter), had a barony in Oxfordshire, and his brother William held Godington under the King (Domesday).

CAMOYS, not known anything of before the reign of King John; an interpolation.

CANTELOUP, in Leland, Canntilow: from Chanteloup, near Cherbourg. Not mentioned in Domesday or by Wace. But the name occurs in the reign of Henry II., when one Ralph de Canteloup held two knights' fees under William de Romara.

CHALLONS, not in Wace or Domesday, but it may stand for Calna or Chawn, a name that occurs, not at the time of the Conquest, but in 1200.

CHALLYS, for Schalliers or Escaliers; an interpolation. The name is not found in Normandy till the reign of Philip Augustus. However, as *Scales* it became important in

THE ROLL OF BATTLE ABBEY

England, but can have been introduced only during the English occupation of Guienne. Besides the form *Scales*, the name remains as *Challys* and *Challis*. A professor of astronomy at Cambridge bore that name; so did a gardener of mine.[1]

CHAMBERLAIN. An official title and not at the time a surname.

CHAMPERNOWN. De Campo Arnulphi. A knightly family of great possessions in Devonshire. The present Champernownes are really Harringtons.

CHAMPNEY. From Champigny, in Normandy. Not found in Domesday or in Wace; nor is the name found earlier than 1165.

CHANCEUX. Perhaps from St. Quesney, near St. Saëns. In Wace we have Cahagnes; either a place of that name in the arrondissement of Vire, or another of the same name in that of the Andelys. The name has gone through many changes, as *Keynes, Chesney, Cheyney*.

CHANDUIT. Ralph de Chenduit or Chanuit held lands afterwards included in the barony of Chenduit.

CHANDOS—in Leland, Chaundoys. Robert de Candos was a companion-in-arms of the Conqueror, and he won with his sword a large domain in Wales.

CHAMBERAY—in Leland, Combrai or Coubrai. Combrai is near Falaise. The Sire de Combrai, according to Wace, was one of the knights who challenged King Harold to come forth. Godfrey de Combrai held lands *in capite* in Leicestershire (Domesday).

CHAPES, from Chappes, in Normandy. Osbern de Capis is mentioned in 1079 by Ordericus, but it is doubtful whether he was in the Battle of Hastings. Hence *Capes*.

CHARTRES. Ralph Carnotensis, or de Chartres, held estates in Leicestershire (Domesday). The name is found in Scotland as *Charteris*. It is found also as *Chayter*.

CHAUMONT, not in Wace or Domesday, but early seated in Cornwall. The name became *Chamond*.

CHAUNEY, from Canci, near Amiens; not in Domesday. Now *Chownes* and *Chowen*, the name of my land agent.

[1] Challis may also come from Calais, and also from a chalice-maker.

THE ROLL OF BATTLE ABBEY

CHAVENT, not identified. First comes into notice in the reign of Edward I.

CHAWORTH is supposed to come from Cadurcis (Cahors), in the South of France. Peter de Cadurcis was seated in Gloucestershire towards the end of the Conqueror's reign. He must have been a soldier of fortune. Leland gives the name *Chaward.*

CHENIL, from Quesnel in Normandy. Not met with in England before the reign of Henry III. Probably an interpolation.

CHERCOURT or CHEVRCOURT. Thorold of Chavercourt was enfeoffed of Wyforaby in Leicester, and Carleton in Notts, in 1085.

CLARELL, not found till the thirteenth century; probably an interpolation.

CLAIRVALS, from a castle in Anjou. Hamon de Clairvaux is said to have come over to England in the train of Alan of Brittany, but evidence for the assertion lacks. Croft, near Darlington, was the seat of the family for about 350 years. "A humble race of cadets occurs at Darlington long after the broad lands of their parent tree passed into another name, and they seem to have gradually sunk into utter pauperism. The pedigree will show these to have been nearly related to the main branch, as the Chayters had to buy out any claim they had on Clerveaux Castle" (Longstaffe, "Darlington").

COIGNIERS, the ancestor of the *Conyers* family, long seated in Yorkshire. Wace mentions the Sire de Coignieres as one of those who attended the Conqueror in the invasion of England.

COLEVILLE. William de Colville held lands in Yorkshire (Domesday). A descendant of that most furious knight and valorous enemy, "Sir John Coleville of the Dale," is introduced by Shakespeare as taken prisoner by Falstaff (*Henry IV.*, Part II., IV. III.).

COLOMBIERS, from a place of that name near Bayeux. William de Colombiers is mentioned by Wace. Ralph de Colombiers, or Colombers, in Domesday, held lands in Kent and elsewhere *in capite.* The name remains as *Columbell* and *Columb.*

THE ROLL OF BATTLE ABBEY

COMINES, from Comines in Flanders. Robert de Comines was created Earl of Northumberland by the Conqueror, but on account of his insolence and violence, was killed by the people of Durham in 1069. He must, however, have left kinsmen in the North, for the name was continued as historical in Scotland; but forms of it are found in all parts of England, as *Comings, Cummins, Cooming, Comyns.*

CORBETT, spoken of by Ordericus as "the faithful and very valiant men," *i.e.*, Corbett and his two sons, who were employed by Roger de Montgomerie in the government of his new earldom of Shrewsbury.

CORBYN—in Leland's list, "Corby et Gorbet." Four of the names are entered in Domesday, all of them undertenants.

COUBRAY. Coubray is near Thury Harcourt. Wace mentions the Sire de Coubrai.

COURSON, a branch in Norfolk and Suffolk (Domesday). Now *Curzon.*

COURTENAY, an interpolation. Reginald de Courtenay did not come to England till the reign of Henry II., in consequence of his marriage with the heiress of Robert d'Avranches, Viscount of Devon.

COURTEVILLE.

CREVECŒUR, from a place near Lisieux. The Sire de Crevecœur is mentioned in the "Roman de Rou."

CRESSY—in Leland, Crescy; a seigneury between Dieppe and Rouen. No trace of the family till the middle of the twelfth century. Now *Creasy.*

CRIQUET—in Leland as Griketot. Ansgar de Criquetot held lands in Suffolk from Mandeville in 1086. Criquetot has become *Cricket* and *Crytoft.*

DABERNON. From Abernon, near Lisieux. A subtenant of Richard de Clare in Suffolk and Surrey; he received the Manor of Stoke in the latter county.

DAMOT, actually D'Amiot. The name of Damote occurs in Oxfordshire in the reign of Henry I.

DAUBENY. The descendants of Robert de Toeni bore this name. The son of Robert assumed the name of

THE ROLL OF BATTLE ABBEY

De Albini, and was styled " Brito " to distinguish him from the Albini, the *pincerna*, Earl of Arundel.

DARELL, from Arel, on the River Vire; obtained lands in Yorkshire.

DAUTRE, as abbreviation of De Haute Rive or De Alta Ripa; from Haute Rive in Normandy. Very doubtful if a De Haute Rive attended the Conqueror. Not named in Domesday. Now *Dawtrey*.

DE LA HAY, named by Wace. Niel, son of Humphry de la Haye, is named in a deed of 1060. From La Haye-du-Puits, in the arrondissement of Coûtance. Hence the family name of *Hay* and *Haye*.

DE LA HUSEE, from Le Houssel, north of Rouen. In Domesday William Husee or Hisatus held Charecomb in Somersetshire; of Bath Abbey, as well as other manors in the county. Hence *Hussey*.

DE LA LANDE. William Patric is twice mentioned by Wace. La Lande Patric is in the arrondissement of Domfront. Leland gives the name twice. Leland's name is derived from this family.

DE LA MARCHE. The name first appears at the end of the thirteenth century.

DE LA MARE, from the fief of La Mare, in Autretot, Normandy. The lake is still called Grande-mare. Four of the sons of Norman de la Mare came to England. William FitzNorman held of the King in chief in Gloucester and Hereford. The name has become *Delamare*, *Delamore*, and *Delmar*.

DE LA POLE, an interpolation. The first of the name known was William de la Pole, a merchant of Hull in the reign of Edward III., whose son Nicholas also was a merchant, and was the father of Michael, created Earl of Suffolk by Richard II.

DE LA VALET, from Lanvalle, opposite Dinan. At the beginning of the reign of Henry II. William de Lanvallee held a barony in Essex.

DE LA WARDE, or LAVARDE. Ingelram de Warde is mentioned in Northamptonshire in 1130; but *Ward* or *Guard*

THE ROLL OF BATTLE ABBEY

are names descriptive of office. Leland gives the name again as Warde.

DE L'ISLE, from Lisle in Normandy. Humphry de l'Ile held twenty-seven manors in Wiltshire (Domesday). Hence the name *Lisle, Lesley,* and *Lilly.*

DENNIS or DACUS (the Dane). Not certain, not even probable, that one came over with the Conqueror. An interpolation.

D'EVREUX—in Leland, Deveroys. Richard, Count of Evreux and Archbishop of Rouen, son of Richard I. of Normandy and his mistress, the washerwoman Arletta, had by a concubine three sons—Richard, Count of Evreux: Ralph, Sieur de Gaci, whose son Robert died without issue; and William d'Evreux. The eldest of these brothers, Richard, and his son William fought by the Conqueror's side at Hastings. He died the following year, and William appears in Domesday as holding a great barony in Hampshire, Berkshire, and Oxfordshire. The name remains as *Devereux.*

DE LA VACHE—in Leland, De Wake; not encountered earlier than 1272. An interpolation.

DE VAUX, de Vallibus. Two brothers, Robert and Aitard de Vaux, appear in Domesday as holding lands in Norfolk. The name remains as *Vaux.* The title of Lord Vaux is held by a Mostyn.

DAVERANGES is a duplicate for D'Avranches.

DAYVILLE, repeated as Deville; from Daiville in Normandy. Walter de Daiville accompanied the Conqueror, and had grants from Roger de Musbray, in Yorkshire, with the title of Seneschal. The name remains, but as *Deville* has an unpleasing signification; it has been altered to *Eville.*

DEVERELL, for D'Evrolles. Name found in Sussex in 1165. The Deverells became a Wiltshire family.

DISART. The name we meet with as *Izzard.* No earlier settler of the name is met with than the time of Henry I. (1114-15). The Scottish Dysart is from a different origin.

DISNEY or D'ISENEY, from Isigny, near Bayeux. The name is still extant.

THE ROLL OF BATTLE ABBEY

DISPENSER, a title of office as a steward, whence *Spenser, Spencer*.

DORENY, perhaps for D'Orenge.

DOYNELL, not in Domesday, but found in Essex forty or fifty years after the Conquest.

DRUELL or DE RUELLES, from Ruelles, near Vernon, in Normandy. Does not occur in England before 1130.

DUYLY or D'OYLEY, from Ouilly-le-Basset, in the arrondissement of Falaise. They were a branch of the Bassets. Robert D'Oily became through the Conqueror's favour one of the most potent Barons in the country. He was made Baron of Oxford, where he built the castle. A John D'Oyley was created a baronet in 1821, but left no issue male. Hence the name *Doyle*.

DURANT, not a surname, but a personal name, that occurs frequently in Domesday.

ESTOTEVILLE. This is given twice in Leland—in the second place as Soucheville. Wace mentions the name as Esteville. The man who accompanied the Conqueror was Front-de-Bœuf, who was Sire d'Estoville according to some authorities. There are two places in Normandy that bear the name. The name does not appear in Domesday.

ESTRANGER, probably of Breton origin. The name occurs in the reign of Henry I. The name is still in England as *L'Estrange*, also as *Stranger*, which is that of a draper in Tavistock.

ESTOURNAY. Richard and Ralph came over with the Conqueror, and were given lands in Hampshire, Wilts, and Surrey. The name became *Stormey, Sturmer*, and *Sturmyn*.

EUSTACE stands for Eustace, a personal name; and *Fitz Eustace* also occurs; now *Stacy*.

FANCOURT, printed Fovecourt, from a place near Beauvais. Not in Domesday, but occurs early. Spelt also Vancort and Pencourt.

FERRERS, from Ferrières St. Hilaire, near Bernai. William and Henry, sons of Walkelin de Ferrieres, were with William; also another of the name Hermerus. William and Hermerus are among the Domesday Barons.

THE ROLL OF BATTLE ABBEY

FINERE—in Leland, Feniers. Not mentioned in Domesday or by Wace, and first comes into notice much later than the Conquest. Hence the *Finmore, Filmer,* and *Phillimore* names.

FERMBAUD, not named elsewhere till much later, in Bedfordshire.

FICHENT for Fecamp. Remigius, chaplain of Fecamp, "a man of small stature, but of lofty soul," was the first Norman ever appointed to an English see, and became Bishop of Dorchester in 1067. He translated the see to Lincoln. Some of his needy relatives probably came over, for we find the name among landowners later; or, what is as likely, there were other natives of Fecamp settled here, who were called after the place whence they came.

FIENNES—in Leland, Fenes; a baronial family from Fiennes, in the county of Guines. The family was seated in Kent at an early date, and held the office of hereditary castellans of Dover.

FILLIOL. Ralph de Filliol was one of the benefactors of Battle Abbey. The name signifies "little son" or "godson," but whose godson he was is not known.

FITZALAN, FITZBRIAN, etc. As these names are patronymic, and did not necessarily pass into surnames, we may pass them over.

FOLLEVILLE, from the name of a place in Picardy. The family was seated in Leicestershire in the reign of King Stephen. Probably *Foley* and *Folly* come from that name. The ancestor of Lord Foley was but a common workman, yet he may have been descended from the Sieur de Folleville.

FRESSEL, a family of Touraine. Simon Fressel came to England with the Conqueror. He was the ancestor of the Scottish *Frazer* family.

FREYVILLE, held land in Cambridgeshire. Sir Anselm de Fraeville, son of the De Freyville who came over with the Conqueror, was a benefactor to Battle Abbey. His son Roger took a fancy to a dog, and the father gave him the dog on condition that he agreed to surrender an acre of meadowland to the abbey.

THE ROLL OF BATTLE ABBEY

FRISSON. This name implies no more than that a Frisian adventurer shared in the exploit of the Conqueror. From it comes the name *Frize*, the name of a shoemaker and postman at Lew Down.

FURNEAUX, from a place of the name near Coûtance. Odo de Furnell held lands in Somerset (Domesday).

FURNIVEL, an interpolation. The first of the name in England was Gerard de Furnival, who went to the Holy Land with Richard Cœur de Lion.

GALOFER. William Gulafre had great estates in Suffolk (Domesday). Hence *Guliver*.

GARRE. Probably the same as De la War.

GAUSY, from Gauçy, near L'Aigle, in Normandy. The Gausy barony was created in Northumberland. The name has become *Gaze*.

GAUNT, from Ghent, but perhaps a misprint for Graunt.

GERNOUN. Robert Guernon held a great barony in Essex (Domesday).

GIFFARD. Three brothers of this name are entered as holding baronies in England after the Conquest. They were the sons of Osbern, Baron of Bolbec.

GLANCOURT, not in Wace or Domesday. Perhaps, however, Grancourt, which does appear in the Survey.

GOBAUD, not in Domesday, but the name occurs in the reign of Henry I., in which a Robert FitzGubold is named.

GORGES, from Gaurges, in the Cotentin. The family became famous, but there is no evidence that it was represented at the Conquest.

GOWER. This is very suspicious. It seems to be taken from the district of Gower in South Wales. Gower occurs in the "Annales Cambriæ" under date 954, and is mentioned in the "Book of Llan Dav" in 1150.

GILEBOT, from Quillebœuf in Normandy. The family won lands in Brecon, but ruined itself by extravagance. The name became *Walbeoffe*, and still more recently *Gilby*.

GRACY. In the printed Leland, "Grauncon et Tracy," where the T is apparently a misprint for G. It stands for Grancey, on the confines of Champagne and Burgundy, and gave its

THE ROLL OF BATTLE ABBEY

name to a great Burgundian family. There is no evidence that any Grancy was present at the Conquest. The modern form of the name is possibly *Grace*.

GRANDISON, Leland's Grauncon; an interpolation. The Grandisons were a Burgundian family. William de Grandison was the first to come to England, in the reign of Edward I. John de Grandison was Bishop of Exeter in 1327.

GRAY, perhaps an interpolation. It is true that an Architel de Grey is mentioned in Domesday, but it was not till the marriage of Edward IV. with Elizabeth Woodville that the Grays became important people, and then efforts were made to concoct for them a specious pedigree. Grey or Gray was a descriptive name, and we cannot be sure that all Greys or Grays belonged to the descendants of Architel de Grey.

GRAUNT or GRANT, from Le Grand. They may be traced back in Normandy till 985, but such pedigrees are suspicious, as the name is descriptive of height of stature, and was not a surname. There is no mention of a Grant in Domesday, unless that of Hugo Grando de Scoca, an under-tenant in Berkshire, be taken as one; but Grent de Everwick is found in the reign of Henry I. In the printed edition of Leland the name is Gaunt.

GRANDYN, no other than Grendon; an interpolation, from Grendon in Warwickshire.

GRESLEY—in Leland, Greilly; from Gresilé in Anjou. Albert Greslet occurs in Domesday as Baron of Manchester. The name has assumed the form of *Gredley* and *Greely*.

GRENVILLE—in Leland, G[r]enevile; from Grenneville in the Cotentin. This illustrious house is descended from Robert de Grenville, who accompanied the Conqueror to England, and received three knight's-fees in the county of Buckingham.

GREVILLE is disguised in Leland as Gruyele. It comes from a castle of the name in the Cotentin; but the existing Greville family is thought to be a branch of the Grenvilles.

GURDON, from a town of that name in the department of

THE ROLL OF BATTLE ABBEY

Lot, on the limestone Causses. How a Gurdon drifted north to join the expedition is hard to say, and almost certainly the name is an interpolation. The first Gurdon of whom we know received a grant of half a knight's-fee in Selbourn from Richard Cœur de Lion, and this is intelligible enough, as all the district of Cahors and the South was then under the English Crown.

GUBBION. Guido Gobio witnessed a charter of Geoffrey of Dinan in 1070, and was one of his knights; as the latter came to England with the Conqueror, Gobio doubtless accompanied him. Hugh Gubion is found in Hampshire in 1130. What induced Shakespeare to adopt the name for the two Gobbos we do not know. The name has become *Gibbon* and *Gubbins*.

GURNEY, from Gournai-en-Bray. The name is of note in the history of the Conquest. It is one that is now widely spread in England.

HAMELIN, a personal name, and not a surname. Several are named in Domesday. In Cornwall, Hamelin held twenty-two manors under the Earl of Mortaine. He is supposed to have been the ancestor of the Trelawney family; but the name *Hamlyn* remains in Devon and Cornwall.

HANSARD, not mentioned in Domesday; but the Hansards appear as Barons in the palatinate of Durham in the twelfth century. This is probably an interpolation.

HARCOURT. Enguerand de Harcourt was in the Conqueror's army at Hastings. The family was largely rewarded in later times. But the name is not in Domesday. We find a Harcourt among the dependents of Henry I. in 1123.

HAREVILLE, not heard of before the reign of Edward III. The name of Harivel means actually a dealer in harins, an inferior sort of horse, at fairs. An interpolation.

HASTINGS. Robert de Venoix was the first Mareschal or Portreeve of Hastings. He came from Venoix, near Caen. Robert is named in Domesday as FitzRalph and de Hastings and le Mareschal. It must not hastily be concluded that everyone bearing the name of Hastings is descended from

THE ROLL OF BATTLE ABBEY

Robert de Venoix; many a man was so named simply because a native of that place.

HAWARD, or HAYWARD, as Leland has it. This is not a Norman-French name; it is from the Norse Hávard, and has the same origin as Howard.

HAULEY, from La Haulle in Normandy. We do not find the name before the twelfth century, when Warin de Haulla held a barony of eight fees in Devon. In Dartmouth Church is a brass of a Hawley, a merchant (1408), possibly the origin of the name *Holley*.

HAUTENEY—in Leland, Hauteyn. Godwin Haldein held in Norfolk (Domesday), but his personal name is Saxon, and Haldein stands for Halfdan. He held the lordship of Gratyngton in the time of the Conqueror, and was not only permitted to retain it, but received a grant of three other manors after the Conquest. This looks much as if Godwin had been a traitor to his King and country, and had fought under the banner of the Bastard adventurer. It is curious to note the transformation of the name Halfdan or Haldane into Hautein and Hauteney by a Norman scribe. The name is now represented by *Haldane*: the Norman scribe supposed it meant a turn-up nose.

HAUTEVILLE. In Domesday, Ralph de Hauteville held a barony in Wilts.

HERNOUR, not heard of before 1324.

HERCY, from Hericy in Normandy; not noticed in Domesday.

HERON, from a place of that name near Rouen. Tihel de Heroun held lands in Essex (Domesday). The name survives both in the original form of *Heron* and as *Herne*. I remember a nurse of the latter name.

HERYCE. The family of Herice is supposed to descend from a son of the Count of Vendôme, but no evidence is forthcoming other than the bearing of his allusive arms, three "herissons," or hedgehogs, which still appear in the coats of the Earls of Malmesbury and Lord Herries. But the Earls of Malmesbury derived from a William Harris, an inhabitant of Salisbury in 1469. I dare say a good many

THE ROLL OF BATTLE ABBEY

Harrises would like to be supposed to derive from the companion of the Conqueror, Robert, named in Domesday. The name has become *Hersee, Herries.*

HOWELL, a possible companion of Alan the Red, Duke of Brittany, but probably the same as the family of Le Tourneur, near Vire.

HURELL. The name Haurell or Harell is found in Normandy, but not in England, before the latter part of the twelfth century.

JARDINE. The first of that name on record is found in Scotland before 1153. In England there have been *Gardens* from the end of the twelfth century.

JAY or GAI, not in Domesday, but the name is found in the first half of the twelfth century. Probably a descriptive appellation. The modern form of the name is *Gaye* and *Jaye.*

KANCEIS in Leland's list is really *Chauncy,* from Canci, near Amiens. An Anschar de Canci is found to have flourished in the reign of Henry I. The name has continued not only as *Chawncey,* but also as *Chance.*

KEVELERS, from Cauville, in Seine-Inférieure.

KYRIEL stands for Criol. Robert, youngest son of Robert, Count of Eu, obtained from him Criol, near Eu. He held Ashburnham of his kinsman, the Count of Eu. The name became *Creale* and *Crole, Curlle* and *Kyrle.*

LACY, from Lassy, in the arrondissement of Vire. Walter and Ilbert de Lassi took part in the Conquest of England. Roger de Lassi, son of Walter, held 100 manors in five counties.

LASSELS—in Leland, Lascels. Picot Lascels was a vassal of Alan Fergeant, Duke of Brittany and Earl of Richmond, and he held lands under the Earl in Yorkshire.

LATYMER, an interpreter; not uncommon.

LA MUILE in Leland is none other than *Moels* or *Meules.* Baldwin de Moels—from Meulles, near Orbec, arrondissement of Lisieux—had estates in Devonshire filling eleven columns in Domesday. A hairdresser in Launceston bears the name of *Mules.*

THE ROLL OF BATTLE ABBEY

LEVETOT—in Leland, Levecote. From Levetot in Lower Normandy. Not in Domesday, but shortly after.

LIFFARD, a misreading for *Oliffard*.

LIOF ET LIMERS, another misreading or misprint. Liof was a Saxon who held under Edward the Confessor.

LISOURS, from the Lisière, or verge of the Forest of Lyons, a favourite hunting ground for the Dukes of Normandy. Fulk de Lisours attended William to England, and was given Sprotburgh.

LONGCHAMP, not in Domesday, but appears under Henry I., when Hugh de Longchamps was granted the Manor of Wilton in Herefordshire. An interpolation.

LONGESPEE. Longsword held in Norfolk (Domesday). A mere nickname; possibly enough an interpolation for the bastard son of Henry II. and the fair Rosamond.

LONGVAL and LONGVILLE, perhaps the same, a branch of the House of Giffard, Barons of Longueville and Bolbec, near Dieppe. The name *Longville* still exists in England. Leland gives also *Longvillers*.

LORING, for Lorraine; a native of that province. The name *Lovering* exists. I had a cook so named.

LOVEDAY, from Louday, near Toulouse. An interpolation, as the family can have come to England only at the time of the English occupation of Aquitaine. It is also not heard of before the thirteenth century in England.

LOVELL, a name, "the Wolfing," given to Aseline de Breherval, who became Lord of Castle Cary in England. He received the nickname on account of his ferocious character.

LOUVAIN—in Leland, Lovein. An adventurer from Louvain in Flanders. Twice in Leland; possibly from Louveny, or Louvigny, near Bernay.

LOVERAC held an estate in Wiltshire after the Conquest; changed to *Loveries*.

LOWNEY, from Launai in Normandy. Not found in England till about the reign of Edward III. Modern form of the name, *Luny*, that of a charming seascape-painter in Devonshire.

THE ROLL OF BATTLE ABBEY

LUCY, from a place of that name near Rouen. The Lucys performed the office of Castle Guard at Dover for seven knight's-fees in Kent, Norfolk, and Suffolk. The name remains in its original form, and as *Luce*, a yeoman name in Devon.

LYMESAY, from a place of that name in the Pays de Caux, near Pasilly. The ancestor of the *Lindsays*.

MALHERMER should be Monthermer. An interpolation. The name first occurs in 1296, when Ralph de Monthermer, "a plain esquire," made a love-match with Joan, daughter of Edward I. He was summoned to Parliament as Earl of Gloucester and Hereford *jure uxoris* in 1299.

MAINARD, an under-tenant in Essex and Lincolnshire, but the name occurs as holding in Wilts, Hants, and Norfolk, in the reign of Edward the Confessor. It is a Teutonic name, Meginhard, and he has no right to appear as one of William's assistants at Hastings, unless, indeed, he were a traitor. Now *Maynard*.

MAINGUN is a misreading for Mayenne. Judael de Mayenne had a vast barony in Devon (Domesday); Geoffrey de Mayenne is named by Wace. Now *Maine* and *Mayne*.

MALEBURGH, for Merleberge. A great Baron in 1086; had been a landowner in England previous to the Conquest. He was certainly one of Edward the Confessor's Norman favourites, and after the Conquest he was not dispossessed, but was given lands that had belonged to Harold. The name became *Maleberg* and *Malborough*.

MALEBOUCHE, a nickname for a foul-mouthed fellow. There are plenty of the kind now, but not descendants.

MALEBYS, a nickname for Mal-bête. In Latin it is *Mala bestia*. The name occurs in England in 1142. Richard Malbysse, or "Ricardus vero agnomine Mala Bestia," says William of Newburgh, bears the blame of having, with two others, instigated the massacre of the Jews of York in 1189. The name became *Malby*.

MALET, a great favourite with the Conqueror, who appointed William Malet to hold his newly-built castle in York.

THE ROLL OF BATTLE ABBEY

MALCAKE. The name occurs as Maletoc in the reign of King Stephen.

MALMAYNE, a bad-hand; a nickname.

MALVILLE, from a barony in the Pays de Caux. William de Malavilla appears in Domesday as holding lands in Suffolk. Hence the Scottish *Melville*.

MANCEL, a native of Le Mans. Wace mentions a contingent thence.

MANDEVILLE, for Magnaville, from a place near Creuilly. Geoffrey, Sire de Magnaville, is mentioned by Wace, and was given estates in many counties. Hence *Manville*.

MANGYSIR, for Mont Gissart. Nothing known of the family.

MANNERS, properly Myners, from Mesnières, near Rouen. Richard de Manieres came to England with the Conqueror, and held under Odo, Bishop of Bayeux, land in Kent and Surrey (Domesday).

MARNY, formerly De Marreiny, from a fief in Normandy. The first mentioned is William de Marney, in 1166, who held a knight's-fee in Essex.

MARTIN, Sire of Tour, near Bayeux. Came over with the Bastard in 1066, and conquered the territory of Kemys in Pembrokeshire, which was erected into a palatine barony.

MASEY, from Maçy, near Coûtances. In 1086 Hugh de Maci held lands in Huntingdonshire (Domesday), and Hamo de Maci nine manors of Hugh Lupus in Cheshire. The name remains as *Massey*.

MAULE, from a town of that name in the Vexin Français. Guarin de Maule came over with the Conqueror, and received the Manor of Hatton and some other lands in Cleveland.[1] The name remains not only in its original form, but perhaps also as *Moll*.

MAULAY, de Malo Lacu. The first who came over to England was Peter de Maulay, a Poitevin, brought here by King John, who employed him to murder his nephew Arthur. In reward for this he was given in marriage the

[1] Ordericus Vitalis gives an account of this family (v. 19).

THE ROLL OF BATTLE ABBEY

heiress of Doncaster, who brought him the barony of Mulgrave.

MAUCLERK, MAUCOVENANT, MAUFÉ, MAULOVEL, MAUREWARDE (for *regarde*), MAUTALENT, MAUVOISIN, are all nicknames—the bad clerk, the bad covenant, bad faith, the bad young wolf, the evil eye, bad talent, bad neighbour—not likely to be passed on as surnames. *De Mauney* is, however, not bad nose, but a place-name; more of this presently.

MAUDIT might have been supposed to have been the name given to one excommunicated, but it was not so; it was from a place, Mauduit, near Nantes. Geoffrey Maudet held lands in Wiltshire, and his brother William also in Hampshire (Domesday). The name has been shortened into *Maude*.

MAULEVRIER or MALEVRIER, from a place near Rouen. Helto de Mauleverer held lands in Kent (Domesday).

MENYLE, for Menesville, or Mesnil, near Grandmesnil, in the arrondissement of Lisieux. Hugh de Grand-Mesnil fought bravely at Hastings, says Wace. He "was that day in great peril; his horse ran away with him so that he was near falling, for in leaping over a bank the bridle-rein broke, and the horse plunged forward. The English, seeing him, ran to meet him with their axes raised, but the horse took fright, and, turning quickly round, brought him safe back again." He was created Count of Leicestershire and Hampshire. The name remains as *Meynell*.

MERKINGFEL, not a Norman name, nor heard of till 1309, and then in Yorkshire.

MOWBRAY, from the Castle of Molbrai, near St. Lô, in the Cotentin. Three of the family were in the Conqueror's train. Robert, Earl of Northumberland, was the son of one of these; he was thrown into a dungeon by William Rufus, where he lingered for thirty-four years, and his newly-wedded wife, Maud de l'Aigle, was married to Nigel de Albini; and Nigel's eldest son, Roger, by King Henry's command, assumed the name of Mowbray, and from him the later Mowbrays are descended.

MOHUN—in Leland Mooun. From Moion, near St. Lô in Normandy. Wace tells us that "Old William de Moion had

THE ROLL OF BATTLE ABBEY

with him many companions at the Battle of Hastings." He was rewarded for his services by the grant of not less than fifty-five manors in Somerset, besides two in Wilts and Dorset. The name remains nearer to the early spelling than Mohun, as *Moon*, which is that of a music-seller in Plymouth.

MONCEAUX, "le Sire de Monceals" of Wace. The place is south-east of Bayeux. Became a famous family in Sussex, and gave benefactions to Battle Abbey; the name remains corrupted into *Monseer*. In Leland the name is Monceus.

MONTAIGUE, from a place of the name in the arrondissement of Coûtances. Two of the name appear in Domesday, both richly endowed, but of these one left no heir. Drogo de Montaigue came in the train of the Earl of Mortaine.

MONTBURGH, from Montebourg, in the Cotentin, which at the time of the Conquest was held by Duke William himself.

MONTFEY, for Montbrai, arrondissement of St. Lô. Giffard de Montbrai attended the Conqueror to England. Name is not in Domesday. Now *Mumfey*.

MONTFICHET, from Montfiquet, arrondissement of Bayeux. Not in Domesday as such, but as Robert Guernon, Baron of Montfiquet, who held a barony in Essex in 1086. The name is found in later times as *Fichett*, and I notice in a newspaper of January 22, 1909, the death of a Mrs. Amelia *Fidgett*, of Mistley, Essex, who died in her 104th year.

MONTFORT, from a place on the Rille, near Brionne, arrondissement of Pont Audemer. Hugh, says Wace, was one of the four knights who mutilated the body of Harold after the battle; he received a barony of 113 English manors. The name remained on as *Mountford* and *Mumford*.

MONTCHESNEY. Hubert de Monte Canisi held a barony in Suffolk (Domesday). The name may remain as *Chesney*.

MONTIGNY, not in Domesday, but Robert de *Mounteney* is found estated in Norfolk in 1161.

MONTPINSON, from Montpinçon near Evreux. Ralph de Montpinçon was "Dapifer" to the Conqueror, as Ordericus tells us. The name became in England *Mompesson*.[1]

[1] Ordericus gives an account of this family (v. 17).

THE ROLL OF BATTLE ABBEY

MONTREVEL, not in Domesday; from Montreuil.

MONTSOREL, from Montsoreau on the Loire. The name first occurs in 1165. There is a Mountsorel in Leicestershire that had estates in it that belonged to the Earl of Chester. Perhaps *Mounsell.*

MONTRAVERS or MALTRAVERS, not named in Domesday, but occurs in the reign of Henry I. The name has been made odious through John, Lord Maltravers, who murdered Edward II. with terrible cruelty. We have the name still as *Maltravers.*

MORLEY. The name does not occur till the reign of Henry I.; probably from Morlaix in Brittany, and the first who came over was a retainer of Alan Fergeant. The name is given again by Leland as Merley.

MORTAINE. Robert, Earl of Mortaine, was the son of Herluin de Couteville, who married Harleva, the cast-off mistress of Duke Robert, and consequently was uterine brother of the Conqueror. When William became Duke of Normandy, he lost no opportunity of raising his kinsfolk from their humble estate, to the disgust and indignation of his nobles, and above all of his relatives on the side of his father. Robert was rewarded for his services in the Conquest of England by being given the whole of Cornwall, comprising 248 manors, 52 in Sussex, 75 in Devon, 10 in Suffolk, 29 in Buckinghamshire, 99 in Northamptonshire, 196 in Yorkshire, besides others in other counties. The name in England has become *Morton,* but all Mortons do not derive from him, as there are places named Morton in England that have given appellations to individuals issuing from them.

MORRICE, a Christian name.

MORTIMER, de Mortuo Mari. From Mortemer, in the Pays de Caux. Roger de Mortemer furnished forty vessels for the invading fleet. He was too old himself to join the expedition, but he sent his son Ralph, the founder of the splendid English lineage that conveyed to the House of York its title to the Crown. The name still continues. I had an undermason working for me some years ago, a singularly handsome man, of the name of *Mortimer.*

THE ROLL OF BATTLE ABBEY

MORTIVAUX or MORTIVAL. The name does not occur before the reign of King John. The name has gone through various forms, one being *Morteville*.

MORVILLE, from a castle of that name in the Cotentin. The first named is Hugh de Morville, the founder of the English house in 1158. He was one of the four knights who went from Normandy to slay Thomas à Becket. The family obtained a high position in the North. It became of great account in Scotland. This is certainly an interpolation. The name in Scotland became *Marvell*.

MOUNCY, from Monchy, near Arras. Drogo de Moncy came to England in 1066, and was in Palestine in 1096. In 1299 Walter de Moncy was summoned to Parliament as a Baron. The name remains as *Mounce*. Some of the name occupied a cottage belonging to my father. They were notorious poachers, and lived on what they caught, and stole their firing. At last one of them, a youth, was caught "robbing hen-roosts," like some of his betters, and was convicted and sent to prison. On leaving, he came to my father with the request that as a magistrate he would send him back to prison, as "it was the only place where he had been treated as a gentleman." Was he a descendant of the Crusader? Also *Mounsey*.

MOYNE, in Leland's copy Maoun (*i.e.*, Monk). The family is found at Owers in Dorset in the reign of Henry I. The Monks, ancestors of the Duke of Albemarle, are found seated at Potheridge in Devonshire as early as the reign of Edward I. *Monk* is still a name not uncommon in Devon. There is a baker and confectioner so called at Tavistock.

MOVET, MAUFÉ. The name does not occur before 1165.

MUSARD. Asculphus Musard held a great barony. Enisard and Hugh Musard are also named in Domesday. A nickname signifying a loafer or loiterer. It has become in later times *Mussard*.

MUSE. The name does not occur in England till the end of the twelfth century. It is probably a nickname from an expression used in hunting.

MUSSET, a name from the bag-pipes the man played.

THE ROLL OF BATTLE ABBEY

Leland gives Muschet. Not mentioned in Domesday. Probably only the piper that played before William. The name remains.

MUSTEYS, for Moûtiers. Robert de Mosters was a tenant of Earl Alan, of Richmond and Brittany, in Yorkshire in 1086. There are several Moûtiers or monasteries in Normandy, whence the name may have come. The name remains as *Musters*.

MUSEGROS, from Mucegros, near Ecouen, was a tenant-in-chief in Herefordshire (Domesday). The ancestor of the *Musgraves, Musgroves*.

MYRIEL does not occur till the end of the twelfth century. The name is probably an interpolation. Now *Murrell*.

NAIRMERE, perhaps for Nemours — Hubert de Nemors was a tenant in Dorset, and William de Nemors an undertenant in Suffolk (Domesday).

NENERS. In the reign of Henry I., Robert Nernoit is met with. The name also occurs as Nermitz.

NEREVILLE in Leland seems to be a copyist's mistake for Oirval, south-west of Coûtances, the men of which place are mentioned as being at Hastings.

NEVILLE, from Neuville-sur-Touque. The first who came to England was Gilbert de Nevill, but he is not named in Domesday. The family was early estated in Lincoln, but by marriage with an heiress moved into the North. This line died out *sans* male issue, and the lands of the heiress passed to a Saxon husband, and with the lands the Norman name was assumed.

NEWBET or NERBET. The name occurs first in Gloucestershire, where William de Nerbert in 1165 held four knight's-fees of the Earl of Gloucester. The name has become *Newbert*.

NEWBURGH, from Neufbourg in Normandy. Henry de Newburgh obtained the earldom of Warwick, his brother Robert that of Leicester. The name became *Newburrow*.

NEWMARCH, from the castle of Neumarché in Normandy. Bernard Newmarch was one of the Conqueror's companions-at-arms, and obtained as his share of the spoil a Welsh principality won by his own good sword.

THE ROLL OF BATTLE ABBEY

NOVERS, for Noyers. William de Noiers, or Nuers, was an under-tenant in Norfolk (Domesday), where he had the custody of thirty-three of the Conqueror's manors.

OLIFARD, not heard of before 1130, when two, Hugh and William, occur in Hampshire and Northamptonshire. It appears in Scotland under David I., 1165. The name there becomes *Oliphant*. Possibly *Lifford* derives from Olifard.

ONATULLE is probably a misreading of Osseville, from Osseville in Normandy. The name does not occur till after 1190.

PAGANEL or PAINELL, a great baronial family in Normandy. The name was probably given to the original Norman founder of the family, who came over with Rollo and obstinately refused to be baptized. So he was called the Pagan, and possibly his sons and grandsons were poor Christians, if Christians at all, so that the name of Pagan adhered to the family. It still remains as *Payne* and *Pennell*. Other derivations shall be mentioned later.

PAIFRER appears in Domesday as Paisfor, Paisforere, and Pastforcire, once a considerable name in Kent.

PAITENY. The name does not occur till the reign of Edward I.

PAVILLY, from a place near Rouen; not in Domesday. Name occurs in the reign of Henry I. The family died out in the tenth century.

PAVILLON, from Pavelion, near Mantes. Appears as Papelion, witness to the charter of William the Conqueror to the Church of Durham, and was present at a Council at Westminster in 1082. Now *Papillon*, but this is a later Huguenot importation.

PECHE. This nickname of a "man of sin" occurs in Domesday. William Pecatum was an under-tenant in Norfolk, Suffolk, and Essex. The name may have been altered to *Beach* and *Beachy*. It has also been found as *Peach* and *Peachy*.

PERCY, from Perci, a fief near Villedieu near Caen. William de Perci was a tenant of the Duke of Normandy. He and Serlo de Perci came over in the time of the

THE ROLL OF BATTLE ABBEY

Conqueror, but neither of them is mentioned as having been present at Hastings.

PERECHAY. Ralph de Perechaie is named as a tenant-in-chief in Berkshire (Domesday). The name comes very near to Percy. I knew some few years ago a taverner on Dartmoor whose name as spelled over his door was *Purcay*.

PEROT, for Pierrot, Peterkin. Peret the Forester occurs in Domesday as a Hampshire Baron, but nothing can be concluded from this. Sir John *Perrott*, Deputy-Governor of Ireland, was an illegitimate son of Henry VIII. He got into trouble with Elizabeth, whom he treated with impertinence. The name still exists. It is that of the well-known family of guides to Dartmoor, living at Chagford.

PERRERS, from Periers, near Evreux. Not in Domesday, but the name found in 1156. Alice Perrers of this family was mistress of, and then wife to, Edward III. She afterwards married Lord Windsor. Another family of entirely different origin, derived from Periers in Brittany, is now represented by *Perry* in Devonshire. It was seated in Devon in 1307. Now a worthy yeoman family.

PERERIS is probably a mistake for Praeres, or Praers now Préaux. There was a barony of the name in the arrondissement of Rouen. Probably some *Priors* and *Pryors* derive hence, and not from a Prior who abandoned his vocation.

PEVERELL, given twice in the list. The name is not territorial. It is rendered in Latin *Piperellus*. William Peverell was reputed to be the son of the Conqueror by a Saxon lady, daughter of Ingelric, whom he gave in marriage to Ralph Peverell. Both Ralph and William Peverell are found as chief tenants in Domesday. William had a barony of 160 manors. The complaisant Ralph was rewarded with sixty-four knight's fees.

PICARD, from Picardy, occurs twice.

PIERREPONT, from a place of that name near St. Sauveur, in the Cotentin. Three brothers of that name occur as under-tenants in Domesday.

PINKNEY, from Pincquigny, a town in Picardy, not far

THE ROLL OF BATTLE ABBEY

from Amiens. Ansculph was created Viscount of Surrey, and his son was William Ansculph, one of the great landowners of Domesday. From two passages in that record we learn that their name was de Pinchingi.

PLACY, an interpolation. The family descends from John de Placetis, a domestic servant of Henry III., who obtained the favour of his weak master, and became Earl of Warwick on marrying Margaret de Newburgh, much against her will, but at the command of the King.

PLAYCE or DU PLAIZ. The family was enfeoffed after the Conquest by Earl Warren. The name remains as *Place* and *Plaice*.

PLUNKET, from Plouquenet, near Rennes. Not in Domesday, but occurs in 1158.

POWER, from Poher in Brittany, a county of which Carhaix was capital; properly Poucaer. *Pou* is the Latin *Pagus*. A branch settled in Devon in 1066 with Alured de Mayenne.

POINZ or DE PONS, the ancestor of the Cliffords; from Pons, in the Saintonge. Pons had four sons who went to England, of whom Drogo FitzPonce and Walter FitzPonce held important baronies (Domesday). The younger brothers were ancestors of the Veseys and Burghs. The name is still to be found as *Bounce* and *Bunce*. I remember a poor, humble-minded servant-lad of that name, who for aught one knows may have been as true a descendant of the Lords of Pons as any Clifford, de Burgh, or Vesey.

PUNCHARDON, from Pontcardon in Normandy. Robert de Pontcardon held lands in Devon in 1080. William de Pontcardon held six fees in Somerset and Devon in 1165. Now *Punchard*, *Pinchard*.

PUGOYS, a probable interpolation. It has been pretended that Ogier de Pugoys came over with the Conqueror, and was given the Manor of Bedingfield in Suffolk, and that his descendants assumed the name of *Bedingfield*. Mr. Freeman throws discredit on this descent. "It is patched up by a deed of which I have a copy before me, and which is plainly one of a class of deeds which were invented to make

THE ROLL OF BATTLE ABBEY

out a pedigree." The name is from Puchay, near Evreux. In England it became *Poggis* and *Boggis*.

PUTEREL. One of the charters of Hugh Lupus, Earl of Chester, names Robert Putrel. Possibly the name may have become *Botrell*.

PYGOT or PIGGOT. The name Picot occurs seven times in Domesday. It was a personal or nickname. The name is a diminutive of *Pygge*, a girl.

QUERRU, probably for Carew, and consequently an interpolation.

QUINCY, from Quinci in Maine. Richard de Quincy was companion-in-arms of the Conqueror, and received from him Bushby in Northamptonshire.

REYNEVILLE, a mistake, either of copyist or of printer, for Roudeville, now Rouville, near Gisors. Not in Domesday, nor does the name occur in England till the thirteenth century.

RIDELL, descended from the Counts of Angoulême. The surname was first assumed by Geoffrey, the second son of Count Geoffrey, in 1048. He had two sons; the second, of the same name as himself, came to England along with William Bigod. He is mentioned in Domesday as receiving large grants of land, and he also succeeded to his father's barony in Guienne. The next in succession was drowned in the *White Ship*, leaving only a daughter, who married Richard Basset; and their son Geoffrey retained the name of Basset, but the second continued that of Ridell. Not to be confounded with the Ridells, descended from the De Ridales, so called from a district in Yorkshire.

RIPERE, from Rupierre, near Caen. William de Rupièrre, who came to England with the Conqueror, is mentioned by Ordericus. The name has become *Rooper*, *Roope*, and *Roper*, when this latter does not signify a cordwainer.

RIVERS, from Reviers, near Creulli, in the arrondissement of Caen, named by Wace. Richard de Reviers held a barony in Dorset in 1086 (Domesday). He was granted the Castle of Plympton, and was created Earl of Devon. Usually called *Redvers*.

THE ROLL OF BATTLE ABBEY

ROCHELLE, called by Leland " Rokel "; from Rochelle, in the Cotentin. Not in Domesday, nor heard of before the reign of Henry II.

Ros. Five of the name are entered in Domesday, deriving their name from the parish of Ros, two miles from Caen. The name has become *Rose*.

ROSCELYN, not in Domesday.

ROSEL, for *Russell;* from the lordship of Rosel, in the Cotentin. In Domesday, Hugh de Rosel appears as holding lands in Dorset as Marshal of the Buttery in England, so that he was one of the flunkey nobles. The fortunes of the family were made under Henry VIII., whom the then Russell served unscrupulously, and was nicknamed the King's Firescreen. He was richly rewarded with Church lands.

RUGETIUS, not to be identified.

RYE, from a place of that name north of Bayeux. Herbert de Rie in 1047 saved the life of William, the future Conquerer of England, when flying from the conspirators of the Cotentin. He died before 1066, but his sons are entered in Domesday. The name remains.

RYVEL, for Rouville or Runeville. Goisrfed de Ryvel held lands in Herts in 1086 (Domesday).

RYSERS, for Richer. The name does not occur before the end of the thirteenth century.

ST. AMANDE, in the Cotentin. Not in Domesday. Almeric de St. Amande witnessed a charter of Henry II. in 1172.

ST. AMARY, not identified, but probably a mistake for Amaury.

ST. BARBE. In Normandy a town and two villages bear the name of St. Barbara. Not in Domesday. William de St. Barbe was Dean of York, and elected Bishop of Durham in 1143. A family of Saintbarbe was in Somerset, tenants of Glastonbury, in the thirteenth century.

ST. CLERE, from a place of that name in the arrondissement of Pont l'Evêque. "This Norman village has bestowed its name upon a Scottish family, an English town, an Irish county, a Cambridge college, a royal dukedom, and a King-

THE ROLL OF BATTLE ABBEY

at-Arms" (I. Taylor). The Sieur de St. Clair is named by Wace as at the Battle of Hastings. This was Richard de St. Clair, who had lands in Suffolk (Domesday). His brother Britel held lands in Somerset (*ibid.*). Now *Sinclere* or *Sinclair*.

SALAWYN. Joceus le Flamangh—*i.e.*, the Fleming—came to England with the Conqueror, and held a third part of a knight's-fee in Cukeney, Nottinghamshire, and two ploughlands of the King by the service of shoeing the King's palfrey; in fact, he was a farrier. His brother, Ralph le Silvan of Woodhouse, was ancestor of the Silvans or Salvins of Woodhouse. They took the name from the fact of living in Sherwood Forest. The name remains as *Salvin* and *Salvyn*.

SANDFORD. Gerard de Tornai—*i.e.*, Tournay—held Sandford in Shropshire, under Earl Roger, and the family took the name from the place.

SAUVAY, not met with till the reign of Edward I.

SAUNZAVER or SANS-AVOIR, the poverty-stricken. Matthew Paris mentions a Walter Sansavoir in the annals of 1096. But the first Sansaver met with in England is in Devon in 1165.

SANSPEUR or SAUNSPOUR, a nickname.

SAGEVILLE, from a place of that name in the Isle de France. Richard de Sacheville occurs as holding lands in Essex in 1086. *Sackville* is the modern form.

SAYE, mentioned by Wace. From Say, nine miles to the west of Eximes, the chief place of the viscounty of Roger de Montgomery in Normandy. Picot de Say is named in Domesday.

SESSE, from Seez, on the Arne, in Normandy. The name not met with before 1130.

SENGRYN or SEGUIN, not in Domesday, and not met with before the reign of Edward I. In 1273 it became Segin, now *Seekins* and *Sequin*.

SOLERS, from Soliers, near Caen. Two of the family are met with in Domesday.

SOMEROY, entered twice by Leland. From Someneri,

THE ROLL OF BATTLE ABBEY

near Rouen. William de Someri held lands in Sussex in the reign of Henry I. The name got in time contracted to *Somers*.

SORELL, not met with before the reign of Henry II. Now *Sarell* and *Serle* and *Searle*, the Norman Serlo, a personal name.

SUYLLY. Raymond de Sully in the time of William Rufus went with Robert FitzHamon to the conquest of Glamorgan, and was one of the twelve knights that shared the territory they had helped to win. The name is now met with as *Soley*. I see *Sulley* on many coal-trucks.

SOULES, from a place of that name near St. Lô. The men of Sole are mentioned by Wace at Hastings, "striking at close quarters, and holding their shields over their heads so as to receive the blows of the hatchet." The family was in early times powerful in Scotland, where it gave its name to the barony of Soulistown, now Saltoun, in East Lothian.

SOVERENY, not accounted for.

SURDEVAL. Richard de Surdeval in 1086 was one of the tenants of the Earl of Mortaine in Yorkshire, holding of him 180 manors. Now *Sordwell*.

TAKEL or TACHEL, first heard of in 1165, when Simon Tachel held a knight's-fee of Roger de Moubray in Yorkshire. Now *Tackle*.

TALBOT. William Talbot came to England in 1066, and had two sons, Richard and Godfrey, who are mentioned as under-tenants in Essex and Bedfordshire (Domesday). A nickname.

TALLY perhaps stands for Tilly. From the castle and barony of Tilly, near Caen. Ralph de Tilly held lands in Devon (Domesday). The name of *Tilly* remains, but it also signified a labourer.

TANY, from Tani in Normandy. Robert de Tani held a barony in Essex (Domesday).

TAY and THAYS are probably the same. Derived from a certain Baldric Teutonicus. He was called later *De Tyas*, and was seated in Yorkshire, Essex, and many other counties. The motto of the family was *Tays en temps*

THE ROLL OF BATTLE ABBEY

(Know when to hold your tongue). Robert Tay, who was engaged in the Wars of the Roses, had a variant of this: "Not to be hanged for talking."

TARTERAY in Leland's list is a misreading or a misprint for Carteray, the ancestor of the *Carterets*.

THORNY, from Tornai in Normandy. Giraud de Torni received eighteen manors from Earl Roger de Montgomeri.

TIBOL, probably for Tilliol, from a place so named near Rouen. Humfrey de Tilleul was the first castellan of the new castle erected at Hastings.

TINGEY, not to be identified.

TINEL. Thurstan Tinel and his wife appear in Domesday as under-tenants in Kent.

TIPITOT, from Thiboutot, in the Pays de Caux. The name does not occur in England till 1165. It got corrupted to *Tiptoft*.

TISOUN, a nickname. From *tison*, a badger; now *Tyson*. The family was so called from the knack they had of laying hold with their claws of all that came in their way and appropriating it. Gilbert Tison, or Tesson, had a barony in York, Notts, and Lincoln (Domesday).

TOURYS. Odo de Turri had large possessions in Warwickshire in the reign of Henry I., at Thoresby. This is curious, that he should have settled at a place with a name so similar to his own. The name *Torre* is still extant in Yorkshire.

TREGOZ, from a castle of that name in the arrondissement of St. Lô. A Tregoz was in the Conqueror's host, and is praised by Wace for his bravery: "He killed two Englishmen, smiting the one through with his lance and braining the other with his sword." No mention of the family in Domesday, and not as of much possessions till the reign of King Stephen.

TRACY. It is uncertain whether Tracy is intended in the entry in Leland. He gives "Graunson et Tracy," and, in accordance with the system adopted in the roll, the name should be Gracy. The Sire de Traci was, however, according to Wace, in the Battle of Hastings. The family does

THE ROLL OF BATTLE ABBEY

not appear to have been of much importance in England before the time of Stephen, who bestowed upon Henry de Tracy the Honour of Barnstaple. William de Tracy, one of the murderers of Thomas à Becket, had extensive estates in Devonshire and Gloucestershire.

TRAVILLE, not identified.

TREVILLE, same as Treilly, from a castle in Manche. The name occurs in England in the twelfth century. Now *Treble*.

TRUSSEL. The name does not occur in England till the twelfth century.

ST. CLOYES, not identified.

ST. JOHN, from St. Jean-le-Thomas, near Avranches. The men of St. Johan are spoken of at Hastings by Wace. Not named in Domesday, but in the reign of William Rufus John de St. John was one of the twelve knights that invaded Glamorgan along with Robert FitzHamon. The name remains.

ST. JORY, not identified; perhaps now *Jury*, unless from residence in the Jewry, or Jews' quarter, in a town.

ST. LEGER, from a place of that name near Avranches. Robert de St. Leger was estated in Sussex (Domesday).

ST. LEO or ST. Lô, from a place near Coûtances; a barony. Simon de St. Laud had grants at the Conquest.

ST. MARTIN, not in Domesday, but Roger de St. Martin was Lord of Hampton, Norfolk, in the reign of Henry I.

ST. MAUR, from a place of that name near Avranches. Wido de St. Maur came to England in 1066, but died before Domesday was compiled. His son, William FitzWido, held a barony in Somerset, Wiltshire, and Gloucestershire, and ten manors in Somerset. The name became *Seamore* and *Seymour*. But see what is said on that name in the chapter on Trade-names.

ST. OMER, in Leland's list St. Thomer. A branch of the house of the Barons of Bethune. Not in Domesday, but William castellan of St. Omer is mentioned in the reign of Henry I. The name is found now as *Stomer*.

ST. PHILIBERT—in Leland, Felebert. From St. Philibert,

THE ROLL OF BATTLE ABBEY

in the arrondisement of Pont Audemer. Not in Domesday, but occurs in 1213; a baronial family.

ST. QUINTIN, from a place so called near Coûtances. Hugh de St. Quintin accompanied the Conqueror to England, and received lands in Essex and Dorset (Domesday). Whether the name of *Quintin* now found points to a descent from the Norman St. Quintin family cannot be said.

ST. TES, for Saintes, capital of the Saintonge. An interpolation, as the bearer of that name must have come during the English occupation of Guienne.

TURLEY, for Torlai or Thorley. Not named before 1272. It may be doubted whether the Thorleys of the Middle Ages were one quarter as well known in England as is the name of *Thorley* now for providing "food for cattle."

TUCHET, from Notre Dame de Touchet, near Mortaine in Normandy. The family was seated at Buglawton and Tattenhall shortly after the Conquest. Sir John Touchet married the eldest daughter and coheiress of Lord Audley in the reign of Edward III., and the barony descended to Sir John's son. The name is now *Tuckett*. There is a confectioner of that name at Plymouth.

TYRELL, printed in Leland "Tyriet," but certainly a mistake for "Tyrell." Fulk, Sieur de Guernaville and Dean of Evreux, married a lady named Onelda, and had by her two children, of whom the youngest—Walter—assumed the name of Tyrell. He is entered in Domesday as Walter Tirelde, tenant of Richard FitzGilbert, Lord of Clare, of whom he held Langdon in Sussex.

UMFRAVILLE, from Amfreville, near Evreux. Robert Umfraville, with the Beard, Lord of Tour and Vian in Normandy, had a grant from the Conqueror of the barony of Prudhoe and the lordship of Redesdale. The name still exists.

VALENCE, from a place of that name in Normandy.

VALLONIS, for Valognes, in the Cotentin. Peter de Valognes, or Vallonis, received from the Conqueror fifty-seven manors, and was created Viscount of Essex.

VAVASOUR. A vavasour is the vassal of a vassal, or the holder under a mesne-lord. But the baronial Vavasours were

THE ROLL OF BATTLE ABBEY

descended from Sir Mauger de Vavasour, porter to William the Conqueror. He is not to be found in Domesday, but his grandson was a landowner in Yorkshire.

VAUX or DE VALLIBUS. Robert of that name was a subtenant in Domesday, as was also Richard de Vaux. The family rose to great distinction.

VAVILLE, properly Wiville or Guideville, held in Normandy under the Toenis. Hugh de Guidville came to England in 1066, and held lands in Northamptonshire and Leicester (Domesday). The name has gone through several changes. The *Woodvilles* derived from this Hugh de Guidville. But the name continued in the form of *Wyville* or *Wyvill* in Yorkshire and in Cornwall. I have working for me an under-carpenter of that name, whose son was my boot-boy and knife-cleaner. Twice in Leland.

VENABLES, from a place between St. Pierre and Vernon on the Seine. It was the seat of the *Veneurs*, or Hereditary Huntsmen, of the Norman Dukes. Gilbert de Venables, or Venator, was one of the Palatine Barons in Cheshire under Hugh Lupus.

VENOUR, also a huntsman. The Grosvenour, or head-huntsman, was the ancestor of the *Grosvenor* family. There were seven Venatores mentioned in Domesday, some bearing Saxon names; but the ancestor of the Grosvenors was Ralph Venator, one of the attendant Barons on Hugh Lupus, who held Stapleford under the Earl.

VERBOIS, from a place near Rouen. The family gave its name as *Warboys* to a village between Huntingdon and Ramsey.

VERDERS, from *verdier*. The Verdier, or verderer, was a judge of petty offences against the forest laws. In England his office was to take care of the *vert*, a word applying to everything that bears a green leaf within the forest that may cover and hide a deer.

VERDON, from a fief in the arrondissement of Avranches. Bertram de Verdon, the founder of the English house, had Farnham Royal in Buckinghamshire of the King (Domesday).

THE ROLL OF BATTLE ABBEY

VERE, from Ver, between Bayeux and Caen. Alberic de Vere was one of the great landowners of Domesday, who had his castle at Hedingham in Essex. His successor and namesake was Viscount under Henry I. in no less than eleven different counties.

VERNON, from Vernon in the arrondissement of Evreux. Richard and Walter appear in Domesday. Richard was one of the Barons of the palatinate of Hugh Lupus in Cheshire, and had a castle at Shipbrook on the Wever.

VESEY, from Vassey, a fief in the Val de Vire, mentioned by Wace as at the Battle of Hastings, under the name of Waacee. Robert and Ivo were there present. Robert received a great barony in Northants, Warwick, Lincoln, and Leicester. The name remains as *Vasey, Facey, Veysey*, and *Voysey*. In the latter form I had a labourer working for me many years who could neither read nor write.

VEYLAND cannot be a Norman name; it is *Wayland*, the English form of the Norse Viglund.

VILLAIN. Hugh de Villana held land at Taunton under the Bishop of Winchester. The name assumed the forms of *Villane, Velayne*, and *Willon*.

VINON, for Vivonne, a seigneurie in Poitou. We do not hear of the family till 1240.

VIPONT, from Vieuxpont-en-Auge, near Caen. Robert, Lord of Vieupont, was at Hastings, and William is also mentioned by Wace. William died the year before the compilation of Domesday, but his son is mentioned in it, who held Hardingstone in Northamptonshire. The name has become *Fippen* and *Fippon*.

VUASTENEYS or GASTINAYS, from the Gastinois, south of Paris and east of Orleans. Goisfrid, described as "homo Roberti de Stafford," who held large tracts of land in the great Stafford barony, was the founder of the De Wastineys in England.

WACE, shall be dealt with elsewhere.

WACELAY, not traced.

WALANGAY, not traced.

WALOYS, variously spelt Le Walleys, Wallais, and

THE ROLL OF BATTLE ABBEY

Latinized Wallonis, means "the Welshman"; now *Walsh* and *Welsh*, also *Wallace*.

WAMERVILLE, for Wannerville; not heard of before the second half of the twelfth century.

WARDE, already mentioned under De la Ward.

WARENNE. William de Warenne, or de Garenne, fought at Hastings, and few of the Duke's followers were as munificently dealt with. He held the great baronies of Castle Aire in Norfolk, Lewes in Sussex, and Coningsburgh in Yorkshire. The last Earl Warren had during the lifetime of his wife lived in open concubinage with Maud de Nerefort, by whom he had a son who bore his arms and was knighted, and inherited through his wife the Cheshire barony of Stockport, and their descendants remained in the county for fourteen generations. It would be unwise to assume that all *Warrens* are descendants of William de Warenne. Most, doubtless, derive their name from some warren, of which the ancestor was warrener.

WARLEY stands for Verlai in Normandy. In 1066 Thurold de Verlai held thirteen lordships in Salop from Earl Roger, of which Chetwynd appears to have been the chief. But Leland enters Werlay as well as Warley. By this Werlay he means *Vesli*. Humfrey de Vesli was a vassal of Ilbert de Lacy in Yorkshire in 1086.

WATERVILLE is a mistake for Vateville on the Seine. Three de Vatevilles are entered in Domesday: William, who held of the King in Essex and Suffolk, etc.; Robert, who held *in capite* in Surrey with five manors in other counties; and Richard, an under-tenant in Surrey. Now *Waterfield*.

WAUNCY, for Vancy, from Vanci or Wanchy, near Neufchâtel in Normandy. Hugh and Osbern "de Wanceo" each held fiefs in Suffolk in 1086.

WEMERLAY, not traced, but probably the English Wamersley and *Walmsley;* an interpolation.

CHAPTER XII

FRENCH NAMES: I. EARLY

THAT Whitsuntide wedding of 1152 when Henry Plantagenet took to wife Eleanor of Guienne, the divorced wife of Louis VII., was an event full of disaster to both England and France. Henry II. was Lord of Anjou, Touraine, and Maine, as well as of Normandy, with suzerainty over Brittany; he was, moreover, King of England. By this marriage his empire stretched from the Flemish border to the Pyrenees, commanding the entire coast of France, with the exception of that on the Mediterranean, which belonged to Provence and Toulouse, covering more than half the soil whose nominal lord paramount was Louis VII.[1]

Eleanor was the daughter and heiress of William X., Duke of Aquitaine and Poitou. She had gone with her husband on Crusade to the Holy Land in 1146; but there scandal had it that she carried on an intrigue with her uncle, Raymond I., Prince of Antioch, the handsomest man among the soldiers of the Cross. A Council was held at Beaugency in 1152, March 21, when the marriage with Louis was dissolved on the convenient plea of consanguinity, and in the ensuing May she married Henry.

A disastrous marriage to England and France alike, for by it the kingdom of France was cut off from the ocean, contracted within narrow bounds, and with a stricture on the arteries of commerce. By it, for 300 years, English wealth and English blood were drained away to be squandered on a foreign soil.

[1] Louis IX. was obliged to buy Aigues Mortes as a port on the Mediterranean for his fleet, when in 1244 he resolved on a Crusade.

EARLY FRENCH NAMES

The broken soldiers of fortune from the French possessions of England drifted to our island in quest of offices about the Court, or came in the service of noblemen, to be rewarded by being settled into farms and lodges on English soil. Cooks and scullions, minstrels and porters, chamberlains and jesters, marshals and foresters, trooped from a land devastated and depopulated, to settle down in the green pastures and among the flowering orchards of England.

But the tenure of all the ports of France on the Channel and the Atlantic served to enrich England, by bringing to it the commerce of the mainland, and merchants arrived to display their wares, at first in booths at fairs, then to settle permanently into shops open all the year round.

Thus it came about that into England were introduced foreign designations of officers in Court and manor, as also those of merchants and traders. Thus it is that side by side we have foreign as well as English names, as Seamer and Tailor, Fletcher and Arrowsmith, Seller and Sadler, Porcher and Swineherd.

Undoubtedly, after Hastings, a considerable number of cautious men, who had waited to see what would be the results of William's venture, crossed over from Normandy with offers of assistance to keep down the English. Those who had come across with him were but a handful, so that he and his successors—the Red King and Henry Beauclerk—were ready enough to accept such aid, and secure such services, without inquiring too closely as to why they had not thrown themselves into the arms of the Bastard when he first planned his invasion.

The inflow must have continued with little diminution under the House of Anjou. But the caution must be made not to assume that those arrivals bearing place-names were Sieurs with territorial estates, or even knights. Many took their names from the places where they had been born.

I shall add more concerning this at the close of the chapter; but I will now deal briefly with the French names that have become rooted among us and have been Anglicized. These fall into four categories: those that are personal—

EARLY FRENCH NAMES

names adopted as patronymics; those that are descriptive of an office or a trade; those that are personally descriptive; and, lastly, such as are place-names. The same four categories are found everywhere in Europe.

1. PERSONAL NAMES.—In a good number—perhaps the majority—of cases where a personal name became a family name, it had begun as a Fitz So-and-so. But Fitz was all very well and understandable among the Norman and French speaking nobles and their retainers, but not among the English dwellers on the land; and when an old servant FitzHameln retired to a little farm or a forest lodge, and exchanged his associates from those of the castle for those on the land, he now shed his Fitz, and was known as Hameln. My hind is named *Hamley*, and is doubtless a descendant from such a pensioned-off retainer, who began life as French Monsieur FitzHamelin, and ended it as Master Hamlyn.

Hammond is from Hamon, a Norman form of the Old Norse Hámundr. Hamo Dentatus, "with the Teeth," had a son Hamo de Crevecœur, "the Break-heart." The Haymans of Somerfield, extinct Baronets, claimed descent from the toothed Hamo. Whether they could prove it is another matter, for Heyman or Hayman signifies a parish servant for keeping the cattle from straying over the grass "heamed up" for hay.

Jordan is from the Norman Jourdain, a Christian name adopted after the Crusades had begun, and Crusaders returned with a bottle of Jordan water, wherewith their sons were baptized, and at the same time were called after the river. I had a gardener once of this name—perhaps, judging by it, of Norman descent.

Drew is from the Norman name Drogo, but in some cases, perhaps, from Dreux. Drogo, the Norman who came over with William, was given large estates in Devonshire, where the name remains to this day.

Emery is from Amaury, as also *Merick*. *Oates* is a name made hateful through the iniquities of Titus Oates. The name is from Odo. FitzOdo came over with the Conqueror. Odo is the same as Otho or Otto, and takes as well the form

EARLY FRENCH NAMES

of Eudes. Odo has likewise become *Ody* and *Hood*. Robin Hood is supposed to have been descended from FitzOtes. There was a family named *Hody* (from Odo) owning much land in Devon. Just outside the parish of Lew Trenchard is a block of cottages on which was painted up "Little White Spit." On consulting the map, it appeared that at some distance was "Great White Spit." The names were corruptions of Little Hody's Bit and Great Hody's Bit, as those patches of land had belonged to the Hody family.

Mrs. *Bardell* of "Pickwick" fame descended from a Bardolf. *Ours*, the Bear, must have been accepted as a personal name, for there was a *Fitzurse*, one of the murderers of Thomas à Becket. This name has descended to Fitzoor, then *Fyshour*, and to *Fisher*. *Goatcher* is from Gautier, the French form of Walter; *Gwillim* is Guillaume, or William; *Wilmot* is Guillaumot, Little Billy. I had a gardener in Yorkshire called *Jaques*, a French form of James. *Rolle* is from Raoul, the Norman French for Rolf—unless Rolle be a place-name, De Ruelles. *Ingram* is Enguerand. *Fookes* and *Vokes* and *Folkes* are from Folko; *Eustace* and *Stacey* from Eustacy; *Reynald* and *Rennell* are Reynaud or Reginald. Pierre has furnished us with our *Pierces* and *Pearces*. Oger has become *Odger*. *Lias* and *Lyass* come from Elias, not an uncommon name among the Normans. Arnoul has become *Arnold*, and Ivo is *Ivey*. *Raymond* and *Gilbert* we derive from Normandy. *Gerard* remains unaltered. Mauger has been transformed into *Major*. In Georgeham Church, Devon, are the monumental effigies of Sir Mauger de St. Albino and his lady; he is in armour. The villagers say that this is the tomb of Major St. Aubyn and his "missus." Milo has become *Miles*. Perhaps from Guido we have the surname *Giddy*. Alured is turned into *Aldred*. From Thibault come the *Tibbets* and *Tippets*. There is, however, a place named Thiboutot in the Pays de Caux, but this place apparently takes its name from a Thibault. The name *Tibbald* is not uncommon among labourers in the neighbourhood of Colchester. *Willett* is from Guillot, a diminutive of Guillaume, but we have it unaltered as the

EARLY FRENCH NAMES

name of one of the first manufacturers of steel pens. *Aubrey* is the English of Alberic; François has given us *Francis* and *Franks*; and Walkelin has supplied us with *Wakling*.

2. OFFICIAL AND TRADE NAMES.—These have been largely dealt with in preceding chapters, and need not here delay us and demand repetition.

There are, however, a few that have not been included in them that may receive notice here. *Wade* and *Wayte* may come from Guet as well as from a ford,[1] or be employed for a watchman; and *Way* may come from *gué*, a ford. *Baynes* and *Baines* may be a name given to a man in charge of a bath, or it may come from one of the French places named Bagnes. The Baines family has adopted canting arms—crossbones—but this is a mistaken derivation. Over the cemetery entrance in a certain place was inscribed in large letters, " De mortuis nil nisi bonum." A father walking that way with his son, fresh from college, asked him the meaning of the sentence. " Oh," answered the youth, " Of the dead nothing remains but bones."

It is interesting to note side by side men of different nationalities pursuing the same trade, yet called by different names, as though the Normans had employed men of their nationality, and the English had given their custom to men of their own. *Norris* is sometimes from *nourice*, nurse. Lord Norris was unquestionably descended from Richard de Norreys, the favourite cook of Eleanor de Provence, wife of Henry III. But he may have been the son of a nurse. And beside the French *Norris* we have also the English surname *Nourse*. Salt-workers employed by the Norman French were Sauniers—whence the surname *Sawner*—whereas the English got the condiment from native *Salters*.

It would appear as if in some instances the Normans brought their serfs over with them, perhaps for the nonce to serve as fighting men, and then rewarded them with a farm, and they retained the designation of the office they held in Normandy. So can one explain the presence among us of *Porchers*: a swineherd would be a Swineherd to the English

---
[1] William atte Wayte was Vicar of Shebbeare, 1356.

EARLY FRENCH NAMES

villagers; set down in their midst as a small farmer, called by his fellow-Normans "Jean le Porcher," he would acquire among the natives the name of Jan Porcher.

To what a large extent the foreigner must have usurped the higher branches of trade and commerce may be seen by the introduction of the word and name of *Merchant*, and the sinking of that of *Monger*. It is only the ironmonger, and the costermonger who hawks his wares from door to door, and the fishmonger, and a few other smaller tradesmen, who retain the good old Saxon designation. All the higher class of tradesmen, in deeds and in registers, write themselves "merchants." The greatest term of contempt that can be given to a dog is that it is a mongrel—a small tradesman, a half-breed.

3. PERSONALLY DESCRIPTIVE NAMES.—These can have been accepted by the family only if complimentary, or because misunderstood, when an old foreign retainer or man-at-arms went to end his days in the village among farmers and villeins, talking to them in broken English. They had heard him spoken of at the hall as Phillipot, or as Fouille-au-pot. It mattered nothing to them whether he were called by his fellow Frenchmen Little Phil, or the scullion, and they called him and his family *Philpotts*. From the same source we have *Willard*, or *gueulard*, a brawler; *Mordaunt*, one biting or sarcastic; *Mutton*, a sheep; *Patey*, from *pateux*, an adhesive person—one such as was Benedict, according to Beatrice: "He will hang upon him like a disease; he is sooner caught than the pestilence, and the taker presently runs mad." *Prouse*, or *Prouze*, from *preux*, chivalrous; *Sale*, dirty;[1] *Capron* and *Capern*, one wearing a short cloak. An old servant who had set up a tavern outside a town called it his "Guinguette," and thence obtained the surname of *Wingate*.

Hachet is either the man with the little axe, or else the name comes from a residence near a wicket-gate. Le Neveu became Le Neave, and then *Neave*. Le Beaufils was shortened

[1] But the surname *Sayles* may signify one living by the *sayles*, or palisading, of a park: Robert à la Sale, 1273, Hundred Rolls.

EARLY FRENCH NAMES

into *Buffets*. *Timble* was the name acquired by the Frenchman who played on the timbal, the kettledrum. *Grice* is from Le Gris, the Grey-haired — unless from *griis*, a pig. *Rouse* is from Le Roux, and *Morell* from a dusky complexion. *Grant* is from Le Grand, and *Petty* from Le Petit. *Trist* is from *triste*, and, on the other hand, *Joyce* from Le Joyeux. *Douce* may be significative of a gentle disposition, but may also signify a Dutch ancestry. A man in my parish who picks up a small livelihood by going round on Saturday, selling penny papers, is surnamed *Curtis*, Le Courtois; and I knew a little farmer named *Poley*, from Le Polis, the polished and refined. A *Fyers* comes from Le Fier, and *Gent* from Le Gentil.

The trees meet us in double form—English and French—in our surnames. We have the Norman *Fail*, or *Fayle*, and the English *Beech*; also *Frein* and *Freyne*, the name coming mediately through Fresne in Calvados. I had a cook once called Freyne; this signifies an *ash*. The hazel-tree we encounter in *Coudray*, the name of a place in Calvados, and also in Kent. *Tallis*, our English composer, took his name from Taillis in Seine-Inférieure, that means underwood. *Wood* is with us as *Boys*, and the Norman-French *Bosc* is recognizable in our family name *Busk*. But we have also *Tallboys*, or woodcutter.

Names expressive of deformity are to be accepted with great hesitation, and only to be explained as above stated, on the assumption that their meaning was not understood by the English. *Chase* may in some instances come from *chassieux*, blear-eyed; but *Cammoys* did come from *cammus*, flat-nosed, and *Courteney* from short nose. *Peggotty*, of "David Copperfield" fame, unquestionably is the Norman-French *picoté*, smallpox-marked. *Comper* may derive from Compère; *Benbow* has no relation to archery — it is a rendering of *bambouche*, a puppet. *Bunyan* has been erroneously deduced from Bon-Jean—it is really Ap-Einion; and *Mytton* in like manner has been derived from *miton*, a spoiled child, whereas it is from Mitton (Mid(de)-Town) in Yorkshire.

4. PLACE-NAMES.—By far the most numerous French

EARLY FRENCH NAMES

names taken into our family nomenclature come from places in Normandy or other portions of the possessions of the Anjou dynasty. A good number of these has been given in the chapter on the Roll of Battle Abbey; but I add some others here, without pretending to give an exhaustive list:

AGNEW does not necessarily come from *agneau*, a lamb, but may also be a place-name, Agneaux, in the department of Manche.

AINGER is Angers, capital of Maine-et-Loire.

ANWYLL, a name now found in Wales, is derived from Anseville.

ARCH, the name of a peasant agitator in Essex, is from Arques in Seine-Inférieure; but there are several other localities of that name.

AVERY is from Evreux.

BARBEY, from Barbey, in Seine-et-Marne.

BARWISE, from Barvaix.

BATTEN and BEATON derive from Bethune in Pas-de-Calais; and BAVE, from Bavey, in the department of Nord.

BAVENT is from a place of that name near Caen.

BARWELL is from Berville in Eure.

BEAVER is not from the beast, but from Beauvoir; and BELCHER from Bellecourt.

Some of the BEARDS do not take their name from "valour's excrement," as Bassanio called it, but from Les Biards, or Biard, as it was formerly, in the arrondissement of Mortaine, near Joigny, the fief of the Avenels.

"Des Biars i fu Avenals,"

says Wace. The Avenels joined the Conqueror with a contingent of lusty men, and doubtless planted some of them in farms and homesteads about their castle at the Peak, and on other lands in their possession. Such would not call themselves Avenels, but Biards, after the place whence they came, and thence *Beards*.

BELLCHAMBERS is from Belencombre, near Dieppe.

BLOMFIELD is from Blonville, near Pont l'Evêque.

BELLASIS is from a place so called near Coulommières.

EARLY FRENCH NAMES

BISSET is from Bissey in Côte-d'Or; and BOFFIN from Bouvignes on the Meuse, nearly over against Dinant, an ancient town commanded by a stately castle.

BLOYE is deducible from Blois.

BONVILL, from Bonneville, near Rouen.

BOOSEY, the music publisher, derives his name from Boussey in Côte-d'Or.

BONNEY, from Bony, near Peronne.

BOSWELL derives from Bosville, in Seine-Inférieure.

BOUTELL, the name of an authority on brasses and on heraldry, has naught to do with bottles, but derives from Boutailles in Dordogne. A migrant during the Hundred Years' War and the Plantagenet possession of Guienne.

BOVEY, when not from Bovey in Devon, is from Bouffay in Eure.

BRAINE may derive from Brain in Côte-d'Or, or from Braine in Oise.

BREWER does not necessarily imply that the ancestor of the Brewers was one who brewed a peck of malt, for it comes from Bruyères in Seine-et-Oise.

BRUDENELL hails from one of the many Brettignolles. One is in Maine.

Although the London BUCKETS came from a German of Heidelberg early in the seventeenth century, whose son became an Alderman of London in 1634, all earlier Buckets deduce their name from Buquet, near St. Malo.

BURDETT is from Bourdet.

BURT is from Bourth in Eure.

Mr. Hall CAINE, the novelist, derives his name remotely from Cahaignes, in the department of Eure; and CAMMIDGE is the same as *Gamidge*, from Gamaches in Somme.

CANN is from Caen; and CHAFFERS, the great authority on hall-marks for plate and on china, draws his name from Caffiers in Pas-de-Calais.

CHAMLEY is Chamilly, Saône-et-Loire; and CHANTRELL is Chanterelle in Cantal.

CAUSE is from the Pays de Caux.

CARRINGTON drew his name from Charenton, in the

EARLY FRENCH NAMES

department of Seine; and CAYLEY from Cailly in Seine-Inférieure.

CHAWNEY is from Chauny, on the Oise; and CHAWNES from Chaulnes.

CHERWELL, from Carville.

CHESNEY, from Chesnais; a widely-spread name.

CHEYNELL is from Quesnel; and CHURCHILL perhaps in some instances may be an anglicizing of Courcelle in Seine-et-Oise.

CLAVELL is from Claville, near Evreux; and CONDY, that supplies a name to the disinfecting fluid, permanganate of potash, as well as CUNDY, come from Condé, in Somme, Eure, and other departments. We cannot count the patentee of Condy's Fluid as a descendant of the great Condé, only as partaking with him in a place-name.

CONQUEST is from Conques in Aveyron—a most interesting place, with a church treasure of almost unsurpassed value, happily saved during the Revolution. English authority extended over this part of the South of France fitfully and disputedly, and the Conquest who came to England must have been one who had thrown in his lot with the losing side.

Sir Roger de COVERLEY's ancestor came from Coveliers.

The CRESSYS and CREASYS deduce from Creçy, the scene of the great victory of Henry V.

A good old nurse, one of the faithful of the past generation, was a CROCKET of ancient Norman extraction, doubtless from Criquetot in Normandy.

CROLEY is from Creuilly.

CUFF and COFFEE, from Coiffy, in Haute Marne.

CUSTANCE, from Coûtances. The Bishop of that see came to England with the Conqueror. Godfrid was his name, and he was richly rewarded with manors. He plundered his estates in England to obtain the money wherewith to build the glorious cathedral of Coûtances. Doubtless the *Custance* family derives from some retainer of the Bishop who remained in England looking after his interests, but certainly not those of his tenants and villeins.

EARLY FRENCH NAMES

DAMPIERRE is a place-name in Seine-Inférieure.

DAVERS is De Havre.

DARK is from D'Arques in Normandy. I know a labouring man so named.

DIMOND derives from Dimont in Nord; and DINHAM from Dinan.

DIPROSE is from De Préaux.

DOMVILLE is from Donville in Manche.

DAY and TOYE, from Douay; and DRUCE, from Dreux.

DUCIE is from Duçy, near Avranches.

DUDNEY may be Dieudonné (the "gift of God") or a place-name in Oise.

DUFFY is D'Auffai.[1]

Dame DURDON, who kept three serving-men, was of Norman ancestry, from Dourdan in Seine-et-Oise. I have a tenant of the name in a cottage, a labouring man.[2]

EVILL is from Yville in Normandy. At first the name was D'Eville, but the *d* was dropped because Devil was the inevitable corruption. Indeed, even then the name did not escape. My uncle had a white-haired curate of the name of Evill, but he went throughout the neighbourhood by the name of "the Old Devil," though a more innocent and gentle soul did not exist.

EYRE is a place-name in Normandy.

FANCOURT is a corruption of Vandelicourt.

FILBERT or FILLBIRD is St. Philibert in Calvados.

FOULGER is from Fougères in Ille-et-Vilaine.

FOLLETT may not be from Folliott, but be a place-name—De Veulette.

FOWELL deduces from Fauvel or Vauvelle in Normandy.

FURSE is the De Forz in some copies of the Battle Abbey Roll, and it occurs in Domesday as Fursa; but it is doubtful if it be a Norman name, and not Saxon. A tenant of one of my farms bore this appellation.

---

[1] Ordericus gives an account of this family (vi. 8).

[2] There is, however, a Dearden near Edenfield, in Lancashire. But Durdon was the famous fortress of the Duke of Ardennes, according to the medieval romance of the Seven Sons of Aymon.

EARLY FRENCH NAMES

GAYLORD is from Château Galliard, on the Seine.

GILBEY, the great wine-merchant, whose crest—a dragon issuing from a tower—is on every bottle he sells, may derive from Quillebœuf in Normandy. There is, however, a Kilby in Leicestershire; and in the Oxford University Register for 1571 is the entry of Richard Gilbye or Kelby of Lincolnshire.

GOAD and GOOD are from Goude; and GORMAN, when not from the Norse Gormundr, is from Gourmont, and this is the more probable as it is a name still widespread in Normandy. Gorman was the name of a policeman in my district in Devon.

GOSLING is Joscelin in Brittany.

GUINNESS, the brewer, derives his name from Guines, near Calais.

HANSOM, the inventor of the cab that takes his name, derives his from Anceaumville in Seine-Inférieure; and HERRICK, the poet, could look back to an ancestor from Heric in Loire-Inférieure.

HOLMES is not always descriptive of one living on a low island, but comes from La Houlme in Seine-Inférieure.

INGHAM might be supposed to be the *ham* or *hame* on the *ing* or *eng*, a field by a river-side. It is not this, however, but is the anglicized form of Engaine; and IVORY derives from Ivry. I remember a baker of that name. Rudolf d'Ivry the uncle of Duke Richard the Good, was the son of a miller who had complaisantly married the cast-off mistress of Duke William Longsword. "No Princes were more lax as to marriage than the Norman Dukes. Both William Longsword and Richard the Fearless were the offspring of unions which were very doubtful in the eye of the Church; and Richard the Good and other children of Richard the Fearless were legitimatized only after the marriage of their parents" ("Encyclopædia Britannica"). So the Ivry family rose from a mill to great splendour and rank, and now is represented by a baker.

JOBLING is from Jublains in Mayenne.

KISSACK and CUSSACK, from Quissac in Lot—arrivals and

EARLY FRENCH NAMES

settlers in England when our arms were being driven out of the South of France. There the petty nobles and knights passed from one side to another without scruple, according to the pay offered, or to the chance of plunder, or to revenge a slight. Some, who had too deeply compromised themselves on the English side, were obliged to abandon their paternal acres and castles built in and out of the limestone rocks, and take ship at Bordeaux and retire to England. The condition of misery in which the people were during the Hundred Years War cannot be realized by those who have not visited the Causses, and seen how the unhappy peasants were constrained to make their houses on the face of a precipice, and at night haul up their cattle to their rock fastnesses.[1]

KNOWLES, if not the short of OLIVER, may be from Noailles.

The names of LILLEY, LYALL, and LISLE, come from Lille, in the department of Nord.

LINE and LYNE are from Luynes in Indre-et-Loire; and LINTOTT from a place of that name in Seine-Inférieure.

LONGFELLOW, the poet, derives a mutilated name from Longueville in Calvados; and LONGSHANKS is a barbarous alteration of Longchamps, in the department of Seine. As I have said before, it by no means follows that all those who bear a place-name had lands and a castle in that place. The De Longchamps were a great baronial race; but William de Longchamps, the Chancellor of Cœur de Lion, did not pertain to it. He and his brother, the Sheriff of York, Norfolk, and Suffolk, were the grandsons of a serf in the Diocese of Beauvais. William, who was Bishop of Ely, bought the chancellorship of Richard for 3,000 marks. "And had he continued in office," said his enemies, "the kingdom would have been wholly exhausted—not a girdle would have remained to the man, nor a bracelet to the woman, nor a gem to a Jew." At his fall he was obliged to make his escape in the disguise of a woman.

LOWRY is from Lowry in Loiret.

MAGNAC, from a place of that name in Haute Vienne.

MAGNAY and MAGNAL, whose dreadful and useless ques-

[1] See my "Deserts of Central France" for these rock refuges.

EARLY FRENCH NAMES

tions were the plague of one's childhood, came from Magny in Calvados.

MAINWARING is from Mont Guerin, and MATCHAM from Muschamp in Normandy.

MANWELL, from Mandeville in Calvados, which gave its name to the great traveller Sir John.

MANSELL is from Le Mans. Wace tells us that many of these went to help in the invasion of England. The existing family, however, derives from John Mansell, in the reign of King Henry III. He was one of the grossest pluralists known in England, for he held 700 livings at one and the same time. He was also Provost of Beverley, Treasurer of York, Chief Justice of England, one of the Privy Council, Chaplain to the King, and his Ambassador to Spain. He had a wife, an heiress (Joan de Beauchamp, daughter of Simon, Baron of Bedford), and left a son (Sir Thomas Mansell), who was a banneret. He feasted at his house at Tothill two Kings and their Queens, with their dependents, and 700 messes of meat scarce served for the first dinner. A Sir Thomas Mansell, a lineal descendant, was created Lord Mansell by Queen Anne in 1711.

MANT also is from Mantes or from Le Mans.

MARVELL is from Merville, near Caen. Andrew Marvell, the poet, must have derived thence.

MAUDE is drawn from Monthaut, a hill in Flintshire on which Robert de la Mare built a castle, now called Mola. But the name has been supposed to derive from Le Mauduit, the excommunicated or accursed one, who came over with the Conqueror.

MAIRE and MAYOR are not necessarily names derived from office, but may come from La Mare.

MAYBRICK derives from Makebranche, that was altered first into Malebrank and then into Maybrick.

MERRIT, and the commoner name MERRY, are due to Merey in Eure; and Sir Thomas MALLORY, who wrote his delightful "Morte d'Arthur" that was printed by Caxton, drew his name from Meilleray in Seine-et-Marne probably, but the name is found in other departments as well.

EARLY FRENCH NAMES

All MILLERS do not necessarily come from the mill, for there was a Norman family De Meslières. A William de Meslières witnessed Richard Builli's foundation charter of Roche Abbey, Yorkshire, in 1146, as well as that of Boxgrove in Sussex.

MONEY is a corruption of De Mauny. Sir Walter Manny or Mauny, afterwards Lord de Manny, and founder of the Charterhouse, was one of the ablest of the soldiers of fortune under Edward III. His father was Jean le Borgne, or the One-Eyed, Lord of Mauny, near Valenciennes, who was killed in a private quarrel in the English camp before La Reole, on the Garonne, in 1327. Walter came to England in the train of Queen Philippa, who made him one of her Esquires, and he was given the governorship of Merioneth, and the keepership of Harlech Castle. He married Margaret, daughter and heiress of Thomas of Brotherton, second son of Edward I., but his only son fell down a well and was drowned in his father's lifetime. He had but one legitimate daughter, who married John Hastings, Earl of Pembroke; but he had two others that were illegitimate, of whom he cannot have been proud, as he gave them the names, the one of Maloisel (a bad bird) and the other of Malpesant (disagreeable). The English Moneys consequently cannot derive from Walter de Manny, but almost surely from some of his attendants, natives of Mauny, who followed him in war and were settled by him on his estates in England. He died in January, 1372.

MOON or MOHUN is from Moyon in Manche.

Some of our MONDAYS and MUNDYS may derive from Mondaye in Calvados, and not from the first day of the week.

MORTICE, from Mortaise in Calvados.

MOTT is from La Motte, a very common name of place and of family in France.

MULLINS is Des Moulins.

NEVILL and NEWELL are from Neville in Manche, and NOEL from Noailles in Oise.

NEWERS and NOYES are derived from Noyers in Eure, and NUGENT from Nogent in Seine.

EARLY FRENCH NAMES

OTLEY is from Otteville. In "Testa de Neville" the name is spelt Ottele.

PEROWNE is from Peronne, in the department of Nord. Poor, humble-minded Tom PINCH may have had a Norman ancestry and come from Penchard in Seine-et-Marne, whence certainly came the PINCHARDS.

PINKERTON is from Pontchardon.

PINKNEY, from Piquigny, near Amiens, and PLACE and PLAICE from either Plaçy in Calvados or Plaçe in Mayenne.

The not very beautiful name of PUDSEY comes from Puisay, in the Orléanois. This place gave its name to one of the chief nobles of France, Everard de Puisay, whose daughter Adelais was the second wife of Roger de Montgomery, Earl of Shrewsbury. She came to England in 1083. During her voyage she was overtaken by a storm, and all despaired of reaching land. However, a priest had a dream in which the Magdalen appeared to him and bade him tell Adelais to build a church in her honour at the spot where she should meet her husband for the first time, and where grew a hollow oak beside a pig-sty. The Countess, obedient to the vision, on reaching the spot vowed to build a church, which is Quatford in Shropshire. Hugh de Pudsey was elected Prince-Bishop of Durham in 1153, when he was Treasurer of York. He had three bastards: Henry became a soldier, Burchard was made Archdeacon of Durham, and Hugh was created Count of Bar-sur-Seine. It is probably from the eldest Henry that the Pudseys of Durham have descended, unless the Archdeacon followed his father's example. They remained in the palatinate till the seventeenth century, and then spread over Yorkshire. I have known Pudseys who kept a lodging-house.

The PUSEYS probably took their name from Peise or Pesci, the manor held by them, and named in Domesday.

The PLUNKET family draws its name from Plonquenet, near Rennes.

Ralph PINEL in 1086 held a barony in Essex and Sussex.

EARLY FRENCH NAMES

The name came from Normandy, where remained for long branches of the family, and gave the name of Le Bois-Pinel to a place near Rennes. There were three Seigneuries of the name in the Cotentin. In England we recognize the name as *Pennell*, unless we derive this from its more probable source, Paganel.

PENLEE, that sounds like a combination of Welsh and Saxon, is no such thing; it comes from Penly, between Tréport and Dieppe.

POYSEY is from Poissy in Seine-et-Oise.

PUNSHON and PUNCHEON come from Ponchon in Oise.

PURSEY, a distinct name from Percy, is from Pourçy in Marne.

RAW is Réau, Seine-et-Marne.

RAYNES is from Rennes.

REVELL, from Réville in Manche.

RICHFIELD, from Richeville in Eure.

RICKETTS from Ricquier.

ROMILLY is in Normandy.

ROMER is Romare.

ROSCOE, from Roscoff in Brittany.

ROWE is De Rohaut. The four sons of Rohaut, a Breton noble living in 1000, accompanied the Conqueror to England, and one of these, Ruald FitzRohaut, held three lordships *in capite* in Devon in 1086. His son Ruald, or Rohaut, was father of Alan FitzRohaut, who married Lady Alicia de Dodbrooke, and acquired additional estates by her in Devon. The Rowes or Rohauts have remained to this day in Devon. One branch at Staverton is extinct, but the other at Lamerton, near Tavistock, flourishes.

ROYE, from a town in Somme.

RUGGLES is from Rugles in Eure.

RULE, from Ruelle in Seine-et-Oise.

RUMBELOW and RUMBOLD are from Rambouillet in Seine-et-Oise.

SACE, from Sassey, in Calvados, or Sace in Mayenne.

SCOFIELD and SHOVELL are all English forms of Escoville in Calvados.

EARLY FRENCH NAMES

SEELEY may possibly hail from Sillé in Sarthe.
SERVICE is from St. Servais in Côtes du Nord.
SHAND, SHANDY, and CHANDOS, from Chandai in Orne.
STUTFIELD is Estoteville in Seine-Inférieure.
SUMMERFIELD and SUMMERVALE derive from Somerville, now Sommervieux, near Caen. Roger de Somerville was summoned to Parliament as a Baron, and died in 1327. Roger's son was the Sir Philip to whom John of Gaunt granted an estate on condition that he should keep a flitch of bacon hanging in his hall at Wichnor at all times of the year except in Lent, to be given to any man who could take oath that he had not repented after having been married a year and a day, and could bring with him a couple of witnesses to confirm his words. "Of the few that have ventured to claim the prize, three couple only have obtained it, one of which, having quarrelled about the mode of preserving it, were adjudged to return it. The other two couples were a sea-officer and his wife, who had not seen each other from the day of their marriage till they met in Wichnor Hall; and a simple couple in the neighbourhood, the husband a good-tempered man and the wife dumb." So little prospect is there of the flitch being claimed that it is now made of wood and hung up in the lodge.

STAPLES, from Estaples.
TEALE is Le Thél in Seine-Inférieure.
Mr. TOOTS, of "Dombey and Son" notoriety, derived his name from Tôtes. Look at his picture by Phiz, and think of him as a descendant of a Norman man-at-arms.
TORRENS comes from a citizen of Torigny in Manche.
TOWERS is an anglicizing of Thouars.
TRAVERS comes from Tévières, between Bayeux and Caen. In the days of the Conqueror, Robert de Travers, or D'Estrivers, Baron of Burgh-upon-Sands, married the daughter of Randulf de Meschines, Lord of Cumberland. He became hereditary forester of Inglewood. "The badge of his office—the jagged branch—is over and over again introduced in the chapel of Naworth Castle, which is so rich with arms and cognizances; and where this jagged branch is, in

EARLY FRENCH NAMES

some places, even thrown across the Dacre's arms fesswise. The forestship of Inglewood was so honourable, and gave so great command, that there is no wonder that the family should wish by every means to set forth their claim to it" (Hutchinson's "Cumberland").

TWOPENNY, perhaps, comes from Tupigny in Flanders.

TURNEY, from Tournai in Orne, or in Belgium.

UDALL is from Oudalle in Seine-Inférieure.

VARVILL and FARWELL and FAREWELL, even FARFIELD, are all from Varaville in Calvados.

VERDON and VERDANT derive from Verdon in Meuse.

VERE, from Verin, in Calvados, or another Ver in Manche.

VERNEY is from Vernai, near Bayeux.

VILLIERS is the name of a place in Manche.

VILLEDIEU has given us the surname *Filldew* or *Pilldew*.

VIZARD is from Visart.

WYLIE is no crafty rogue, but deduces from Vesli.

WORNALL comes from Verneuil.

WYON is from Vian; spelled *Wiun*, as one holding lands in Lincoln in the twelfth century.

VAWDRY is from a place of that name in Calvados.

VOWLES and VOALES is from Veules in Seine-Inférieure, and WATERFIELD very probably from Vatierville, in the same department.

I have left to the last all the corruptions of names of saints. SIMBARBE is Ste. Barbe. SACHEVEREL comes from St. Cheverol. SLODGER is St. Ledger. SLOW is St. Lô; in Latin *Laudus*, that gives us the surname of the Archbishop, *Laud*. SMART comes from Ste. Marte or Martha. STOMER, from St. Omer. SIMPER, from St. Pierre. SIMPOLE, from St. Pol de Léon. SAVILLE, from St. Ville or Vitalis.

If we want nowadays to find the descendants of the Normans, even of those who held vast baronies under the Conqueror and his successors, we look in vain into the modern peerage; only here and there do we find them in

EARLY FRENCH NAMES

Burke's "Landed Gentry." For the most part the representatives of the conquering Normans are found in the lower walks of life, among labourers and artisans, or, at best, among tradesmen. Here and there, indeed, among the titled of the land we may find an ancient Norman name, but it is assumed, either on the grounds of a doubtful pedigree or of a descent in broken falls through the spindle. How great families may decline I will show by a few instances.

I will begin with a notable family — that of the *Grenvilles* of Stowe, whence came the great Sir Bevil and Sir Richard. One branch so sank—and that in the very parish wherein was the splendid mansion of the Grenvilles—that two of them were in receipt of parish relief, and one of them was twice pricked for High Sheriff whilst a pauper.

The *Glanvilles* were of Norman descent. A branch settled near Tavistock and became tanners. From the tanpits rose one who became a great Elizabethan Judge, and built a noble mansion at Kilworthy. One of the last of the Glanvilles was huntsman to Squire Kelly of Kelly, and another was a ferryman at Saltash, whose wife Anne was a famous rower, and was one of the crew of women who beat the French boatmen in a race at Havre in 1850. Anne was stroke. The women were dressed in black skirts, long white bedgowns, and nightcaps. One of them—Mrs. House—was so elated at the victory that on reaching the committee-boat she plunged into the water, dived under the vessel, and came up with dripping and drooping nightcap on the opposite side. The Glanvilles declined in station, and with the declension the name became degraded to Gloyne. In the Sourton parish registers is the entry of the death of Matthew Glanville, *alias* Gloyne—February 24, 1777.

There was not a prouder name amongst those who came over with the Conqueror than the *De Pomeroys*. The family issued from La Pomeraye in Normandy, and a fragment of their stronghold remains at Cinglais, not far from Falaise. Here was the original *pommerai*, or orchard, that gave its name to the place and family. Ralph de Pomeraye is mentioned in Domesday as holding sixty manors *in capite*,

EARLY FRENCH NAMES

all but two in Devonshire, where Berry Pomeroy became the seat of the barony. Ralph built the castle whose ruins now tower above the woods that clothe the hill it crowns. Henry de Pomeroy, unhappily for himself, took sides with John during the absence of Cœur de Lion, and garrisoned St. Michael's Mount for John. But soon arrived the news of the enlargement of Richard from prison, and the story goes, as Fuller relates, "that a sergeant-at-arms of the King's came to the castle of Berry Pomeroy, and there received kind entertainment for certain days together, and at his departure was gratified with a liberal reward. In counterchange whereof he then, and no sooner, revealing his long-concealed errand, flatly arrested his host, to make his immediate appearance before the King, to answer a capital crime. Which unexpected and ill-carried message the gentleman took in such despight that with his dagger he stabbed the messenger to the heart. Then, despairing of pardon in so superlative an offence, he abandoned his house and gat himself to his sister, then abiding in the Island of Mount Michael in Cornwall. Next he bequeathed a large portion of his land to the religious people dwelling there, to pray for the redeeming of his soul; and, lastly (that the remainder of his estate might descend to his heirs), he caused himself to be let bleed to death."

But the misfortunes of the De Pomeroys did not end here. In the reign of Edward VI. Sir Thomas Pomeroy wrought the utter downfall of his family by engaging in the Devonshire rebellion of 1549 against the violent changes in religion. He was involved in ruin. His life indeed was spared, but that was all; the grasping hand of the Seymours was laid on his estate, and his beautiful and noble mansion of Berry passed away from the family for ever.

And now where are the Pomeroys? Our school committee paid five shillings to a Mrs. Pomeroy to clean out the schoolroom, and as I write I have before me a bill for a suit of clothes from Pomeroye, tailor, at Tavistock.[1]

[1] I quote the following from the *Daily Express*, February 23, 1909: "*Paris, February* 22.—The Countess de la Pomière was found dying in a

EARLY FRENCH NAMES

No more splendid family existed in England of the Norman invaders and conquerors than that of the *De Toeni*. Raoul of that family bore at Hastings the consecrated banner that the Pope had sent to William with his blessing to consecrate the wicked invasion. It was a race that mixed its blood with the Plantagenets. They became Earls of Stafford and Dukes of Buckingham. Henry, the second Duke, " made his boast that he had as many liveries of Stafford knots as Richard Nevill, the late great Earl of Warwick, had of ragged staves." He, as may be remembered, was executed at Salisbury in 1483. His son Edward was restored by Henry VIII. to the dukedom and other honours, and was appointed Lord High Constable of England; but he also was to end his life on the scaffold. He had quarrelled with Wolsey. It is said that at a great Court ceremonial, when the Duke was holding a basin to the King, no sooner had His Majesty washed than Wolsey dipped his own hands into the water, and Buckingham, stung at this indignity, "flung the contents of the ewer into the Churchman's shoes." Wolsey swore to be revenged, and how he accomplished his end may be read in Shakespeare's "Henry VIII." With the fall of his head under the axe in 1522 the princely house of Stafford fell to rise no more. His only son, stripped of lands and dignities alike, received back but a scanty portion of the splendid possessions of his family, and was allowed the title of Baron. Edward, fourth Lord Stafford, married his mother's chambermaid, and was succeeded by his grandson Henry, with whom the direct line terminated in 1637; and the claim of the last remaining heir, Roger, was rejected by the House of Lords on account of his

---

miserable garret in Senlis this morning. She had not been seen for some days, and when the neighbours forced their way into her room they found her calling feebly for help. She was lying on a heap of straw in the middle of the room, fighting as well as she could with rats for a crust of bread and a piece of cheese, which she clutched to her breast. Lying all about the floor of the room were bank-notes, bonds, and shares worth more than £6,000. The rats had eaten away portions of the paper. The Countess has been taken to a home at Clermont, but there is little hope of her recovery."

EARLY FRENCH NAMES

extreme poverty. The unfortunate man, *de jure* Lord Stafford, the great-grandson of the last Duke, was then aged sixty-five, and had sunk into so abject a condition that, ashamed to bear his true name, he called himself Floyd, after one of his uncle's servants who had brought him up and been kind to him. He was compelled to surrender his claim to the barony into the hands of Charles I., and died in 1640, unmarried. His only sister, Jane, married a joiner, and had a son who earned a livelihood as a cobbler in 1637 at Newport in Shropshire. As Banks says: "The most zealous advocate for equality must surely here be highly gratified when he is told that the great-granddaughter of Margaret, daughter and heir of George, Duke of Clarence, brother to King Edward IV., was the wife of a common joiner, and her son the *mender of old shoes*."

The *Conyers* were one of the noblest families in the North of England. Roger Conyers was made Constable of Durham Castle by William the Conqueror. Surtees enumerates all the defunct families that had sprung from the parent stock—viz., "Conyers of Hornby Castle, whose peerage is vested by heirs-general in the Duke of Leeds; Conyers of Bowlby, Danby-Wiske, Hutton-Wiske, Thormandby, Pinchinthorpe, Marshe, and High Dinsdale, in Yorkshire; Wynyard, Layton, Horden, Coltham, Conyers, in Co. Durham; and Hopper in Northumberland." The Duchess of Cleveland says: "One by one, some later and some earlier, each of the remaining branches of this famous house had died out. The fair domain of Stockburn went with the heiress of William Conyers to Francis Talbot, eleventh Earl of Shrewsbury, in 1635, and passed through their daughter to the Stonors. Coatham-Conyers, first brought by Scolastica de Coatham in the time of Edward I., was forfeited by Roger Conyers, who joined the rising of the Northern Earls in 1569. Wynyard had been transferred to the Claxtons in the previous century. The line of Layton ended in 1748. Hutton passed to the Mallorys, and Danby to the Scropes, who now hold it. Their possessions dwindled and disappeared year by year. Manor after manor was lost to its

EARLY FRENCH NAMES

ancient lords, estate after estate alienated or carried away by heiresses, till at length they were bereft of all, and in 1810 Surtees found Sir Thomas Conyers, the last of this race, in the workhouse of Chester-le-Street. No other earthly refuge was left him save the pauper's grave. A subscription, proposed by Surtees, and headed by Bishop Barrington, was set on foot to rescue him from his unhappy position, and enough money was raised to remove him to a more fitting abode. The old man only lived, however, a few months afterwards, and with him expired the proud name that had shone in the county annals for the better part of 800 years."

And is this an altogether exceptional case? Has it not been the same thing with many an ancient family that from one cause or another has gone under?

The *Umfravilles* derived from Amfreville, near Evreux. The first of the name who came to England was Robert with the Beard, Lord of Tour and Vian in Normandy, and had a grant from the Conqueror of the barony of Prudhoe. Gilbert III. of Umfraville inherited from his mother, the Countess of Angers, and was created Baron Umfraville by Edward I. in 1295, and Governor of the whole territory of Angers. He was then created Earl of Angers. But the family sank lower and lower, till towards the end of the eighteenth century the last of the baronial race was a chandler in Newcastle-upon-Tyne. He left several daughters and one son, born in 1784, who after the death of the father, were supported by the industry of their mother. The then Duke of Northumberland, whose ancestor had obtained Prudhoe from the Umfravilles, took interest in the lad, then aged fourteen, and provided for him in the navy. He served under Lord Exmouth in the East Indies, eventually rose to the rank of a Captain, retired on half-pay, and died of drink. He still possessed a sword given by Henry V. to his ancestor, which after the death of Mrs. Umfraville was sent to Alnwick Castle.

The Duchess of Cleveland says of the *Vieux-ponts*, or *Viponts*, named by Wace as taking part in the Battle of

EARLY FRENCH NAMES

Hastings, and afterwards advanced to honour : " This great name, like many others presumed to be extinct, has most likely simply merged into obscurity. In 1880 I saw *Vipond* inscribed over the door of a grocer's shop in Middleton in Teesdale, within a dozen miles of the county in which the De Viponts once reigned supreme."

De Vesci was a famous name. It was like the tree in the vision that had its boughs wide extended, and the birds of the air lodged in the branches of it. It stretched into Scotland. It is represented at the present day by Messrs. *Veitch*, the nursery gardeners and seed merchants.

> " Little Miss Muffet
> Sat on a tuffet,
> Eating curds and whey ;
> When by came a spider
> And sat down beside her,
> Which frightened Miss Muffet away."

In Miss *Muffet* we recognize the name, but not the ancestral heroism, of her ancestor, De Maufet or Maufé, who fought at Hastings. Her arms : *Argent*, a lion rampant, *sable*, between nine escallops, *gules*. A lion rampant, and sable, too, and to be frightened by a spider !

Lysons is from Lisons in Calvados.

Memoray is a singular name that appears in Holinshed's list of the warriors who came over with the Conqueror. John de Murmuru was granted half a knight's-fee in Gloucestershire. The family never rose to any distinction. A Brixham fisherman bears the name of *Memory*.

Holinshed includes Totelles among those in the Roll of Battle Abbey. I believe that the *Tootles* of to-day do not occupy a very distinguished place in the social order. At an evening party the butler announced : " Mr. Tootles, Mrs. Tootles, and the two Misses Tootles, too."

Such, the broadside ballad printer, takes his name from Zouche.

Rudeville, now Ruville, is a place near Gisors, and, according to Holinshed's list, a De Rudeville came over with the Conqueror. The name in England became *Rudall*

EARLY FRENCH NAMES

or *Ruddle*. Daniel Defoe published an account of the laying of a ghost by the Rev. Samuel Ruddle, Vicar of Launceston, 1720. He had a family, the living was poor, and his children settled down into humble life in the neighbourhood. A descendant is now a gamekeeper.

There was a worthy carrier between Lew Down and Tavistock, now dead, who could neither read nor write, but never forgot a commission. His name was *Tooke*. Tooke or Touques is a place in the arrondissement of Pont l'Evêque. The Sieur de Touques appeared in the list of those who fought under William the Conqueror. Henry Tooke served Edward I. in his Scottish wars, and obtained from him a grant of lands. Sir Brian *Tuke*, Treasurer under Henry VIII., was one of those drawn by Holbein. "Nicholas *Toke* of Godington, usually called Captain Toke," says Hasted, "Sheriff of Kent in 1663, dying in 1680, was buried in the chancel with his five wives. His portrait, at full length, is in the hall there, and that of Diana, his fifth wife, daughter of the Earl of Winchelsea. There is an anecdote of him in the family, that at the age of ninety-three, having been left a widower, he walked from hence to London to pay his addresses to a sixth wife; but, being taken ill, he presently died. Leaving no male issue by any of his wives, he devised the seat of Godington, with the rest of his estate, to his nephew and heir-at-law, Nicholas Toke of Wye."

Godington Hall is a fine Elizabethan mansion. "In the windows of the staircase are collected all the arms, quarterings, and matches, of the family, in painted glass. The drawing-room upstairs is curiously wainscoted with oak." So in the East of England is a Toke or Tooke estated, with the armorial bearings of his family shining down on his head through the painted glass; and in the West lies, in my churchyard, Tooke or Toke, the illiterate carrier, without a headstone to mark his grave, and he may have been as lineal a descendant of the Sieur de Touques as is the Squire of Godington.

Toustain was the Norman equivalent of the Saxon Tostig. Toustain FitzRou—*i.e.*, son of Rolf—was standard-bearer at

EARLY FRENCH NAMES

Hastings. When Raoul de Conches, to whom this honour belonged by hereditary right, and Walter Giffard, to whom it had been offered, both declined the honour on various excuses, the Duke looked about him for a worthy substitute. "Then," says Wace, "he called to him a knight whom he had heard much praised, Tostan FitzRou le Blanc by name, whose abode was at Bec-en-Caux. To him he delivered the gonfanon; and Tostan accepted it right cheerfully, and bowed low to him in thanks, and bore it gallantly and with a good heart, high aloft in the breeze, and rode by the Duke, going wherever he went. Wherever the Duke turned, he turned also; and wheresoever he stayed his course, there he rested as well. His kindred still have the quittance of all service for their inheritance; on that account they and their heirs are entitled to hold their inheritance for ever."

"For ever," writes Wace, and for ever the grant was made by William the Conqueror. Where now are the acres of the Tostans? Where the descendants of the standard-bearer at Hastings? What has become of the barony, including land in two different counties, granted to the standard-bearer?

The name, if not the blood, remains, and I have little doubt that the blood follows the name made so famous at Hastings. It is now *Dustan*.[1] One of that name is now a coachman, son of the village tailor. He married a dressmaker of the name of *Gerry*, from the adjoining parish. Now, this also is a Norman name, and that also of one that fought at Hastings. He was, indeed, a clerk, and was given a canonry in St. Paul's and lands at Twyford. Either he married and had a considerable family, or his brothers and cousins followed him, as we find the name of *Gueri* or *Gerry* all over the county of Devon in the succeeding reign.

What a palace of delights is *Gamage's* shop to children! What hours of happiness has not Mr. Gamage given to the little ones! Among some copies of the Roll of Battle Abbey occurs the name. If the Sieur did not come over in 1066, he did soon after, drawing his name from the Château de

[1] But another derivation of the name may be *dystain* (Welsh), a steward. *Dustun* (Cornish) is a witness.

EARLY FRENCH NAMES

Gamaches, and his pedigree from Protadius, Mayor of the Palace to Theodoric, King of Orleans, in 604. What peer in his ermine and wearing his coronet can show such an ancestry as the owner of the toy-shop?

William de Valence was a Lusignan, with a water-nymph as ancestress. He was Earl of Pembroke, and half-brother of Henry III. through his mother, Isabella d'Angoulême, widow of King John, who remarried Hugh de Valence or de Lusignan, Count de la Marche. A curse was believed to rest on the family of Aymer de Valence, whose beautiful monument is in Westminster Abbey, because he sat in judgment on his cousin, Thomas of Lancaster, at Pontefract, and condemned him, unheard, to death. His own violent death two years later was held to be a retribution for his "mercenary and time-serving act of infamy." But the fatality did not end with him, for "it was observed that, after that judgment was given, none of the succeeding Earls of Pembroke ever saw his father, nor any father of them took delight in seeing his son."

The name lingered on. A squire of the name had lands in Sennen at the very Land's End. But these lands are gone now, and the last Valence I have met was a small tenant-farmer in an adjoining parish.

I have shown in another chapter that from household domestics, and from those engaged in the forests and in the stables, that also from the booths and workshops of the traders, that even from among the labourers on the land, men have risen to the surface and have flushed our nobility with new and vigorous life. Tailors have cast aside their shears, and ceased to sit cross-legged on the table. Smiths have quitted the bellows and the anvil; coopers have ceased to hammer and tighten the staves of casks; cooks have doffed their white aprons and wiped the gravy from their fingers, to assume the ermine and the coronet. And the butlers have slipped from behind their master's chairs, and the obsequious chamberlains have ceased to cringe, and the forester and the parker to stand, bonnet in hand, and bow before their lords, to step forward and thrust these great

EARLY FRENCH NAMES

seigneurs into the background, and require the namesakes of their lords—probably their descendants in blood—to clean the boots and serve behind the counter, to the great-grandsons of the servants of the haughty possessors of castle and manor.

> " Robert of Sicily, brother of Pope Urbane
> And Valmond, Emperor of Allemaine,
> Apparelled in magnificent attire,
> With retinue of many a knight and squire,
> On St. John's Eve, at vespers, proudly sat,
> And heard the priests chant the Magnificat.
> And as he listened, o'er and o'er again
> Repeated, like a burden or refrain,
> He caught the words ' *Deposuit potentes*
> *De sede, et exaltavit humiles.*'
> And slowly lifting up his kingly head,
> He to a learned clerk beside him said :
> ' What mean these words ?' The clerk made answer meet :
> ' He has put down the mighty from their seat,
> And has exalted them of low degree.'
> Thereat King Robert muttered scornfully :
> "'Tis well that such seditious words are sung
> Only by priests and in the Latin tongue :
> For unto priests and people be it known,
> There is no power can push me from my throne.' "

And so must have thought the great nobles of Norman extraction in the early Middle Ages. But the words of Mary uttered 1,900 years ago proclaimed a great social fact that has prevailed for ever in the world, and ever will prevail. It is a law that the mother impresses on her infant, when she sways it, now to the ceiling, then to the floor, in her hands, and sings :

> " Now we go up, up, up,
> And now we go down, down, down !"

The great human pot must boil, and if it did not do so there would be stagnation :

> " And thus the whirligig of Time brings in his revenges."

CHAPTER XIII

FRENCH NAMES: II. THE HUGUENOT REFUGEES

IT is unnecessary to relate the story of the civil wars of religion in France, and the attempts made by the Crown to crush out Calvinism, that had pervaded the South even more than the North. The refugees from persecution began to come over in the reign of Edward VI., the flow was considerable in that of Elizabeth and of James I., but the great bulk arrived after the Revocation of the Edict of Nantes by Louis XIV. in 1685. The Calvinists—it is a mistake to call them Protestants, for they strongly dissented from the Augsburg Confession, the adherents to which were the true Protestants, and obtained their designation from it —the Calvinists, I say, had obtained liberty from 1577 to build meeting-houses ("temples"). But in 1661 the death of Cardinal Mazarin was the signal for evading the permission hitherto accorded, and between that year and 1673 half their conventicles had been taken from the Huguenots.

They came over in troops. The crypt of Canterbury Cathedral was given up to them for haranguing and psalm-singing; they had places of worship in Austin Friars and Threadneedle Street, London. Before 1685 they had their conventicles in Canterbury, Canvey Island, Colchester, Dover, Faversham, Glastonbury, Ipswich, Maidstone, Norwich, Rye, Sandtoft, Sandwich, Southampton, Stamford, Thetford, Thorne Abbey, Whittlesea, Winchester, Yarmouth; in and after 1685 at Barnstaple, Bideford, Bristol, Chelsea, Dartmouth, Exeter, Greenwich, Hammersmith, Plymouth, Stonehouse, and Thorpe.

Considerable reluctance was felt by the English Govern-

THE HUGUENOT REFUGEES

ment in granting letters of naturalization to these foreigners. It was thought that the great influx of needy strangers would throw many of our own people out of employ. Any Bill to allow them a share of the Englishman's right was unpopular with the City of London, and with all boroughs and corporations; and naturalization was doled out reluctantly to individuals only, by letters patent and by private Acts of Parliament. In 1681 naturalization was accorded to eleven men only and six women, but to as many as thirty-eight with their wives and children in one day, March 21, 1682. A royal bounty was accorded to the refugees, consisting of money raised throughout the kingdom, but these Huguenots speedily settled into trades. There were, however, some persons of quality who were unable or unwilling to work with their hands, and these had to be provided for out of the alms gathered through the land. Large sums had been subscribed in 1681, and in the two or three ensuing years, for it appears that in 1685 there remained a balance of £17,950 undistributed. In 1686 another collection was made, and something like £40,000 was raised.

The funds were faithfully administered. To this, one of the refugees, Misson, bore witness in 1697. He wrote: "The sums of money that have been collected have always been deposited in the hands of four or five noblemen, who have referred the division and administration thereof to a chosen set of men picked out from among the refugees themselves. Nothing can be more laudable than the charity, equity, moderation, compassion, fidelity, and diligence, with which these gentlemen acquit themselves of the employment which their goodness induced them to accept. It is impossible to express the sentiments of acknowledgment, esteem, and love, which all the poor, and all the refugees in general, have in their hearts for these good and pious administrators." In 1696 the House of Commons voted an annual grant of £16,000 for the distressed French Calvinists, of which £14,000 was for the laity and £3,000 for their ministers.

In 1711 Harley and Bolingbroke stopped the annuity.

THE HUGUENOT REFUGEES

They thought—and perhaps thought justly—that these French had received quite enough English money, and had had time to learn to shift for themselves. But on the accession of George I. the payments were resumed, and they continued at the same rate until the death of Sir Robert Walpole. The sum of £1,718 4s. per annum is still paid without diminution to the French pastors in England.

In 1694 a Bill for naturalizing all Protestant strangers came up for a second reading in the House of Commons, but was dropped, so strong a feeling against it was entertained in the country. It was hoped that these immigrants had come to remain for a while only, till the tyranny was overpast, and would then return to their own country; and, in fact, a good many of the refugees entertained the expectation of going back to their old homes.

Sir John Knight, M.P. for Bristol, published an elaborate oration in 1694 relative to the Bill: "That the sergeant be commanded to open the doors, and let us first kick the Bill out of the House, and then foreigners out of the kingdom." One of the reasons given for the introduction of the Bill was that England was in need of husbandmen to till the ground. On this Sir John wrote: "Of the 40,000 French come into England, how many . . . at this time follow the ploughtail? It's my firm opinion, that not only the French, but any other nation this Bill will let in upon us, will never transplant themselves for the benefit of going to the plough. They will contentedly leave the English the sole monopoly of that slavery."

William of Orange, who had a special dislike for the doctrines of the Anglican Church and Episcopal order, encouraged the influx to the utmost, especially of Dutch, who had no need to escape, and he desired to leaven the British population with Calvinism. This the Tory and High Church party resented.

However, a Bill for the Naturalization of Foreign Protestants was brought into the House of Commons on February 14, 1709, and passed on March 23. The qualification was the taking of the usual oaths, and there was also

THE HUGUENOT REFUGEES

a proviso : " That no person shall be naturalized, etc., unless he shall have received the Sacrament in some Protestant or Reformed congregation within the kingdom."

Bishop Burnet says hereon : " An Act passed this session that was much desired, and had been often attempted, but had been laid aside in so many former Parliaments, that there was scarce any hope left to encourage a new attempt. It was for naturalizing all foreign Protestants upon their taking the oaths to the Government, and their receiving the Sacrament in any Protestant church. Those who were against the Act soon perceived that they could have no strength if they should set themselves directly to oppose it, so they studied to limit strangers in the receiving of the Sacrament to the way of the Church of England. This probably would not have hindered many who were otherwise disposed to come among us; for the much greater part of the French came into the way of our Church. But it was thought best to cast the door as wide open as possible for the encouragement of strangers. And therefore, since, upon their first coming over, some might choose the way to which they had been accustomed beyond the sea, it seemed the more inviting method to admit of all who were in any Protestant communion. This was carried in the House of Commons with a great majority. But all those who appeared for this large and comprehensive way were first reproached for their coldness and indifference to the concerns of the Church, and in that I had a large share, as I spoke copiously for it when it was brought up to the Lords. The Bishop of Chester (Sir William Dawes) spoke as zealously against it, for he seemed resolved to distinguish himself as a zealot for that which was called the High Church. The Bill passed with very little opposition."

A good many of the merchants and manufacturers who came over brought their money with them. Those immigrants who were of noble family were younger sons, and fortune-hunters, who looked out for rich widows and heiresses in England, and with their French manners and flattering tongues soon wheedled themselves into their affec-

THE HUGUENOT REFUGEES

tions and married them. On the whole, the refugees did very well in England, and managed to feather their nests comfortably. The pastors did uncommonly well, what with the grants made to them and their chances with amorous and rich widows of citizens; and they took good care to have their sons brought up in the faith of the English Church, so as to qualify them for plump livings and still higher preferments.

The Marquis de Rouvigny was created Earl of Galway by William III. Jean Louis Ligonier was raised to the peerage as a Viscount Ligonier of Enniskillen in 1757, and Earl in 1776; Edward Ligonier was created Earl Ligonier in 1776. He was the son of Francis Ligonier. Lord de Blaquière is descended from a refugee, Jean de Blaquière, who took up his abode in England in 1685. Baron de Tessier comes from a refugee, Jacques, who came to England in 1712 and founded a wealthy merchant-house. Claude Armand was naturalized in 1698. His son George was created a Baronet in 1764. A French refugee named De Bailleu settled in Cambridgeshire before the Revocation, and was the ancestor of Sir John Bayley, Bart., 1834. Another refugee, Boileau, was the ancestor of Sir John Peter Boileau, Bart. Elie Bouhéreau, son of a pastor at La Rochelle, founded the family of Borough, Baronets. De Crespigny is another Baronet of Huguenot ancestry; also Lambert, Baronet; also Larpent; also Pechell. Earl Clancarty is a Trench descended from the Huguenot family of Trenche.[1] The Earl of Radnor is a Bouverie, whose ancestor was Laurent des Bouveries, a silk-manufacturer, who fled to England from French Flanders. Sir John Houblon, Lord Mayor of London in 1695, and a Lord of the Admiralty, was also of Huguenot extraction. In 1689 was naturalized that soldier of fortune, Count Schomberg, whom William III. at once elevated to the English peerage,

---

[1] In the Patent Rolls, March 17, 1715, George I. declares: "We are graciously pleased to allow for and towards the maintenance of the late Countess of Clancarty's children, and for their education in the Protestant religion, the annuity or yearly pension of £1,000."

THE HUGUENOT REFUGEES

with the titles of Baron of Teyes, Earl of Brentford, Marquis of Harwich, and Duke of Schomberg. His son Charles, naturalized in 1691, was created Duke of Leinster, and afterwards succeeded to his father's English dukedom.

Frederick William de Roy, de la Rochefoucauld, who was naturalized in 1694, was created Earl of Lifford. Armand de Liremont, a second son, was given the title of Earl of Faversham by Charles II. Swift says that he was "a very dull old fellow"; and Burnet: "Both his brothers changing their religion, though he continued himself a Protestant, made that his religion was not much trusted to. He was an honest, brave, and good-natured man, but weak to a degree, not easy to be conceived." However, he knew on which side his bread was buttered.

Cavalier, the Camisard, a baker's boy, was given a commission in the British army as Major-General, and made Governor of Jersey. Tassin d'Allonne was made Secretary to Queen Mary, and granted the lands, manors, and lordship, of Pickering, and the manor and lordship of Scalby, for ninety-nine years after the death of the Queen. A good many of the pastors were provided for to serve the refugee congregations in London, Plymouth, Colchester, Norwich, and elsewhere; and with the £200 per annum granted them out of the Royal Bounty Fund, and the money that flowed in from their flock, they were in pretty comfortable circumstances, far better off than they had been in their own land, and infinitely better than many a poor English curate.

Where a pastor could not find a congregation of refugees, he swallowed his scruples, signed the Thirty-nine Articles, submitted to ordination, and was given a cure in England or Ireland, which he had no hesitation in accepting, though unable to speak the language of the people to whom he was supposed to minister. Daniel Lombard was given the rectories of Lanteglos and Advent in Cornwall, with the borough town of Camelford in it, a mile and a half from the parish church, worth at the present day £385 per annum. He rode to take possession of his living, but, being unable to make himself understood when he asked his way, rode on to

THE HUGUENOT REFUGEES

the Land's End, and there had to turn and ride back to the eastern confines of the county. Jacques Abbadie was made Dean of Killaloe, and, not content with that, clamoured for the deanery of St. Patrick's. Charles Bertheau, pastor of the French chapel in Threadneedle Street, left £1,000 to his nephew and £4,000 to the poor. Jacques Pineton de Chambrun was made domestic chaplain to William of Orange, and Canon of Windsor. The pastor Eland Grosteste de la Motte feathered his nest so well in England, that in 1713 he was able to bequeath to his brother-in-law Robethon £1,200, another £1,200 to his brother Jacques, £500 to a godson, and all the rest of his money to his wife. De Montandre was made Master of the Ordnance in Ireland, and Field-Marshal. Josias de Champagne married Lady Jane Forbes, daughter of the Earl of Granard, and his son was given the deanery of Clonmacnois; his grandson became a Lieutenant-General; another grandson, Rector of Twickenham and Canon of Windsor; another became General Sir Josias Champagne. The refugee Jean Crommelin left to his three sons £10,000 apiece. Louis Crommelin became Director of the Royal Linen Manufactory, with a patent, and petitioned for a pension of £500 a year, "having lost his only son, who managed all his affairs," and he would have to pay an assistant to do the work for him.

From the pastor Aufere the family of Aufere of Hoveton and Foulsham Old Hall descends in direct succession. The pastor's second son, George René, had one child Sophia, the ancestress of the Earls of Yarborough. The following notice appeared in the *Scots Magazine*: Died 1st September, 1804, Mrs. Aufere, mother-in-law of Lord Yarborough. By the death of this venerable lady his lordship will come into possession of £50,000 ready money, and one of the finest collections of paintings in this country. The late Sir Joshua Reynolds frequently said that it contained a greater variety of pieces by the first masters of the Italian, Dutch, French, and Flemish schools than any other private collection in England, and estimated it at £200,000. It is

THE HUGUENOT REFUGEES

supposed that the deceased, in conformity with her promises frequently repeated, has besides left a legacy of £10,000 to each of his lordship's daughters. His lordship's two sons, it is also supposed, will enjoy £20,000 each beside the Chelsea estate." This lady was a Miss Bate. George René was the second son of the Calvinist minister Israel Antoine Aufere. Pretty well done for the second son of a runaway Huguenot pastor, it must be allowed!

The Portals were refugees. Henri Portal become a paper-manufacturer, and was granted the privilege of making the notes of the Bank of England, which his descendants inherited. Jean François Portal's son, Guillaume, was given the rectory of Fanebridge, Essex, and Clowne, in the county of Derby, and was made tutor to Prince George, afterwards George III. The family is now well estated in Hampshire, and represented by Melville Portal of Laverstoke, M.P. for North Hants in 1849-1851, and High Sheriff in 1863.

Louis Paul, son of a refugee druggist, was ancestor of the Baronets of that name. Elie Bouhéreau, son of a pastor at La Rochelle, was ordained and made Chanter of St. Patrick's Cathedral, Dublin, and Librarian. The descendants call themselves Borough. Sir John Chardin, the traveller, was another refugee. He was knighted in 1681; the daughter, Julia, married Sir Christopher Musgrave, Bart., of Hartley Castle. Henri Justel, on coming to England in 1681, was made Keeper of the King's Library in St. James's Palace, with a salary of £200 per annum.

James and Peter Auriole were refugees. James became a wealthy merchant in Lisbon, whence he went from London. His eldest son, James Peter, as well as his brother, obtained lucrative appointments in India. The second, Charles, became a General in the royal service. James Peter was the father of Edward Auriol, Rector of St. Dunstan, in the West of London, and Prebendary of St. Paul's. Peter Auriol was the father of Henrietta Auriol, ancestress of the Earls of Kinnoull, whose marriage is thus recorded in the *Gentleman's Magazine*: "Married, 31st January, 1719, the Right Rev. Robert Drummond, Bishop of St. Asaph, to the eldest

THE HUGUENOT REFUGEES

daughter of Mr. Auriol, merchant, in Coleman Street." With her, as dowry, £30,000 went to the Bishop.

This prelate was by birth the Hon. Robert Hay, second son of the seventh Earl of Kinnoull. He assumed the name of Drummond in 1739, on succeeding to the estates of the first Viscount Strathallan. From being Bishop of St. Asaph in 1748, he was promoted to be Bishop of Salisbury in 1761, and in the same year was made Archbishop of York. He had six sons by his wife. The eldest became ninth Earl of Kinnoull.

M. David de Montolieu was made General of Foot in the English army. He left £1,500 to his only daughter. Louis Jacques Puissard, the refugee, was granted several forfeited estates in 1697, yielding £607 per annum. Gabriel de Quesne was made Commissioner of Fortifications in the British service at Port Royal, and his son Thomas Roger was given the vicarage of East Tuddenham and made Prebendary of Ely. Mathieu Hullin de Gastine was another refugee. He left to his son £3,666 7s. 9d. Jacques de Gastigny, a Huguenot refugee from Holland, was created Master of the Buckhounds to the Prince of Orange. He followed him to England, and died in 1708. He must have done pretty well for himself, as he left £500 to the pesthouse, £500 for the hospital, and numerous legacies.

In the *Gentleman's Magazine* the death is recorded of Paul Dufour, a Huguenot refugee, "Treasurer of the French Hospital, to which he left £10,000." There were other numerous and large bequests.

David Bosanquet came to England from Lyons in 1685. His son Samuel married the heiress of William Dunster, and his grandson, also named Samuel, became Director of the Bank of England and Deputy-Governor of the Levant Company. James Whatonau Bosanquet married the only daughter and heiress of the Lord Chief Justice Sir Nicolas Conyngham Tindal, and his descendants are the Tindal-Bosanquets.

The family of Esdaile of Cothelestone claims descent from a Huguenot refugee. Sir James Esdaile, Kt., was the father of William Esdaile, a London banker. Zacharie Fonnereau was another who escaped to England at the Revocation, and

THE HUGUENOT REFUGEES

his son Claude died a merchant-prince in 1740, leaving to his eldest son, Thomas, £40,000, and to three other sons, Abel, Philip, and Peter, £20,000 apiece, and to another son, the Rev. Claude, £25,000, and to his four daughters, each £10,000. To his widow £400 per annum. Nicholas Gambier came to England at the same time. His son James became a barrister in good practice, whose daughter Susan married Sir Samuel Cornish, Bart., and Margaret, Sir Charles Middleton, Bart., created Lord Barham. The son James became an Admiral.

Augustine Prévost came to England from Geneva, where was no persecution whatever, and became a Major-General in the British army. He was the father of Sir George Prévost, created Baronet, Governor-General, and Commander-in-Chief of the Forces in North America, where he disgraced himself at Saratoga, and had to be recalled, and only by his death escaped a court-martial.

Sir Samuel Romilly was the son of a Huguenot jeweller refugee. Sir Samuel's eldest son was called to the Upper House as Baron Romilly of Barry.

Baron de Tessier was descended from Jacques, who took refuge in Switzerland, but whose son of the same name thought he could better his fortunes by coming to England.

William III. found means to accommodate a large number of the refugees by raising French regiments to serve in Ireland. There was one of cavalry, one of dragoons, and three infantry regiments. These were disbanded at the Peace of Ryswick, but were reorganized in 1706-07. But that was not sufficient. An English infantry regiment was placed under Colonel Puissar, and an English regiment of cavalry under Sir John Lanier, both Frenchmen.

De la Roche wrote: "A clergyman well acquainted with Isaac Vossius told me that one day he asked that Prebendary of Windsor what was become of a certain person. 'He has taken Orders,' replied Vossius. 'He has got a living in the country—*sacrificulus decipit populum.*'"

There is this excuse for the way in which William III. and George I. thrust French and Dutch pastors into English

THE HUGUENOT REFUGEES

livings and prebendal stalls after having had them ordained, that the main body of the English clergy were Jacobite and High Church, even such as had not joined the Nonjuror schism. It was the policy of both to flood the English Church with Calvinism and Whiggery. That those preferred either could not speak English at all, or spoke it with such an accent and so broken as not to be "understanded by the people," was not a matter that concerned them greatly. William was highly incensed at the rejection by Convocation of his and Burnet's Bill for the revision of the Liturgy, in order to admit Dissenters, by adopting certain alterations and making the use of certain ceremonies discretionary. He revenged himself on the Church by heaping benefices and dignities on the Calvinist foreign refugees.

Pierre Allix was a Huguenot pastor and the son of a pastor. When he came to England he submitted to ordination. Woodrow wrote: "Mr. Webster tells me that he had an account that, when they were forced out of France in 1685, Monsieur Allix was the first who submitted to reordination in England; that he was so choked [shocked] when he saw Monsieur Allix reordained, and a declaration made that he was [had been] no minister, and the reflection cast on the whole ministry of France and the Reformed Churches, that he could not bear it, but came to Scotland."

Allix had several sons. Peter became incumbent of Castle Camps in Cambridgeshire, and Chaplain-in-Ordinary to the King; then Dean of Gloucester, and next Dean of Ely. His wife was Elizabeth, niece of Admiral Sir Charles Wager, and his descendants are the well-estated families of Allix of Willoughby Hall and of Swaffham.

Charles Daubuz, another refugee, became Vicar of Brotherton in Yorkshire. Théophile de l'Anger was made Vicar of Tenterden, Rector of Shargate, and Minister of Goodmestone—in fact, a pluralist, as was also his son, John Maximilian, who obtained the rectories of Danbury and Woodhamferrier, and was also Minister of Goodmestone. Pierre Dresincourt, whose grandfather was either a shoemaker or soap-boiler, was given the archdeaconry of Leigh-

THE HUGUENOT REFUGEES

ton, and the rectory and deanery of Armagh. He bequeathed £500 to the French Church in Dublin, £700 to a charity school in Wales, £800 to a hospital in Dublin, £1,000 for charities in Armagh, £2,000 to his own and his wife's relations. His only child, Anne, married Viscount Primrose. John Armand du Bourdieu was given the rectory of Sawtry-All-Saints in Huntingdonshire.

Jacques Jerome was presented to the vicarages of Mullingar and Rathconnell, and then to the rectories of Churchtowne and Piercetowne, and finally to the rectories of Clonegan and Newtownclenan. Jacques Sartres, a native of Montpellier, was ordained by the Bishop of London in 1684, and in 1688 was made Prebendary of Westminster. Daniel Amiard, another French refugee, was accorded the rectory of Holdenby, and was given a canonry in Peterborough Cathedral.

Antoine Ligonier, a pastor, became a military chaplain in Britain, and retired with a pension of 3s. 4d. a day in 1702.

The Barbaulds were refugees. One of them was the father of Théophile Louis, who was presented by George II. to the rectory of St. Vedast in London. His son reverted to Calvinism, and became a Dissenting preacher. The wife of this latter was the at one time famed Anna Lætitia Barbauld, *née* Aikin. She visited Geneva in 1785, and saw there Calvinist worship as appointed by the founder of the religion : " As soon as the text is named, the minister puts on his hat, in which he is followed by all the congregation, except those whose hats and heads have never any connection (for you well know that to put his hat upon his head is the last use a well-dressed Frenchman would think of putting it to). At proper periods of the discourse the minister stops short and turns his back upon you to blow his nose, which is a signal for all the congregation to do the same ; and a glorious concert it is if the weather is already severe and people have got colds. I am told, too, that he takes this time to refresh his memory by peeping at his sermon, which lies behind him in the pulpit."

Bernard Majendie was a Calvinist preacher at Orthez.

THE HUGUENOT REFUGEES

His son André, born in 1601, was pastor at Sauveterre; the brother Jacques came to England and was naturalized in 1704, and had a son, who was made Canon of Worcester. The Canon's son became Bishop of Chester in 1809. James Saurin, a descendant of Jean Saurin, Sieur de la Blaquier, was made Bishop of Dromore in 1819. The Very Reverend Daniel Letablière, Dean of Tuam, Vicar of Laragh-Brian, a Prebendary of Maynooth, who died in 1775, was the son of René de Lestables, who on the Revocation of the Edict of Nantes escaped to Ireland. Dean Gabriel James Mathurin was grandson of the pastor Gabriel Maturin, a foundling who was picked up in the streets of Paris by the coachman of a lady of the name of Maturin. Archdeacon Fleury of Waterford, Prebendary of Kilgobenet, was descended from the pastor Louis Fleury of Tours. Daniel Augustus Beaufort, Archdeacon of Tuam, was the son of a pastor to French congregations in London. Archdeacon Jortin was son of René Jortin, a refugee. Isaac Thellusson was a refugee at Geneva. His son Peter came to London to better his position. He prospered, and purchased the Manor of Broadsworth in Yorkshire. His eldest son was created Baron Rendlesham. Peter Thellusson, whose will is dated 1796, left £4,500 a year in landed property and £60,000 of personal estate. Andrew Boevy, a native of Courtrai, came to England, and became a merchant in London. His son William, who died in 1661, left £30,000 in real estate and personality. James Boevy and his brother William in 1647 bought Flaxley Abbey in Gloucestershire, now the residence of the Baronet Crawley-Boevy. Theodore Janssen was a refugee; he was created a Baronet by Queen Anne. He brought with him to England £20,000, which he improved to £300,000 in 1720, but, being involved in the South Sea Company, lost £220,000, nearly half of his then real estate. Richard Chenevix, of another refugee family, was given the bishoprics of Waterford and Lismore, and he at once began to provide in the Irish Church for other descendants of refugees.

A Trenche was created Lord Ashtown; another was made Archbishop of Tuam.

THE HUGUENOT REFUGEES

Of later beneficed clergy of Huguenot descent it is not necessary to write. I may but name Archbishop Chenevix-Trench, Huguenot on both sides; Turton, Bishop of Ely; Lefroy, Dean òf Norwich and Bishop of Lahore; and Dean Pigou.

When, in the reign of Queen Anne, the Tories came into favour, there was a fear entertained by the refugees that they would not be favoured and pampered as they had been, and a certain number, but not many, returned to their native land. But the majority found themselves far too comfortable in the positions they had acquired through favour, or by their own merits and abilities, and with the accession of William of Orange there was another rush of foreign Calvinists to England. With George I. there came in many more. Industrious and inventive, they did much to enhance the manufacturing and mercantile prosperity of England, and although at first they ousted many of our native men of business and workmen from their places, eventually they proved of material and intellectual advantage to the country of their adoption.

Numerous well-to-do county families derive from Huguenot refugee ancestors. Beside those already mentioned are Layard, Barclay, Pigou, Chamier, Carpenter - Garnier, Garrett, Jeune, Papillon, Blanchard, Blondell, Boileau, Bourdillon, Boyer, Brocas, Bulmer, Champion, Courtauld, Cramer, Daubney, Cazenove, Rivière, Gambier - Parry, Hassard, La Touche, Le Fanu, Luard, Martineau, Morrell, Ouvry, Sperling, Lefevre, Houblon, and many more names known in banks, manufactures, and trades.

During the reign of William III. many Dutch were naturalized who were not in any way refugees from persecution; they came to make their fortunes in England. In France, moreover, persecution had come to an end about 1688, but Huguenots continued to drift over in considerable numbers, hearing that their kinsmen and coreligionists were having "a good time" in England, and settling in green pastures. In fact, in one day—July 3, 1701—as many as 303 persons were naturalized.

THE HUGUENOT REFUGEES

For complete lists of refugees and naturalized foreigners, see the Camden Society volume, " Lists of Foreign Protestants and Aliens resident in England, 1618-1688 " (London, 1862) ; Agnew (D.), " Protestant Exiles from France in the Reign of Louis XIV." (London, 1871-1874) ; Burn (J. S.), " History of French, Walloon, Dutch, and other Foreign Protestant Refugees settled in England " (London, 1846) ; and the third volume of Weiss's " Histoire des Réfugiés Protestants de France " (1854).

In looking through these lists, one is struck with a number of names included in them, such as Lambert, Godfrey, Gilbert, Gervase, Michael, Martin, Roger, Charles, and the like, that would become English at once without any alteration. But there are others with which we are familiar : Percy occurs ; Roussell repeatedly. Dherby, an immigrant in 1684, would drop the *h* and become Derby. There are several Smiths in the lists, presumably arriving from the Netherlands. The old Norman name of Houssaye comes in several times ; so do Hardy, More, Hayes, Faulconier, Rose, Mercer, Marchant, Courtis, Carr, Emery, Nisbet, Neel, Ogelby, Paget, Paulet, Boyd, Blondell, Cooke, Pratt, Pain, Lee, King, Wildgoose, Johnson, Stockey, Jay, Davies, Best, Kemp, Wilkins, Pryor, Dove, Fox, Hudshon (soon to shed the *h*), White, Bush, Greenwood, Highstreet, etc.

Langue would speedily become *Lang*, and *Boreau* become *Borough* ; *Grangier* be converted into *Granger*, and *Goudron* into *Gordon* ; *Guillard* would become *Gillard*, and *Blond* be written and pronounced *Blunt*. How some of the names given above that seem to be distinctly English, as Greenwood and Highstreet, come into the lists is puzzling, and we can only suppose that the immigrants translated their French names into the corresponding English, as Boisvert into Greenwood, and Hauterue into Highstreet.

A large number of names of the refugees still remain among us, recognizable ; nevertheless, a large percentage has disappeared. Either these fugitives translated or anglicized their names, or else dropped them altogether and assumed such as were purely English. Some, again, have become so

THE HUGUENOT REFUGEES

corrupted that there is no discovering what they originally were without reference to parochial registers, in which the modification and final transformation may be traced. On the whole, we may be thankful for the infusion of vigorous Huguenot blood. The Conquest had brought some freshness into what was dull Saxon life, and this new importation helped further to salt the soup. Although a good many of those who came to England bore territorial names, with *De* this or that, and accounted themselves to be nobles, we must bear in mind that a French noble, unless of the highest class, was on a level with an English squire. Not even that always. There were in France, as also in Germany, two classes, the noblesse and the bourgeoisie, beside the peasants. Only the noblesse had any right to a coat of arms, and every son, grandson, great-grandson, of some petty *De* considered himself, and was considered, a member of the class of nobles. In England it was always quite different. The wars in which France was constantly engaged killed off a host of the junior scions of nobility; but for that, they would have swarmed like flies. For these needy offshoots of scrubby plants considered themselves too good to soil their fingers with trade or commerce. There were but three professions open to them as gentlemen—the Army, the Law, and the Church.

"The unfortunate custom in France," says White in his "History of France," "which made all the members of a family as noble as its chief, so that a simple Viscount with ten stalwart and penniless sons gave ten stalwart and penniless Viscounts to the aristocracy of his country, had filled the whole land with a race of men proud of their origin, filled with reckless courage, careless of life, and despising all the honest means of employment by which their fortunes might have been improved. Mounted on a sorry horse, and begirt with a sword of good steel, the young cavalier took his way from the miserable castle on a rock, where his noble father tried to keep up the appearance of daily dinners and wondered how in the world all his remaining sons and daughters were to be clothed and fed, and made his way to Paris. There he pushed his future, fighting, bullying,

THE HUGUENOT REFUGEES

gambling, and was probably stabbed by some drunken companion and flung into the Seine."

We must not be dazzled by the pretensions of some of the Huguenot pastors to be members of noble families. That meant very little—no more than that they were not descendants of honest tradesmen. Some needy second, third, or fourth son of a starved, ragged Count or Viscount, or even Marquis, found that he could still remain a gentleman if he became a pastor, which suited him better than to be a *curé*, debarred from marriage. The titled class in France did not by any means represent the corresponding class in England. After the time of Louis XI. the representatives of the old feudal aristocracy were few and far between. They were left like pillars in an almost universal inundation, and were themselves finally sapped and overthrown by the force of the prevailing tide. A second aristocracy arose among the descendants and survivors of the English and Italian wars. They claimed their rank as proprietors of petty estates. Three thousand acres of sandy soil or barren limestone were ample to invest the owner with the title of Marquis. A third aristocracy also came up, the creation of Court favour—possessors of a nominal rank without lands, and without corresponding duties.

Enriched tax-gatherers, or others who had fattened on the royal favour, ascended above their original position by the purchase of lands that were recognized or assumed as carrying with them a title, and this became so general that at last an edict was passed to deprive them of a pre-eminence derived solely from the purchase of these lands.

Among the "nobles" who came over there were very few indeed who left behind them anything of any value, and the merchants managed to sell their businesses, as appears from the large sums of money they brought over with them; and they had previously well-established relations with substantial firms in England.

In the end of February, 1744 (N.S.), the merchants of the City of London presented a loyal address to the King in consequence of His Majesty's message to the Houses of

THE HUGUENOT REFUGEES

Parliament regarding designs "in favour of a Popish pretender to disturb the peace and quiet of your Majesty's kingdom," declaring themselves resolved to hazard their lives and fortunes "in defence of your Majesty's sacred person and government, and for the security of the Protestant succession in your Royal Family." Among the 542 signatures are those of ninety-four French names, chiefly Huguenot. I give these, as of interest, in the Appendix.

CHAPTER XIV

NICK- AND DESCRIPTIVE NAMES

ALMOST invariably in the nursery a child is given by brothers and sisters some name which, if not a contraction of the baptismal name, bears no relation to it. Margaret is indeed crumpled into Maggie, Mary reduced to May, Elizabeth to Betty or Lizzie, Catherine to Kate; William is contracted and altered to Bill, Harry to Hal, Richard to Dick, and Robert to Bob. But often the names given are capricious and unaccountable, as Bunchy, Pim, Stubbly, Topsy, Dott, Tittums. If they escape this in the nursery, they do not do so at school, where personalities often rule the giving of a name, as Ginger, Carrots, from the hair; Snout, Beak, Nosey, from the nose; Goggles, from the eyes; Bat, from the projecting ears; Frowsky, from indifference to outdoor sports.

Moreover, it is not easy to get rid of such a name. A girl known at home to parents, as well as to brothers and sisters and cousins, by a pet name carries it with her to her husband's house, and the boy leaving school and entering the army is saluted with his nickname at the regimental mess. A Colonel Smith was spending a winter in a certain German town. He possessed a daughter who went in the family by the name of Jack Spratt. This she acquired as a little child by her revulsion against fat with her meat; and as the nursery rhyme avers:

> "Jack Spratt could eat no fat,
> His wife could eat no lean;
> And so between them both
> They licked the platter clean."

NICK- AND DESCRIPTIVE NAMES

She grew up to woman's estate, and neither parents nor brothers and sisters had shaken off the habit of calling her Jack Spratt, although her Christian name was Isabella.

When aged twenty-three she became engaged to a gentleman who was visiting in the aforesaid German town. On his return to England he wrote to her; and as lovers fall into strange lunes, he addressed his letter to her—Miss Jack Spratt!

Two days later a messenger arrived at Colonel Smith's door with a summons to attend at the post-office next morning, between 8 a.m. and noon. He obeyed, and found that it concerned the letter. Who was Jack Spratt? How long had he been an inmate of the Colonel's house? No intimation of such a person had been sent to the police, and, according to law, no stranger could reside for over three days in the town without legitimation by the police. The Colonel in broken German explained that his daughter was familiarly known as Jack Spratt. He was requested to take a seat whilst the police were communicated with. Half an hour later the head of the police arrived, and the matter was discussed between him and the postmaster. The former then, turning to the Colonel, stated that he had the paper of legitimation of Miss Isabella Smith, but not of Jack Spratt. In vain did Colonel Smith reiterate his statement that this was a joke. German officials do not comprehend jokes, and it was finally concluded that the letter must be opened to ascertain to whom it actually was addressed. An interpreter was introduced. The letter was opened, and began:

"MY DEAR JACK,
 "You are a regular ripper——"

When this was translated, the face of the Oberpolizei became grave.

"Der wahrhaftige Aufschneider!" he exclaimed. "We have at last obtained a clue to the discovery of the criminal who a few years ago committed such atrocious acts in London, and who has been the author of similar cases recently in Berlin."

The Colonel explained that *ripper* was a term of admira-

NICK- AND DESCRIPTIVE NAMES

tion and endearment much affected by lovers and young ladies.

The police-officer assumed a still sterner expression.

" Herr Oberst," said he, " this passes everything—that a person calling himself a gentleman should address to a lady delicately brought up a disgusting and horrible epithet derived from the acts of Jack the Ripper as a term of endearment and commendation. Herr Oberst, you must understand that, under the circumstances, your house must be subjected to a domiciliary visit !"

The employment of nicknames is so common among navvies that they know each other solely by them. It is the same with colliers.

An attorney's clerk was employed to serve a process on a collier. After a great deal of inquiry as to the whereabouts of the fellow, he was about to abandon the search as hopeless, when a young woman who had witnessed his labour volunteered to assist him.

" Oy say, Bull'yed," cried she to the first person they met, " does thee know a man named Adam Green ?"

The bull-head was shaken in token of ignorance.

" Loy-a-bed, dost thee ?"

Lie-a-bed's opportunities of making acquaintances had been limited, and she could not resolve the difficulty.

Stumpy (a man with a wooden leg), Cowskin, Spindleshanks, Cockeye, and Pigtail were severally invoked, but in vain, and the querist fell into a brown study, in which she remained for some time. At length, however, her eyes suddenly brightened, and, slapping one of her companions on the shoulder, she exclaimed triumphantly :

" Dash my wig! whoy, he means my feyther !" And then, turning to the gentleman, added : " Ye should 'a ax'd for Ole Blackbird."

A correspondent of *Knight's Quarterly Magazine* wrote : " I knew an apothecary in the collieries who, as a matter of decorum, always entered the paternal names of his patients in his books—that is, when he could ascertain them. But they stood there only for ornament; for use he found it

NICK- AND DESCRIPTIVE NAMES

necessary to append the sobriquet, which he did with true medical formality, as, for instance, 'Thomas Williams, *vulgo dict.* Old Puff.'"

Precisely the same is found elsewhere. A writer in *Blackwood's Magazine* in 1842 gives the following account of the peculiarities of nomenclature among Scottish fisherfolk: "The fishers are generally in want of surnames. There are seldom more than two or three surnames in a fish-town. The grocers, in 'booking' their fisher customers, invariably insert the nickname, or *fee*-name, and, in the case of married men, write down the wife's along with the husband's name. Unmarried debtors have the names of their parents inserted with their own. In the town register of Peterhead these signatures occur: Elizabeth Taylor, spouse to John Thomson, 'Souples'; Agnes Farquhar, spouse to W. Findlater, 'Stonttie.' It is amusing enough to turn over the leaves of a grocer's ledger and see the fee-names as they come up: *Buckie, Beauty, Bam, Biggelugs, Collop, Hilldom, the King, the Provost, Rockie, Stoatie, Sillerton, the Smack, Snipe, Snuffers, Toothie, Todlowrie.* Among the twenty-five George Cowies in Buckie there are George Cowie 'Doodle,' George Cowie 'Carrot,' and George Cowie 'Nap.'"

In 1844 John Geddes, *alias* Jock Jack, was indicted at the assizes in spring at Aberdeen for assaulting John Cowie, *alias* Pum. Some of the witnesses were Margaret Cowie "Pum," daughter of the person assaulted; John Reid, *alias* Joccles; James Green, *alias* Rovie; John Geddes, *alius* Jackson; Alexander, *alias* Duke, and John Reid, *alias* Dey—all described as fishermen. The only trace in this list of a nickname developing into a surname is in the case of Margaret Cowie, who was called "Pum," as well as her father.

Among primitive peoples, as already said, nicknames were employed to conceal the real name of a person, lest an enemy, by getting hold of it, should work mischief on the owner of the name by magical arts.

But this fear of the name being misused must have soon died away, whereas the notion remained that by invoking the name, not of a saint only, but of some man of renown,

NICK- AND DESCRIPTIVE NAMES

help would come from the person so called on. There are several such instances in the Icelandic sagas—as when, in a storm, an Icelander invoked King Olaf, who was still alive; then Olaf responded by appearing and tendering his assistance.

Among the Kings nicknames were common, as Ethelred the Unready, Edmund Ironside, Harold Harefoot, Henry Beauclerk, Richard Cœur de Lion, John Lackland, Edward Longshanks, Richard Crookback. The Welsh Princes, moreover, had descriptive epithets attached to their names, as Calcfynedd the Whitewasher, Lauhir Longhand, Mynfaur the Courteous. Sometimes a nickname displaced a baptismal mame. Thus, Brendon the Voyager was christened Mobi; but, because there was an auroral display at his birth, he was known through life as Brenain. St. Patrick had four names, of which Succat, Cothraigh, and Magonius were the others. Cadoc's real name was Cathmael.

Roger de Amandeville, Seneschal of Remigius, Bishop of Lincoln (one of the compilers of Domesday), and by him endowed with four Lincolnshire manors, for some unaccountable reason called himself *Humfine*, and the head of the family was so named for several generations. What the meaning and how it originated we cannot tell.

Hugh d'Avranches, the Earl of Chester, went generally by the name of Hugh Lupus (the Wolf), and bore on his banner a wolf's head *arg.* on a blue field.

Richard d'Avranches, the father of Hugh Lupus, went by the name of Le Goz or Le Gotz, a name borne by the family long after its significance had been forgotten. It was actually a name designating the ancestor, who had come over with Rollo, as a Gothlander, a native of that southern portion of Sweden which lies as a belt across it, and included the Wener and Wetter lakes. Rollo's companions were otherwise Norwegians. But although the family spoke of themselves as Gotzes, they do not seem to have assumed this designation as a fixed surname.

Among the Scandinavians descriptive names were common. A Danish King was Harald Bluetooth; another Harald was

NICK- AND DESCRIPTIVE NAMES

called Wartusk; another, called Ivar, was known as Widefathom, from the stretch of his extended arms.

Harald of Norway vowed that he would not suffer his hair to be clipped or combed till he had forced all the petty Kings in the land to fly the country, or had killed them. At the time he went by the designation of Shockhead; but when he had brought the whole of Norway under his sway, he subjected his poll to a treatment—become, one would suppose, indispensable—and thenceforth, from the beauty of his golden locks, was named Fairhair.

Harald II. had his Court near the sea, where was a haven. One day a vessel belonging to some chapmen came to harbour from England, laden with grey felt cloth, very stout and serviceable, but not showy. No one would buy, so the chapmen complained to the King. "I will soon satisfy you," he said, and went to the vessel and purchased a sufficient supply of the cloth to make several suits for himself. At once the fashion was set; the courtiers hastened to buy, and the vessel was cleared of its burden. Thenceforth Harald was known as Greyfell.

His brother Eric, who became for a short while King of Northumbria, was called Bloodaxe. He burned his half-brother, Björn the Chapman, and all his company in a wooden house, because he coveted his petty realm. Björn was the only one of the brothers who pursued a quiet life, and, because he traded, acquired the name of Chapman.

Among the Swedes nicknames were also given. One King was Illrede, one Eric the Victorious; another Eric was named Windhat.

Usually, when a nickname was given, it was customary for the giver to make a present to the man thus furnished, as a "name-fastener."

Hrolf, son of Helgi, was sent to the Court of the Swedish King to demand certain dues that were in arrears, claimed by the King of Zealand. The mission was perilous, and Hrolf, on reaching Upsala, drew his hood over his face. As he sat in the royal hall, a man came up to him, and, noticing his dark face under the shadow of the hood and his pro-

NICK- AND DESCRIPTIVE NAMES

truding nose, exclaimed: "Whom have we here—a crow?" "You have given me a nickname; give me also a name-fastener," said Hrolf.

"Alas!" replied the man, "I am poor as a rat; but what I will give you is my promise that, should you die a violent death, I will avenge you."

"I accept that with the name," said Hrolf, and thenceforth he was known as Kraki. Nobly and faithfully did the man fulfil his undertaking.

But none of these nicknames were hereditary: they died along with the men who bore them. The sole instance to the contrary with which I am acquainted is that of Ragnar Lodbrog and his descendants.

Ragnar acquired the descriptive epithet of Shaggy-brogues, from his having fashioned for himself a pair of gaiters of coarse wadmal, sopped in pitch, and hardened. He died in or about the year 794. He had sons with nicknames—Björn Ironside, Sigurd Worm-i'-th'-eye, Ivar the Boneless, and Whitesark, all known as Lodbrog's sons. But some seventy to eighty years later we know, from the English and Norman Chronicles, that Lodbrog's sons were harrying the coasts. Two of them, Hingvar and Hubba, put Edmund, King of the East Angles, to a cruel death in 870, and Ingvar, or Ivar, became King of Dublin, and ruled from 871 to 873. It is, of course, impossible that these can have been the sons of the original Lodbrog, and we are driven to the conclusion that the name of Shaggy-brogues had become hereditary.

We see in early characters that nicknames were common in England, but not that they were hereditary. Among those who came over with the Conqueror, several bore nicknames, as Humfrid Vis-de-lew (Wolf's-face), Rudolf Tortemains (Twisted-hands), Roger Deus-salvet-dominas (God-save-the-ladies). There was Front-de-bœuf (Oxbrow) and Pêché (the Man-of-sin). Pinel, who obtained a great barony from William I., we may suppose shed his name of Pinel—that signifies one devoid of means—when it ceased to apply.

NICK- AND DESCRIPTIVE NAMES

> "The naked file
> Distinguishes the swift, the slow, the subtle,
> The housekeeper, hunter, everyone,
> According to the gift, which bounteous Nature
> Hath in him closed, whereby he does receive
> Particular addition from the bill
> That writes them all alike."
> *Macbeth*, II. 1.

These descriptive names applied to the individual only, and in rare instances descended to their sons and grandsons. One Anglo-Saxon instance of *Hatte* has, however, been given in the first chapter, and we have instanced one of Hairy-brogues among the Scandinavians. Some also, as that of *Louvel*, became hereditary among the Norman settlers in England. Whether all the *Pennels* derive from the Baron Pinel, or whether the description of "needy men" was applied all round to several who were impecunious, we cannot say.

In the Peterborough Chronicle we read: "Ronald, monk, had made his brother Hugh a monk when he was a boy. This Hugh had suffered from a bloody flux when a child, and he was consequently called Hugh White, because he was so pale and good-looking."[1]

When Archbishop Henry de Londres took possession of the See of Dublin, he called together the tenants of the see to show the nature of their tenures; and after they had produced their evidences, he ordered the charters of the villeins to be burnt. Thereupon he acquired the nickname of Scorch-villeins.

Among those who made grants to Battle Abbey occur such names as these: Walter le Bœuf, John God-me-fetch, Bartholomew le Swan, Roger le Bunch.

Naturally, many nicknames are unintelligible to us, as we know nothing of the circumstances which induced their application. They were given out of mere caprice, out of scorn, or were pet-names.

In "Cocke-Lorell's Bote," a satirical poem printed by Wynkyn de Worde, we have this:

[1] Leland, "Collectanea," i., p. 15.

NICK- AND DESCRIPTIVE NAMES

> "The Pardoner sayd, I will rede my roll,
> And ye shall here the names poll by poll.
>   *   *   *   *   *
> Pers Potter of Brydgewater,
> Saunders Sely, the Mustard-maker,
> With Jenkyn Jangler.
> Here is Jenkyne Berward of Barwyke,
> And Tom Tombler of Warwick,
> With Phylypp Fletcher of Ffernam [Farnham].
> Here is Wyll Wyly the Millpecker,
> And Patrycke Pevysshe Beerbeter,
> And lusty Harry Hangeman.
> Also Matthew Toothe-drawer of London,
> And Sybby Sole, milkwyfe of Islington,
> With Davy Drawelacke of Rockyngam."

There are many more lines to that effect. Although these are the names of imaginary persons, they are framed in the mould of nomenclature then in process of shaping; but there is no evidence that they passed from father to son. In most of the registers in which offensive nicknames occur such names were entered for identification by the scribe, and were probably not accepted by the bearer. If we look into the episcopal registers of the Middle Ages for the names of ordinands and of clergy inducted into livings, we encounter none of these nicknames, for the very good reason that the parsons there enrolled named themselves, and were not named by others. In these registers the clergy are usually designated by the place of their birth, or as the son of So-and-so.

When the beasts were brought before Adam, he gave them names, from the characteristics observable in each. And there is something of the Adam in every man. He is not disposed to call one of his fellows by that name which he gives himself, but to invent and apply one of his own devising. Caius Cæsar was known to his dying day as Caligula (Little Boots), the name given to him by the soldiers at Cologne.

Daniel Finch, Earl of Nottingham, had such a dark complexion and so solemn a face that he went by the name of Don Dismallo. John Sheffield, Earl of Mulgrave, was commonly spoken of as Lord Allpride.

NICK- AND DESCRIPTIVE NAMES

When and *how* nicknames as well as other names became fixed and hereditary must now be considered. In 1538 King Henry VIII. ordered that in every parish should be kept a register of the births, deaths, and marriages that took place therein, with the Christian name and the surname of the parties. The result must have been a precipitation of names hitherto fluid and in suspense. Now let us suppose cases that must have occurred in every parish throughout the length and breadth of the land:

John, a humble rural village labourer, required the parish priest to baptize his child and call it Philip. As the godparents and nurse are about to leave the church, the parson recalls them.

" There is a new law published : we have to enter every baptism, and give the father's Christian name and surname."

The peasant scratches his head.

" I don't reckon I have any other than John, sir."

" But by the law you must have one. You are an honest man. What say you to being called Goodman ?"

" As your reverence wishes. I don't understand about these matters."

So Philip, the son of John Goodman, is registered, and thence come all those of that name in England.

Peter and Margery appear before the altar to be married. All goes smoothly enough in the service : " I, Peter, take thee, Margery, to my wedded wife, to have and to hold from this day forward, for better for worse, for richer for poorer, in sickness and in health, till death us do part." But when they retire to the vestry, and the new book, with parchment leaves, bound in calfskin, is produced, along with the inkhorn, then the difficulties begin. Neither bridegroom nor bride has a surname. " They do call me sometimes Snout," says the former, colouring, " because I have a big nose, but I shouldn't like *that* to be written down in the book."

" Then, what am I to call you ?"

Both are at a nonplus. The priest endeavours to help them out of their difficulty.

" Peter, your father is the village blacksmith, and

NICK- AND DESCRIPTIVE NAMES

Margery, you are the daughter of the tinman or whitesmith. Suppose that I enter you, Peter, as son of James Blacksmith, and Margery as daughter of Simon Whitesmith?"

"Aren't the names a bit long?" protests the bridegroom.

"Perhaps so. Well, we will cut them down to Black and White."

Digory the fuller has just buried his father. He is summoned by the parson to have his old parent duly registered:

"What was his name?"

"Roger, your reverence."

"I mean his surname."

"He had none."

"Then, what was your grandfather's name?"

"Digory."

"Shall I enter him as Roger Digoryson or Digges?"

"That will not do, axing your pardon, as it will seem as though you had buried my son Roger instead of the old man; and my Roger is bad with the thrush, and giving my wife a deal of trouble just now, but will pull through all right."

"Then, what shall I call him?"

A dead silence and much pondering. Presently Digory brightens up, and says:

"My wife always did say that dad was an old pennyfather [screw]."

"Very well, I have registered him as Roger Pennyfather. Now, mind you, Digory, any child you may have in future will have to be recorded as that of Digory Pennyfather; and when you are buried, it will be under that name."

"Lord ha' mercy on my soul! I don't want that. Can't I change it and call my father by the trade—Fuller?"

But the parson is a martinet. "What I have written I have written. Pennyfather you remain till the Judgment Day."

Some such scenes must have occurred again and again on the first introduction of parish registers. Maybe, in a careless mood, some man put down his not very complimentary nick-

NICK- AND DESCRIPTIVE NAMES

name, without a thought that thereby he was riveting it upon generations yet unborn. Some dull minds were content to be called after their fathers—as Thomson and Johnson—and some after their place of residence—as Leigh or Coombe—and others, again, after their trade or after the sign that swung over their shop.

In the eighteenth century the Emperor Joseph II. required all Jews throughout the Empire to assume surnames. Hitherto they had had none, and were so slippery that, when the law desired to lay hold of a Hebrew, he generally succeeded in gliding away. At once throughout Germany the Israelites had to give themselves surnames, so as to be enrolled upon a certain day. Some, with florid imaginations, adopted such names as Rothschild (Red Shield), Lilienthal (Vale of Lilies), Rosenberg (Mountain of Roses), or such as pertained to heraldic beasts—Hirsch, Löwe, Wolf. Others, less ambitious and less rich in fancy, contented themselves with being stereotyped as Lazarus, Levi, and Samuel. Others, again, took appellations from their places of residence, as Bamberger, Augsburger, Feldberger; and a few from their trade, as Goldschmidt.

What took place in Germany in 1782 was much like what had taken place in England in 1538. In the latter country, however, the process had begun some time before.

But nevertheless there remained a good deal of uncertainty in family names. Some bore two simultaneously, as Jones *alias* Vallence and Gilbert *alias* Webber. At the present day is to be found, in the parish of Cheriton Bishop in Devon, an ancient yeoman family named Lambert *alias* Gorwyn.

The original name of the family to which John Hooker (d. 1601), the first Chamberlain of Exeter, and his famous nephew, Richard, "the judicious Hooker," belonged, was Vowell; but in the fifteenth century members of it called themselves Vowell *alias* Hooker, or Hoker, and in the sixteenth century the original name was gradually dropped. John Veysey, or Voysey (d. 1554), *alias* Harman, adopted the name of Veysey, but he was actually the son of

NICK- AND DESCRIPTIVE NAMES

Richard Harman. Anthony À Wood asserts that this was done in compliment to a member of the Veysey family who had educated him.

A writer in *Devon Notes and Queries* observes that in the registers of Parkham a family is entered as Tenant *alias* Penington. Other such names were Mortimer *alias* Tanner, Uphill *alias* Helman, Combe *alias* Bidlake.

Some four or five centuries ago persons did change their family names without a grant from the crown, if no property were involved, and the law regarded such a proceeding with complacency. Lord Coke says: "It is required that a purchaser be named by the name of baptism and his surname, and that special heed be taken to the name of baptism, as he may have divers surnames." And again: "It is holden in our ancient books that a man may have divers *names* at divers times, not divers Christian names."

The following anecdote, given by Mr. Lower from the life of Lackington, will serve to show how easily, even in modern times, a nickname may usurp the place of the family name: "The parish clerk of Langford, near Wellington, was called Red Cock for many years before his death for having one Sunday slept in church, and dreaming that he was at a cock-fighting, he bawled out, 'A shilling upon the Red Cock!' 'And behold,' says Lackington, 'the family are called Red Cock to this day.'"

Considerable caution has to be observed in fixing, as such, names that appear to be nicknames, for not infrequently they are so in appearance only. Thus, as shown above, *White* and *Black* are not necessarily to be taken as expressive of the colour of the person, nor is Brown; for these are contractions of Whitesmith, Blacksmith, and Copper- or Brownsmith. *Hoare*, or *Hore*, is not indicative of a grizzled head; it may come from the Norse *hár*, tall. A man was not *Green* because so named, but because he was wont to represent the Jack-in-the-Green on May Day, or because he was the taverner under the sign of the Green Man. *Tallboys* was a name not given to a family of gaunt brothers. The name is from *taillebois*, woodcutting, which was their

NICK- AND DESCRIPTIVE NAMES

trade. The *Hansoms* do not take their name from great personal beauty; it is a corruption of a Norman place-name. Nor were the *Thynnes* remarkable for their meagreness of aspect; they derive, so it is said, from John de Botteville, in the reign of Edward IV., who studied in one of the Inns of Court, and acquired thence the designation of John-o'-th'-Inne, or John Thynn. The *Quicks* were not necessarily lively individuals, rapid in their movements. Quick is but a form of "wick," from the Latin *vicus*, and its equivalents are *Wyke* and *Weekes*. Nor was a man named *Fleet* because swift of foot, but because he lived at Fleet, on a tidal river. Mr. Lower supposes *Dummerel* or *Dumbril* to signify a silent person, but it is really an anglicizing of D'Aumerle. On the other hand, there are names that are expressive of bodily or mental characteristics, that have lost their signification in English, or at all events in Modern English. Thus, *Wace* is from the Norse *hvasi*, and signifies keen or quick. Who would have supposed that Bishop Bonner derived his name from Le Bonair, kind or gracious. The Cornish name *Bolitho* signifies Big Belly, and *Eldridge* is Oldish. Some Welsh expletives have formed names on the marches, as *Gam*, crooked, *Goch*, red, *Gwyn*, white, and Danish terms have attached themselves to persons in Northumbria and East Anglia, as *Gamel* and *Bloed*, foolish, the origin, probably, of the name of *Blood*. So from the French: *Blount* is Le Blond, *Camoys* is one with a turned-up nose, *Courtenay* is Short Nose. *Allfraye* is Le Balafré, the scarred. *Bright* does not signify a lively personage, but is a title (A.S. *brytta*, from *breótan*), the man who dispensed the bread and other food among the thralls, and he was a headman over them.[1] *Arber* has no connection with an arbour; it signifies an heir, from the A.S. *arb*, Gothic *arbi*.

As I have pointed out elsewhere, in entries made by men themselves, as in lists of ordinands and clerics instituted to livings, nick- and descriptive names are conspicuously absent. In probably nine cases out of ten, where a surname seems to be descriptive of personal characteristics, it is a corruption —that is to say, when it has become hereditary.

[1] Munch, "Der Norskefolks Historie," iii. 965.

NICK- AND DESCRIPTIVE NAMES

Strange and ill-understood names, and even ordinary words, get altered. Asparagus is rendered Sparrow Grass, Cucumber is rendered Cowcumber. I have heard Chocolat Ménier spoken of as Chocolate Manure.

A servant-girl got a fortune left her. In high exultation she exclaimed: "Now I shall have a house with indecent [incandescent] lights, and a damnation [Dalmatian] dog, and a cloak lined with vermin [ermine]. But"—her face fell—" I fear I shall not live long to enjoy it all, for I get the browntitus [bronchitis] every winter, I have an ulster [ulcer] in my stomach, and the doctor said I had slugs in my liver [a sluggish liver]. However, I intend to enjoy life while I have it, and eat blue mange [blancmange] every day."

An old woman received a letter from a son in the tropics, in which he complained of the mosquitoes. " Dear life!" she exclaimed, " how forward young women are in foreign parts! My Tom has to shut his windows every night against the Miss Kitties who try to get in to him."

I had an illiterate gardener, who informed me he was getting up a lot of lumbago [plumbago]. "I wish, gardener, you would give it to my worst enemy." "I'm rearing, also, a lot of citizens [cytisus]," he added. "Bless me!" said I, "how shocking! I was unaware that you were married."

Surnames have been treated in precisely the same manner, and have been adapted to something understood by the people; and as those who bore these names were often illiterate and uneducated themselves, they have accepted the alteration without compunction.

We will now take some of the principal characteristics of man—physical, moral, and mental—that may have given to some their surnames.

We find such as *Long* and *Short* and *Shorter*, but we cannot predicate that Long or Short are not contractions of some place-names, such as Longacre and Shortridge. *Dark* is formed from D'Arcques; but we have *Fair*, that stands for *Phayre* and *Motley;* but this latter may be due to the first who assumed the name legally having been a clown:

"Motley is the only wear."

NICK- AND DESCRIPTIVE NAMES

The jester has contributed other surnames, as *Patch*, from his patchwork garment :

"The patch is kind enough."

Also *Pye*, from his pied suit.

Roux, le Roux, Redman, and in some cases *Ruddiman, Redhead*, come from the colour of the hair or complexion. *Reid, Reed, Read*, are all forms of Red. Chaucer speaks of "houses both white and rede." *Scarlett* perhaps is from the habit usually worn. *Blakelock* is not a black-headed man, but a black and lock smith. *Longman* probably means tallness, or long-hand. *Snell* is the Norse *snjall*, the quick; King Halfdan was so designated. *Basset* signifies a man of stunted growth. *Fairfax* is one fair-headed. *Giffard* is a ready giver. *Trottman* is a man of trust, and not a trotter.[1] We have also *Brightman, Goodman, Goodchild, Goodfellow, Allgood, Best, Goodenough, Toogood, Joliffe*, joyous, and *Doughty. Hussey* is no good-for-nothing girl; the name comes from Houssaye in Normandy, and is found in the Roll of Battle Abbey. *Crookshanks, Sheepshanks*, denote infirmity. *Cockayne* is the French *coquin*, a rascal. *Kennard* is the French *caignard*, "you hound!" a sordid rogue. *Pennyfather* is, as already said, a miser. *Moody* may be Le Maudit, the accursed or excommunicated one. A good many names come from the upper ranks of society, given to men whose ancestors never enjoyed any place so high as that of a tradesman, as *King, Duke, Earl, Baron, Knight, Squire;* also *Pope, Bishop,* and *Parson*.

When names had to be registered, and poor country folk beat about for some by which to call themselves, we may well suppose that some men would be inclined to indemnify themselves for their humble position in life by assuming a name indicative of a high position in the State, in Society, or in the Church. How else are we to account for the multitude of Kings we come across everywhere? Or some pompous fellow, full of bluff in the alehouse, may have acquired

---

[1] From the same source come *Troyte, Trott, Trout*, possibly *Trood*, unless this comes from Atte Rood, one living by the Cross.

NICK- AND DESCRIPTIVE NAMES

among his fellows the sobriquet of the Duke or the Squire, and, when he came to register his son, was but too pleased to adopt the name accorded to him in the parish. Another source of these names was the morality plays, when strolling actors assumed the parts of Kings, Dukes, and Angels; and when obliged to record their full appellations, Christian name and surname, the whole company, instead of entering themselves as John and Harry, Bill and Timothy, *Player*, adopted the titles of their parts, and wrote themselves down as John *King*, Harry *Duke*, Bill *Earl*, and Timothy *Angel*.

The acting in mysteries belonged largely to certain families, and parts were probably hereditary, just as in Oxfordshire and the Midlands to this day remain certain families of hereditary morris-dancers, whose ancestors have bedizened themselves and capered for some four or five hundred years; and much as in Ober-Ammergau and other Alpine villages special parts in miracle plays remain in certain families.

That the term *Bastard* should have been accepted without demur as a surname is not so surprising as might appear. William the Conqueror in his charters did not shrink from describing himself as William the Bastard. The name has been borne by an ancient and honourable family in the West of England. *Liefchild* is a love-child, a provincialism for one that is illegitimate. *Parish* was a name often given to a child that was a foundling, and brought up by the community in a village. *Parsons* may designate the child of the parish priest before the marriage of the clergy was suffered, or even when it was a new thing, and not relished by the people. But in most cases it is a corruption of Pierson, or Peter's son, The name *Burrell* comes from the Old English word employed by Chaucer for a layman. But why one layman out of all the parish should assume this title to himself is due to this: that Burrell is a contraction for Borelclerk, a lay clerk in a cathedral or collegiate church.

Child, as already said, was a title applied to the eldest son of a King, or noble, or knight; thus we have "the child of Elle." On Dartmoor is a cross of granite called Childe's

NICK- AND DESCRIPTIVE NAMES

grave. At some time that is uncertain, a Childe of Plymstock was hunting on the moor, where he was overtaken by a snowstorm; and unable to find his way to habitable country, and suffering from the cold, he cut open his horse, crept inside, and, with his finger dipped in blood, scribbled on a stone:

"He who finds and brings me to my grave,
My lands of Plymstock he shall have."

When the monks of Buckland and those of Tavistock heard of this, each sent forth a party to secure the body. Those of Tavistock were successful, and till the Dissolution Plymstock was a priory attached to the Abbey of Tavistock.

Some names bearing on social relations came out oddly enough. Mr. Lower quotes the following from the newspaper:

"Died on Tuesday week, Mr. Young of Newton, aged 97.

"Died on the 10th instant, Miss Bridget Younghusband, spinster, aged 84.

"Birth. Mrs. A. Batchelor, of a son, being her thirteenth."

Some names that seem plain enough do not really mean what they seem. Thus, *Summer* or *Summers* is from Somner, as already stated, and *Winter* is perhaps a vintner, a publican. *Day*, as already pointed out, is used of a dairymaid. So Dull says of Jacquenetta: "For this damsel, I must keep her at the park. She is allowed for a day-woman." *Gaunt* is not descriptive of a rawboned figure; it signifies "of Ghent." I know a carrier whose name is *Death*. This does not describe him as one who conveys man to his long home. It is really De Ath. And we cannot be sure that a *Leeman* derives from a female of light character, as the name may come from Le Mans. When men were suddenly called upon to find a surname for themselves, in their perplexity they laid hold of the days of the week, or the month, or the seasons of the Church, and this has given rise in some cases —but these are not certain—to the *Mondays*, or *Mundays*, and

NICK- AND DESCRIPTIVE NAMES

Sundays, to the names of *Noel* or *Christmas, Paschal, Easter,* and *Middlemas,* or *Michaelmas,* and to *Holiday* and *Hockaday.*

Crabbe, in his "Parish Register," says that foundlings were named after the day of the week in which they were picked up. After agreeing that the child should be christened Richard, the vestry

> "Next enquired the day when, passing by,
> Th' unlucky peasant heard the stranger cry.
> This known, how food and raiment they might give
> Was next debated, for the rogue would live.
> Back to their homes the prudent vestry went,
> And Richard Monday to the workhouse sent."

In Iceland, one of the first to embrace Christianity was Thorkell Krabla. He was a foundling, and he received his nickname of Krabla from this circumstance: that when picked up as a babe he had scrabbled the linen cloth over his face above his mouth, so that his screams became audible for a long way round. But Thorkell Krabla did not pass on his nickname to his children, whereas Richard Monday would do so.

Mr. Lower says: "There resided in 1849, at no great distance from Lewes, a farmer whose family name was Brookes, to which the odd dissyllable of Napkin was prefixed as a Christian name. Both these names he inherited from his grandfather, a foundling, who was exposed at some place in Surrey, tied up in a *napkin,* and laid on the margin of a *brook,* and who, as no traces of his individual parents could be found, received the very appropriate though somewhat cacophonous name of Napkin Brookes."

A family in Sussex bears the name of By the Sea, because, according to tradition, the first of it was discovered as an infant lying on the beach.

How names were given that were purely applied to one person appears from the case of William Faber. He had been in the service of William, Duke of Normandy, and he acquired the name of Faber (the Smith) from this circumstance: As he was one day hunting with the Duke, the party fell short of arrows, and thereupon recourse was had for

NICK- AND DESCRIPTIVE NAMES

more to the nearest smith, who proved to be unacquainted with this branch of his trade. William, the attendant, thereupon seized the tools, and presently made an arrow, whereupon he was named Faber. Afterwards, changing his profession, he became a monk of Marmoutier; but it is quite possible, had he remained in the world, and married, and left a posterity, that the posterity would have continued to bear the name of Faber given to the ancestor by Duke William.

One might suppose that the *Loveday* forefather was so designated from his being a child of light. But it was not so ; he came from Loudet, in Haute Garonne, during the English domination of Guienne.

Bacon is not of the pig, piggy, but comes from Bascoin, the amily name of the Seigneurs of Molai. Anchetel Bascoin before the Conquest made grants of his lordship of Molai to Ste. Barbe-en-Auge; and William Bacon, Lord of Molai, in 1082 founded Holy Trinity, Caen; in 1154 Rogier Bacon is mentioned as of Ville-en-Molai, who held as well estates in Wiltshire.

In Domesday are many nicknames among the English tenants, but such names perished with the bearer, they were never handed on to his descendants.

The Magni Rotuli Saccarii Normanniæ (twelfth century) contain numerous nicknames. Men are noted for their good looks, and doubtless were gratified to be called Belhomme, Belteste, Bellejamb, De Bella Visa, Le Merveilleux, and he with the handsome beard, Bellebarbe (we have already had among those who were at Hastings Barbe d'Or, the golden-bearded man). On the other hand, there were men named for their ugliness: Vis de Chien ; Vis de Loup ; the badly shaped man, Maltaille ; the pushing man, Tireavant ; the solemn man, " Qui non Ridet "; the short man, Petitsire, Courtecuisse ; the man who cocked his cap, Tortchapel ; the man with twisted neck, Tortcol, or hands, Tortemains ; the man of doubtful lineage, Sansmesle; the grasping man, Prenstout. Moral characters are named as Preuxhomme, Le Malvenu, Sanschef (Brainless). Œil de Larun was a thief ; others are Œil de Bœuf, Bat les Boes (Beat the Oxen),

NICK- AND DESCRIPTIVE NAMES

Folenfant (Foolish Child), Peu de Lit, Ammerherbe (Bitterherb), Embrasse Terre, Bailleabien, Escorchebœuf (Skinflint, doubtless), and many more.

Sir Robert Umfraville, Knight of the Garter and Vice-Admiral of England, had a nickname, as Stowe tells us "he bought such plenty of clothes and corn and other valuable commodities from Scotland that he was called *Robin Mendmarket*. Other writers say that he sold the Scots round pennyworths of their own goods taken in plunder."

Can we doubt that Miss *Mowcher* derived her name from an ancestor who created great amazement in his village by breaking away from the primitive method of blowing his nose with his fingers, and using instead a *mouchoir*?

Duncalf is a corruption of Duncroft; *Goodlad* of Good Lathe—*i.e.*, a good barn. *Monkey* stands for Monkhaugh, and *Giltpen* is a miswritten and misunderstood Gilpin. *Halfnaked* is derived from Half-an-acre, tenanted by the nominal ancestor, who went by the name of the Half-an-acred, whence the transition was easy. *Greatraikes*, or *Greatrex*, and *Raikes*, by no means indicate that the founder of the family was a scamp; it is from "raik," a cutting or sheeptrack in the fells in the North of England. The surname *Graygoose* is an anglicizing of Gregoise. My father had a coachman named Pengelly, whom we took with us when driving to the South of France. The French invariably gallicized his name to Pain-au-lait, and in like manner we have altered French names.

Godliman is a corruption of Godalming. *Golightly*, also found as Gelatley, has nothing to do with a trippant toe, but signifies the ley of some Geljat. *Midwinter* probably means a mead-vintner, and *Midnight* a mead-knecht, or servant who served out the mead. A *Medlar* is not an obtrusive person, but one who came from a township of that name in Kirkham, Lancashire. *Luckman* does not imply peculiar good fortune—the name signifies the serving-man of Luke; and *Littleboys* is the French Lillebois, as pronounced by English tongues. *Spittle* is the name of one who had a house at the spital, or hospital.

NICK- AND DESCRIPTIVE NAMES

The habit of leering at the ladies was not hereditary in the family of the *Ogles;* it comes from the Norse *Ogvaldr.*

John de Grandisson was Bishop of Exeter between the years 1327 and 1369. During his tenure of the see there were 1420 incumbents in this diocese in Devon. Of these the vast majority bore place-names. They give *de* this place or that, or *atte* some other place, or else bore a simple place-name without a prefix. A few—a very few—had trade names, as *Baker* or *Pistor,* that has the same meaning, or *Carpenter, Bolter, Farman, Gardiner, Hawker, Page, Piper, Ridler, Sumpter, Ward, Warriner, Woodman,* but nicknames are most rare. The few that exist in the record are *Coupgorge, Besta* (that is doubtful), *Dieudonné, Foot, Fox, Gambon, Kene, Maidgood, Maloysel, Merrey, Peticrue, Rake, Short, Swift, Tryst, Whitehead, Wolf,* and *Young.*

In the Cornish portion of the diocese there were 597 institutions. Almost all instituted bore place-names; the few exceptions were a Tailor, a Taverner, a Le Soor, a Le Conk. The sole nicknames are *Mackerel, Fox,* and one William *Jaune* de Trebursy, appointed Dean of Crantock 1348; a *Truwe,* a *Strong,* a *Rover,* and a *Prechour.* If we look among the patrons of livings in Devon and Cornwall in the same Bishop's tenure of the see, the only nicknames that appear are *Taundefer* for Dent-de-fer, *Prouz, Gambon,* and *Inkepenne;* but as this last is preceded by a *de,* it must be a place-name. And such it is: Inkpen is a parish in Berkshire.

Everything goes to show that we must be very cautious in accepting the face signification of a name that looks and sounds as a nickname.

At the same time it is impossible to deny that such names did get taken up and became accepted hereditary family appellations. Such were Barfoot, Crookshanks, Sheepshanks, Halfpenny, etc.; but many were French sobriquets applied by French men-at-arms and domestics to Englishmen with whom they were brought in contact, and accepted without any comprehension as to the meaning. Thus we have the surname of *Bunker* from Boncœur, *Bunting* from

NICK- AND DESCRIPTIVE NAMES

Bonnetin; *Pettifer* is Pied-de-fer, and *Firebrace* is Ferrebras. Joseph *Centlivre* was cook to Queen Anne; but the name, translated into *Hundredpounds*, occurs in 1417, when a William of that name was Mayor of Lynn. Possibly enough the original name Centlivre was a mistake for St. Livaire, who is venerated at Metz. We should look to every other source for the interpretation of a grotesque surname before accepting it as a genuine nickname.

CHAPTER XV

PREFIXES AND SUFFIXES

A NAME without a prefix is like a cup without a handle—at least, it is so in general estimation—but a suffix, instead of enhancing the worth of a name, generally derogates from its value, and is often, accordingly, dropped or disguised.

Prefixes were introduced by the Normans, but they were of a simple description, and consisted of *de* or *le*. The article had, indeed, been employed in Anglo-Saxon nicknames, but had never been handed down with the to-name to a son.

De always preceded the name of a place whence the Norman came, and where he had a castle or an earthwork crowned by a wooden structure, in which he and his family lived. At the time of the Conquest very few nobles and knights had stone dwellings. It sufficed him to throw up a tump—in French *motte*—and to crown it with a house built of wood, reached by a ladder, little better than a hen-roost. It accommodated himself and his wife and children —no more—and his men-at-arms lived in hutches below in the *basse-court* — hutches not much superior to pigsties. But when these ruffians came over with William, they swaggered as great nobles, and called themselves De This and De That, after those fowl-houses perched on top of a mound; and the simple English whom they trampled on supposed that the places after which their masters called themselves were like the stone castles William and his Barons set to work to build on English soil so as to keep the natives down.

PREFIXES AND SUFFIXES

A good many, but not all, of these adventurers, De Pierrepont, De Mortaigne, D'Evreux, or from wherever they came, on obtaining estates in England, assumed the names of their English estates, with the *De* prefixed, as De Newmarch (Newmarket), De Ford, De Ashburnham, De Newton, for on them they were able to cut a very different figure from that they had borne in the mouldy burghs in Normandy, Flanders, and Bretagne.

After a while, when these foreigners bearing such names had become thoroughly anglicized and spoke English, they let slip the *De*, and called themselves simply Ford, Ashburnham, and Newton.

But of late years it has become the fashion to reassume the *De*, sometimes where it does not pertain. We may instance De Foe.[1] Such a use of the *De* is an affectation, and is absurd, unless prefixed to a place-name. The Frenchman would make a fool of himself by calling himself De Grosjean or De Rouge. It is otherwise in Germany, with the ennobling of burghers, so that we there do meet with a Von Schneider, Von Schäffer, and a Von Schornsteinfeger—Of Tailor, Of Shepherd, Of Chimney-sweep. Of a Von Falkenstein or a Von Rabeneck, one may predicate that they can boast that their names have been inscribed in history, probably in letters of blood; but of a Herr von Pumpernickel nothing is known save that his forbears ate black bread from the days of Arminius, and were honest peasants, plundered and maltreated by the Vons periodically.

In cases where the place-name began with a vowel, the *De* adhered to it so closely as to defy being ripped away, and thus we have *Danvers* (D'Anvers), *Devreux*, *Daubigny*, *Darcy*, and *Dawney*.

A man was often named after his place of birth, irrespective of his having any land there. Thus, William of Wykeham's father was surnamed *Long*, and William Waynflete was the son of Richard *Pallen*, also called the Barber.

So of late years, when the painter Schnorr made himself a name in Germany as a clever limner, he elected to subscribe himself Schnorr von Carolsfeld.

[1] Daniel Defoe was the son of James Foe, a butcher.

PREFIXES AND SUFFIXES

There was a certain linden-tree at Seckendorf under which the villagers met and watched the youngsters at their sports. In 950 the Emperor Otto arrived there on his return from Italy, seated himself beneath the tree, and watched the young villagers disporting themselves. The day was hot and the flies troublesome, so Otto asked for a branch wherewith to fan his face and brush the insects away. At once a young peasant climbed the tree and returned to the Emperor with a bough, which he tendered with such grace, and with a speech so well turned, that Otto said: "I dare be sworn that you are as ready with your hand as you are glib with your tongue. I will take you into my service!" Such was the origin of the illustrious family of Seckendorf, that bore the name of the native village of the founder, who owned not so much soil in it as he could put his foot upon and call it his freehold.

The *Le* introduced by the Normans was the prefix before a descriptive name of a trade or else of a functionary, or expressing some personal characteristic: Le Roux, he of the ruddy complexion or with red hair; Le Portier, the doorward. L'Estranger has suffered, like the White Cat, with the loss of its head; it has become *Stranger*. With its tail cut off it is *L'Estrange*. Le also preceded the designation of a man from foreign parts, as Le Brabazon, Le Breton. The prefix still remains in some names, as *Le Neveu, Legard, Lenoir, Legatt*. Sometimes it has fallen away, like *Brune* for *Le Brun* and *Neeves* for *Le Neveu*.

In England generally *the* took the place of *le*, and a tradesman was called John the Smith, William the Cook, Hal the Baker. But the definite article was speedily dispensed with. In the second part of "Henry IV." we have Justice Shallow say to his steward Davy: "A couple of short-legged hens, a joint of mutton, and any pretty little tiny kickshaws, tell William Cook."

In 1479 Robert Ricart was elected Town Clerk of Bristol, and, at the instance of the Mayor, William Spencer wrote a Chronicle or Mayor's Kalendar of Bristol.[1] He gives a list

---
[1] "The Maire of Bristowe is Kalender," ed. Camden Society, 1872.

PREFIXES AND SUFFIXES

of the Mayors, Provosts, and Sheriffs of the town from 1217, and this list is of interest, as it shows us the formation, modification, and transformation of surnames. At first the majority are either *at, de, à, le*: Adam le Page, Philip le Cok (Cook), Thomas le Spycer, Thomas le Chalnere (Chaloner), Henry le Cheynere (chain-maker); also David le Wight (White), John le Longe, Thomas le Roux, Robert le Bele (le Bel, the Good-looking); also Walter le Fraunceis and Henry le Walleys (the Welshman). But *de* prevails: Richard de Bury, William de Chiltone, Elyas de Axbridge, and many more. We have also Richard atte Ok (at the Oak), Radulph atte Slupe, John at Wall, John at Knolle, Robert at Woode, Robert at Welle. But sometimes the *at* is omitted, as Thomas Upditch, Hugh Upwell; and also the *le* occasionally falls away, as William Clerk, Robert Parmenter, Galfredus Ussher.

But what is especially interesting with regard to the *de* and *le* is that both totally disappear after 1355, when Richard le Spycer was Mayor, and Richard de Dene was Bailiff. After that date we have Reynold French, Walter Derby, Robert Chedder, John Slow, John Kene, Richard Spicer, William Draper, John Fisher, Richard Hatter, and the like.

The episcopal registers of the thirteenth century show us that the clergy who were ordained, and those inducted into livings, were known by the villages and manors whence they came. Almost invariably they bore place-names. It was with extreme rarity that they bore such names as were indicative of trade. Not but that many of them may have been the sons of tradesmen or of officials, but that trade and official names had not become surnames to those who were not in trade or office. The register of Bishop Brondescombe of Exeter (1257-1280) contains one name only indicative of an office in a couple of pages of entries: it is that of Le Botillere. Farther on we get one of a trade, almost an unique instance—Le Teinturier (the Dyer), Prior of Launceston—and no nicknames whatsoever; but what it does reveal to us is that many names that now appear to us as

PREFIXES AND SUFFIXES

nicknames are actually corruptions, usually of place-names. They ceased to be generally understood, and were assimilated to some name more or less phonetically equivalent, as *Greenhorn* for Grenoven, a place near Tavistock; *Parrott* for Pierrot; *Loveless* for Lovelace; Vairshield became *Fairchild*. *Vair* is an heraldic tincture.

Now we pass on to the close of the fourteenth and beginning of the fifteenth century, to the register of Stafford, Bishop of Exeter (1395-1419). We shall find that the condition of affairs as touching surnames is completely changed. *De* and *le* have fallen away altogether, and there are fewer place-names and a considerable number of trade-names.

In like manner the *de* falls away, but *atte* lingers on. Atte Ford, Atte Haye, Atte Mill, Atte Stone, Atte Water, Atte Well, Atte Wood, soon, however, to be incorporated into the name, as Atwell, Atwood, and Aston, or to fall away altogether, and leave Ford, Haye, Stone as surnames.

Some demur has been raised relative to the termination "cock" and "cox," as signifying "the cook." Mr. Lower —and after him Dr. Barber—will have it that this is a diminutive; according to the latter, brought in by the Flemings.[1]

But le Coq occurs at the time of the Conqueror, and wherever the termination does occur, it is conjoined to an abbreviated Christian name, as *Willcox*, *Hancock* (John), *Badcock* (Bartholomew), *Sandercock* Alexander), *Simcox* and *Simcoe* (Simon the Cook).

Indeed, William Bitton, Bishop of Exeter, who died in 1307, in his will leaves a bequest "Symoni Coco"; and Richard de Gravesend, Bishop of London, who died in 1303, makes a bequest to "Magistro Johano Coco." Stephen le Cokke was Provost of Bristol in 1261, and James Cokkys

[1] Pott ("Personen-namen") does not recognize "cock" as a diminutive in the Germanic languages. Quoting Ehrentraut's "Frisische Archæologie," i. 3, he points out that many Dutch surnames are trade-names, and that the article has fallen away, as Hinrek Kok. The numerous Koks found in the Netherlands are descendants of cooks (pp. 547, 548).

PREFIXES AND SUFFIXES

Bailiff in 1407. We can hardly doubt that Symon Coc would become Simcox, and James Cokkis be turned into Jacocks.[1] Chaucer spells " Cook " as *Cok*. Le Coq is still a surname in Normandy and Brittany; indeed, it is the name of a banker at Dinan. In a nobleman's house the official in the kitchen was William le Coq, but that of the English squire was William the Cook; so we get both names, *Willcock* and William *Cook*.

But the termination *cox* or *cock* does not always represent a professor of the culinary art, for it is occasionally used in place of *cott*. *Glasscock* is from Glascote, in Tamworth parish. *Woodcock* is really Woodcott. Cottswold as a surname has become *Coxwold*, and Cottswell is turned into *Coxwell*. Geoffrey le Coq has left us his name in both forms, *Jeffcot* and *Jeffcock*.

I have spoken elsewhere of the prefixes *O'* and *Mac*, and will say no more about them, or of the Welsh *ap*, that has given us such names as Bunyan (ap Einion), Price (ap Rice), Bevan (ap Ewan), Bowen (ap Owen), etc.

Sometimes, where the original name began with *th*, it has been altered by the employment instead of *st*, as *Sturgess* for Thurgis—*i.e.*, Thorgisl, the hostage of Thor. But, on the other hand, the *s* initial letter has more frequently fallen away. Spigurnell has become *Pickernell*, and *Pillsbury* stands for Spillsbury.

Ph has taken the place of *f*, or the reverse. *Physick* stands for Fishwick, and *Philbrick* for Felbrigg in Norfolk. *Filpott* stands for Phillipot, and *Phillimore* for Finmoor.

Ch has taken the place of *j*. Thus Job has become first *Jubb*, and then *Chubb* and *Chope*. *Choice* is another form of Joyce, and *Challand* of Jalland; that also is found in *Yelland*. *V* and *f* are interchangeable in the West of England, as *Facey* for Vesci, *Vowell* for *Fowell*, and *Vowler* for Fowler. Indeed, among the Devonshire peasantry no distinction is made between the letters. *Vokes* is the same as *Foulkes*, and

[1] When we get such an entry as Joannes Alcokson, 1379, it certainly looks as though John were the son of Allen the Cook. So also William Wilkocson, 1379, is William the son of Will the Cook.

PREFIXES AND SUFFIXES

Venner as *Fenner*. *At* and *atten*, as prefixes, have been spoken of sufficiently. The suffix *ot* has also been mentioned as a diminutive brought from Normandy. Jeanot signifies Little John; Mariot is Little Mary. Shakespeare uses Carlot as a diminutive of Churl. Some difficulty has been found in discovering the origin of the name *Piggot*. It has been supposed to stand for *picoté*, one small pox-marked. The famous family of Pegotty, no doubt, did thence derive its name, but we cannot suppose that so early as the Conquest the final syllable of *picoté* had already fallen away. It is more probable that the surname was derived from *pigge*, the Scandinavian for a girl, and that the family descended from some captive wench, the prey of a Norse settler.

From Margot, the diminutive of Margaret, comes *Margotson*. The termination *ot* is a common French diminutive: *archerot* is a small archer, *augelot* a little ditch. *Baggot* may be a diminutive of *bague*, and designate the man with the small gold ring.

Another diminutive is the termination *et*. We speak of a leaflet, a hamlet, a ringlet. And *Harriett* is the feminine, but actually the diminutive, of Henry. So *Hamlet* is that of Hamo, and *Paulett* of Paul. But of this more presently.

The Normans affected changing an ending in *elle* into *eau*, and *al* into *aux*. Isabelle became Isabeau, and this was turned in English into Isbet and Ebbet, whence our surname *Ibbotson*.

The *ot* is sometimes softened down to *y*. Thus *Polliot* becomes *Pawley*, Lancelot is reduced to *Lancey*, and Hallet to *Halley*.

Another diminutive is *et*. Thus *Corbett* from *corbeau*, and we have the name *Hewett* for Little Hugh, and *Marcett* for Little Mark.

The suffix *ing* signifies "the son of" or "descendants of." This fact has been pretty well worked to death by Mr. Kemble and Mr. Ferguson. The former makes out some 220 tribes to have colonized England, solely deducing this from the termination *ing* or *ingas* found scattered over the country. But Glaestingabyrg (Glastonbury) does not draw its name from any imaginary Saxon family of

PREFIXES AND SUFFIXES

Glaestingas, but from Glasynys, the British for "Green Island." Carlingham, Fotheringay, Warrington, Pocklington, may very possibly derive from the settlements of the sons of Carl, Fothere, Ware, and Folko; but *ing* as a termination often enough has the signification of " dwellers at."

Again, *ing* takes the place of *win*. *Golding* replaces Goldwin, *Gunning* stands for Gunnwin, *Harding* for Hardwin, *Browning* for Brunwin. So that we must not be peremptory in grouping all the names ending in *ing* as tribal designations. But this has been already shown.

The termination *ey* or *y* often signifies an island; but not always. It is occasionally a softening of *eg*, *edge*. *Anstey* is Atten-steg, at the stile. The *y* or *ie*, again, is a diminutive, as Baby for Babe, Brandy for Brand (burnt wine). In Scotland the *ie* takes the place of the English *y*. *Dick* becomes Dixie; in English it would be Dicky. *Hankey* is the diminutive of Hans, or John, and *Sankey* of Alexander. *Wilkie* is the same of William. In nine cases out of ten in place-names, *ey* and *ay* as an ending represents *hey* or *hay*, a hedge, as Fotheringay, Goldingay.

Lin or *lyn* is equivalent to the German *lein*, and becomes *ling* at the end of a name. Hamelin is a diminutive of Hamo. *Wakeling* stands for Wakelin, Little Wake. *Kin* or *kyn* corresponds to the German *chen*. *Peterkin* is Small Peter, and a pipkin is a little pot. In an old poem entitled " A Litol soth Sormun " it is said of the maiden Malekyn (Little Male or Mary) and Janekyn:

> " Masses and matins
> Ne kepeth they nouht,
> But Wilekyn and Watekyn
> Be in their thouht."

Kin as a termination has nothing to do with kindred. *Kin* and *kins* often get abbreviated to *iss* and *es*. Hence *Perkins* becomes *Perkiss*, and finally *Perks*; *Tonkins* is reduced to *Tonks*, *Dawkins* to *Dawkes*. In Anglo-Saxon there were two endings for the genitive case. When a name ended in *a* or *e*, it took *n*, and became *an* or *en* in the possessive; otherwise it took *s*. Thus *Puttenham* and *Tottenham* were the homes of Putta and Totta. But we cannot say that

PREFIXES AND SUFFIXES

Sydenham was the home of *Syd*, or even that it was a southern homestead, for *sid* is the Anglo-Saxon for unenclosed land, and a Sydenham is a Newtake.

The termination *by*, for a farm or dwelling, in Normandy became *bœuf*, as Elbœuf, in English rendered *Elbow*, the name of one of Shakespeare's foolish constables. Volney, the French traveller, had for his real name Chassebœuf, but was so afraid lest it should be said of him that he was descended from a bullock-driver, that, like a snob, he altered his name. The termination *el* is found in German diminutives, as *Handel, Mendel, Hirschell;* but the ending does not always imply a German origin, as in *Coterell* and *Cockrell*.

The termination *ard* is usually Norman-French, as Camisard, pillard. Hence we have *Hansard, Collard, Ballard, Cowlard*. Another termination is *iff*. Some French names ending in *val* become *vau*, and *vau* in English becomes *iff*. *Joliff* stands for Jollivau. We might suppose *Stiff* was a corruption of Estivau, if we did not hold it to be an abbreviation of Stephen.

Sop is a corruption of "hope," as *Blenkinsop* for Blenkin's-hope, or hill. This I have already shown. *Allsopp* for Ellis (or Elias) hope. *Skog* (forest) is often reduced to *scoe*, as *Briscoe* and *Jellicoe*, for the scog of Giolla and of Brice.

Ship, again, is a corruption of *hope*, as *Nettleship* for Nettlehope.

White also is a corruption of *Thwaite, Applewhite*. We have both forms *Hebblethwaite* and *Hebblewhite*, denoting a clearing for apples. *Musslewhite* is Musslethwaite, the same as *Micklethwaite*.

Thorpe, as already pointed out, becomes *throp* or *thrup—Winthrop* for *Winthorpe*. *Thrupp* is no other than *Thorpe*.

The suffix *man* has four or five distinct meanings:

1. Usually it is given as the equivalent of "servant."[1] Thus, *Higman* is the serving-man of Hick, or Richard; *Merriman* is the servant of Mary; *Pulman*, that of Paul;

[1] In some cases merely devotional surnames, formed like Gill-Christ, Gill-Patrick. He who assumed the name was by no means necessarily a domestic servant, but one who placed himself under the protection of a saint.

PREFIXES AND SUFFIXES

Houseman is a house domestic. *Kingsman* or *Kinsman* is the King's servant.

2. It signifies also the dweller at a certain place: *Heathman* is the dweller on the heath; *Woodman* may be either he who lives in the wood or he who is a woodcutter by his trade; *Bridgeman* may be the man who lives by the bridge or the toll-taker on the bridge; *Yeatman* is he who occupies a cottage by the gate.

3. It also represents an occupation, as *Cheeseman*, a cheesemonger; *Portman*, the gatekeeper or porter; *Palfreyman*, the stableman in charge of the ladies' palfreys; *Stoneman*, the stonecutter; *Bateman*, the bear-baiter.

4. It is as well a corruption of the termination *ham* in place-names. *Tottman* stands for Tottenham; *Packman* alike for the packer by trade and for him who comes from Pakenham; *Gillman* may well be a corruption of Gillingham. *Heyman* is either the man who looked after the hay or is a corruption of Highnam in Gloucestershire. *High* is very generally pronounced by countryfolk *hey*, as Hightor is called Heytor. *Lyman* is Lyneham.

5. It stands as a modification of *mond* in personal names, as *Gorman* for Gormund, *Wyman* for Wymond. Again, it is not infrequently a corruption of *ham*. *Deadman* may stand equally for a corruption of Debenham and for a dudman (old clothes man).

Hewer as a suffix resolves itself into *y*. *Woodyer* is properly wood-hewer. Sometimes even that letter falls away, as *Stoner* for Stone-hewer, and *Flesher* for Flesh-hewer, a butcher. But *y* is often introduced for euphony, as *Locky*er for Locker, *Sawyer* for Sawer, *Bowyer* for Bower.

Wright occasionally gets altered into *rich*, as *Woodrich* for Woodwright; Kenwright is changed into *Kendrick*.

Son as a termination has sometimes displaced *ston* or *stone*, thus converting a local into a personal name, as *Baldison* for Balderston or Balderstone, *Shillson* for Shilston, and *Kilson* for Kelston. Shakerley has become a personal name—*Shakelady*. *S* is occasionally added to a monosyllabic place-name, as *Stokes* for " of Stoke."

CHAPTER XVI

NAME STORIES

A GENTLEMAN attending service at St. Andrews, Wells Street, London, for the first time, at the conclusion inquired of the churchwarden what was the name of the preacher.

" Mr. Stonewig."

" And of the clergyman who sang the Office ? "

" Mr. Griffinhoof."

" Sir," said the stranger, flushing red, " I asked for information, and not to be insulted."

Actually these were the names of two curates at that time. Griffinhoof was an English rendering of the name Greifenclau, borne by a noble and distinguished family in Germany, derived from the possession by it of a narwhal's tooth, which it fondly believed to be the claw of a griffin slain by an ancestor in deadly conflict. A member of this house settling in England had translated its name into corresponding English. Stonewig is probably also a version of the German Steinveg, which would be more properly rendered Stoneway or Stanway.

At a great Court ball given in Vienna, where all were masked, appeared a stately and graceful youth, who danced several times with one of the Princesses. The Emperor, marvelling who he was, bade him unmask, when he was recognized as the hangman's son. " You have come to Court as a rascal, and as a rascal dared to dance with my daughter," said the Kaiser, " and the name of a rascal you shall bear ! Kneel down. It ill behoves a Princess to have

NAME STORIES

a common citizen as partner. I ennoble you as Schelm [rascal] of Bergen." The family died out in the male line in 1844.

A considerable number of family names have legends attaching to them that attempt to explain their origin. The name is due to some incident in the story of the founder, or else is a clumsy fabrication to account for the device on the crest or coat of arms. There are comparatively few English families that have stories connected with their names; but this is not the case with the Scotch, and such tales are common enough on the Continent. In a few instances the traditions may have a substantial basis. For instance, as Elizabeth of Hungary was on her way to Thuringia to be married to the Margrave Louis, one day the cavalcade passed a pale, half-starved woman, with a babe at her breast and a lean boy at her side. She begged for food, but the knights swept by, disregarding her appeal, and all the squires exhibited a like indifference, save one, who gave to the beggar-woman his day's portion of bread and wine. Elizabeth was so pleased that she called him to her side, knighted him on the spot, and bade him thenceforth be *Schenk* (butler) at the Wartburg.

She further favoured him by obtaining from Louis of Thuringia a grant of land, and Schenk became the progenitor of a knightly family that assumed the title of "butler" as a surname and occupied the castle of Schweinsburg.

Snooks, it must be admitted, is not a beautiful name, yet it has a sufficiently respectable origin. A male child was found deserted by his mother at Sevenoaks. It was taken up by kindly people, who reared it, and eventually put it out in life, after having it baptized with the name of William, and called it Sevenoaks, after the place where found. William de Sevenoaks became Lord Mayor of London in the sixth year of Henry V., was knighted, and died in 1432. He left benefactions to his native place, that were doubtless misused, as was his name when degenerated to Snooks.

In the county of Devon, on the Exe, lived for many

NAME STORIES

generations a yeoman family of the name of Suckbitch. It has but recently become extinct in the male line. A story accounts for this remarkable name.

A West Saxon chief was hunting in the forest one day when he discovered a male child in the wood, with none near it save a large bitch, that was suckling it. The parents could not be discovered. The chieftain accordingly adopted the child and gave it the name of Suckbitch, which it and all its descendants were to bear, and he further conferred upon it an estate near the Exe where it was found.

Before it became extinct some of the family altered the designation to Suckbury.

Many a legend explaining the derivation of a name is an afterthought. A story has been invented to account for what seemed peculiar.

Thus the story of the origin of the name *Napier* is distinctly a fabrication. Napier comes, as already said, from a napper, the official at Court who looked after the nappery, or table-linen. But this did not please the family, so the following tale was invented and promulgated:

"One of the ancient Earls of Lennox in Scotland had issue three sons: the eldest succeeded him in the earldom; the second, whose name was Donald; and the third named Sillchrist (probably Gilchrist). The then King of Scots, having wars, did convocate his lieges to the battle. Amongst them that were commanded was the Earl of Lennox, who, keeping his eldest son at home, sent his second son to serve for him with the forces under his command. The battle went hard with the Scots, for the enemy, pressing furiously upon them, forced them to lose ground, until at last they fell to flat running away, which, being perceived by Donald, he pulled his father's standard from the bearer thereof, and, valiantly encountering the foe (being well followed up by the Earl of Lennox's men), he repulsed the enemy, and changed the fortune of the day, whereby a great victory was got. After the battle, as the manner is, everyone advancing and setting forth his own acts, the King said unto them: 'Ye have all done valiantly, but there is one amongst you that

NAME STORIES

hath *na pier!'* [no equal]; and calling Donald into his presence, commanded him, in regard of his worth, service, and augmentation of his honour, to change his name from Lennox to Napier, and gave him lands in Fife and the lands of Goffurd, and made him his own servant." This story is as old as the reign of Charles I., for it occurs in a manuscript written by Sir W. Segar, Garter King-of-Arms.

Equally fabulous is the legend of the origin of the name of *Hay*, borne by the Earl of Errol. It is related that the founder of that family, with his two sons, held successfully the pass of Lancarty against the Danes in 942 by shouting as he smote the invaders, "Hay! hay! hay!" Actually, the name came from a hedged-in enclosure.

The tale circulates that once upon a time a Yorkshire gentleman, being about to let slip a brace of greyhounds to run after a hare, held them so unskilfully as to strangle the hounds; whence he obtained the sobriquet of *Maleverer*—in Latin, *Malus Leporarius*, the bad hare-hunter, whereas actually the name comes from *Malus Operarius*, the bad workman. It occurs in Domesday in Essex: "Terra Adamis filii Dusandi de Malis Operibus" (Durand of bad deeds; in fact, a ne'er-do-weel).

Of the great family of the Corvini in Rome it was related that on a certain occasion a Tribune, Marcus Valerius, was challenged by a Gaul to single combat. He accepted the challenge. At the moment of conflict a crow appeared and attacked the eyes of the Gaul, and so distracted him that he fell an easy prey to the Roman. The story was invented to explain the fact that the crow was a totem of a family in the Valerian gens.

A very important family among the first settlers in Iceland was that descended from Kveldulf (the evening wolf). How he got that designation is explained by a legend. He was said, as soon as the sun set, to change his character from one of good-humour to that of wolfish ferocity. On one occasion, in the evening, his son, a mere child, offended him, and he rushed to slaughter him, when the nurse interposed, and old Kveldulf literally tore her to pieces.

NAME STORIES

The legendary explanation of the origin of the family name of *Ayre*, or *Eyre*, is altogether absurd.

"The first of the family was named Truelove, but at the Battle of Hastings, October 14, 1066, William was flung from his horse and his helmet beaten into his face, which Truelove observing, pulled it off and horsed him again. The Duke told him: 'Thou shalt hereafter from Truelove be called Eyre [or Air], because thou hast given me the air I breathe.' After the battle the Duke, on inquiry respecting him, found him severely wounded (his leg and thigh having been struck off), and ordered him the utmost care, and on his recovery gave him lands in Derby in reward for his services, and the leg and thigh in armour cut off for his crest, an honorary badge still worn by all the Eyres in England."[1]

The story is obviously apocryphal. There is no Truelove, an English and not a Norman name, in the Roll of Battle Abbey, and the tale supposes William the Bastard to have spoken English, a language of which he understood not one word. The tale has been made up to account for the name and the crest.

Very different is the story of the origin of the name *Lockhart*. This may be true: that a follower of James, Lord Douglas, who accompanied him to the Holy Land, was requested by his master, who died in the Crusade, to convey his heart back to Scotland, and this the retainer did in a locked casket. In consequence of this, the family bears as its arms a heart clasped by a padlock. That the story is possibly true is due to the fact that at the period of the Crusades it was by no means unusual for the hearts of knights and nobles dying abroad to be conveyed home. There are not a few "heart-stones" in the churches of England; there is one at Molland in Devon, containing the heart of a Courtenay, and the heart of Richard Cœur de Lion is preserved at Rouen in the museum.

Fabulous is the story of the *Osbornes*. This name is Scandinavian, and signifies the Bear of the Aesir, the Divine ancestors of the Norse race. But all knowledge of the

[1] Thorpe, "Catalogue of the Deeds of Battle Abbey."

NAME STORIES

signification was lost in the days when Christianity had been accepted, and a story was invented to explain the origin of the name. Walter, a Norman knight, playing at chess with William the Bastard one summer evening on the banks of the Ouse, succeeded in every game. The King threw down the board, saying that he had no more stakes to risk. "Sir," said Sir Walter, "here is land." "There is so," said William, "and if thou beatest me in this game also, thine shall be all the land on this side of the burn which thou canst see from the seat on which thou art now seated." Sir Walter again defeated the Conqueror, and William, clapping him on the shoulder, said : " Henceforth thou shalt be called Ouseburne."

This story labours under the same defect as that which accounts for the origin of the name of Eyre.

The *Thirlwalls* are said to be so called from an ancestor, a Saxon chief named Wade, who built a fort upon the Roman wall which he *thirled* or broke through.

A legendary tale is attached to the name of *Montmorris*: that it was borne by a Moor who lived in the mountains—the Atlas, we suppose—and that he joined Charlemagne and became a good Christian and a paladin. This is nonsense. The name comes from Mont St. Maurice. St. Maurice was an exceedingly popular saint among knights, as he was a soldier martyr.

The story of the origin of the name of Field-Marshal *Blücher* is this: His ancestor, serving under Prince Borwin of Mecklenburg against the pagan Wends, on one occasion single-handed defended a chapel against them when they sought to desecrate it. When succour arrived, he was found covered with blood, and he handed the keys of the chapel to the Prince, who thereupon bade him assume the name of Blütiger, or the Bloody, and adopt the keys as crest and coat of arms. Blütiger has been corrupted to Blücher.

The noble family of Bojanowsky in Poland was originally called Baran (sheep), but it changed its name to Jundisza (bridegroom). One day a Baran was going to the altar with his bride when he received summons to attend his Prince

NAME STORIES

immediately. He at once obeyed, leaving his bride in the church. In commemoration of this prompt obedience, his name was changed from Sheep to Bridegroom.

The family of *Turnbull* is supposed to derive from an ancestor Ruel, who saved Robert Bruce from being gored in Stirling Park by catching the bull by its horns and turning it about. Actually Turnbull comes from the Anglo-Saxon *Trumbold*.

In 1003 the family of Wrschowcen in Bohemia formed a plot to murder the reigning Duke, so as to win the ducal throne for one of themselves. To attain this object some of the brothers lured the young Duke Jaromir into the forest to hunt, and drawing him from his retinue, bound him to an oak, and were proceeding to shoot him, when a common forester, named Howorra, emerged from the bushes. The brothers at once seized and bound him to a lime-tree, to kill him also, lest he should betray them. Before his arm was fastened he begged to be suffered to sound his horn. This was granted. He blew so loud a blast that the Duke's retainers came up before the brothers had put their plot into complete execution. The Duke and the huntsman were released and the brothers slain. In reward for what he had done, Jaromir ennobled the man, who had two sons, and one was named Duba (an oak) and the other Lippa, or Laba (a lime-tree), and they bore on their shield two boughs crossed—the one of an oak, the other of a lime.

Equally fabulous is the story of the origin of the name of *Purseglove*. In one of the commotions in the North of England a gentleman deemed it advisable to fly his country, and he did so with such precipitation that he took no money with him. He would have fared badly but that he managed to pick up on the highway a purse in a glove. This he took to himself, and settled in the South, and there founded a family. Deeming it well to keep his original name a secret, he called himself thenceforth Purseglove. There was a Thomas Pursglove, or Purslow, Bishop of Hull. Purslow is in Shropshire, and Purslow is probably the correct form of the name, the *low* being the tumulus of one Brusi.

NAME STORIES

Camden relates that a certain Frenchman who had craftily smuggled one Crioll, a feudal lord in Kent, out of France in the reign of Edward II., when he was in great danger of imprisonment, if not of his life, and brought him over the Channel into his own county, received from the nobleman in return for his services the estate of Swinfield, and on account of the *finesse* displayed by him on this occasion, he adopted the surname of Finesse, originating that of *Fynnes*.

Between the Waag and the Moldau, Prince Pirwina was hunting and lost his way. A poor bird-snarer gave him shelter for the night and food. Next day the Prince granted him the land on which stood his hut as far as to the bank of the Moldau, and dubbed him knight. As the fellow, whose name was Welen, was going about his acquired estate, he climbed a hill, on which he thought he might build a castle. He was barefooted, and struck his toe against a stone, and it bled. "Ha!" thought he, "henceforth I need go no longer barefoot" (*go nedger boskowice*). Thenceforth he took Boskowice, or Barefoot, as his family name.

The Crivelli family pretend that in the reign of Augustus an ancestress was a vestal virgin at Rome. She was accused of having broken her vows. She offered to prove her innocence by carrying water from the Tiber in a sieve. She performed this feat. Afterwards, when her time as a vestal had expired, she married and founded the Crivelli family, which in its name (Ital., *crivallo*, a sieve) and in its arms recalls the story of its origin.

The following story may possibly be true:

In the disturbances in Bohemia in 1212, when the Chancellor Scornir was driven out of the country, the people raged against his family, burnt his castle, and massacred his sons. One of these latter alone was saved, a little boy, whom his nurse concealed in a hole that is still shown in the chimney of the castle of Chudenitz. When the rioters had departed he was drawn forth, and was so covered with soot that he was passed off as Czerny (black), because it was still unsafe for it to be known that he was a Scornir. As

NAME STORIES

this latter name long remained hateful in the land, the descendants of this lad elected to call themselves *Czerny*.

The name of *Fortescue* is said to have been bestowed on Sir Richard le Fort, one of those who attended William the Bastard to England. In the Battle of Hastings he protected his chief from the arrows of the English archers by extending his shield before him, whereupon the Conqueror said : " Forte scutum salus Ducum " (a strong shield is the safety of commanders), and the family has preserved this as their motto, and call themselves no longer Le Fort, but Fortescue.

Not one of those who record the history of the battle mentions such an incident. Moreover, in Normandy there were two noble families, quite distinct—one Le Fort, the other Fortescue. The story is mere fable.

The German noble family of *Kalkreuth* had its origin from this : A nobleman suspected his wife of being too fond of his page, and he determined to have him put out of the way. So he went to his limekilns, and bade the burner throw in the first of his lord's servants who arrived and asked whether he had done his duty. Then he bade the page go with this question to the kilns. Before leaving, the Countess required the youth to enter a chapel on the way and pray for her son, who was ill of a fever.

The Count next despatched another servant, the man who had maligned the page to his master. He passed the chapel whilst the other was engaged in prayer.

Presently the page rose from his knees, went to the kiln, and asked whether his master's commands had been obeyed. The lime-burner pointed to the kiln and laughed. " He is there," said he. On his return the Count recognized the hand of God in this. The page was knighted and assumed the name of Limekiln, or Kalkreuth, and for crest a kilner holding a lime-rake in his hand.

The name of *Lepell* is not unknown in England, as one of a family that came over with George I. from Hanover ; and there is a song on a great beauty of that name, which was once in great vogue ; she married Lord Hervey :

NAME STORIES

"Had I Hanover, Bremen, and Varding,
And likewise the Duchy of Zell,
I would part with them all for a farthing,
To win my sweet Molly Lepell.
Were I but the King of Great Britain,
I'd govern the Ministry well;
To support the great throne that I sit in,
I'd have none but my Molly Lepell."

The family originated in Pomerania. In a battle the nine brothers perished. Then, at the request of the Sovereign, the Pope released the sisters from their vows in the convent where they had been placed, and they married; but in commemoration of their brothers they assumed as the family crest a damsel with a hat, in the band of which are stuck nine spoons (Löffel, or, in the vulgar tongue, Leppel).

A Slavonic knight went to serve in Spain with a Moorish Prince. One day the Moorish Princess asked him to play chess with her. "What is to be the reward of the winner?" he asked.

"To smash the board on the head of the defeated," said she.

The Slavonic knight won, and, taking the board, banged the Princess on the head and made it bleed, so that she was obliged to bind it up with a kerchief.

After that the knight thought it best to get back to his native land, where he assumed the name of *Bretwitz*, or the witty chessboard-player, and the chessboard as his arms, and as his crest the Moorish Princess with bound head.

Among the Anglo-Saxon families who resisted the domination of William was that of *Bulstrode*. The head of the family was despoiled of his estate by the victorious Norman, who presented it to one of his own followers, and furnished him with a body of men to seize it by force.

The Saxon called in the aid of some neighbours to defend his ancestral acres, and entrenched himself within an earthwork. The besieged had no horses, so they were fain to bestride certain bulls which they had brought into the enclosure, and thus mounted they made a sally and routed the Norman assailants. William, on hearing of this exploit,

NAME STORIES

invited the brave Saxon to visit him; so the chief and his seven sons once more bestrode their bulls and proceeded to Court. William was so pleased that he bade them remain in undisturbed possession of their land, and ever after bear the name of *Bulstrode*.

In 1192, at the Battle of Ascalon, a young knight of the House of Arundel, clad all in white, fought with such gallantry that when he came out of the battle his maiden armour was bespattered with Saracen blood. Richard Cœur de Lion granted him as arms a lion gules in a field argent, between six crosslets of the first, and for motto, *Tinctus cruore Saraceno*. His descendants thence assumed the surname of *Tynte* (*tincti*), and settled in Somerset.

The *La Scala* family derive both name and arms from an achievement in scaling a tower; the *La Saca* from an ancestor who always went into battle with a sack of provisions over his shoulder. " I cannot fight," said he, " unless I eat. Fighting is hungry work."

A Bavarian noble family is that of *Notschaft*. A knight of Wernberg went to the Crusades, and was absent twelve years. When he returned he was a wayworn, ragged, and grey pilgrim, and none recognized him save his old dog, that wagged its tail and fawned on him. In commemoration of this he assumed the dog's head as his crest, and because of the need he had endured he took the name of Notschaft.

The German family of *Fleming* is not content with the reasonable derivation of the name from immigrants from Flanders, but pretends that their ancestors were Flaminii, who went to Britain when the Romans held the isle, and remained there. One branch passed over to the land of the Teutons, but other of the Flaminii hung on in England, and their descendants are the English family of Flemings.

The name of *Knott* is common enough in the North of England. It is the English form of the Danish *Knut* or *Knud*, that has been Latinized into Canute. The story concerns a King of Jutland. Gorm the Bairnless found ale such as the Northmen drank somewhat heady, and he had acquired a liking for the light wines of the Rhine. Accord-

NAME STORIES

ingly he sent some thralls into Holstein to purchase for him a supply. They were on their way back to Jutland with a train of horses laden with wine-kegs, when they were overtaken by night in the Forest of Mirkwood.

Unable to proceed farther, they camped out under the trees, lighted a fire, and cast themselves down to sleep, after having tethered their horses. The moon shone and smote through the foliage, forming patches of silver on the sward. The owls hooted and the night-jars cried, but what disturbed the men most was the incessant wailing of a child, and they found that under the circumstances sleep was impossible. Next morning they went in quest of the babe. The undergrowth was dense, and they had to hack their way through thorns, sloe-bushes, and brambles, till they reached the spot whence came the sobbing. There they found a babe wrapped in fine linen, that was fastened in a knot over the breast, and in untying this out fell three gold rings. Moreover, the child was folded about with a silken mantle.

The little creature stretched out its arms, and its cheeks were beblubbered with tears. When one of the men took it up, and the babe laid hold of his nose and sucked vigorously, his heart became so soft that he protested the infant must not be left to perish. So the thralls took the child with them, and conveyed it to King Gorm.

To him they excused themselves for being so late by the fact that they had been delayed on account of the babe. They had been obliged to feed it with milk. It had a ravenous appetite, and, being unprovided with the natural apparatus for nourishing an infant, they had been constrained to dip their fingers in milk, and feed the child by this slow and unsatisfactory method.

King Gorm took the child on his lap, liked its appearance, poured water over it, and gave it the name of Knut, or "the knot," because of the knotted linen on its breast that had contained the gold rings.

The fact of Gorm taking the child on his knee constituted legal adoption. He now passed over the little foundling to women to be nursed, better adapted in every way to this end than rough thralls, or even than a King upon his throne. Gorm had the child brought to him every day, and became vastly attached to it. "One may be sure," said he, "that he comes of a good family—he is so beautiful, and has in his face a look of true nobility. Moreover, the rings and silk found on him are tokens that he is the issue of no common folk."

As the little Knut grew up he became more handsome and intelligent, and wormed his way into the innermost heart of old King Gorm. At length the King fell sick, so he called his counsellors about him, and said that, as he was childless, it was his intention to set over Jutland a King to succeed him, who would be generally acceptable to his people; and as to the Overking of Sweden and Denmark, so long as the customary tribute was paid, he cared not who was lord in the land. Then he named Knut the foundling. The people assented, and when Gorm died Knut was accepted without demur.

One of the first acts of King Knut was to summon a Thing, or assembly, of the people, and announce his intention to reward liberally any man who could enlighten him as to who were his parents. This was rumoured far and wide.

One evening two Saxon men arrived at the King's hall, and asked to be presented before King Knut, as they had important information to communicate. When introduced, they said: "Is it true, sire, that you have promised rewards to those who shall inform you whence you are sprung?"

The King replied that it was so.

Then said they: "Will you observe your promise to any, whether they be thralls or freemen?"

Knut assured them that their condition would make no difference.

Then the spokesman said: "In the first place, King, I must inform you that I and my comrade are thralls to an Earl in Saxon land; and, in the next place, that we are in a position to afford you all the information you desire to obtain."

Then he told a tale: Knut was the son of Earl Arngrim of Holstein, but a scandal was attached to his birth, and to conceal this the Earl had bidden his two most trusted thralls

NAME STORIES

to carry the child away; but before parting with it he had wrapped it in silk and fine linen, and three gold rings were knotted in the wrap upon its breast. They had taken the infant to Mirkwood, and had deposited it there, hoping that some good folk might find and foster it. Then they described the rings and the place where they had laid the infant. On investigation it was found that this account tallied with that told by the thralls who had rescued Knut.

Then the King gave the men money wherewith to purchase their freedom, and bade them return to him. A few weeks later they reappeared, and the King was as good as his word. He conferred on them dignities, and they speedily became rich men.

It was by this means that the name of Knut came into the Danish Royal Family; and as Knut the Great became King of England, the name of *Knott* entered the island with him, and is with us even unto this day, indicating an unmistakable Danish origin.

There was a noble family in France—the *De Levis*—who pretended that they were of the family of the Virgin Mary, descended from the elder branch, and of the tribe of Levi. They produced a pedigree to establish the descent, complete in every stage. That Our Lady did not pertain to the tribe of Levi was a small matter. An old painting still extant in the Château of Mirepois represents the ancestor of the family, the kinsman of St. Mary, taking off his hat to the Queen of Heaven as she sits enthroned in the clouds. "Couvrez vous, mon cousin," says she. "C'est pour ma commodité, ma cousine," replies the De Levis, desirous to be courteous, but careful not to compromise his dignity. As a matter of sober fact, the De Levis do not draw their name from any Jewish Levi, but from a Château de Levis, near Chevreusse.

The story of the origin of the name *l'Estrange* is this: William Peverel advertised through many lands a tournament to be held at his castle in the Peak, whereat he who acquitted himself best should have to wife his youngest niece, Meletta, and with her the lordship of Whittingdon in

NAME STORIES

Shropshire. To this tournament came Gharin of Louvain and the ten sons of John, Duke of Brittany. The knight of Louvain won his bride; but one the sons of the Duke John, Guy by name, who called himself " the Stranger," remained in England, and obtained many lordships by his sword; and of his issue are the l'Estranges. The story is utterly fabulous. There never was a Duke John of Brittany. They actually derive from a FitzAlan early in the reign of Henry I.

A story, not older than the seventeenth century, accounts for the origin of the name *Fraser* as follows: A certain Jules de Berri presented a dish of strawberries to Charles the Simple, King of France, who thereupon bade him change his name from Berry to Strawberry—*i.e.*, *Fraises*—and to assume strawberry flowers on his arms. As it happens, the Frasers derive from the family of Fresel in Normandy, and Simon Fresel settled in Scotland in the middle of the twelfth century, going thither out of England.

Norton Malreward is in Somersetshire. It was, as its name implies, the seat of the family of *Mauregard* (Evil Eye). But the real significance of the name did not please them, and a story was devised to give it a different signification. Sir John Hauteville was a great favourite of King Edward I. He was a man of prodigious strength. The King having one day expressed a desire to see the full extent of his power, the knight undertook to carry three of his lustiest men-at-arms to the top of Norton Church tower. This he effected by taking one under each arm, and the third he sustained by his teeth. Those under his arms kicked and resisted, whereupon Sir John squeezed the breath out of their bodies, but the third was conveyed safely to the top.

For this feat of strength the King gave Sir John all the estate lying in the parish of Norton, observing at the same time that it was a *mal-reward* for so great an achievement. Thenceforth the knight changed his name from Hauteville to Malreward. The trifling circumstance that two of his stoutest men-at-arms had been squeezed to death in the process does not seem to have occurred to the mind of King Edward as a matter of moment.

NAME STORIES

Once upon a time a German Emperor of the House of Austria proclaimed a tilting at the ring, and whoever proved most successful was to be rewarded with the hand of his daughter. A knight without heraldic cognizance proved the victor. He carried off six rings. When he came to demand his reward, it was found that he was the imperial keeper of the falcons, Musegraff. So he was ennobled and given the Princess, and for arms six golden annulets. He came to England and founded the family of the *Musgroves*. Unhappily for the story, the Musgroves derive from Muse Gros, near Ecouen, and came over with the Conqueror, and the annulets refer to the arms of the De Viponts, Barons and hereditary Sheriffs of Westmorland, under whom they held lands.

The *Skenes* are said to derive their name from the following incident: The first of the clan was a Robertson of Struan, who killed a gigantic wolf, that threatened the life of Malcolm III. in the royal forest of Stocket, with his *skene* (dagger). Hence the family arms are: Gules, three dirks or skenes, supported by three wolves' heads. The motto is, *Virtutis regia merces*.

The story of the *Dalziels* is this: A friend of one of the Scottish Kings was caught in a border raid and promptly hanged by his captors. The King was sore distressed, and exclaimed: " Who will dare to recover for me my friend's body, that it may be given Christian burial?" Whereupon one of his guard exclaimed: "I dare!" He crossed the border, and cut down the body from the gallows, flung it across the pommel of his saddle, and brought it to Scotland. Hence the motto of the Dalziels is "I dare!" and their coat of arms a naked corpse suspended from a gallows-tree. Of late years, however, the gibbet has been discarded. According to the common version of the story, Dalziel signifies in Gaelic "I dare!" As a matter of fact it does nothing of the sort; it means "the yellow field." *Dal* signify " a part" originally, then " a field." *Dalhousie* is Dalchoisne, the corner field, and *Dalmahoi* the field of the north.

The story of the origin of the name *Forbes* is that an

NAME STORIES

ancestor slew a mighty bear that was a terror of the neighbourhood, and so he was nicknamed For-beast, as he "went for" the Bruin.

The *Guthries* were so called from gutting three haddocks for King David II., his entertainment when he landed hungry on the Brae of Bervie after his French voyage. Whereupon the King said:

> "Gut three
> Thy name shall be!"

CHAPTER XVII

THE EVOLUTION AND DISINTEGRATION OF SURNAMES

I SHALL have in this chapter to go over some ground already trodden to pick up threads and sum up what has been discussed. When Hop-o'-my-Thumb went forth he strewed behind him white pebbles, and as he came home in the evening he picked them up again, and by them returned to the point whence he had started.

If we look over the mapped-out period of history to that beyond enveloped in blue haze, and without a hedge and a cultivated patch, and consider the Aryan stock before it broke away from its Asiatic primeval seat and moved west, dividing as it sped into diverse streams, we note that one system of nomenclature prevailed before the migration began, for that same system is found to exist in all the branches of this remarkable people.

The system was this: The name given to a person was formed out of two words—perhaps two nouns substantive glued together, perhaps a noun substantive with a qualifying adjective. Thus, in Greek we have Stratonikos (Lord Victor); in Welsh, Cadwaladr (Lord in Battle), Aelhaiarn (Iron Brow); in Norse, Arinbjörn (Eagle-Bear); in German, Friedrich (King Peace); in Old Gallic, Devagnata (Daughter of God); in Serb, Bratogub (Brother Dear); in Sanskrit, Devadathas (Gift of God); in Anglo-Saxon, Eadward (Defender of his Possessions).

But the length of some of these names led to their being curtailed, at least in common use; in most cases this was done by retaining one member only of the original name, as

THE EVOLUTION AND

Zeuxis, the famous painter, from Zeuxippos (the Horse of Zeus). So in Teutonic nomenclature, names were clipped for convenience. Ulf was used for Arnulf; in Anglo-Saxon, Edi for Eadward; and in Welsh, Cattwg for Cathmail. Another method for avoiding the entire mouth-filling name was to take one member and tack on to it a diminutive, as Wulfila (the Little Wolf) for Wulfhild. The other portion of the name, having fallen away, had been forgotten. The Irish Moaedan become Madoc. At the present day, in Germany, Margaretta is contracted into Gretli or Gretchen, and with us into Maggy. The principle of a component name did not last after a people had become to some extent civilized; it was a stage at the beginning of the history of nomenclature.

A common but not an invariable rule among the Greeks, Germans, and Scandinavians, was to give to a child one of the parts of the father's name, coupling with it some other expletive, so as to make it resemble, and yet be different. Dinokrates was the son of Dinokles; Andronikos, the son of Nikokles. In German, Waldbert and Wolfbert were the sons of Humbert; Winegaud was the son of Winaburgis. In Norse, Arnmod was the son of Arnvid; Vigfus was the son of Viga-Glum, in this latter case the son taking the nickname of his father into composition. This breaking up of the paternal name, and the coupling it with some other word, often led to the new compound having an incongruous meaning, as Wolfdag (Wolfday) and Fridigund (Peace-War).

Early Greek names expressed some quality held in high estimation, or bore some reference to a god whose protection was solicited, as Callimachus (Exultant Fighter), Apollodorus (Gift of Apollo).

The Romans in prehistoric times followed the Indo-Germanic principle of nomenclature. Originally every man had his personal distinctive name, and no other; but already in the time of the Republic each man was provided with three. The *nomen* was that of the *gens*, or clan, to which he belonged, and which almost invariably ended in

DISINTEGRATION OF SURNAMES

ius, as Publius, Fabricius. The *prænomen* went before this, and indicated the family in the tribe to which the individual belonged. Lastly came his own individual name. Thus we have Caius (*prænomen*) Julius (*nomen*) Cæsar (*cognomen*), or Marcus Tullius Cicero. Roman names were less ambitious and far less poetical than those of the Greeks. Agricola (a husbandman), Fabius (a bean), Lentullus (the slow), Cicero (a vetch), Porcius (a pig-breeder), Assinius (asinine). From appearance they were named Niger, Rufus, Flavius, Livius, Longus, Paullus, Crassus, Macer, Calvus, Naso, Pætus, Balbus, Claudius, and Plautus (flat-footed). Parents, in the barrenness of their imaginations, descended to numerals, and a father labelled his sons as No. 2, No. 3, etc.: Secundus, Tertius, Quartus, Quintus, and Sextus. Roman nomenclature exhibits the utmost poverty of invention when compared with that of the Germans and Scandinavians. An additional name, *agnomen*, was sometimes tacked on in commemoration of an heroic achievement or of some military expedition, as Coriolanus, Germanicus, Africanus.

Among the Angles, Saxons, Teutons of Germany, and Scandinavians, an almost unlimited variety of personal names existed. These could be formed with facility by combinations, in which the designations of gods, beasts, and birds, even of inanimate objects, could be made use of, with expletives added.

The deities from whom they drew their origin, who reigned in Valhalla, who ruled the course of events, were the Æsir, the singular of which is As. Hence came such names as Asbjörn, Osborn (the Divine Bear); Asmund, Osmund (the Hand of the God); Aswald, Oswald (the Power of the As); Oswin (the Friend of the Ancestral Deity).

Or, again, a special deity was honoured, as Thorr, the Thunderer; Thorfrid is the Peace of Thor; Thorbjörn, the Bear of Thor. An Archbishop of York who died in 1140 was Thurstan—the Sacrifical Stone of Thor, across which the spine of the victim was snapped.

In the temples and at religious feasts a caldron was

employed, filled with blood, that was splashed over the image, and which was used as well for boiling the horseflesh for the sacrificial feast. This was the *kettil*, and hence we have Thorketill and Osketill.[1]

Frey was another god. Freymund was the Hand of God, and Freystan—still among us as a surname, *Freestone*—the Stone of Frey.

Gud was a name employed before Christianity was finally accepted, as a name of God, without any very fixed idea being attached to it; but when the English were converted it entered into numerous combinations, as Guthfrid (the Peace of God), Guthric (the Power of God), Godwin (the Friend of God).

Arn, the Eagle into which, according to myth, Wuotan had transformed himself, gave names, as Arnor (the Eagle Arrow), Arnvid (the Eagle Wood), Arnkill (the sacrifical kettle of Odin the Eagle). The Finns, from whom tribute was taken by the Norwegian Kings, were regarded with not a little awe as necromancers, but marriages were entered into with them, and the name of Finn penetrated into the

---

[1] The following passage from the Saga of King Hakon the God is of interest: " It was an old custom that, when there was to be a sacrifice, all the bonders should come to the spot where the temple stood, and bring with them all that they required while the festival of the sacrifice lasted. To this festival all the men brought ale; and all kinds of cattle, as well as horses, were slaughtered, and all the blood that came from them was called *laut*, and the vessels in which it was collected were called laut-vessels. Laut-branches were cut, like sprinkling-brushes, with which the whole of the altars and the temple walls, both outside and inside, were splashed over, and also the people were sprinkled with the blood; but the flesh was boiled into savoury meat for those present. The fire was in the midst of the floor of the temple, and over it hung the kettles, and the full goblets were handed across the fire; and he who made the feast, and was a chief, blessed the full goblets and all the meat of the sacrifice. And first Odin's goblet was emptied for victory and power to the King; thereafter Niord's and Frey's goblets, for peace and for a good season. Then it was the custom of many to empty the Braga-goblet; and then the guests emptied a goblet to the memory of departed friends, called the remembrance-bowl" (*Heimskringla*, saga iv., c. 16). Customs die hard. This was the origin of drinking healths.

DISINTEGRATION OF SURNAMES

nomenclature of the offspring, as Finnlog, Thorfin; or the name Halfdan was employed, indicative of mixed blood.

Qualities also entered into the composition of names, as Ethelburg (the noble stronghold), Ethelred (the noble counsellor), Eadward (the defender of his property). The list might be greatly extended, but this must suffice.

Among the Christian Anglo-Saxons and Scandinavians, no scruple whatever was felt in the employment of names redolent of paganism, any more than there was hesitation in retaining the pagan designations of the days of the week. And as such a wide field existed for the formation of personal names, the necessity for surnames was not immediately felt. Individuals might have, and did have, nicknames applied to them, but these were ephemeral.

But with the advent of the Normans the conditions changed. It must be borne in mind that the invasion of England by William the Conqueror was a crusade carried out in the name of religion against a people whom Rome regarded as faulty in the faith. As Freeman says: "England's crime in the eyes of Rome—the crime to punish which the crusade of William was approved and blessed—was the independence still retained by the island Church and nation. . . . Rome was watchful, ever mindful, had not forgotten the note of insular defiance, when the heart of England spoke by the mouth of Tostig, and threatened the Pontiff on his throne." A Bull was published by Alexander II. authorizing the invasion of England. "The cause of the invasion was blessed, and precious gifts were sent as visible exponents of the blessing—among others a consecrated banner to hallow the cause of fraud and usurpation—and a crusade preached against England."[1]

Thenceforth the Church was Latinized, and all that spoke of independence was hushed, all that recalled the past of England was frowned down as tainted with heresy. Even the names of children suffered. The clergy pointed out the duty, the necessity, of every Christian being given a patron in heaven, and such a patron could be acquired by his being

[1] "Norman Conquest," ii. 458.

furnished with the name of a saint in the calendar. One concession was made: the application to an English child of the name of a Norman master. He must have a patron somewhere, either in heaven or in the hall. In a canon attributed, but falsely, to the Council of Nicæa, but at all events very ancient—for it is mentioned by Theodoret and alluded to by St. John Chrysostom—parents were forbidden to give to their children the names of their forefathers, and were required to call them after saints. The Roman *Rituale* orders: " Let the parish priest take care that to a child shall be given no name that is obscene, fabulous, or ridiculous; nor one smacking of the vanity of the gods or the impieties of the heathen; but rather, as far as can be enforced, the names of saints by whose example they may be stirred to live, and that they may obtain their patronage."

Each diocese had its own calendar, and such were scantily provided with names. It was not then, as now, that the Roman Calendar and Martyrology were universally accepted, stuffed as they are with names, two, three, a dozen, for each day in the year. The old English calendars were not more richly provided than is that of the Anglican Church of the present day. In the Sherborne Calendar are but nine names in February, and seven in March. Consequently parents, when naming their children, had a limited range, and Johns and Peters, Philips and Thomases, became thick as blackberries, dense in a parish as sparrows in a bush. For the simple life of the early centuries, so long as life was limited within a narrow compass, one name sufficed a person. Population was stationary, and to a large extent rooted to the soil. The serf, the villein, could not leave it; he was *adscriptus glebæ*. But so also was the Lord of the Manor, for thence he drew all his revenue. Everyone knew his neighbour, held his nose over his neighbour's chimney-top and knew when he fried a rasher, and who sat round the table to eat it. There was little migration from one district to another; the only strangers who penetrated to it were the wandering pedlars and gleemen. Trade was insignificant, as most people had small requirements, and such as they had

DISINTEGRATION OF SURNAMES

they were able to supply themselves with at home. They grew their own kail and corn, wove their own cloth, and made their own pots. A second name was as little required in a village among peasants as in a palace among Princes. But conditions altered, though not rapidly. The population became dense, and at the same time acquired fluidity. The Crusades and the French wars created a different condition of affairs. Properties changed hands.

> " Oh, many
> Have broke their backs with laying manors on them
> For this great journey."

Merchants, lawyers, Churchmen, bought the lands the knights sold to furnish themselves for war. Trade and commerce increased, and contracts had to be drawn and registers to be kept. The single name no longer sufficed. This was especially the case in towns, the centres of life and activity. There the necessity for some more particularizing of the persons dealt with in commercial transactions became imperious. Among the *minstrales* of the Archbishop of Cologne in 1141, consisting of fifty-nine individuals, there were twelve Hermans. How could the Elector summon one to his presence without giving him some particular epithet to distinguish him from the other eleven?

In England, even if in a village, a parent gave to his son a Norman in place of a saintly name; the number of such names at his choice cannot have been great. He was acquainted with only such foreign Christian names as were to be found among his lord's children and servants. Thus, as said above, a parish swarmed with men of the same name, and the action of the Church in treading out the old English nomenclature, and forcing Scriptural and foreign names on the people, tended largely to the adoption of surnames.

In "The Chronicle of Battle Abbey"[1] we have a list of the tenants of the Abbey whilst it was building, and this list is very instructive, for it shows us a great number of Saxon names, but also along with them Norman names, not of

[1] Lower, M. A., "The Chronicle of Battle Abbey," London, 1851.

knights and nobles, but of plain common tradesmen, and among these latter is a Russell.

"The Leuga being brought into the possession of the abbey, and the building of the abbey meanwhile going forward, a goodly number of men were brought hither out of the neighbouring counties, and some even from foreign countries. And to each of these the brethren who managed the building allotted a dwelling-place of certain dimensions around the circuit of the abbey, and these still remain as they were then first apportioned with their customary rent or service."

The order of the messuages is as follows (I do not give particulars in full):

1. Brihtwin, who had been Bedell.
2. Reinbald de Beche (Bec in Normandy) to pay 7d. per annum, and find a man for one day only, to make hay in the meadows of Bodeham.
3. Wulmer, also 7d. and like obligation.
4. Malgar the Smith.
5. Ælfric Dot.
6. William the Shoemaker.
7. Edward Gotcild (Godchild).
8. Ralph Ducg.
9. Gilbert the Weaver.
10. Dering Pionius.
11. Legard.
12. Elfwin Trewa.
13. Godieve.
14. Godwin, son of Colsuein.
15. Godwin the Cook.
16. Edward the Scourer.
17. Robert the Miller.
18. Robert de Havena.
19. Selaf the Herdsman.
20. Wulric the Goldsmith.
21. William Pinel.
22. Lambert the Shoemaker.
23. Orderic the Swineherd.
24, 25. Sevugel Cochec.
26. Blackeni the Cowherd.
27. William Grei (Grey).
28. Robert, the son of Siflet.
29. Seward Gris (the Pig).
30. Ælfric the Steward.
31. Wulfin Hert (Hart).
32, 33. Lefwi Nuc.
34. Gilbert the Stranger (l'Estrange).
35. Ælfric de Dengemareis (Dengemarsh).
36. Bennet the Sewer.
37. Maurice.
38. Ædric, who cast the bells.
39. Gunnild.
40. Burnulf the Carpenter.
41. Ælfric Cild (Child).
42. Æilnod the Shoemaker.
43. Francefant.
44, 45. Ældwin the Cook.
46. Emma.
47. Ælstrild Nonna (the Nun).

DISINTEGRATION OF SURNAMES

48. Peter the Baker.
49, 50. Sewin.
51. Robert de Cirisi.
52. Mathelgar Ruff.
53. Siward Stigerop (Stirrup).
54. Goldwin.
55. Edwin the Smith.
56, 57. Sevugel (Sea-fowl).
58. Gotseln (Joscelyn).
59. Russell.
60. Lambert.
61. Ailric the Baker.
62. Æilnod, the son of Fareman.
63. Gilbert the Clerk.
64. Lefwin the Baker.
65. Herod.
66. Orgar.
67. Chebel (Keble).
68. Dering.
69. Leffelm.
70. Benwold Gest (Guest).
71. Wulfric the Swineherd.
72. Emma.
73. Slote.
74. Gosfrid the Cook.
75. Godfrey.
76. Lefwin Hunger.
77. Edwin Knight.
78. Goldstan.
79. Wulbald Winnoc.
80. Brembel.
81. Robert Barate (Barret).
82. Lefflet Lounge (Long).
83. Edilda Tipa.
84, 85. Golding.
86. Ælfric Curlebasse.
87. Wulfwin Scot.
88. Hugh the Secretary.
89. Humfrey the Priest.
90. Pagan Peche.
91. Durand.
92. Juliot Wolf.
93. Ælfwin Abbat.
94. Siward Crull.
95. Sevugel Cannarius (the Dog-trainer).
96. Brictric the Gardener.
97. Ælwin the Secretary.
98. Cheneward (the Dog-keeper).
99. Baldwin the Shoemaker.
100. Osbert Pechet.
101. Cochard.
102. Ælfwin Hachet.
103. Æilnoth Heca.
104. Blacheman of Bodeherstegate.
105. Reinbald Genester.
106. Ælfric Corveiser (the man employed in forced labour).
107. Brictric Barke (for Barker).
108. Ælfwin Turpin.
109. Roger Braceur (for Brassour the Brewer).
110. Walter Ruff (le Roux—the Red).
111. Humfrey Genester.
112. Godwin Gisard (perhaps the Lie-a-bed).
113. Siward Crull.
114. Brunreve.
115. Wulfwin the Carpenter.

The list is very instructive, and deserves to be analyzed. It must be borne in mind that, when the Conqueror came over, his knights and nobles brought with them their

THE EVOLUTION AND

contingents of men-at-arms, and that these men could not be dispensed with and sent back to their homes in Normandy and Brittany and Flanders. They were needed to control the restless English. They were employed to conquer Wales and to devastate Northumbria. They were retained as garrisons in all the fortresses dotted over the land. Not one of these men brought with him a hereditary surname. Their masters were only beginning to learn the advantage of having a family *to-name*. But William had to do more than lodge fighting men throughout the land. He had to bring over masons and builders to erect castles and churches, for the English knew nothing of building fortresses of stone, and their efforts at church-building were rudimentary.

That the nobles and knights should bring as well their stewards, butlers, and porters and huntsmen, we can well understand. But we were not prepared to learn, as we do from the above list, that various petty tradesmen also came over and settled in England. Out of the four shoemakers enumerated, one alone was English. There were three cooks, but one of these was Norman. The baker, the brewer, the smith, the weaver, the miller, were all Norman-French.

Out of 115 householders in Battle, there were 39 Normans.

But that is not all. Some of these men, working at the building of this abbey or supplying the needs of the workers, bear the names of their noble and knightly masters with whom they had come over, as William Pinel, Paganus Peche, Osbert Pechet, Gilbert l'Estrange, Madelgar Ruff (le Roux), Russell, Robert Barret, Walter Ruff. And, what is still more curious, Siward twice occurs with the to-name of Crull—*i.e.*, Criol, a famous name among the nobles of William's retinue. Yet Siward is a Danish name, and he seems to have accommodated himself with a French surname, so as to identify himself with the winning party.

Some of the foreign settlers at Battle were known after the place whence they came, as Robert de Havena, Robert de Cerise; but one of the oddest assumptions is that of Ralph, who called himself Ducq, or the Duke, perhaps

DISINTEGRATION OF SURNAMES

because he came over in the immediate retinue of William the Bastard. Some designate themselves, or are designated, as "son of"; but of these there are three only, as Battle was a newly-constructed village, and, of the settlers in it, few knew the parentage of their fellow-settlers.

One thing this list teaches us—that we are not to suppose that all the bearers in this day of Norman names were blood descendants of the Barons who first assumed them; they may be the issue of their humble retainers who adopted their masters' names.

So as not to be tedious, I will refer to only a few lists of benefactors, etc., to show how gradually surnames crept into general use.

Here is a list of those who contributed to the building of the Franciscan convent at Newgate, London, between the years 1225 and 1327.

John Ewin, citizen of London, first founder; *William Joyner* built the choir, 1225; *Henry Walleis* built the nave; Alderman *William Porter* founded the chapter-house; *Gregory Bokesley* made the dormitory; *Bartholomew de Castello* made the refectory; *Peter de Helliland* erected the infirmary; *Bogo Bond*, the herald King-at-Arms, built the museum (*sic*). Then comes in a bevy of noble names. Next *William Taylor*, "sutor regis Henrici III.," gave the water-supply. Then, later, *Richard Whittington*—of cat celebrity—founded the library in 1429.

Observe in the list that William, King Henry's tailor, adopts Taylor as his surname.

The Feet of Fines are profitable reading for the purpose of elucidating the progress of nomenclature. If I take those for the county of Devon in 1238, it will suffice to show us how the process of acquisition of surnames was in progression during the first half of the thirteenth century. There are several instructive features in this catalogue. The first names are those of the plaintiffs, generally landowners, and the defendants are tenants.

In several cases these landowners have no surnames at all, but are described as "son of" or "daughter of" the father who had a Christian name alone.

THE EVOLUTION AND

In the next place, the tenant in a great number of instances is described as "de" his farm, for which he paid rent, and from which he might be evicted, and this becomes a surname.

Another peculiar feature is that already in the first half of the thirteenth century some of the best surnames are found among the tenants. In one case John le English is master of the land, and William Peverel, with a good Norman name, is tenant; and again is this the case with John de Langefurlong, probably ancestor of the Furlong family, and Geoffrey de Dynant, a descendant of one of those who came over with the Conqueror. In both cases—and there are others like them—the old lords of the land are parting with portions of their estates to English yeomen, and dropping into the position of tenants. In the case of Michael, son of Godfrey without a surname, he acquires lands in Lew Trenchard of William Trenchard, whose ancestors had held the land as a knight's-fee from the Conquest, "and for this Michael gave to William one sore sparrow hawk." So the land went.

In the list are few surnames that indicate professions. There is a Cryer, a Mason, and also a Dispenser, the latter as a tenant, and only one that may be taken as a nickname—"Youngknight." Any number of documents might be quoted, but they would all tell the same story—the slow progress made in the adoption of surnames.

It is worthy of note that the thirty-four first Archbishops of Canterbury had no surnames. Ralph d'Escures in 1114 is the first to whom a second or to-name is accorded, and even later there were four, of whom Boniface, in 1246, was the last to remain undistinguished by an addition to his Christian name.

The first thirty-three Bishops of London had no to-names. The first to be designated as "of" a place is Hugh de Orivalle, in 1075; his successor had but his baptismal name, but after that double names became the rule. And yet we cannot say of them for some time that they were properly family surnames.

DISINTEGRATION OF SURNAMES

Further, in the English Book of Common Prayer there is no recognition of such a thing as a surname in either the Baptismal or the Marriage Service, or the Catechism. So far as the Church is concerned, the person is possessed of none.

On February 25, 1909, a woman applied to the North London Police Court in great perplexity. On the preceding day she had been married, and the man had given in registration a false surname. Was the marriage valid? she inquired. "Certainly," replied the magistrate. "You are wedded to the man, and not to the name. His Christian name remains immutable; but as to his surname, he may change it at pleasure. It is a luxury and not a necessity."

And he was right according to law. Law and liturgy date from a period when surnames were unfixed.

Now let us suppose the case—and it was a case that occurred repeatedly, almost universally—of there being Johns many and Toms many in the same parish. If not distinguished by their trades, as John the Smith and John the Baker, Tom the Brewer and Tom the Mason, they would probably be differentiated by the place of their residence—John of the Townsend, Tom at the Well, John under the Wood, and Tom at the Ridgeway, becoming in time Townsend, Atwell, Underwood, and Ridgeway. Now let us suppose that the families of these respective Johns and Toms lived on for several generations at the Town's End, at the Well, under the Wood, and by the Old Roman Road or Ridgeway. The personal names John and Tom would be replaced by others, and gradually the place-name would adhere to the family; and although the descendant of John at the Town's End might move his residence into the middle of the town, he would carry with him the name of Townsend. So the great-grandson of Tom at the Well may have set up shop in the town, but he would have come to call himself Atwell.

There is a spur of highland running into the valley in which I live; it was once, and to some extent it is now, covered with heather; and when this is in flame in the glow

THE EVOLUTION AND

of the evening sun, the whole tongue of land is crimson. Even when the heather is out of flower, its dry branches are russet, and the hill-spur has still a red glow; this is the more noteworthy as it stands out against green woods clothing the other hills. Hence this ridge has the name of Raddon. On it are three farms—one Upper, one Middle, and the third Lower, or Nether.

When the first settling in the land by the Saxons took place, one boor planted himself at the upper end of a spur of land, another in the middle, and a third lower down; each built his habitation of wood, and enclosed a patch of land about it with a wall, and this patch of land was manured plentifully from his stalls, and produced richer and greener grass than any of his meadow-land. This he called his *tun;* and so came into existence three farms—an Upperton, Middleton, and a Netherton. But if, instead of a man of some consequence, with servants under him, it was a poor villein who planted his humble lodge, then there would spring up an Upcot, a Middlecot or Medlicott, and a Nethercot.

Or perhaps in level land there were four settlements roughly taken at the points of the compass. One would be a Norton or a Northcot, another a Southton or Sutton, or a Southcot, a third an Easton or Eastcot, and the fourth a Weston or Westcot, according to who made the settlement, a freeman or a serf. In time the families living in these farms or cottages would come to appropriate to themselves the names of their habitations, or, rather, these names would be given to them by their fellow-parishioners, as a simple and intelligible way of describing the families so situated.

The late Mr. Robert Ferguson, when he mounted a hobby, rode it to death. He wrote books to prove that the majority of English surnames were of Saxon origin. In our simplicity we believed that Seamore and Seymour were derived from either the Old English Seamer, a tailor, or from the Norman St. Maur. But no; according to Mr. Ferguson, it is derived from the Teutonic Sigimar; and so pleased is he with this derivation that he gives it in five different places.

DISINTEGRATION OF SURNAMES

There are undoubtedly some Saxon names that have lingered on; others are of late introduction from Germany and Flanders. A good many Scandinavian names have filtered in, much altered through the Normans; other Scandinavian names remain little changed in the land north of the Humber.

But what vitiates his argument is this: it presupposes that surnames—and those Saxon—were assumed and continued from the time of the Conquest to the present day, whereas nothing of the sort took place.

That there are Saxon and Norse names that have become surnames is not to be doubted, but it has usually taken place in a roundabout manner. A Saxon or a Scandinavian gave his name to a place; then, when surnames began to come in, the family living in this place assumed or were accorded the place-name. By no means infrequently the latter portion, signifying that it was the *thorp*, or *by*, or *ton*, or *cot*, of the original settler, fell away, and the name of the more modern possessor reverted to that of the original settler. But there was no blood relationship in nine hundred and ninety-nine out of a thousand cases.

Ægelweard was the name of a Saxon who gave his name to a *tun*, and from Ægelweardestun came Aylwardston, and then, the place-name becoming a surname, it was contracted to Aylward. Coton gave his name to a clearing in the forest, Cotonesfeld, and thence came Cottonsfield, and finally the surname Cottonsfield was reduced to Cotton. Lidgeard built a fortress, Lidgeardesbeork, and thence came Ledgardsboro, and at last, by shortening, Ledgard.

When the Scandinavians Ormr, Thoroldr, and Viglundr, came to Northumbria, there was a fine threatening vibration of the tongue over the final letter, that was sounded like the rattle of a snake; but hardly had they settled themselves on English ground than they shed the rough *r* at the end of their names, and became Orme, Thorold, and Wayland. Yet, strange to say, Olafr retained the *r*, but was softened to Oliver or Olver. But this name has wheeled about and come over through Normandy.

THE EVOLUTION AND

Such an ending as *ig*—as Copsig, Sigtrygg—the English ear disliked. Such names, whether they came through the Norse or through the Danes, were scraped and smoothed down.

Near Launceston is a farm that stands on a rocky scarp, and bore the name of Carig; this means rock. It was the nursery of a family that spread far and wide, carrying with it as its name that of its nursery, as a newly hatched chicken bears off part of the shell upon its back. But the name was softened into *Carey* and *Carew*. The story goes that two of the name appeared before Queen Elizabeth, members of widely parted branches of the same stock, and disputed before Her Majesty as to the correct pronunciation of the name. Then said the Queen to one: "Carey you shall be, and what *care I* ?" and to the other: "Carew shall you be, and what *care you* ?"

And now see the caprice there is in the pronunciation of names. The present Sir Reginald Pole Carew pronounces his name *Poole Carey*. Wulfsig in time became *Wolsey*. Strange alterations have been made in names by the English tongue, that has a tendency, it must be admitted, to vulgarize them. Stigand was a ferocious Scandinavian Viking, who after rapine and murder settled down in England, was baptized, and beat his sword into a ploughshare. His namesake—perhaps a grandson—was Canute's priest at Assandune, and then Archbishop of Canterbury, where his sturdy independence and contemptuous refusal to obey citations to Rome caused his excommunication by five successive Popes, and William declined to be crowned by him, and deposed him in 1070.

Brother *Stiggins*, whose head Sam Weller held under the pump, was his nominal descendant. But, oh, what a falling-off was there! I can recall, some fifty years ago, a London sexton, the living prototype of Mr. Snawley in Phiz's picture in "Nicholas Nickleby." Discussing the man's name, *Holybone*, with a friend, he conjectured that his ancestor had been the guardian of some relic-shrine. But Holybone was a corruption, in fact, of Hallbjörn, the *r* having dropped away.

DISINTEGRATION OF SURNAMES

The ancestor of this mild individual in semi-clerical costume, with pompous manners and a hand curved for the reception of tips, had come to England in a dragon-ship, with white sail swelling, and oars flashing, and the gilded figure-head flaring in the sun, to plunder and burn churches and massacre priests.

I have already mentioned Thustan, the Conqueror's standard-bearer. The name signifies the stone heaved and "put" by a Thus or Thurs, a Northern giant. The stone was lost in the lapse of ages, and the name degenerated to *Dust*. A story is told of a Miss Deeks, who against the wishes of the family married a man of the name of Dust; he turned out to be a good-for-naught, and she repented of her folly. At two o'clock in the morning she returned to her home, and knocked at the door, soliciting reception. Old Mr. Deeks protruded his head from the bedroom window and refused to open. "No, no! Dust thou art, and unto Dust shalt thou return."

Mr. Ferguson mentions another instance of the elision of the letter *r*. It occurred in a name of Norse origin, Bedbjorg, that became first *Bedburg;* and then the English or American tongue let the *r* slip, and it resolved itself into *Bedbug*. Now, in America every beetle is a bug, but there can be no disguising the objectionable character of one that is a bedbug, and the possessor of the name changed it.

In Wyckliffe's Bible the verse of the psalm, "The pestilence that walketh in darkness, nor for the sickness that destroyeth in the noonday," is rendered in the first part "the bug that walketh in darkness." "Bug" remains as "bogie." It is the Sclavonic word for God, and the man who can call himself by the surname of *Bugg* can boast that he is of Divine origin as much as any Angle or Saxon King.

If the English tongue be a rasp roughening some names, it is a smoothing iron passed over others. The name Nagle has been turned to *Nayle*. Wighardt, dropping the *r*, is *Wyatt*, and Radbod (the ferocious) is tamed into *Rabbit*. Sigebert we meet with in *Sibthorpe*, the thorp of Sigebert. I see, in an advertisement of the Church Lads' Brigade, Lewis

THE EVOLUTION AND

Wigram as hon. treasurer. The object of the institution is the training of lads under military discipline. Salt of the past must remain in the treasurer. Wigram signifies "strong in war." *Honeybun* comes from Honeyburn, the *r* being again omitted. Letters also are transposed to enable a name to slide past the lips the readier. Sir John Fastolf is altered by Shakespeare into *Falstaff*, and the Anglo-Saxon Trumbald, as already mentioned, has become *Turnbull*. In some names ending in *ulf*, the wolf has been banished in name as in reality, and Godenulf, the Divine Wolf, is now the innocuous *Goodenough*, and Ricenulf, the Strong Wolf, is what no man will admit that he is, *Richenough*.

The *De Poers*, a family that issued from the county of Poher in Brittany, of which Carhaix is the capital, did not relish having their name, when in England, Latinized into *Pauper* and *Pauperculus*, and so took to calling themselves *Power*.

The *Malebys* (Mala-bestia), bad beasts, preferred to be regarded as issuing from a malt-house than to be considered evil beasts, and so entitled themselves *Maltby*. The noble name of Douglas, on this side of the Tyne, has been vulgarized into *Diggles*. Ap Odger is now *Podger*, and Ap Roger *Prodger*. St. Ethelreda is turned into *Audrey* and *Taudry*; and Renshaw, the wood of the Norse Ragnar, into *Wrencher*. Beautiful Bruges has given us Mr. *Briggs*, the butt of many of Leech's humorous sketches in *Punch*.

Mountjoie was a name given to a height whence the first sight of Jerusalem burst on the Crusaders. Then it became a surname. I sent my boots once to be resoled and heeled by a *Mungay*, a cobbler. As I paid him, I looked hard in his face, and tried to think back from this man to the ancestor on the height, crying "Joie! joie!" when the roofs of Jerusalem burst on his view, and he threw up the visor of his helmet to obtain a good sight of the object of his long journey. Who would not suppose that the name *Physick* was due to an ancestor having been a physician? Yet this name is actually the corruption of *Fishacre*. An ancient house and estate on the borders of Dartmoor is called

DISINTEGRATION OF SURNAMES

Colovin; by corruption it would seem to have become the family name of *Coffin*.

De la Chambre has become in English mouths *Dealchamber*, and *Troublefield* represents De Tourbeville, and Chaddlehanger near Tavistock gives *Challinger*.

In Tavistock, at the time of the siege of Plymouth by the Royalists, Sir Richard Grenville—" Rascal " Grenville—had his headquarters. Ever since then there have been *Greenfields* in the town. One now prints the *Tavistock Gazette*. Lord Lyttleton and Earl Temple had a dispute relative to the antiquity of their several families. " Little-town," said Lord Lyttleton, " must have preceded Grande-ville. But if you choose to call yourself Greenfield, I allow you greater antiquity." The name *Mummery* is a corruption of the Norman De Momerie. If I remember aright, a few years ago a Mr. Mummery wrote strongly against Ritualism. The list might be indefinitely extended. The English tongue is impatient of foreign sounds, and insists on rounding or roughing them into some semblance to a known English word, as *Shovell* out of Escoville. But even good plain English names are not left alone. Thus, Caldwell has been resolved into *Caudle*, Comberford to *Comfort*.

Tricks have been played with the letter H. Othere, the traveller, appeared before King Alfred, and gave him an accurate account of Norway and Finland and the White Sea. Othere has branched on the one side into *Otter*, and on the other side into *Hodder*, the name of an eminent publisher.

How names may be assumed is shown by the instance of an Italian cabin-boy named Benito, who among the English sailors acquired the name of Ben Eaton. He accepted the change, was sent to school in America, was entered as Benjamin Eaton, married and settled in the States, and now his descendants come to England and look with fond admiration at the towers of Eaton Hall, the supposed ancestral home of the family.

It does not by any means follow that individuals found in humble walks of life, bearing good names, such as Courteney,

THE EVOLUTION AND

Neville, Howard, Champernowne, are descendants in blood of these ancient families, though I am far from denying that in a good many cases they are such. But it must be remembered that it was not unusual for servants, having no family names of their own, to adopt those of their masters. The case will at once occur to the memory of the reader of Shakespeare, when Christopher Sly called Cicely, "the maid of the house" to Marian Hacket, the fat alewife of Wincot, by her mistress's name, Cicely Hacket.

But it is at the same time most true that

> "Ebbing men, indeed,
> Most often do so near the bottom run
> By their own fear or sloth"

—either through their own fault or through misfortune many an ancient and honourable name has been brought very low. There is a certain good humour noticeable in the English genius. It disguises the origin of names that reek with paganism, so as to escape the censure of the clergy. What parson could object to a *Thorogood*? And yet the origin of the name is Thorgautr, the hog of Thor the Thunderer, that drew his car through the storm as he hurled his flaming bolts. It must have been with a qualm of conscience that a priest baptized a child by the name of Paganus, when making a Christian of it, and it is perhaps due to refusal to give this as a Christian name that we have it as a surname in the form of *Payne*.

At the Restoration the name of *Cromwell* was odious, and it underwent a slight change so as to disguise it. But what a descent there is from Thomas Cromwell, Earl of Essex, and Oliver, the Lord Protector, to Mr. Vincent *Crummels*, in whose company Nicholas Nickleby acted Romeo.

A series of Cumberland names end in *staff*, as Langstaff, Wagstaff, Everstaff. They have, however, nothing to do with quarter-staves (*pace* Twisden in *The Tatler*, No. 11, 1709). A more primitive form remains in *Bickersteth*, and the last syllable is the Scandinavian *sta* — the *th* has in many cases become *ff*. A *sta*—in German *stadt*—is the

DISINTEGRATION OF SURNAMES

Old English *stead*, a place of abode, a farm, a settlement. *Wagstaff* is the watch or lookout station, and Bickersteth is the stede or stead of Beck or Bako, a name that occurs in the Durham "Liber Vitæ," and Everstaff is that of Ever.

We have seen how the ending *th* has become *ff* in Cumberland, but the *ff* becomes *p* in some cases. In North Devon lived a family named *Cutcliff*, named from a cleve that was cut as with an axe, where it resided. But a member of the family moved south, and enclosed land and made a *tun* near Tavistock, on the edge of Dartmoor, and called the place Cutcliffton. In process of time this became Cudliptown. Anyone might suppose at first glance that *Cudlip*, a name now pretty widely distributed in the neighbourhood, was given as a nickname to some man owing to a malformation of the mouth—in fact, to a harelip—did we not know its real origin. *Lipton*, again, is Cliffton. We must always observe great caution in deriving surnames from nicknames of merely personal application, due to some peculiarity of appearance, for such are most unlikely to adhere to the posterity of the man so marked. Usually such a name is a corruption of a place-name. I have said this before, and I repeat it. The double *f* in Cliff in the midst of a name may be altered into *b*, and the preceding vowel changed. Thus Cliffbury has become *Clobbury*. The well-known publishing firm of *Lippincott*, in Philadelphia, derives from an immigrant to America called Luffincott, from a small parish in Devon. In German, our word "cliff" is *clippe*. *Metcalf* is the Middle Cliff.

The name of *Lamprey* does not derive from the fish, through overeating of which Henry I. died, but from Landfrith (the Peace of the Land), and there was probably a Landfrithstead; but a family living at one time at this stede or stead left the paternal acres, and in drifting about dropped the *stead*, and reverted to the name of the founder of the settlement. Vowels get strangely altered. *Clutterbuck* is the same name as the German Lauterbach—*i.e.*, the clear (A.S. *hlutter*) beck or brook. It is of Dutch importation.

In the West of England the ear cannot endure a harsh

THE EVOLUTION AND

conjunction of consonants, and in place-names *a* is inserted to soften the sound; thus, Blackbrook becomes *Blackabrook*, Woolstone is more pleasant when pronounced *Woolaston*, and *Woolcombe* is the name of one family, and *Wollacombe* of another, both deriving from the same combe and both bearing the same arms.

I have already mentioned the word "hope," employed mainly in the North as an opening in a wood or in a range of hills. Indeed, I have been directed thus: " You go straight along the edge of the wood till you come to an ope: turn up there." Hence the name *Hopwood*, but also *Hopgood*, which is not Hopegood or Goodhope, but the same as Hopwood, an ope in the wood. A consonant is often misplaced for the sake of smoothness in pronunciation. Thus Crossford, Crosswell, Crosslake, become *Kersford, Kerswell*, and *Kerslake*. A lake is not a sheet of water but a lead or leat—a channel for bringing water to a house or a mine or a mill.

Some names must always remain uncertain as to the germ from which they have evolved. *Sternhold* has been supposed to be a corruption of St. Arnold, but it may also be Stjörn (Star), the hauld; or landholder. A "hold," or Norse *hauld*, was a superior yeoman holding allodial land.[1] In ancient Norway the churchyards were divided into four circles. The innermost was reserved for the lender-men, the next for the haulds, the third for the freemen, the fourth— next to the outer wall—for the thralls. Our surname *Old* may derive from a Hold, and may not be descriptive of the age of any one member of a family.

There is a village in Oxfordshire of the name of Finmore. The name has gone through changes, as Fynemore, Phinnemore, *Phillimore*. The Kentish family of *Filmer* is clearly of the same stock.

The name of *Shakespeare* has probably nothing to do with a spear. The name is derived from Schalkesbœr, the knave's farm. Neither schalk nor knave originally implied anything but what was honourable. Schalk was a servant, and enters into the names Godshalk, God's servant.

[1] Harald Harf. Saga, c. 62.

DISINTEGRATION OF SURNAMES

Indeed, the Anglo-Saxon *scealc* was used as a designation of a warrior. Adrian IV.—or Nicolas *Breakspeare*, as he was called before his elevation to the Papacy—took his name from Bragi's-bœr, the farm of Bragi.

On one side of the Tamar lived the family of *Monk*, with a pedigree more or less fictitious, worked out by the heralds when George Monk became Duke of Albemarle. On the other side of the Tamar was a poor tinminer named *Lemon*. In the second generation after George, Duke of Albemarle, the Monk house went down like a pack of cards. A century later the miner's family had risen to affluence, and Sir Charles Lemon was created a Baronet. But Lemon is Le Moine, the Monk. The ancestor of each was a truant from his monastery, who had trampled on his cowl, taken to himself a wife, and founded a family.

Landseer is not a surveyor, but is l'Ansier, the handle-maker to mugs and pots. While the potter moulded the vessel on the wheel, the ansier was engaged on shaping the handles to be affixed to them.

Peascod is a surname met with occasionally, but is not common. But the surname Peascod has nothing in its origin to do with the vegetable kingdom. It is from the Welsh Pys-coed. The ancient name of Tenby was Dinbych-y-Pyscoed.

Caprices of spelling have given occasion to divergencies from a common origin. Some of these have arisen unconsciously; others are modern affectations. Into what contortions the name Smith has been thrown! In the register of the University of Oxford is entered in 1556 George Guldeford, or Gilford, or Kifford. How readily would Kifford become Giffard, and a descendant pose as of the Norman family of Giffards.

Dr. Barker, quoting from the register of the parish of Pechletin, Leicester, gives the variations of the name *Weewall* between 1735 and 1750. It appears as Whewaugh, Whewvaugh, Wheeraw, Weway, Weewa, Wheewhal, Whewwhaw, Whealwhal, Weewall, Wheewall. And these are all forms of the name Whewell borne by a former very pompous Master of Trinity College, Cambridge.

THE EVOLUTION AND

An affectation is to employ the letter *y* in place of *i*, or as an interpolation. *Smith* is made into *Smythe*, *White* into *Whyte*, *Sands* into *Sandys*, *Light* into *Lyte*. And another affectation has been the use of the double f as Ffinch, Ffoukes, Ffrench.

A pile of fossils is placed before a geologist, and he sets to work to sort them into several heaps, according to the strata to which they pertain. Here go those of the Chalk, there such as belong to the Greensand. This collection represents the Lias, and that the Oolite, and another the Red Sandstone, and this small accumulation those of the Silurian beds.

In like manner, out of the great heap of our English nomenclature, it is possible to distinguish the names that belong to the different historic strata. We can put in one pile all the Anglo-Saxon names, heap up those that are Norman and Angevin-French—and this accumulation is considerable—then the few that are Celtic, mostly introductions from Ireland and the Highlands of Scotland, and from Cornwall and Wales. Next comes a small accumulation of Flemish names, then a whole heap of Huguenot French importations, many that are German, and a promiscuous pile of odds and ends from Sweden, Poland, Italy, etc. And we can give an approximate date for the formation of these names or their introduction into England, for we have our series of records from Domesday, through the Rotuli Normannorum, the Hundred Rolls, the Feet of Fines, the charters, and innumerable other documents, by means of which we can see when these names first appear, and can follow them in their permutations.

But the geologist does more than determine the age and succession of the fossils in the various strata: he arranges those in each into distinct groups, according to their kind or genus. And we do the same with nomenclature. There are the four main classifications into Sire-names, Place-names, Trade-names, and Nick-names. We can tell whether a sire-name be of Norman or English origin; in place-names, whether that place be in England or abroad. In trade-

DISINTEGRATION OF SURNAMES

names he can point out that some represent importations from France or Germany, and others are English, as *Tailor* and *Marchant* are French, whereas *Seamer* and *Chapman* are English.

But when all this sorting and arrangement has been accomplished, there still remains a great heap of names that he cannot classify. In the New Red Sandstone are beds of crushed, split, and pinched pebbles. Pressure, if it has not broken these rolled stones, has squeezed them out of shape. And in English nomenclature there is a deposit of these crushed, splintered, and pinched names, the origin and original shape of which is most difficult to determine. But from these rubble beds of the Red Sandstone patient research has been able to track every stone to the mountain whence it was wrenched, and far from which it has been rolled, and so it is possible by patient and persevering study to trace back every eccentric and distorted surname to its origin. But that is not a task to be undertaken in such a volume as this, which aims only at accounting for the bulk of English names falling under the four categories, and such as are uncommon and strange must be left to elucidation by special research.

CHAPTER XVIII

SCOTTISH AND IRISH SURNAMES

MOST tragic has been the fate of the great Celtic race that at one time occupied the greater part of Western Europe—France, the British Isles, Southern Germany, Spain, the Alps, and Upper Italy—and which even established itself in Asia Minor. Everywhere, with a few marked exceptions, it has abandoned its native tongue. The only places in which it lingers are Wales, Brittany, Ireland, the Isle of Man, and the Highlands of Scotland; and year by year it is being driven back still farther, and the doom of final extinction hangs over it, overwhelmed in Brittany by French, and elsewhere by English. In Asia Minor the separate existence of the intrusive Gauls in Galatia has been locally forgotten.

The language is not all that it has lost. Other national characteristics have gone as well. Its tribal organization, so similar to that of the Early Romans, has failed to develop into a higher form. The tribal condition is, and always has been, a stage in the course of social and political development that all peoples have gone through that have reached the nobler and more perfect organization of the nation. But the Celts have had their natural social and political growth arrested, and the organization went to pieces at once, and they have been constrained to accept from outside what they were not suffered to reach from within by an orderly and natural process.

The organization of the people, whether in Ireland, Wales, or Scotland, was substantially identical. The highest virtue demanded of a tribesman was loyalty to the chief, for whom

SCOTTISH AND IRISH SURNAMES

life and everything precious in life was to be sacrificed when required.

The chief was no arbitrary despot. He was controlled by a council of elders. His place of residence was not his own exclusively: it belonged to the tribe or clan. He could not shut himself within and bar the door. Every clansman had a right of access and of speech with the chief.

A race in Gaelic is *slioch* or *siol*, and the people comprising it, supposed to be of one blood, are termed *cineal*, *tuath*, or *fine*, without there being any very fixed distinction drawn between these terms. A *siol* was divided into clans. *Clan* signifies literally "offspring, children"—in Irish *cland*, in Welsh *plant*. Latin writers, when describing clans, employ the word *filii*, as Filii Gadran, Filii Ædan.

Duncan Forbes, in "Culloden Papers," says: "A Highland clan is a set of men, all having the same surname, and believing themselves to be related the one to the other, and to be descendants from the same common ancestor."

Thus the clan is supposed to be the expansion of the family. Each male member of the clan was called Mac, son of the reputed ancestor. Each member of, say, the clan MacLeod was a MacLeod, of the clan Aulay was MacAulay. But to distinguish man from man his Christian name was employed. But even that did not suffice, as there might well be several Ians in the same clan. Accordingly, some characteristic was added, as the colour of his hair, or the name of his father, and perhaps also the name of the grandfather was brought in.

But simple and beautiful as the system of the clan was, it produced many difficulties in practice. As a tribe increased in numbers, it inevitably broke up into septs. A great chief had, let us say, three sons, and each gathered about him a set of followers, ravaged a neighbour's lands, and planted his followers on the soil from which he had expelled the former holders. Then each son became a new head, giving his name to his followers and to his descendants, and the original clan was broken up into three, at a later period to undergo further division.

SCOTTISH AND IRISH SURNAMES

Thus the clan Alpine consisted of seven subclans: the MacGregors, Grants, MacIntosh, MacNab, MacPhies, MacGarries, and MacAulays. The ancient clan Chattan comprised as many as sixteen, of which the principal were the Camerons, with their subsection clan MacBean, the clans Farquharson, and MacDuff. The clan Campbell has its Argyll, Breadalbane, Cawdor, and Loudon branches, and also the MacArthurs.

Burt, in his "Letters from a Gentleman" in 1726, says: "The Highlanders are divided into tribes or clans, under chiefs or chieftains, as they are called in the laws of Scotland; and each clan, again, is divided into branches from the main stock, who have chieftains over them. These are subdivided into smaller branches, of fifty to sixty men, who deduce their original from their particular chieftains, and rely upon them as their more immediate protectors and defenders."

But the notion that the clan consisted wholly of those related in blood was a fiction. An inner ring was indeed so composed. But there existed an outer circle, made up of captives taken in war, thralls, and runaways from other clans—"broken men," as they were termed, who had been excluded from their own clan for some offence, and had solicited and obtained admission into another. The Macraes of Glensheals were thralls under the MacLeods; but after a battle, in which most of the men of the MacLeods had fallen, their widows and daughters took to them husbands of the Macraes, so as to fill up once more the depleted tribe. But that all in the clan were connected by blood, as they were by name, was a fiction that could impose on few. An Earl made a grant of land to a favourite tenant. Whereupon that servant invented a tartan, obliged all who lived on his land to assume it, and call themselves his sons. The ancestor of the Colquhouns was Humphry Kirkpatrick, who was granted the lands of Colquhoun in the reign of Alexander II. The first to assume the name of Colquhoun was his successor Ingram. In this case—and this is only one among several—the clansmen, who wore his badge, the dogberry, and assumed the tartan, had not a drop of Kirkpatrick blood in their veins.

SCOTTISH AND IRISH SURNAMES

Siol Fhinian is the name of the clan MacLennan. It was founded by the son of Gillie Gorm of the Logans, in Ross-shire, in the thirteenth century. He was deformed, and was educated for the ecclesiastical profession, took priest's orders, and had several sons, whom he called Gillie Fhinian, and from them came the clan MacGilleInain, now corrupted to *MacLennan*, but we cannot suppose that the entire clan is the fruit of his loins.

The *MacNabs* form a clan descended from the Abbot of Glendockart, who lived between 1150 and 1180. All his lands—plundered from the abbey—were in the valley of that name. He had sons, and they constituted, with the retainers poached from the Church, the clan of MacNab—*i.e.*, sons of the Abbot.

Ewan, grandson of the chief of the clan Chattan, in the reign of David I. became Abbot of Kingussie, till 1153, when his elder brother died without issue, whereupon he obtained a dispensation from the Pope, married, and had two sons. From him rose the clan *MacPherson*, or Sons of the Parson, that is divided into two branches, that of Cluny and that of Invereshie, to which latter belong the Gillieses and the Gillespies. But that is not all. The heads of some sixteen or seventeen clans are descended from Norman-French or Scandinavian founders. But of this more hereafter.

Further, owing to subdivision, many of the clans cannot trace back to a remote antiquity. They came into being in the twelfth or thirteenth century, some even later than that. The *MacQueens* were founded as a clan in the fifteenth century. The clan *Matheson* originates with John Matheson, a man believed to have been of foreign extraction, who was killed in 1587.

The chief in his *dun* was surrounded by functionaries, and, as Sir John Carr wrote in his " Caledonian Sketches," 1809: " When a chief undertook a journey, he used to be attended by the following officers and servants : the Henchman; Bard; Piper's Gilly, who carried the pipe ; Peadier, the spokesman; Gillimore, the broadsword-bearer ; Gilli-astflue, to carry the chieftain, when on foot, over the ford ; Gilli-constraine, leader

SCOTTISH AND IRISH SURNAMES

of the horse in rough and dangerous ways; Gilli-trushan-urich, baggage-man."

The Highlanders bore an implacable hatred towards the Lowlanders, whom they regarded as Sassenachs, who had dispossessed them of their richest lands, and in former days one of their main resources in hard times was to issue from their passes and raid the Lowlands.

But Sassenachs the Lowlanders were not; the whole of Bernicia, that extended from the Firth of Forth, had been conquered and colonized by the Angles, and after that there had been an infusion among them of Danish and Norse blood. The old kingdom of Scotland was of very limited extent. It stretched from the Firth of Forth to the Moray Firth in the north; all the west was Gaelic peopled from the North-West of Ireland; and all Caithness, Sutherland, Argyll, and the Western Isles, together with Orkney and the Shetlands, were held by Scandinavians.

As might be expected, in the Lowlands surnames are formed in the same way as those in England, and resemble such as are common in Northumberland and Durham; but in the Highlands, where Gaelic prevails, it is otherwise.

How widely through Scotland foreign blood has flowed, and penetrated into even Gaelic veins, may be seen when we look at some of the principal families, and even clans, in Scotland. Let us take some. The *Grant* clan is purely Celtic, a branch of the very ancient clan MacAlpine, and carried the badge of that clan. But the name is unmistakably Norman—Le Grand. Gervase of Tilbury, in his " Otia Imperialia," tells us that Grant or Graunt was the English name for a giant or monster. The story is told of an old Earl of Seafield who desired to establish beyond dispute the antiquity of his family, and accordingly altered in the family Bible one letter in Gen. vi. 4, so that it read, " There were Grants in the earth in those days"—before the Flood. "But," said a sceptical friend, " the Deluge came and swept them all away." The Earl fixed on him a stony glance, and replied haughtily: "That verse has been misplaced, and should have come after the Flood."

SCOTTISH AND IRISH SURNAMES

Cummin is from De Comines. William the Conqueror sent Robert de Comines to be Earl of Northumbria, but he was killed by the people of Durham in 1069. A kinsman went north beyond the Tweed, and his descendants have constituted a powerful clan, and wear the cummin as their badge and have their own tartan.

Frazer is really De Frezel, a family of Touraine. René Frezel's second son came to England with the Conqueror. A descendant found favour and land with David I., who was a great importer of Anglo-Norman blood. The Frazers have their tartan and their badge, the yew.

The *Kerrs*, again, are of similar origin. Two brothers settled in Scotland in the thirteenth century. None knew which was the elder of the two, and neither would yield superiority to the other, and this led to such bitter animosity that in 1590 Robert Kerr of Cessford killed William Kerr of Ancrum in a dispute as to precedence.

The *Lindsays*, also, are not of Scottish ancestors; they were originally De Limesay from the Pays de Caux, near Pavilly, north of Rouen. Radolf de Limesay, thought to have been sister's son to the Conqueror, was the first of the stock to settle in England. David I. brought them to Scotland.

The *Melvilles* derive their name from Malaville, in the Pays de Caux, whence a William de Malaville is reported to have come to England with the Conqueror. Galfrid de Maleville settled in Scotland under David I., and was the first Justiciary of Scotland on record.

Oliphant is also an Anglo-Norman name. The first to go to Scotland was David, who had served in the army of King Stephen against the Empress Maud in 1141.

Bruce is Norman, from Bruys or Brix. Wace tells how "they of Bruys" accompanied the Conqueror to England.

Balliol is from Bailleul, near Argentan in Normandy.

Gordon is De Gourdon, from a small town on the Limestone Causses in Quercy. The Gourdons must have come to England at the time of the English occupation of Guienne. They did wisely to abandon the sterile plateau for the lush plains of England. The first heard of is Adam de Gourdon,

SCOTTISH AND IRISH SURNAMES

"the King's servant" under Richard I. The Scottish Gordons, however, assert that they derive from another Anglo-Norman family seated at Gordon in Berwickshire. But Adam has been for generations a Christian name in both Gordon families, that in Scotland and that seated in Suffolk. Richard was Baron of Gordon in the Merse in the middle of the twelfth century. The Gordons have their tartan and their badge, rock-ivy.

The *Stuarts*, or *Stewarts*, derive from a Norman—Alan, Lord of Oswestry. His son Walter was one of the importations into Scotland by David I. in the twelfth century, and the King granted him by charter the burgh and lands of Renfrew, and Malcolm IV. made the office of High Steward hereditary in the family. Alan Dapifer's son Walter was content to call himself Walter FitzAlan, and Walter's son was called Alan FitzWalter, with the addition of Seneschallus (Scotice, *Steward*), from his hereditary office, which soon became the fixed surname of the descendants.[1] Although the family was not of Scottish origin, almost immediately after its settlement in Scotland it became completely identified with the nationality of the new country, to such an extent that Scotland has accepted the Stuart badge, the thistle, as its national emblem. "No Scotchman," says Sir Bernard Burke, "should ever forget the title to honour and respect which the family of Stewart acquired before they began to reign, by their undeviating and zealous defence of their native land against the wanton aggressions of the English. Wherever the banner of freedom was unfurled, it was sure to be bravely defended by the Lord High Steward and all the nobles of his race."

Leslie is descended from a chief of Norman descent, a De l'Isle. The first of the name heard of in Scotland is in the reign of William the Lion (1165-1214).

Maitland is actually Mautalent, "Little-wit," or, to be more exact, Bad-wit.

[1] The arms assumed by the Stuarts two generations after their settlement in Scotland were the fess chequy (the *checquer*, used for computing before the introduction of Arabic numerals), in allusion to their office at the Exchequer table.

SCOTTISH AND IRISH SURNAMES

Hay is also a Norman name, from La Haye-de-Puits in Manche. "Hence came the great Eudo Dapifer," says Sir Francis Palgrave, "who acquired, whether by force or favour, the largest proportions by robbery, called Conquest, in the counties of Sussex, Essex, and Suffolk." William de la Hay settled in Lothian in the middle of the twelfth century, and was Chief Butler of Scotland in the reigns of Malcolm IV. and William the Lion.

Ross is, again, most probably Norman. Five of the name Le Roux are entered in Domesday. The origin of the clan is, however, attributed to one Paul Mactire, who was granted lands in Gairloch in 1366 by William, Earl of Ross and Lord of Skye.

Campbell is supposed to be De Campobello, or Beauchamp, but this is very doubtful. The clan rose upon the ruin of the MacDonalds, and its whole policy for ages was to supplant and ruin that race, leading to the massacre of Glencoe, that has left an indelible stain on its badge of the wild-myrtle.

The clan first appears on record at the end of the thirteenth century. The name occurs at the same time as a good many other Anglo-Norman importations into Scotland. The Campbells were allied with the Norman Bruce, and there can exist very little doubt that they are of Anglo-Norman descent.

Chisholm.—The chieftain of this clan is also asserted to be of foreign origin. An old chief of the clan was wont to say that there were but three persons in the world entitled to be called *the*—the King, the Pope, and the Chisholm.

The *Drummonds*, according to tradition, descend from Maurice, grandson of Andrew, King of Hungary, who, it is pretended, accompanied Edgar Etheling into Scotland, and received a grant of the lands of Drummond in Stirlingshire from Malcolm III. This is probably not true, but points to the belief that the headship of the clan was in a family of foreign origin.

Dundas.—The family descends from one Serlo, in the time of William the Lion. The name Serlo indicates a Norman origin.

SCOTTISH AND IRISH SURNAMES

Gunn.—This clan is probably derived from a Norse chief of the name of Gunnar, in Caithness, which was entirely in the hands of the Scandinavian Earls of Orkney.

MacDougal.—A clan that descends from Somerled of the Isles. Somerled is a Norse name, and signifies a Viking harrying in the summer. He died in 1164. He married the granddaughter of Godred Crovan, a Norse King of Man. Olaf Bitling, his father, had spent his youth at the Court of Henry I. of England; he married the daughter of Fergus, Lord of Galloway, a granddaughter of Henry I. Somerled was the Scandinavian Lord of Argyll.

The *MacLeods* also form a clan subdivided into two subclans, issuing from two Norsemen—Thorkell and Thormod.

The *Menzies*, pronounced "Menies," derive from the Norman family of Menières, Sieurs de la Gaudinière. In England, Gilbert de Menières held three parts of a knight's-fee of the Archbishop of York in the reign of Henry II. In Scotland we find Alexander de Meyners, son of Robert, the Chancellor of Scotland, holding the lands of Durrosdeer in Annandale in 1248; he was of the retinue of the Queen of Scotland. It was not till the reign of Malcolm III. that surnames were introduced into Scotland, and that of Menzies was among the first that were adopted.

The noble family of *Lion* of Strathmore is of Norman extraction; so are the *Maules*.

Maccus was the name of one of David I.'s foreign favourites — probably Anglo-Norman — and he was given large possessions. He called his chief place of residence Maccusville, and this became *Maxwell*.[1]

Sinclair is also a family and name of Norman origin. The Sire de St. Claire is named in the "Roman de Rou" as having been present at the Battle of Hastings. This was Richard de St. Clair. His brother was Britel, and it was in all probability William Britel's son who received the grant of Rosslyn in Midlothian from David I. From him are descended the Sinclairs, Earls of Orkney and Caithness.

---

[1] A Maccus was one of the gallant three who defended the bridge at Maldon in 991.

SCOTTISH AND IRISH SURNAMES

Besides William, another of the family sought his fortunes in Scotland, Henry de St. Clair, who was made Constable of Scotland in 1160, and was the founder of the House of Herdmanston, now represented by Lord Sinclair.

Elliott, moreover, is a Franco-Norman name, a diminutive of Elli or Elias, as we have Henriot, Philipot, etc.

The *Hamiltons*, again, are of Norman descent, and derive from Walter FitzGilbert. The power and consequence of the Hamiltons were of comparatively late date, not before the royal marriage by which they acquired the earldom of Arran.

Barclay is De Berkelai. *Cheyne* is Le Chesne. *Mowat* is De Mont haut (De Monte alto), *Muschets* is Montfichet (De Monte fixo), *Veitch* is De Vesci, and *Weir* De Vere.

But if Scotland has been invaded by foreigners, and its very clans headed by or named after chieftains not of Scottish race, Scotland has known how to repay the world. Where are not Scotchmen now to be found? Half the noble families in Sweden are of Scottish ancestry. In India, in South Africa, in America, they are everywhere, and everywhere to the fore. But perhaps the oddest of all instances is that of Mogador in Morocco, if the story be true.

It is said that a venturesome Macdonald from the Land of Cakes settled at that, the most southern point of Morocco, and, not finding any great difference in creed between the fatalism of the Koran and the predestination of the Lesser Catechism, accommodated himself to his surroundings, and lived to be accounted a saint by the Moors. When he died he was canonized, and a shrine (*kouba*) was built over his body. He was called Sid Mogdoul, or Mogdour; pilgrimages were made to it, and prayers offered to him; and thus arose the town of Mogador.[1]

The clans were by no means early in assuming uniform fixed surnames instead of fluctuating patronymics. The MacDonalds and others had no recognized general surname till the eighteenth century. Moreover, as may be guessed from what has been said above, the settlement of a powerful

[1] *Chambers's Edinburgh Journal*, March, 1909.

SCOTTISH AND IRISH SURNAMES

Southern or foreign family in the Highlands was followed by the sudden spread of their name throughout the dwellers in the neighbouring glens, although not in the smallest degree akin in blood; but the native inhabitants, having no surnames of their own, and being desirous of placing themselves under the protection of these foreign newcomers, readily adopted the name of their lords. Even after surnames had become common in the Highlands, we find that clans or groups of natives made petition to assume such names. Some small clans of the Braes of Angus by this means acquired the surname of *Lyon*. Many more in Argyll and the Isles abandoned their name of Awe, and called themselves *Maccallummore*. The Anglo-French family of *Gordon* was hardly settled in Strathbolgy before the whole country round swarmed with men who called themselves Gordons.[1]

The *Camerons*, or Crooked Noses, are undoubtedly a sept of the ancient clan Chattan. The clan Dhaibhidh, or *Davidsons*, are almost certainly of Gaelic origin; so also the *Douglas* family and the *Farquharsons* issued from the clan Chattan; probably also the *Grahams*, and certainly the *Lomonds*. The *MacAlisters* are descended from Alister Mor, Lord of the Isles and Kintyre in 1284. The *MacAlpine* clan is, along with the clan *Chattan*, the most ancient that exist, but both are broken up into subclans. The old Gaelic saying, "Cnuic is willt is Ailpeanaich," intimates that the clan is as venerable as the hills. The crest of the MacAlpines was a boar's head couped, dripping blood, with the motto in Gaelic, "Remember the death of Alpin," referring to the murder of King Alpin by Brude, King of the Picts, in 834, but looks farther back to the totem of the tribe, a boar.

The *MacBeans* form a clan that is a sept of the Camerons. The name has been anglicized into *Baynes*.

The *MacDonald* clan is of high antiquity, and descends from Gille Brude, a Pict. There are branches, those of Glencoe, of Clanronald, of Glengarry, of the Isles and Sleat; also there are Macdonalds of Staffa. Their badge is the common heath.

[1] Innes, Cosmo, "Concerning some Scotch Surnames." Edinburgh, 1860.

SCOTTISH AND IRISH SURNAMES

The *Macduff* clan is formed out of the clan Chattan. Its badge is a sprig of box.

Macfarlane is a clan occupying the western bank of Loch Lomond. The name signifies Son of Bartholomew, and derives from one so called, grandson of Duncan MacGilchrist, a younger brother of Malduin, Earl of Lennox. The badge is the cranberry.

MacIntosh, a branch of the clan Chattan.

MacInnes, the clan of the sons of Angus, hereditary bowmen to the chiefs of MacKinnon. *MacIntyre* is a branch of the MacDonalds.

Mackay.—Siol Mhorgain was the ancient name of the Mackays, a Celtic stock that retreated into the mountains before the invading Northmen. The badge is a bulrush.

MacKenzie, the clan of the sons of Kenneth.

MacKinlay, the sons of Fionnladh, anglicized into Finlay.

MacKinnon, a sept of MacAlpine. *MacLachlan*, in Argyllshire, in Strathlachlan; their badge is a sprig of ash.

Maclaren.—This clan is of Celtic origin, and occupied a narrow strip of country extending from Lochearnhead to the lands of the *MacGregor* of Glengyle. These latter are of the MacAlpine stock.

MacLean (actually Mac-giolla-Ean), signifies the son of the servant of John. The badge is the same as that of the Mackenzies—a sprig of holly—indicating a common origin. The clan is said to have originated with the sons of Gill-ian, "with the battle-axe," a Celtic chief whose date is undetermined. The lands of the clan are in the Isle of Mull. So also are those of the *MacLaines*, which issues from Hector Reganach, brother of Lauchlan Labanach, from whom sprang the *MacLeans* of Duast. The *MacMillans* were dependents on the clan Cameron.

MacNaughten.—This clan descends from Nectan, a Pictish King. The lands were in the Isle of Lorn, and its badge the trailing wild-azalea.

The *MacNeils*, divided into two septs, occupying the western isles of Gigha and Barra, have the same badge as the Lamonts, the clover or trefoil, and probably have the same origin.

The clan *MacQuarrie* is very ancient, and is descended

SCOTTISH AND IRISH SURNAMES

from the Dalriadic Scottish Princes. It is a branch of the clan MacAlpine. *Munro* is an ancient clan, planted on the north side of the Cromarty Firth. The badge is the club-moss. *Murray* also is an ancient Celtic clan, its badge the butcher's-broon. *Robertson*, a clan in Perthshire, called in the Highlands the clan Domnachie, is descended from the House of Athole. *Rose* is the clan Na Rosaich of Kilravoch, the badge a sprig of rosemary. *Skene* is a Celtic clan in Aberdeenshire. The *Sutherland* clan is made up of refugees from the depredations of the Norsemen. *Urquhart* is a clan so called from the district of that name in Inverness. Its badge is the wallflower.

Indeed, a considerable number of Scottish surnames are derived from places. Such are *Crawford, Dundas, Cunninghame* (the home of the King), *Dunbar, Wemyss,* and *Moncrieff.*

Gill is the Celtic for "servant," and *Gilderoy* is the King's servant, *Gillchrist* the servant of our Lord, *Gillpatrick* the servant of Patrick, *Gilmory* the servant of Mary, *Gillescop* or *Gillespie* the Bishop's servant, *Gilmore* the head-servant. *Gillie* is really Gill-Jesus.

Another word was in use to describe one in subjection, and that was *Gwaeth* or *Gwas*. This we have in *Gospatrick*. This meant that the person so named was placed under the special patronage of the saint whose name he bore. We have a corruption of Gwas in *Gossoon*. *Mael* in composition signifies the bald or shaven devotee of a saint. *Malcolm* means the servant of Columba. A word that enters into several Scottish surnames, as *Dalhousie, Dalrymple, Dalziel,* is *Dal*. This signified first of all a portion, and is akin to the German *theil*. It came later to designate a field, as something taken out of the common.

By an Act of the Scottish Privy Council, April 3, 1603, the name of *MacGregor* was expressly abolished, and those who had hitherto borne it were commanded to change it for other surnames, the pain of death being denounced against those who should call themselves Gregor or MacGregor, their clan names. By a subsequent Act of Council, June 24, 1613,

SCOTTISH AND IRISH SURNAMES

death was denounced against any person of the clan found still bearing either of these names. Again, by an Act of Parliament, 1617, these laws were reinforced and extended to the rising generation, inasmuch as great numbers of the children of those against whom the Acts of the Privy Council had been directed were stated to be then approaching to maturity, who, if permitted to resume the name of their parents, would render the clan as strong as it was before. On the Restoration, King Charles II., in the first Scottish Parliament of his reign (1661), annulled the various Acts against the clan MacGregor, and restored the members to the full use of the name.

We will now turn to Ireland. There there were large tribes. In the South, for instance, were the Hy Faelain, Hy Failghe, Hy Bairche, Hy Cinnselach, Hy Liadhain, Hy Fiachach, Corca Laighe, Corca Duibhne, Hy Cearbhail, Hy Fidgeinte, etc. But in Ireland as in Scotland every tribe was broken up into septs. What the sept was to the tribe, that the homestead was to the sept. The head of a tribe, or *tuath*, was called *rig*. The head of a clan, or *fine*, was entitled *ceanfine*, and the head of a household was an *aire*. But an *aire* whose family had occupied the same house and land for three generations was entitled to be called a *flaith*, or lord, and was ripe to become the head of a fresh segregation of children and followers in a subclan.

The flaiths of the different septs were vassals of the *rig*, and performed certain functions for him, which in course of time became hereditary.

I have already referred to the word *dal* as signifying a part or portion. The word was applied to that division of the clan Riada that migrated from Ireland into Alba, as it was then called.[1] Then it was that most of Scotland fell under the domination of the Irish Gaels, the Dalriadic Scots who conferred the name of Scotland on North Britain.

In Ireland the head of a tribe gave his name to his descendants and followers, who called themselves by his name, preceded by *hua* or *hy*, meaning grandson; and this has been

[1] Bede, " Hist. Eccl.," i. 1.

SCOTTISH AND IRISH SURNAMES

anglicized into O', as *O'Neal,* for Hua Nial. Hua Conchabair has become in English *O'Connor,* and Hua Suilleabhain is *O'Sullivan.*

The ancient Irish, like the Gaelic Highlanders, had their personal names, and that of the sept to which they belonged. Should there be need for discrimination between those of the same Christian name, the same mode of distinguishing one from another was pursued in Ireland as in the Scottish Highlands.

In the tenth century King Brian Boru is said to have issued an edict that the descendants of the heads of tribes and families then in power should take name from them, either from the fathers or grandfathers, and that these names should become hereditary and fixed for ever. In compliance with this mandate, the *O'Brians* of Thomond took their name from the monarch Brian Boru himself, who was slain in the Battle of Clontarf in the year 1014. Other family names were formed either from the name of the chieftains who had fought in the battle or from those of their sons or fathers. Thus, the *O'Mahonys* of Desmond are named from Mahon, the son of Kian, King of Desmond, who fought in that battle; the *O'Donohues* from Donogh, whose father Donnell was the second in command over the Eugenian forces in the same battle; the *O'Donovans* from Donovan, whose son Cathel commanded the Hy Caibre in the same battle; the *O'Dugans* of Fermoy from Dugan, whose son Gevenagh commanded the sept of the Druid Mogh Roth in the same battle; the *O'Faelans* or *Phelans,* of the Desiis, derived from Faolan, whose son Mothla commanded the Desii of Munster in the same memorable battle; the *MacMurroughs* of Leinster deduced their descent from Murrough, whose son Mael Mordha, King of Leinster, assisted the Danes against the Irish monarch. The *MacCarthys* of Desmond are named after Carthach, who is mentioned in the Irish annals as having fought in the Battle of Maelkenny in 1043; the *O'Conors* of Connaught from Conor, or Concowar, who died in 971; the *O'Melaghlins* of Meath, the chief of the Southern Hy Nial race, from Maelseachlainn, or Malachy II., monarch

SCOTTISH AND IRISH SURNAMES

of Ireland, who died in the year 1022; the *Mogillapatricks*, or *Fitzpatricks*, of Ossory, from Gillapatrick, chief of Ossory, who was killed in the year 995; etc.

It does not at all follow in Ireland, any more than in Scotland, that those who bear the tribal name have any blood of the family in their veins, as there existed from a very early period a system of adoption into a tribe. Runaways could obtain absorption if they had committed a murder or some other crime that would bring on them either death or a heavy fine.

Irish names went through great fluctuations subsequent to their first introduction, and names that have been borne for two or more generations were exchanged for others. Thus the *O'Malbrogi* of Moybrugh became *MacDermot*, and *O'Laughlin*, head of the Northern Hy Niall, *MacLaughlin*.

Families, when assuming a surname went back many generations, so as to be able to call themselves after the most illustrious name in the race. Thus the *O'Neills* and the *MacNeills* derive from Niall of the Nine Hostages, who received St. Patrick, and died in 405.

Mr. O'Donovan, quoted by Lower, mentions an instance of a John Mageoghan of Galway who applied to King George IV. for licence to reject the surname which his family had borne for eight centuries, derived from the illustrious King Eoghain, in order that he might adopt a new name from a still more ancient and illustrious ancestor—to wit, that same Niall of the Nine Hostages who lived in the fourth and fifth centuries, and his son and successor wrote himself John Augustus O'Neill. In the fourteenth and fifteenth centuries, when the Irish families had increased, and their territories underwent subdivision among branches of the same sept, each chieftain for distinction's sake adopted some addition to the family name as a means of distinction. Thus there was *the* MacDermot, the head of the race, and the branch-lines of MacDermot Roe (the Red), and MacDermot Gull (the anglicized); again, MacCarthy Mor (the Great), and MacCarthy Reagh (the Swarthy), and MacCarthy Muscreragh (of Muskerry, the place of his residence); and, again, O'Connor Roe (the

SCOTTISH AND IRISH SURNAMES

Red-haired) and O'Connor Don (the Brown-haired). All these additional names were perpetuated by the representatives of each branch for a long period, and even now are not extinct. Mr. O'Donovan says: "After the murder in 1333 of William de Burgo, third Earl of Ulster of that name, and the lessening of the English power which resulted from it, many, if not all, the Anglo-Norman families located in Connaught became Hibernicized—*Hibernis ipsis Hiberniores*—spoke the Irish language, and assumed surnames in imitation of the Irish by prefixing ' Mac ' to the Christian names of their ancestors. Thus the De Burgos took the name of MacWilliam from their ancestor William de Burgo, 'from whom sprang many offshoots, who took other names from their respective ancestors.' Thus originated the Mac-Davids, MacShoneens (from John, and now changed to Jennings), MacGibbons, MacAndrew, and many others, the very plebeian name of MacPhaudeen from an ancestor called Paudeen, or Little Patrick. The De Exeters assumed the name of MacJordan from Jordan de Exeter, the founder of that family, and the Nangles that of MacCostello; ... a branch of the Butlers took the name MacPierce, and the Powers or Poers that of MacShere.

" On the other hand, the Irish families who lived within the English pale and in its vicinity gradually conformed to the English custom and assumed English surnames, and their doing so was deemed to be of such political importance that it was thought worthy of consideration by Parliament."

In 1485 an Act was passed entitled " An Act that the Irishmen dwelling in the counties of Dublin, Myeth, Wriall, and Kildare, shall gae apparelled like English men, and ware their heads after the English maner, sweare allegiance, and take English surnames." This Act directed every Irishman whom it concerned to " take to him an English surname of one towne, as *Sutton, Chester, Trym, Skryne, Corke, Kinsale,* or colour as *White, Blacke, Browne;* and that he and his issue shall use this name under payne of forfeiting of his goods yearly till the premises be done."

Thus constrained, the Mac- and O'Gowans became *Smiths;*

SCOTTISH AND IRISH SURNAMES

the Shonachs, *Foxes*; the MacIntires, *Carpenters*; the Mac-Cogrys, *l'Estranges*; and the MacKillies, *Cocks*.

The process of anglicizing Irish surnames has gone on since then to our own times. After the Battles of Aughrim and the Boyne, and the complete overthrow of James II., numerous families of all ranks assimilated their names to the English by the rejection of their old characteristic prefixes, and by an accommodated orthography. One Felim O'Neill, a gentleman, changed his name to Felix *Neele*. O'Marachain became *Markham*, and O'Beirne has been altered into *Byron*, O'Dulaine to *Delany*.

Other families Gallicized their names, as O'Ducy to *D'Arcy*, O'Malley to *Du Maillet*, O'Melaville to *Lavelle*, O'Dowling to *Du Laing*.

Old names have gone through abrasion. MacGennis is now *Guinness*, *Conry* is short for O'Mulconry, *Kilkenny* for MacGillakenny. The process of assimilation has extended to Christian names. Conor has been supplanted by *Cornelius*, Eoghain by *Eugene*, Aidan by *Hugh*, Donogh by *Denis*, Moriartagh by *Mortimer*, Donnell by *Daniel*, Ardgal by *Arnold*, Ferdorogh by *Ferdinand*, and Mogue by *Moses*.

Some Irish names were simply translated into English. Thus Shannach became *Fox*, and MacChoghree became *Kingstone*. From Joscelin de Angelo came the surname of *Nangle*, and from MacGostelin that of *Costello*. Sir Odo, the Archdeacon, had a son MacOdo, which has been vulgarized into *Cody*.

To such an extent have names been altered in Ireland that in some cases it is only possible by a reference to parish registers and to wills to discover to what race a family belongs, whether Irish or English.

A large number of Scotchmen and some English entered the service of Gustavus Adolphus in the Thirty Years' War. The Marquis of Hamilton raised a troop in 1631 for the Swedish service, under the guidance of his maternal relative Alexander Leslie. Many of these remained in Sweden, and were there enrolled. But there had been levies long before that. Scottish soldiers formed part of the army of Sweden

SCOTTISH AND IRISH SURNAMES

as early as 1563. On July 30 King Eric XIV. wrote to a Master Marten to raise 2,000 men in Scotland. The officers of this first levy were William Colquhoun—whom the Swedes called Kahun—James Henderson, William Ruthven, Thomas Buchan, and Robert Crichton. But in 1566 we hear of others of the names of Stuart, Wallace, Fullerton, Murray, Monraff (? Monroe), Young, Greig, Bisset, Lockhart, Galloway, and Kerr.

In 1573 was another levy of Scottish soldiers; in 1591 there was a third; and in 1595 we find the following Scottish names of officers in Swedish pay: Williamson, Johnston, King, Cunninghame—called by the Swedes Kunnigam—Allan, Wetterson, and Robinson. In 1598 we meet also with a Keith and a Neafre, whom the Swedes entitled Näf. He belonged to an ancient family in Forfar, now extinct.

Gustavus Adolphus in 1612 had more Scottish mercenaries fighting under his banner, commanded by Colonel Rutherford, Captain Learmouth, Waucorse, and Greig. King James and the Council forbade this levying of recruits in Scotland; but the service was lucrative, and many managed to escape. In the fall of the year 1612 a party of these, to the number of 300, under Colonel Ramsay and Captains Hay and Sinclair, landed in Norway, but were massacred by the peasants. The site is still marked and pointed out to travellers. Brook, in his " Travels through Sweden and Norway " (1823), gives an illustration representing the monument on the site of the tragedy.

In 1630 the Marquis of Hamilton brought over 1,000 Scots to fight under "the Lion of the North." There were further levies in 1636 and 1638. Charles XII. was accompanied on his campaigns by a large number of Scottish officers—mostly scions of families whose members had served his father and grandfather, or even won laurels under the great Gustavus. Among them we meet with the Douglases, Hamiltons, Macdougals—who in Sweden figured as Duwalls—Ramsays, Spensers, and Sinclairs. But it was not only in the army that Scots appeared in Sweden; they

SCOTTISH AND IRISH SURNAMES

came and settled there as merchants as well, and there amassed large fortunes.

Scottish names, however, became curiously disguised in the families they founded, and, indeed, in the contemporary army lists. Robsahm stands for Robson or Robinson; Sinckler for Sinclair; Wudd for Wood; Forbus is Forbes; Boij is Boyes; Bothwell becomes Bossveld; Bruce is spelled Brux and Bryssz; Colquhoun is rendered not only Kahun, but also Canonhjelm; Douglas becomes Duglitz, and Findlay is rendered Finlaij; Greig expands into Greiggenschildt; and some entirely changed their names.

An interesting account of "The Scots in Sweden" is by Th. A. Fischer (Edinburgh, 1907). A list of those there ennobled is to be found in Horace Marryatt's "One Year in Sweden" (London, 1862, vol. ii., appendix).

But Scots also settled extensively in Poland and Eastern Prussia as tradesmen and merchants, married, and there founded families. Their names are to be found in the town registers of Warsaw, Cracow, Danzig, Tilsit, Memel, Posen, etc. Strangely altered some of them are in spelling, as Agnitz for Agnew, Bethon for Beaton, Kaubrun for Cockburn, Gloch for Gloag, Erdthur for Arthur. For a full account of "The Scots in Germany," see a work bearing that title by Fischer (Edinburgh, 1902).

Nor must it be forgotten that the Scottish Guard had a glorious career in France. He who desires information on this interesting subject must consult Michel (F.), "Les Écossais en France, et les Français en Écosse" (London, 1862); and Burton (J. H.), "The Scot Abroad" (Edinburgh, 1898, vol. i.).

CHAPTER XIX

CHANGED NAMES

THE great family of Mowbray was really De Albini. In 1095 Robert de Mowbray, Earl of Northumberland, rebelled against William Rufus, and was captured at Tynemouth and brought to Windsor, where he was confined in a subterranean dungeon for thirty-four miserable years. He had but recently married Maude de l'Aigle, but the Pope's licence was purchased and her marriage dissolved, and she was then married to Nigel de Albini; and her son, Robert, by this second husband, born whilst the first husband was still alive and languishing in a dungeon, assumed the name of Mowbray along with his father by order of Henry I.

Nigel, bow-bearer to William Rufus and Henry I., had dismounted Robert, Duke of Normandy, in the Battle of Tenchbray, and had brought him prisoner to the King, his brother. It was in reward for this achievement that Henry granted him, in 1106, the lands of the attainted Mowbray as well as the name of the unfortunate man. This name of Mowbray the De Albinis retained as long as the issue male continued, which determined in John Mowbray, Duke of Norfolk, in the time of King Edward IV., and his heiresses married into the families of Howard and Berkley. There is this to be said in excuse for the change of name—that Nigel d'Albini's mother had been a Mowbray.

In the reign of Edward I., one of the nobles of his Court, holding hereditary honours and lands, had no surname at all. Each successor to his father was known as Fitz So-and-so. This noble was John FitzRobert, but, on account of the bewilderment caused by the continuous change of designa-

CHANGED NAMES

tion, Edward required him thenceforth to bear the name of his barony, Clavering; this he did accordingly, and thenceforth was known as John de Clavering.

Richard Williams, a gentleman of Wales, who had married a sister of Thomas Cromwell, whom Henry VIII. created Earl of Essex just before cutting off his head for having saddled him with Anne of Cleves for a wife, was ordered by the King to assume the name of Cromwell; he did so, and became an ancestor of the Protector.

These instances show that the Crown claimed as a privilege the right to give or to change a name. At the same time, it is quite certain that it was a claim not enforced, and that the vast majority of people called themselves by whatever names they liked. Sir Charles Somerset, bastard son of Beaufort, Duke of Somerset, assumed his father's surname of Beaufort; but, on the other hand, the original Beaufort, illegitimate son of John of Gaunt, was not suffered to call himself Plantagenet. Yet another bastard, the Viscount de l'Isle, was allowed by the Crown to name himself Plantagenet. The surname of Stuart was vetoed to the Dukes of Richmond, Grafton, St. Albans, and Monmouth, all base slips of Charles II., and they were constrained to call themselves Lennox, Fitzroy, Beauclerk.

A considerable number of our nobility have changed their surnames, or have pieced on an additional name to that which is theirs by lineal descent on the paternal side.

The great Duke of Wellington was not a Wellesley, but a Colley. His grandfather, Richard Colley, assumed the name of a relative Wesley, but expanded it to Wellesley. Another branch of the family still retains the name of Colley, but altered into Cowley, as less reminiscent of the nursery rhyme of "Colley, my Cow."

> "A story, a story, I'll tell you just now,
> It's all about killing of Colly, my cow;
> Ah! my pretty Colly, poor Colly, my cow!
> Poor Colly will give no more milk to me now,
> And that is the way my fortune doth go."

The Duke of Northumberland is not a Percy, but a Smithson, his ancestor, Sir Hugh Smithson, having acquired the

CHANGED NAMES

honours of the House of Percy through his grandmother. Lord Clarendon is not a Hyde, but a Villiers; the Duke of Marlborough not a Churchill, but a Spencer. Lord Dacre is not a Trevor, but a Brand. Lord Wilton is not an Egerton, but a Grosvenor; Lord de Tabley not a Warren, but a Leicester. Earl Nelson is a Bolton; his grandfather was Thomas Bolton, who married the sister of the great Admiral.

The late Lord Anglesea was not a Paget, but a Bayley. Viscount Clifden, Lord Robartes, is not a Robartes, but an Agar; but the great estates in Cornwall come through the Robartes family, properly Roberts. The Earl of Haddington is not a Hamilton, but an Arden; Viscount Montmorency is not a Montmorency, but a Morres; the Earl of Shrewsbury is not a Talbot, but a Chetwynd.

The Sieur de Monceaux came over with the Conqueror, and was given large estates in Sussex. His family ended in a distaff, and the heiress married a country squire named Hurst, who assumed her surname on coming into the extensive possessions of the Monceaux, and built the mansion which combined their names—Hurst-Monceaux. But in the reign of Edward III. this new line ended in an heiress again, and she carried all into the family of Fiennes.

Geoffrey Nevill married Emma, the heiress of a great Norman Baron, Bertram de Bulmer. Their son died without issue, and their daughter Isabel married Robert, son of Maldred, of the Anglian race of Earls of Northumbria. This son was Geoffrey, who assumed the name of Nevill, though properly FitzMaldred, and is the true ancestor of the existing family of *Neville*.

The *Cavendishes* were Guernons, a branch of the family of Montfichet. Alured Guernon, brother of William de Montfichet, was given estates in Essex and Middlesex in 1130. He had a grandson, Ralph, father of William Guernon, whose son Geoffrey assumed the surname of Cavendish from his residence of the name in Suffolk. This Geoffrey was the grandfather of Sir John Cavendish, Chief Justice in the reign of Richard II.

CHANGED NAMES

Lord Herries is not a Herries, but a Constable. In 1758 William Hagerston Constable married the heiress of Herries and assumed her name.

The Viscounts Doneraile are not St. Leger, but Aldworth. The last St. Leger, Viscount Doneraile, died without issue in 1767, whereupon his estates devolved on his sister Elizabeth, the wife of Richard Aldworth, who assumed the surname of St. Leger, and was created Viscount Doneraile in 1785. She is said to have been the only woman in the world who became a Freemason. Her father, a zealous Mason, sometimes opened the lodge at Doneraile. His daughter, curious to witness the rite of initiation, hid herself in a clock-case in the room. After witnessing the first two steps in the ceremony, she became frightened and tried to escape, but was caught. According to the story, the Masons were for putting her to death, but were induced to spare her life at the entreaty of her brother, on condition of her going through the two steps she had already seen. The diploma that she received is carefully preserved, and her portrait, with a glass case containing the apron and jewel she was wont to wear, remain in the lodge-room at Cork.

The *De Traffords* were *De Villiers*. Alan de Villiers, second son of the Baron of Warrington, was enfeoffed by his father in Trafford in the time of Henry I., whereupon his descendants have borne the name of Trafford to this day. The crest of the family is a labouring man with a flail in his hand, thrashing, and the motto is " Now thus." The story goes that the ancestor fought in the army of Harold against the Normans, but after fled the rout, and, disguising himself, went into his barn, and was thrashing corn when the pursuers entered. Being suspected by some of them, he was asked why he so abased himself, and he replied : " Now thus." The story is mythical, for the De Villiers was a Norman.

Lord Saye and Sele is not a *Fiennes*, but a Twistleton. The eighth Viscount and last male heir of the Fiennes family died out in 1781, when his barony was claimed by Thomas Twistleton, as representative of his great-great-grandmother, Elizabeth Fiennes, eldest daughter of the second Viscount,

CHANGED NAMES

who had married John Twistleton. The name was thereupon assumed.

The *Mainwarings* of Over Peover in Cheshire are not Mainwarings, have not one drop of Mainwaring blood in their veins. The Mainwarings descended from Mesnil-Garin, a Norman house. But in 1797 Sir Henry Mainwaring, Bart., the last of his race, left all the family estates and the mansion to his half-brother, Thomas Wetenhall, son of his mother by a former marriage, who on succeeding assumed the name of Mainwaring, and a baronetcy followed in the next generation.

Lord Mostyn is not a Mostyn, but a Lloyd. Sir Edward Pryce-Lloyd, Bart., married the sister and co-heir of Sir Thomas Mostyn, Bart., and was created Baron Mostyn, and assumed his wife's name in addition to his own.

Charles Stewart Vane-Tempest, Marquis of Londonderry, is in reality a Stewart. The third Marquis for his second wife married, in 1819, the only daughter and heir of Sir Harry Vane-Tempest, and on his marriage assumed, in 1829, the surname of Vane-Tempest. Sir Godfrey Charles Morgan, Viscount Tredegar, is not a Morgan, but a Gould. Sir Charles Gould, created Baronet in 1792, assumed the name and arms of Morgan only, having married the daughter and heiress of Thomas Morgan of Tredegar.

Bastardy is liberally represented in the Gilded Chamber. The Dukes of Beaufort descend through a double bastardy. A glance through an illustrated Peerage will show how many coats of arms are debruised by the bar sinister, or have the bordure componé azure and argent. There are other peers besides Dukes that originate out of bastard slips, and not from royalty alone. The heralds of the last century were more complaisant to disguise the badge than were those of the reign of Charles II.

Vanity was the occasion of the change of a good number of names in Germany in the sixteenth century.

Writers, dissatisfied with their humble names, and not being entitled to call themselves *von*, altered them into equivalents in Greek or Latin. Melanchthon, the Reformer,

CHANGED NAMES

was ashamed of his father's name of Schwarzerde, and Œcolampadius was equally put to the blush by being designated, as was his father, Hausschein. A Schmidt became a Faber or Fabricius, a Schneider flourished as Sartorius, Didier became Erasmus.

Fuchs transformed his name into Vulpius; Lehman, mistaking the derivation of his name, called himself Argilander. Holzmann became Xylander; Bienemann, Melinander; and Mitscherlich extended his name to Midsscherliex. A certain Bienenwitz, a mathematician, born at Leising in Saxony in 1495, Latinized his name into Apionius. He was highly esteemed by the Emperor Charles V. After the Battle of Mühlberg, April 21, 1547, Ferdinand, the Emperor's brother, went to Leising, and, as the citizens had maltreated some of the Spanish mercenaries in the imperial army, he ordered the place to be given over to pillage. Happily, one of his officers saw above the door of a house the shield bearing bees as a cognizance of Apionius, and learned that Peter Bienenwitz had been born there, and also possessed the house as his paternal inheritance.

The order for general pillage was rescinded.

Towards the middle of the fifteenth century it was the fancy of the wits and learned men of Italy to change their baptismal names for such as were classical. Samazarius, for instance, altered his own plain Jacopo to Actius Syncerus. Numbers did the same; and among the rest Platina, the historian of the Popes, who, not without solemn ceremonial, took the name of Callimachus instead of Philip. Paul II., who occupied the sessorial chair at the time, was suspicious, illiterate, and dull of comprehension. He had no idea that persons other than Popes could wish to alter their names unless they had some bad design, and he did not scruple to employ imprisonment and the rack to discover the fancied mystery. Platina was cruelly tortured on this frivolous account. He had nothing to confess, so the Pope, after endeavouring in vain to convict him of heresy, sedition, etc., released him after a long imprisonment.

CHANGED NAMES

The surnames were also sometimes altered, but generally sufficed when given a Latin termination.

In England it is easy for anyone to change the surname. Burglars and shoplifters have many an alias. But others can do the same without a royal licence. There is a story in an Icelandic saga of some Vikings who had plundered a shrine in Bjarmaland, by the White Sea, then escaped to their ships by strewing wood-ashes behind them, so that even bloodhounds lost all scent. When the settlers in America broke their tie to the mother-country, they burnt the records of their family that told of their connection with their old home, and now many an American family would pay thousands of dollars to recover the records proving their link with the old land. So there are foolish people who, by changing their names, because these are not well-sounding and aristocratic, and assuming others more resonant, think that they have acquired a better station, or may be able to pose as persons of greater consequence. Vin Ordinaire is not to be converted to Old Port by change of label. But it is a grievous mistake. They are obliterating the traces whereby in future times their filiation might be followed, and some of the plainest and most vulgar names may be, and often are, the most ancient and most reputable.

Sir Joseph Jekyll, in the case of Barlow *versus* Bateman, said: " I am satisfied the usage of passing Acts of Parliament for the taking upon one a surname is but modern, and that anyone may take upon him what surname and as many surnames as he pleases, without an Act of Parliament." But this decision was reversed by the House of Lords. The Peers said, upon deciding the matter, "that the individual ought to have inherited by birth, or have obtained an authority for using the same." Nevertheless, it is now an established fact that simple notification in the newspapers of purpose to change a name is deemed sufficient. A *Bugg*, not relishing his ancient and honourable designation, announced in the papers his intention thenceforth to assume the name of *Norfolk Howard*; a *Todd* has become a *De Vere*, and a *Catt* a *Clifford*.

CHANGED NAMES

Lord Byron, desirous of linking his name on to the French ducal house of *Biron*, affected to change the *y* into *i*. Napoleon the Great, to disguise to French eyes his Italian origin, altered Buonaparte to *Bonaparte*.

The Italian Tyrolese name Tunicoto, from a short tunic, became in German *Thunichtgut* (Do-no-good). As this did not please, it was again altered to *Thugut* (Do-good); but when one so called became Minister to Maria Theresa, he flourished as *Von Thugut*. A certain Mr. Walker, afflicted with a squint, assuredly made a mistake when he changed his name to *Izod*.

In America there has been a considerable assumption of good names. There is one who for his name—how procured we do not know—a *Guise*, claims descent from the Dukes of that name, and who owns a county newspaper at Amityville, Long Island. A *Tell* pretending to trace his descent from the apocryphal William is a blacksmith at Broadripple, Ind. At Brownville, Pa., is a *Lafayette*, as to whose connection with the family of the Count at his château, Haute Loire, that family is supremely ignorant. A few years ago I remember Frau von Hillern, the authoress, whose husband was Chamberlain to the Grand Duke of Baden, and a Judge, was very wroth because a Miss von Hillern was advertised as walking for a wager against any man in the States. No relation—the name was assumed as that of a distinguished authoress and as well-sounding. My own name was used of late by a vendor of quack medicines for rheumatism, who had no right to it whatever.

" Why, this is flat knavery," says Petruchio, " to take on you another man's name."

Foundlings were sometimes given very good names. Brownlow, in his " Chronicles of the Foundling Hospital," says : " It has been the practice of the Governors from the earliest period to the present time to name the children at their own will and pleasure whether their parents should have been known or not. At the baptism of the children first taken into the hospital, which was on March 29, 1741, it is recorded that 'there was at the ceremony a fine appear-

CHANGED NAMES

ance of persons of quality and distinction; his Grace the Duke of Bedford, our president, their graces the Duke and Duchess of Richmond, the Countess of Pembroke, and several others, honouring the children with their names and being their sponsors.' Thus the register of the period presents the courtly names of Abercorn, Bedford, Bentinck, Montague, Marlborough, Newcastle, Norfolk, Pomfret, Pembroke, Richmond, Vernon, etc., as well as those of numerous other living individuals, great and small, who at that time took an interest in the establishment. When these names were exhausted, the authorities stole those of eminent deceased personages, their first attack being upon the Church. Hence we have a Wickliffe, Huss, Ridley, Latimer, Laud, Sancroft, Tillotson, Tennison, Sherlock, etc. Then came the mighty dead of the poetical race, viz.: Geoffrey Chaucer, William Shakespeare, John Milton, etc. Of the philosophers, Francis Bacon stands pre-eminently conspicuous. As they proceeded, the Governors who were warlike in their notions brought from their graves Philip Sidney, Francis Drake, Oliver Cromwell, John Hampden, Admiral Benbow, and Cloudesley Shovel. A more peaceful list followed this, viz.: Peter Paul Rubens, Anthony Vandyke, Michael Angelo, and Godfrey Kneller, William Hogarth and Jane his wife, of course, not being forgotten. Another class was borrowed from popular novels of the day, which accounts for Charles Allworthy, Tom Jones, Sophia Western, and Clarissa Harlowe. The gentle Izaak stands alone. So long as the admission of children was confined within reasonable bounds, it was an easy matter to find names for them; but during the Parliamentary era of the hospital, when the gates were thrown open to all comers, and each day brought its regiment of infantry to the establishment, the Governors were sometimes in difficulties; and when this was the case they took a zoological view of the subject, and named them after the creeping things and beasts of the earth, or created a nomenclature from various handicrafts or trades. In 1801 the hero of the Nile and some of his friends honoured the establishment with a visit, and stood sponsors

CHANGED NAMES

for several of the children. The names given on this occasion were Baltic Nelson, William and Emma Hamilton, Hyde Parker, etc. Up to a very late period the Governors were sometimes in the habit of naming the children after themselves and their friends, but it was found to be an inconvenient and objectionable course, inasmuch as, when they grew to man- or womanhood, *they were apt to lay claim to some affinity of blood with their nomenclators."*

Vanity has had a good deal to do with the alteration of names. Swift in the *Examiner* (No. 40, 1711) says: "I know a citizen who adds or alters a letter in his name with every plum he acquires; he now wants only the change of a vowel to be allied to a sovereign prince in Italy, and that perhaps he may contrive to be done by a mistake of the graver upon his tombstone." This was Sir Henry Furnese, whose real name was Furnace, which he altered into Furnice, Furnise, Furness, and Furnese; with an *a* in place of *u*, it would become Farnese.

Mr. Cosmo Innes has the following story: "A Dublin citizen (I think a dealer in snuff and tobacco), about the end of last century, had lived to a good age and in good repute, under the name of *Halfpenny*. He throve in trade, and his children prevailed on him in his latter years to change his name, which they thought undignified, and this he did by simply dropping the last letter. He died, and was buried as Mr. *Halfpen*. The fortune of the family did not recede, and the son of our citizen thought proper to renounce retail dealing, and at the same time looked about for an euphonious change of name. He made no scruple of dropping the unnecessary *h*; and that being done, it was easy to go into the Celtic rage which Sir Walter Scott and 'The Lady of the Lake' had just raised to a great height, and he who had run the streets as little Kenny Halfpenny came out (in full Rob Roy tartan, I trust) at the levees of the day as Kenneth *MacAlpin*, the descendant of a hundred Kings."[1]

In Scotland formerly, the false assumption of a name was

[1] 'Concerning Some Scotch Surnames." Edinburgh, 1860.

CHANGED NAMES

held to be equal to the false assumption of coat-armour, and was punished as a forgery.

In Prussia the law enacts: "Whoever, even without illegal intention, assumes a family name, or arms, without right, shall be forbidden the assumption under pain of an arbitrary but limited fine." A decree of October 30, 1816, enacts: "Since experience has taught us that the bearing of assumed or invented names is injurious to the security of civil intercourse, as well as to the efficiency of police regulation, we hereby order the following: (1) That no one shall, under the pain of a fine of from five to fifty thalers or a proportionate imprisonment, make use of a name which does not belong to him. (2) That if the assumption or invention of a name take place with intent to deceive, the regulations of the general penal laws come into effect."

In France, as in Germany, every individual is registered by his true name, and he cannot possibly alter it in any legal transaction without having received from the State authority to do so.

In the South of France many of the old castles have been restored and fitted up, and have become the residences during the summer of bourgeois, rich wine-merchants or manufacturers, who during the summer flourish as M. le Marquis du Pontlevis, M. le Baron de Roque-fiché, M. le Comte de Valdieu, but when they have to register their children's births or transact any legal business are forced to subscribe their genuine names of Pons, Brouet, Bazin, or Grosjean. Jacques Le Roy, the soldier who served so well the purposes of Louis Napoleon in shooting down the people in the streets of Paris, and was created a Marshal of the Second Empire, who was associated with Lord Raglan in the Crimea, wrote himself, and was allowed to call himself, Achille de St. Arnaud. " He impersonated," as Kinglake says, "with singular exactness the idea which our forefathers had in their minds when they spoke of what they called 'a Frenchman'; for although (by cowing the rich and filling the poor with envy) the great French Revolution had thrown a lasting gloom on the national character, it left

CHANGED NAMES

this man untouched. He was bold, gay, reckless, and vain; but beneath the mere glitter of the surface there was a great capacity for administrative business, and a more than common willingness to take away human life." In the United States there have been wilful alteration of names: *Berners* has been changed to *Barnes*, *Renault* to *Reno*, and *St. Jean* to *Session*. There may be cases, in which some horrible scandal is attached to a name, where it is advisable and justifiable to change it, to hide the stain from generations yet to come; but where the name is simply homely, and has been borne by honest labourers or worthy tradesmen, there it is an outrage on their memories to be so ashamed of it as to abandon it for one to which no real claim can be laid, and to parade, like the jackdaw of the fable, in borrowed plumes. That they are borrowed everyone knows, and everyone laughs behind the bearer's back.

> " Nil me pœniteat sanum patris hujus : eoque
> Non, ut magna dolo factum negat esse suo pars,
> Quod non ingenuos habeat clarosque parentes,
> Sic me defendam. Longe mea discrepat istis
> Et vox et ratio. Nam si natura juberet
> A certis annis ævum remeare peractum
> Atque alios legere ad fastum quoscumque parentes,
> Optaret sibi quisque ; meis contentus honestos
> Fascibus et sellis nollem mihi sumere."
>
> HORACE : *Sat.* i. 6.

CHAPTER XX

COMPOUND NAMES

DURING the last quarter of a century a fashion has set in for double names. Double names are legitimate where property is represented that has descended through an heiress, and it is right that the family that for several generations held the estate should be remembered in the name of the present proprietor. Such a double name is a record. But such have the warrant of royal licence. No objection can be raised to such double names as Agar-Robartes, Prideaux-Brune, Godolphin - Osborne, Spencer - Churchill, because each surname represents a fact in the history of the family—the extinction of one family and the devolution of its estate on another.

But the majority of double names have no such warrant. In some cases the Christian name is linked on to the surname, where that Christian name happens to be a surname derived from some marriage in the family, or godfather, or some supposed connection with a titled race.

In such cases the first member would naturally fall away when the bearer of the Christian name died; but, as a matter of fact, it does not always do so.

It not infrequently happens that the added name has no authority whatever to back it. It is assumed, it is not even a Christian name of the assumer.

There is, however, some justification or excuse for these additions when the true surname is common or insipid. It is sought to fortify it. In nomenclature we add whisky to water, never water to whisky.

When a number of Smiths, Bakers, Thomsons, Halls,

COMPOUND NAMES

Johnsons, jostle in a country town, it is but according to precedent that the bearers of the same name should seek to distinguish themselves and family from their namesakes. In former days this was done by the tacking on of a nickname after the personal name; now it is done by prefixing another family name. Thus such combinations as Bourcher-Smith, Cadwalader-Jones, Neville-Browne, and Gordon-Charlesworth (assumed by an impostor who has made some noise). In many cases the name prefixed has got the slenderest or no justification for its assumption. I know a family that always calls itself Godolphin-Browne, the sole reason for the taking up of the former name being that Lord Godolphin was one of two godfathers to a great-grandfather. I know another that hyphens an ancient Norman name to its actual surname, which latter is common, because in the seventeenth century one of this family married into the other; but, as he had no issue, not a drop of the Norman blood through this channel flows in the veins of those who flourish the name at present. Again, a third family supposes that at some date unspecified it was allied to a noble family, that of the Lord Knowswho, and accordingly writes itself Knowswho-Butcher.

In like manner some people wear titles, as Duke-Coleridge, Baron-Lethbridge, Squire-Bancroft; and there is a menagerie travels the country under a proprietor styled Lord George Sanger. In the first instance this was due to a marriage with one of the family of Duke of Otterton; and as the Coleridges rose from a very obscure origin, they were glad to engraft on their name that of an ancient county family. In the second, the name of Baron was that of the old estated family of Tregeare in Cornwall, whose heiress married a Lethbridge, and the duplicate name is justly held.

When a resonant Norman name is linked to one that is English and dull of sound, the effect is somewhat like that described and ridiculed by Horace:

" Humano capiti cervicem pictor equinam
Jungere si velit, et varias inducere plumas
Undique collatis membris, ut turpiter atrum
Desinat in piscem mulier formosa superne,
Spectatum admissi risum teneatis amici ?"

COMPOUND NAMES

And yet, possibly enough, the English name may be the better of the two, and the conjunction illustrates the final triumph over the invader by the subjugated native Saxon.

The English custom was formerly for the surname of the godfather and godmother to be given at baptism to the child, and this has led to its assumption and grafting on to the true surname.

"I tell you I have a presentiment that it must be a girl," said Miss Betsey Trotwood to Mrs. Copperfield, when that lady was in an interesting condition. "Don't contradict! From the moment of this girl's birth I intend to be her friend. I intend to be her godmother, and I beg you'll call her Betsey Trotwood Copperfield." But when the expected arrived, it proved to be a boy, whereupon Miss Betsey put on her bonnet and departed. But when in after-years little David, neglected and maltreated, flies for refuge to the aunt, she adopts him. "Mr. Dick," says she, "I have been thinking that I might call him Trotwood."

"Certainly, certainly! Call him Trotwood, certainly!" said Mr. Dick. "David's son's Trotwood."

"Trotwood Copperfield, you mean," returned the aunt.

"Yes, to be sure—Trotwood Copperfield," said Mr. Dick, a little abashed.

"My aunt took so kindly to the notion that some ready-made clothes, which were purchased for me that afternoon, were marked *Trotwood Copperfield* in her own handwriting, and in indelible marking-ink." And if David had a family and descendants, the name thenceforth would be Trotwood-Copperfield. And this would be justifiable, for it would be a record of the kind old lady who found him "naked and she clothed him."

If we look through the Peerage, what a host of compound names do we find!

Baillie-Hamilton-Arden is the conjunction of names borne by the Earl of Haddington. Viscount Galway is a Monckton-Arundell. The Duke of Atholl is a Stewart-Murray. Giustiniani-Bandini is the name of the Earl of Newburgh. De-la-Poer-Beresford is that of the Marquis of Waterford,

COMPOUND NAMES

Fitzhardinge-Berkeley that of Baron Fitzhardinge, Wentworth-Fitzwilliam that of Earl Fitzwilliam. Pleydell-Bouverie is the family name of the Earl of Radnor.

Baron Thurlow bears a number of names, Hovell-Thurlow-Cumming-Bruce. The family of Thurlow descends from a country parson in Suffolk who married an Elizabeth Smith, daughter of a Robert Smith, who had been a Hovell; so the Smith was dropped and the Hovell assumed in 1814. The fifth Baron, having married Lady Elma Bruce, daughter of James, Earl of Elgin, by his first wife, Elizabeth Mary Cumming-Bruce, assumed the additional names and surnames of his wife's mother in 1874. Verily the family has gone far afield to scrape together names to tack on to Thurlow, which was respectable enough by itself.

Lord Churston is a Yarde-Buller, the Earl of Shewsbury a Chetwynd-Talbot, the Duke of Newcastle a Pelham-Clinton. Earl Somers is a Somers-Cocks, the Earl of Shaftesbury an Ashley-Cooper. Earl Belmore is a Lowry-Correy, Lord Teynham a Roper-Curzon, the Earl of Portarlington a Dawson-Damer. The Duke of Hamilton is a Douglas-Hamilton, Lord Braye a Vernon-Cave. Viscount Clifden is an Agar-Robartes; Baron Saye and Sele is a Twistleton-Wykeham-Fiennes; Lord Carbery is an Evans-Freke. Leveson-Gower is the family name of Earl Granville and of the Duke of Sutherland. The Earl of Buckinghamshire rejoices in four surnames, Hobart-Hampden-Mercer-Henderson, whereof the penultimate points back to a silk-mercer behind his counter, and the last to a progenitor so insignificant as to have no surname, and to have been known as Andrew's son only.

Lord Vernon is a Venables-Vernon. The Archbishop of York of that family assumed the additional surname of Harcourt on inheriting the estates of the last Earl Harcourt in 1831. George John, the fifth Baron, however, dropped the Venables-Vernon, and assumed the surname and arms of Warren only in 1837, but the sixth Baron resumed them. Charles Vernon, who died in 1874, married the daughter of Nathaniel Evans of Oldtown, co. Cork, and she assumed

COMPOUND NAMES

the name of Gore. Her daughter, Ellen Caroline, married Sir Gustavus Hume, and by royal licence adopted the surname of Gore in addition to Hume. Henry Charles Edward Ligonier Hamilton Vernon in 1800 changed his name to Graham, but tired of it, and shifted back to Vernon in 1838. Frederick William Thomas Vernon assumed the additional surname of Wentworth in 1804; George Vernon took on him the name of Venables, in addition to Vernon, in 1728. Henry, third Baron Vernon, having married the illegitimate daughter of that disreputable Baronet, Sir Charles Sedley, actually assumed the surname and arms of Sedley in 1779. There has been, accordingly, an astonishing shifting of names in this family.

Earl Cranbrooke is a Gathorne-Hardy; the Earl of Kingston is a King-Tenison. James, fifth Earl of Loudon, was a Campbell. His only child Flora married Francis Rawdon Hastings, Earl of Moira, who was created Viscount Loudon and Marquis of Hastings in 1816. His son George Augustus Francis, second Marquis, married Barbara Yelverton, daughter of Edward Gould, twentieth Lord Grey de Ruthyn. She remarried Sir Hastings Reginald Henry, who assumed the name of Yelverton in 1849. Her second son as well as her first died without issue, whereupon her daughter, Edith Maud Hastings, became Countess of Loudon. She married Charles Frederick Abney-Hastings, created Lord Donington, and had by him the present Earl, Charles Edward Hastings Abney-Hastings.

The Earl of Winchelsea is a Finch-Hatton; the Earl of Donoughmore is a Hely-Hutchinson. Lord Muskerry is a Deane-Morgan, the Duke of Leeds a Godolphin-Osborne. The Earl of Plymouth is a Windsor-Clive. Lord Penrhyn is a Douglas-Pennant, the Earl of Yarborough an Anderson-Pelham—properly Anderson, but the name of Pelham was assumed by Charles Anderson as heir to his great-uncle, Charles Pelham, Recorder of Grimsby in 1786. Lord Bolton is an Orde-Powlett; Viscount Boyne is a Hamilton-Russell, and Baron Brabourne a Knatchbull-Hugessen. The Duke of Portland is a Cavendish-Bentinck. The Earl of

COMPOUND NAMES

Ilchester's family name is Fox-Strangeways. Viscount Canterbury is a Manners-Sutton, Lord Londonderry a Vane-Tempest, Lord Eversley a Shaw-Lefevre, Lord Sudeley a Hanbury-Leigh, Lord Wentworth a Noel-Milbanke.

The list might be greatly extended. In almost every case there is historic justification for the linking together of two or more family names. But, as already said, this cannot be always said of such double names as are flourished daily around us, where the additional name has not been assumed by royal licence, and is simply due to personal vanity or caprice.

Sometimes we obtain very odd combinations, as *Hunt-Grubb, Pyne-Coffin, Beerbohm-Tree* for Beerbaum, a berry-bearing shrub, *Corny-Graine*. A witness at a Poplar inquest on July 14, 1909, was named John *North East West*. A clergyman, with the deciduous name of *Field-Flowers-Goe*, was chosen to be a Bishop in Australia. *Bubb-Dodington* was a well-known man in his day, who hid the quaint combination under a title as Lord Melcombe.

In a recent clergy list occur such double names as these: *Dimond-Hogg, Forrest-Bell, Gabe-Jones, Golding-Bird, Haire-Forster, Hughes-Death, Keys-Wells, Master-Whitaker, Nunn-Rivers, Roosmale-Cocq, Teed-Heaver, Teignmouth-Shore, White-Bell.*

And now I must close. The subject is one so interesting and with so many ramifications that it might be dealt with lengthily, but not exhaustively. I have attempted no more than to give indications of the road by which some with names difficult to riddle out, or giving a wrong idea of their signification on the surface, may be traced to their true origin; and also to point out some of the pitfalls that beset the path of the unwary, some of the blind alleys in which they may wander, in that wood of errors, Family Nomenclature.

"Claudite jam rivos, pueri, sat prata biberunt."

APPENDIX TO CHAPTER IX

ANGLO-SAXON AND DANISH NAMES IN DOMESDAY

ABEN (Lincs), Abo (Yorks).
Achi (Wilts, Chesh., Suff., etc.),
    Acum (Lincs), Acun (Yorks).
Ædric Grim (Suff.).
Ælfag (Notts), Elfag (Derb.).
Ærgrim (Salop).
Ailm (Corn.), Ailmar melc (Ess.).
Aki (Suff.).
Aldene tope (Lincs).
Algrim (Yorks).
Alli (Bucks, Beds).
Alnod Grutt (Herts).
Alric (Bucks, Suff., Beds).
Alsi Bolla (Ess.).
Alured biga (Kent).
Aluric (Herts, Cambs, Dev., Oxf.,
    Ess., Suff., Herts).
Alward (many counties).
Alwin (many counties).
Amod, *fem.* (Suff.).
Andrac (Hants).
Anunt dacus (Ess.), properly
    "Önund the Dane."
Ape (Somers.), Appe (Wilts).
Archilbar (Lincs).
Ardegrip (Lincs, Yorks).
Aregrim (Chesh.), properly Arngrim.
Aschilbar (Lincs).
Aseloc (Notts).
Auti (several counties).
Azor (several counties).
Baco (Lincs).
Bar (Yorks. Suff., Middx, Norf.),
    also Ber (Yorks).
Basin (Yorks).
Biga (Suss.).
Bil (Glouc.).

Boda (Hants), Bode (Wilts), Boddus (Ess.).
Bou (Norf.), Bu (Yorks), Boui
    (several counties).
Bricstoward (Somers.).
Brictuar Bubba (Suff.).
Brihtuold (Suff.).
Bunda, Bonde, Bondi, Bundi,
    Bondo, etc. (in various counties).
Caflo (Somers.).
Cava, Cave, Cavo, Cavus (Suss.).
Celcott (Suff.).
Cheteber (Yorks), Chetelber (Lincs,
    and several other counties).
Chetelbern (Notts, Lincs, Norf.),
    properly Ketilbjörn.
Clac (Lincs).
Col (Lincs), Cola (Suss.), Cole
    (Suss., Derb.), Colle (Dev.), Colo
    (many counties), Coole (Wilts).
Couta (Suff.).
Crin (Yorks.).
Dedol (Chesh.), Doda, Dode, Dodo
    (various counties).
Don, Done, Donne, Donnus, etc.
    (various counties).
Edlouedief (Dev.).
Edmer (Herts, Middx., Bucks,
    Dev.).
Edric (in numerous counties).
Edwin (Leics, Heref.)
Edward wit (Beds).
Eldille (Dev.).
Elsi jillinge (Notts), a native of
    Jutland.
Epy (Bucks).
Ergrim (Heref.).
Esber biga (Kent), properly Osbern.

APPENDIX TO CHAPTER IX

Eurewacre (Dev.)
Felaga (Ess.).
Fot (Chesh., Kent).
Fuglo (Beds).
Gam (Yorks), Game (Leics, Yorks), Gamel (in various counties).
Gamelcarl (Yorks), Gamilbar, Gumelbar, Gamiltorf (Yorks).
Gethne (Salop).
Gilepatric (Yorks).
Glunier (Yorks).
Godtovi (Surr.)
Goleathegn (Dev.)
Gold (Cambs).
Golnil (Bucks).
Gos (Hunts).
Gribol (Lincs).
Grimulf (Warw.).
Haltor, Heltor (Yorks).
Huna, Hunus (Suff.), Hunc (Yorks), Huni, Hunic, Hunni, Hunnet, etc. (Salop).
Jalf (Lincs).
Jaul (Cornw.).
Juin (Dev.), Juing (Somers.).
Kee (Norf.).
Kettelbern, Kettelbert (Worc.). See above, Cheteber.
Lambecarl (Lincs).
Leswin croc (Suff.).
Lewric coccus (Suff.).
Lewin calvus (Suff.).
Lurc (Suff.).
Maban (Yorks).
Mannius swert (Suff.), Magno Suert (Surr.).
Moithar (Norf.).
Offa (Surr., Suff.).
Osbert masculus (Suff.).
Oslac albus (Northants).
Phin (Suff., Ess.), Phin dacus (Ess.), Pin (Glouc.). Properly, Finn dacus signifies "the Dane."
Ram (Yorks), Ramechil (Yorks).

Roc (Suff.).
Rozo (Wilts), a Norman, Le Roux.
Saloman (Yorks).
Salpus (Suff.).
Sbern (many counties). Should be Osbern.
Scheit, Scett (Norf.).
Scotcol (Yorks).
Seiar, Seiard bar (Norf., Glouc.), Siward Bar (Yorks and Lincs).
Siward barn, for Björn, (Warw., Norf., Lincs).
Sessi (Salop).
Sindi (Yorks).
Snellinc (Cambs).
Snode, Snot (Dev.).
Sol (Heref.).
Spirites and Spirtes (many counties), Spert (Yorks).
Stam (Yorks).
Stanker (Suff.).
Ster, Sterr, Sterre, Stur, Strui (many counties).
Suartcol (Yorks).
Swenus Suart (Ess.), a Dane.
Thol, Thole, Tholi, Tol, Toli (various counties).
Thor (Northants), Tor (Yorks, Lincs, Norf.).
Tou, Toul, Tovi, Towi (various counties).
Turloga (Yorks), properly "Thorlaug."
Ulward wit (Dors).
Unfac (Notts).
Wadel (Kent, Derb., Cornwall); Wadels (Derb.), Wadhel (Cornwall), Wadelo (Derb.).
Welp (Yorks).
Wilegrip (Suff., Salop).
Wit (as a surname repeatedly in many counties).
Wlward Levet (Beds).
Wardrou (Derb.).

APPENDIX I. TO CHAPTER X

APPENDIX I. TO CHAPTER X

SCANDINAVIAN NAMES

[It does not follow that these surnames certainly derive from the Norse or Danish. Some are common to the Anglo-Saxons. But also, some of our family names may derive from the Scandinavian, when encountered in ancient Northumbria, whereas the same name may have a different origin elsewhere. Hozier may derive from a hosier, or from Ozzur, and Brusi may have originated some Bruces, as well as the Norman place-name Bruix. Some Burns may deduce their name from Björn, others from a brook. Freeman may in some cases be an anglicizing of Freimund, in others describes the quality is a Franklin. The terminal letter *r* in a Norse name was shed at once on English soil.]

Alford	from	Hallvarðr.	Day	from	Dagr.
Alstone	,,	Hallstein.	Eagle	,,	Egill.
Alt	,,	Hjalti.	Elgar	,,	Alfgarr.
Airey	,,	Eyarr.	Ewins	,,	Eyvind.
Algar / Ager	,,	Alfgar.	Easton	,,	Eystein.
			Featherstone	,,	Friðestan.
Arkell	,,	Arnketill.	Freeman	,,	Freimundr.
Arnott	,,	Arnoðr.	Freestone	,,	Freysteinn.
Askell / Haskell	,,	Askulfr.	Froude	,,	Froði.
			Galt	,,	Galti.
Askew	,,	Höskuldr.	Gamell	,,	Gamel.
Atlay	,,	Atli.	Gayer / Geer, Gerry	,,	Geirr.
Barth	,,	Barðr.			
Beale	,,	Bjolli.	Gell	,,	Gellir.
Bligh / Blythe	,,	Bligr.	Goodly	,,	Guðleifr.
			Goodlake	,,	Guðleikr.
Blund	,,	Blúndr.	Goodman	,,	Guðmundr.
Boddy	,,	Boði.[1]	Gorman	,,	Gormundr.
Bowles	,,	Bolli.	Goodrich	,,	Guðrekr.
Brand	,,	Brandr.	Grundy	,,	Grundi or Gundrod.
Broad	,,	Broddi.			
Bruce	,,	Brusi.	Grymes	,,	Grímr.
Burk	,,	Börkr.[2]	Grain	,,	Gráni.
Burn	,,	Björn.	Guest	,,	Gestr.
Carr	,,	Kárr.	Gunn	,,	Gunnar.
Colburn	,,	Kolbjörn.	Gunstone	,,	Gunnsteinn.
Cole and Colley	,,	Kolli and Kollr.	Guthrie	,,	Guðrodr.
			Hake	,,	Háki.
Curtain	,,	Kjartan.	Haldane	,,	Hálfdan.

---

[1] A messenger, Ivarr Boddi, occurs in 1215, Fornmanna Sögur.
[2] The Irish Burks are from de Burgh.

APPENDIX I. TO CHAPTER X

Hall	from	Hallr.	Ronald } Reynolds }	from	Rögnvaldr.
Hammond	,,	Hámundr.			
Harvey	,,	Hávarðr.	Salmon	,,	Salmundr.
Hassel	,,	Asculfr.	Scholey	,,	Skúli, a son of Earl Tostig.
Halford	,,	Hallvarðr.			
Hemming	,,	Hemmingr.	Scorey	,,	Skari.
Herman	,,	Hermundr.	Seaward	,,	Sigurðr.
Holker	,,	Hallkarr.	Smaley } Smale }	,,	{ Smali (a shepherd.)
Holybone	,,	Hallbjörn.			
Hozier	,,	Ozzur.	Snell	,,	Snjall.
Hyde	,,	Hide.[1]	Soley	,,	Sölvi.
Humphry	,,	Holmfrið.	Stiggins	,,	Stigandi.
Inchbald	,,	Ingibaldr.	Stone	,,	Steinn.
Ingle	,,	Ingolfr.	Stoner	,,	Steinarr.
Ingledew	,,	Ingjaldr.	Somerley	,,	Somerlið.
Ingram	,,	Ingiramr.	Steer	,,	Styrr.
Jekyll	,,	Jökull.	Sturgess	,,	Thorgísl.
Jelf	,	Jólfr.	Symonds	,,	Sígmundr.
Kettle } Kiddle }	,,	Ketill.	Swinburn	,,	Sveinbjörn.
			Swayne	,,	Svein.
Knott, Nott	,,	Knutr.	Taite	,,	Teitr.
Lamb	,,	Lambi.	Thorburn	,,	Thorbjörn.
Leefe, Lever	,,	Leifr.	Thorley	,,	Thorleifr.
Lover	,,	Hloðver.	Thurkell	,,	Thorkell.
Luard	,,	Lavard.	Thorold	,,	Thorvaldr.
Magnus	,,	Magnus.	Thurstan	,,	Thorsteinn.
Maule } Moll }	,,	{ Maull, Dan. Möll occurs 1209.	Tooke, Toke	,,	Tóki.
			Triggs	,,	Tryggvi.
Odger	,,	Oddgeir.	Turpin	,,	Thorfinn.
Orme	,,	Ormr.	Uhtred	,,	Útryggr.
Osborne	,,	Asbjörn.	Ussher	,,	Ozzur.
Osegood	,,	Asgautr.	Vickary	,,	Víkarri.
Osmund	,,	Asmundr.	Wayburn	,,	Vébjörn.
Oswald	,,	Asvaldr.	Wrath } Wroth }	,,	Rauðr.
Raven	,,	Hrafn.			
Rayner	,,	Ragnar.	Waymand	,,	Vémundr.
Rayne	,,	Hrani.	Wayland	,,	Víglundr.
Rolf	,,	Hrolfr.	Wyvill	,,	Vífill.

[1] The name of the half-brother of King Sverrir; he fell in 1191. Another Hide was a captain in Sverrir's army, 1201.

APPENDIX II. TO CHAPTER X

APPENDIX II. TO CHAPTER X

SURNAMES OF THE FIFTEENTH CENTURY IN THE "LIBER VITÆ"

Dominus Thomas Burrelle.
" Richardus Murtone.
" Radulphus Blaxtone.
" Christopherus Wyllye.
" Johannes Cartelle.
" Christopherus Hemynborogh.

Dominus Edwardus Hymmers.
" Jacobus Dukket.
" Willelmus Pykryng.
" Johannes Baylay.
" Thomas Baylay.
" Willelmus Foster.

Roger Bill, Cuthbert Dowffe, Johannes Tod, Willelmus Hakfurthe, Johannes Belle, Thomas Sperke, J. Blunt, Johannes Ellnett, Johannes Burghe, Edwardus Hardynk, Willelmus Clyltone, Willelmus Bennet, Georgius Corfurthe, Nicholas Wynter, Thomas and John Wynter, magister Johannes Clerke, Johannes Manneres, Juliana, Margaret, Katerina and Elizabeth Clerke, Dominus Thomas Jonson, Ricardus Poole, feretrarius (the shrineward), Henricus Wylom, Willelmus Dynshburne, Johannes Hudrynsen, Christopherus Wardell, Willelmus Huchenson, Alyson, Edmundus et Thomas, Willelmus Burton, Christopherus Ryffhley, Willelmus Tode, Willm. Brantyngham, Nicholas Rychardson, Robertus Hychesson, Johanna Rychardson, Johannes Rychardson, John Payrnell et Kateryna et Thomas, Helena Mayre, Thomas Coky et Thos., junior, Wyllms et Genett Coky, Thom. Bryntlay.

The rest of the surnames I will give without the Christian names; they are: Richardson, Belle, Weldon, Felton, Peyrson (Pierson), Thomson, Browelle, Morley, Heppell, Nicholl, Hogyln, Scott, Swanston, Kethe (Keith), Heryngton (Harrington), Coode, Todd, Foster, Skipton, Hymers, Hawkwell, Durham, Worlay, Trumpwhett, Brune, Edwarde, Blunt, Eland, Yonge, Cane, Babyngton, Eysdon, Stroder, Carr, Wylem, Barnes, Pule, Kendall, Home, Rawe, Duckett, Robinson, Hegington, Hebburne, Caly, Wardale, Cuthbert, Gray, Hylton, Emerson, Hale, Lawson.

APPENDIX TO CHAPTER XI

LIST OF THOSE WHO ATTENDED WILLIAM THE CONQUEROR TO ENGLAND, ACCORDING TO WACE, "ROMAN DE ROU"

The numbers refer to the line in the edition of Anderson.

Abbeville, Eustache d', 8453.
Alan Fergant, Duke of Brittany, 7679, 8715, 8721.
Anisi, the men of, 8442.
Annebault, Sire d', 8643.
Argentan, the men of, 8441.

Asnieres, Gilbert d', 8557.
Aubigny, Sire d' (Daubeny), 8494.
Aumale, Stephen, Sire d' (Albemarle), 8443.
Aunay, Sire d' (Dawney), 8669.
Aunou, Sire d', 8450.

APPENDIX TO CHAPTER XI

Auvillars, Sire d', 8642.
Avenel of Les Biards, Sire d', 8523.
Avranches, Richard, Sire d', 8491.
Bagueville, Martel de (Baskerville), 8545.
Beaufou, Robert de (Beaufort), 8449.
Beaumont, Roger (mistaken for Richard) de, 8353, 8356.
Bertram, Richard, 8525.
Bienfaite, Richard de, 8560.
Bigot, Roger, 8571.
Biards, Les (same as Avenel), 8492.
Bohun, Humfrey de, 8474.
Bolbec, Hugh de, 8559.
Bonnebosq, Sire de, 8561.
Boutevilain, 8605.
Bray, the men of, 8480.
Brehal, Sire de, 8536.
Breteuil, the men of, 8531.
Brix, or Bruis (Bruce), the men of, 8667
Caen, men of, 8440.
Cahagnes, Sire de, 8558.
Cailly, Sire de (Cailey), 8543.
Carteret, Humfrey and Mauger de, 8475.
Caux, knights of, 8625.
Cayle, Ingulf de, 8483.
Coisnieres, Sire de (Conyers), 8558.
Cinglars, Rodulf de, 8513.
Cintheaux, Sire de, 8547.
Colombiers, William de, 8556.
Combray, Sire de, 8669.
Cotentin, Barons of, 8378, 8379, 8517.
Conches, Radolf de, 7602.
Courcy, Sire de (mistake for Torcy), 8505, 8550.
Crevecœur, Sire de, 8666.
Epinay (for Pins), or Espines, 8504.
Estouteville, 8452.
Eu, Robert, Count of, 8726.
Falaise, men of, 8441.
Ferte, La, Sire de, 8601.
Fitz Erneis, Robert, 8645.
Fitz Osbern, 7511, 7673.
Fontenay, Sire de, 8670.
Fougeres, Sire de, 8387.
Gace, Chevalier de, 8552.
Gael, Rudolf de, 6393, 8518.

Glos, Sire de, 8562.
Gournai, Hugh de, 8479.
Gouvix, Sire de, 8547.
Grandmesnil, Sire de, or de Lisieux, 8461.
Haie La, Sire de, 8595.
Harcourt, Sire de, 8663.
Hommet, Le, the men of, 8537.
Jort, Sire de, 8505.
L'Aigle, Ingulf de, 8483.
La Lande, William Patric de, 8609, 8623.
Lassy, Chevalier de (Lacy), 8551.
Lithaire, Sire de, 8445.
Lucy, Sire de, 8495.
Magneville, Sire de (Mandeville), 8454.
Mayenne, Geoffrey de, 8473.
Mallet, William, 8363, 8375.
Mare, La, Sire de, 8446.
Marmion, Roger, 8514.
Mathieu, the men of, 8442.
Monceaux, Sire de, 8548.
Montfray, Giffard, Sire de, 8600.
Montfiquet, Sire de, 8569.
Montfort, Hugh de, 8370.
Montgomerie, Roger de, 8306, 8727.
Morlai, Sire de, 8671.
Mortain, Robert, Count of, 8659, 10514.
Mortemer, Hugh (Christian name wrong), 8641.
Moulins, William de (Mullins), 8457.
Moyon, William de (Mohun), 8511.
Nehou, Sire de, 8447.
Orval, the men of, 8535.
Ouilly, Chevalier de (D'Oiley), 8553.
Pacy, Sire de (Pace), 8549.
Paisnel des Moutiers Humbert (Paganel), 8524.
Peeleit, de (Bellet), 6391.
Pins, Sire des (same as l'Epines), 8458.
Pirou, Chevalier de, 8448.
Port, Sire de, 8504.
Preaux, Sire de, 8546.
Presles, Sire de, 8555.
Taison, Rudolf de, or de Cinglais, 8513.

APPENDIX TO CHAPTER XII

Reviers, Sire de, Richard, 8507.
Rollo (Rou le Blanc), father of Thustan, the standard-bearer of William, 7657, 8698.
Rouen, citizens of, 8439.
Roubercy, Sire De, 8671.
Roumare, William de, 8447.
Sacy, De, Chevalier, 8553.
Sai, Sire de, 8600.
Saint Clair, Sire de (Sinclair), 8643.
Saint Jean, De, 8536.
Saint Martin, Sire de, 8456.
Saint Saens, Sire de, 8543.
Saint Valery, Sire de, 8725.
Sap, Le Sire de, 8562.
Semilly, Sire de, 8544.
Sole, men of, 8535.
Subligny, Sire of, 8493.
Tancarville, Sire de, 8453.
Tellieres, Gilbert Crispin, commander of, 8390.
Touques, Sire de, 8446.
Tourneur Le, Sire de, 8555.
Tracy, Sire de, 8496.
Trougots, Sire de, 8563.
Troussebot, 8605.
Thurstin, or Thustan, standard-bearer, 7657, 8698, 8701.
Urine, Sire de (Origny), 8599.
Valdaire, Sire de, 8496.
Varenne, de, William, 8477.
Vassy, Sire de (Veysey), 8534.
Vaudreuil, the crossbowmen of, 8529.
Viez Molei, Sire de, William Bacon, 8548.
Vitre, Sire de, 8495.
Vieux Pont, William de, 8371

APPENDIX TO CHAPTER XII

HUGUENOT IMMIGRANTS' SUBSCRIPTIONS TO A LOYAL ADDRESS, 1744

Jacob Albert.
Gilbert Allix.
George Aymand.
Claude Aubert.
George Aufere.
J. Auriol.
Nathaniel Bassnet.
Allard Belin.
Claude Bennet.
J. Lewis Berchere.
J. David Billon.
John Blaquiere.
J. Beter.
Thomos Le Blanc.
Henry Blommart.
Charles de Blon.
John Boitier.
Samuel Bosanquet.
John Boucher.
James Bourdieu.
Stephen Cabibel.
Peter Challifies.
James Caulet.
James Chalie.
Honore Combauld.
Peter Cuisserat.
Daniel Crespin.
Peter Devisme.
Peter Des Champs.
Peter Du Cane.
C. Desmaretz.
Andrew Devesne.
Philip Devesne.
William Dobree.
John Dorrien.
Samuel Dutresnay.
J. Dulamont.
Charles Duroure.
Alexander Eynard.
Willm. Fauquier.
Am. Faure.
Abel Fonnereau.
Zac. Phil. Fonnereau.
Isaac Fiput de Gabay.
Peter Gaussen.
Francis Gaussen.
James Guinard.
Henry Guinard.

APPENDIX TO CHAPTER XII

Stephen Guion.
William Hollier.
John Jamineau.
Stephen Theodore Janssen.
John Lagiere Lamotte.
P. Lebefure.
Gideon Leglize.
Cæsar Le Maistre.
David Le Quesne.
Benj. Longuet,
Samuel Longuet.
John Louis Loubier.
Henry Loubier.
Charles Loubier.
Jo. L. Loubier.
J. Aut. Loubier.
Peter Luard.
Gabriel de Limage.
Willm. Minet.
Wm. Morin.

Pulerand Mourgrue.
Francis Noguier.
Peter Nouaille.
Ph. Jacob de Neufville.
Joseph de Pontieu.
Francis Perier.
Pearson Pettit.
John Pettit.
Joseph Ponchon.
Philip Rigail.
Cypre Rondeau.
Stephen Teissier.
Matt. Testas.
Thomas Tryon.
Aut. Vazeille.
Dan. Vernezobre.
Dan. Vialers.
Thomas Vigne.
Willm. Vigor.
Peter Waldo.

INDEX

Many surnames that end in *s* are formed from the name of the father. *Watts* is the son of Walter, but *Watt* is Walter himself. *Lawes* is the equivalent to *Lawson*.
Many names taken from animals, etc., have an *e* added. Thus, *Lambe* for Lamb, *Crosse* for Cross, *Locke* for Lock.

ABBADIE, 283
Abby, 54
Abdey, 175
Abeillard, 89
Abel, 61
Able, 89
Ablin, 61
Achurch, 176
Ackland, 176
Adam, 131
Adams, 53
Adamson, 53
Adcock, 53
Addison, 53
Adkyns, 53
Adye, 53
Adyman, 53
Affleck, 181-2
Agar, 392
Agate, 175
Ager, 410
Agnew, 255
Aicheson, 54
Aikebaum, 18
Aikenhead, 167
Aincourt, 207
Ainger, 255
Ainsley, 182
Airey, 410
Alabaster, 132
Alanson, 54
Alardice, 53
Albany, 207
Albemarle, 207
Aldborough, 176
Aldershot, 167
Alderson, 54
Aldrich, 170, 187
Aldridge, 170
Aldus, 168
Aldworth, 393
Alexander, 54
Alford, 410
Algar, 13, 410
Alkey, 54
Allan, 54
Allanson, 54
Allard, 65

Allbone, 54
Allbright, 54
Allcock, 54
Allen, 53
Allgood, 310
Allfraye, 308
Allison, 61
Allix, 287
Allonne, 283
Allsopp, 326
Alstone, 410
Alward, 53
Amadys, 65
Amelot, 65
Amery, 206
Amiard, 287
Amory, 206
Amphlet, 164, 175
Amye, 61, 69
Anderson, 54
Andrew, 54
Andrews, 54
Angell, 95, 311
Anger, 287
Anniott, 61
Ansell, 54, 132, 182
Anson, 54, 61
Anstice, 61
Ansty, 61
Anthony, 54
Antliffe, 182
Anwyll, 255
Ape, 70-1
Aplin, 61
Applethwaite, 172
Appleyard, 176
Arber, 308
Arbor, 109
Arbour, 109
Arch, 258
Archbutt, 54
Archer, 132
Archeson, 54
Archibald, 54
Arden, 392
Argent, 207
Arkell, 410
Arkle, 54

Arkwright, 132
Armand, 281
Armiger, 105
Armitage, 176
Armour, 132
Arnold, 251, 387
Arnott, 416
Arrowsmith, 129, 132, 249
Arthur, 54
Artle, 54
Arundell, 207
Ashburner, 118
Ashe, 176
Ashman, 118, 150
Ashridge, 170
Askell, 410
Askew, 410
Aspinall, 178
Astor, 105
Atford, 176
Atkins, 53
Atkinson, 53
Atkirk, 176
Atkynson, 195
Atley, 410
Atock, 176
Attenborough, 176
Atfield, 176
Atthill, 176
Attley, 176, 410
Attmore, 176
Attridge, 176
Attwood, 176
Atty, 54
Attye, 174
Atwell, 357
Atworth, 176
Aubrey, 54, 65
Aubrison, 54
Audley, 202, 207
Audrey, 362
Aufere, 283
Augsburger, 306
Auriol, 284
Austringer, 105
Avenell, 202, 203
Avery, 255
Avis, 61

417 DD

INDEX

Avison, 61
Awdry, 61
Aylward, 53, 187
Ayre, 331

Babb, 61
Backhouse, 176
Bacon, 107, 187, 314
Badcock, 54, 107
Badger, 89, 118
Baggot, 324
Bagster, 132
Bailleu, 281
Baird, 67
Baker, 132, 316, 357
Balancer, 132
Balderson, 54
Baldison, 327
Baldock, 54
Baldwin, 54, 67, 208
Balhatchet, 165
Baliol, 208, 375
Ballard, 89, 362
Balliol, 375
Ballister, 132
Bamberger, 306
Bamfield, 210
Bancroft, 163
Banister, 132, 208
Barbauld, 288
Barbe, 61
Barber, 132
Barbey, 255
Barbor, 133
Barbour, 133
Barclay, 290, 379
Bardell, 251
Bardolf, 208
Bardsay, 163
Barkiss, 176
Barman, 106
Barnby, 54
Barnes, 54, 252
Barnfield, 210
Barnstaple, 172
Barnum, 166
Baron, 310, 402
Barr, 176
Barrett, 208
Barrow, 159
Barry, 202, 208
Barth, 14, 54, 410
Bartholomew, 54
Bartle, 54
Bartlett, 54
Bartley, 54
Barwell, 255
Barwise, 255
Baskerville, 209
Basset, 208, 310
Bastard, 209, 311
Bateman, 106, 327
Bates, 54, 106
Batson, 54
Battey, 54
Bave, 255
Bavent, 209, 255
Bawcock, 54
Bawden, 54, 65
Bawkin, 54
Bawson, 54
Baxter, 132

Bayard, 67-8
Bayes, 209
Bayldon, 208
Bayley, 281, 392
Baylie, 105
Bayne, 380
Baynes, 252
Baynham, 65
Bayouse, 209
Beach, 235
Beacham, 209
Beachy, 235
Beadale, 105
Beadell, 105
Beale, 440
Beamish, 177
Beamsley, 118
Bearman, 106
Beard, 255
Beare, 159
Beater, 133
Beatie, 61
Beaton, 61, 255
Beauclerk, 391
Beaufort, 2079, 289, 391
Beaumont, 182, 210
Beavan, 43
Beaver, 255
Beck, 159
Beckett, 159, 167
Beckwith, 174
Bedbug, 361
Bedburg, 361
Beddingfield, 237
Bedell, 105
Bedmaker, 133
Bedoe, 55
Bedward, 65
Beeman, 182
Beere, 187
Belcher, 255
Belfield, 210
Bell, 61, 88, 97, 187
Bellasis, 255
Bellchamber, 255
Bellew, 210
Bellman, 61, 133
Bellsetter, 133
Benbow, 254
Bencher, 133
Benison, 54
Benjamin, 54
Benn, 54
Bennett, 54, 212
Bennetson, 54
Benny, 210
Benoi, 19
Benson, 55
Bent, 159
Bentinck, 19
Bentley, 159
Bercher, 118
Bere, 159
Berger, 118
Berham, 210
Berkley, 167
Berman, 106
Bernard, 54
Bernardson, 54
Berners, 105
Berneville, 202
Berrill, 182

Berry, 160, 202
Beryll, 182
Bertheau, 283
Bertram, 210
Best, 310
Betson, 61
Bettison, 61
Betts, 61
Betty, 61
Bevan, 57, 323
Beveridge, 170
Bevers, 210
Bevill, 212
Bevis, 67
Beyouse, 209
Bewes, 209
Bickerstaffe, 180, 365
Bickersteth, 365
Bickle, 159
Bickley, 159
Bidder, 133
Biddle, 105
Bidlake, 176, 307
Biffen, 176
Biford, 209
Bigger, 133
Bigott, 211
Bill, 59
Billet, 61
Billiter, 132
Billman, 133
Bilson, 59
Binder, 133
Bird, 135
Birdwhistle, 174
Biron, 211
Bishop, 310
Bisset, 256
Black, 133, 186, 305, 307, 386
Blackall, 176
Blackburn, 176
Blacker, 133
Blackett, 167
Blackister, 133
Blackleach, ix
Blackmore, 169
Blacksmith, 133
Blackstone, 176
Blackwell, 176
Blackwood, 176
Blades, 133
Bladesmith, 133
Blaine, 211
Blake, 133
Blakeley, 176
Blakelock, 310
Blampy, 19
Blanchard, 290
Blaquiere, 281
Blaydes, 133
Blayne, 211
Blaxter, 133
Blenkinsopp, 167, 326
Blewett, 211
Bligh, 410
Blocker, 133
Blomfield, 255
Blompay, 19
Blondell, 211, 290
Blood, 307
Bloomer, 133

INDEX

Blore, 133
Blount, 211, 308
Blow, 106, 133
Blower, 133
Bloye, 256
Bloyne, 211
Blucher, 333
Bluett, 211
Blund, 410
Blunt, 211
Blythe, 410
Boarder, 116
Boardman, 116
Bodkin, 54
Body, 54, 159, 187, 410
Boevy, 289
Boggis, 238
Boileau, 281, 284
Bold, 159
Bokerley, 355
Bolitho, 308
Bolter, 119
Bolton, 159, 392
Bomgartner, 18
Bonaparte, 397
Bond, 116, 186, 190
Bone, 211
Bonner, 308
Bonney, 256
Bonville, 212, 256
Boone, 211
Boosey, 256
Borman, 106
Borough, 281, 284
Bosanquet, 285
Boswell, 256
Botcher, 134
Boteller, 134, 212
Bothwell, 159
Botwell, 238
Bottle, 159
Bottome, 160
Boucher, 134
Boult, 119
Bounce, 237
Bourder, 134
Bourdes, 134
Bourdieu, 280
Bourdillon, 290
Boutell, 256
Boutereau, 281, 284
Boutflower, 96
Bouverie, 210, 281
Bovey, 256
Bow, 187
Bowdler, 14
Bower, 134
Bowen, 43, 58, 323
Bowerman, 134
Bowles, 134, 187, 410
Bowyer, 134, 327
Boyer, 134, 290
Boys, 211, 254
Brabant, 178
Brabazon, 178, 212
Bracegirdle, 134
Braine, 256
Bramble, 182
Brame, 178
Brammel, 182
Brand, 188, 212, 392, 410
Brass, 212

Brassey, 212
Brathwaite, 173
Braund, 212
Bray, 213
Brayler, 134
Brazier, 134
Breakspeare, 367
Brend, 160
Breton, 178, 213
Brett, 178, 219
Bretwitz, 337
Brewer, 134, 256, 357
Brewster, 134
Briant, 213
Brice, 54
Bridgeman, 134, 327
Bridger, 134
Bridges, 177
Bridgwater, 160
Briggs, 60, 177, 362
Bright, 308
Brightman, 310
Brimmel, 182
Briscoe, 326
Brison, 54
Bristol, 160, 172
Broadbent, 159
Brocas, 290
Brock, 89
Brockhurst, 167
Brodie, 187
Brogger, 134
Bromsgrove, 165
Brooke, 160
Brookes, 313
Broom, 96
Brothers, 65
Browker, 134
Browne, 213, 307, 386
Browning, 325
Brownsmith, 135
Browse, 176, 213
Bruce, 73, 213, 375, 410
Brune, 320
Bryan, 213
Bryant, 313
Bryce, 54
Bryson, 54
Bubb, 407
Buck, 93, 106
Buckett, 256
Buckle, 135, 159
Buckler, 97
Budd, 54
Buffer, 65
Buffler, 96
Buffets, 254
Bugg, 361
Bull, 90
Bullen, 178
Buller, 14, 119
Bullinger, 132
Bullivant, 182
Bullock, 90
Bulmer, 290
Bulstrod, 337
Bunce, 237
Bunker, 316
Bunting, 370
Bunyon, 254, 323
Burder, 134
Burdett, 256

Burdon, 214
Burgen, 178
Burgh, 160, 214
Burgoyne, 178
Burman, 106
Burnard, 54
Burrell, 214, 410
Burke, 214, 410
Burne, 410
Burr, 115
Burt, 265
Bush, 119, 254
Butcher, 138
Butler, 102, 134, 149, 212
Button, 135
Butts, 132, 160
Byatt, 176
Byatts, 176
Byden, 176
Byfield, 176
Byford, 176, 209
Bygrove, 176
Bythesea, 176, 313
Bywood, 135
Byrd, 135
Byrder, 135
Byron, 211, 287, 397
Bywater, 176

Cable, 94
Cade, 135
Cader, 135
Cadman, 135
Cæsar, 54, 82
Cailley, 214
Caine, 256
Caird, 135
Calcraft, 135
Calf, 90
Call, 135
Callender, 135
Callman, 135
Calthrop, 135, 149, 172
Calverley, 169
Calvert, 119
Cameron, 36, 380
Cammoys, 254, 308
Campbell, 377
Candy, 178
Cann, 256
Cassel, 93
Capern, 253
Capper, 136
Capes, 215
Capron, 253
Carder, 136
Cardmaker, 136
Carew, 360
Carey, 360
Caroll, 117
Carnaby, 161
Carpenter, 119, 136, 299, 387
Carr, 160, 410
Carrington, 256
Carter, 119
Carteret, 119, 242
Cartwright, 119, 124, 136
Carver, 106
Cass, 61
Cassell, 20
Castello, 355

419 DD 2

INDEX

Castle, 106
Catchpole, 119
Catchpool, 119
Cater, 105, 136
Catlin, 61
Catt, 90, 396
Caudle, 363
Caunter, 136
Cause, 256
Cavalier, 282
Cave, 187
Cavendish, 392
Cayley, 257
Cayzer, 54
Cazenove, 290
Cecil, 61
Centlivre, 317
Chalk, 112
Chalker, 119
Challand, 323
Challinger, 363
Challis, Challice, 136
Challoner, 136
Challys, 136, 214, 215
Chamberlaine, -layne, 102, 103-4, 106, 215
Chambers, 106
Chamier, 134, 290
Chamley, 256
Chamond, 215
Champagne, 283
Champernowne, 215
Champion, 290
Champney, 178, 215
Chance, 226
Chancellor, 106
Chandos, 215
Chanter, 136
Chantrell, 356
Chapell, 136
Chapman, 136, 150
Chardon, 284
Charger, 93
Charles, 54, 116
Charlesworth, 174
Charley, 54, 117
Charter, 105
Charteris, 215
Chase, 254
Chaucer, 120, 136, 144
Chauncy, 226
Chawnes, 136, 215, 257
Chawney, 257
Cheeseman, 136, 327
Chenevix, 289, 290
Cherry, 19
Cherwell, 257
Chesney, 215, 231
Chester, 161, 386
Chaworth, 216
Chetwynd, 392
Cheyne, 379
Cheynell, 257
Cheyney, 215
Chilcott, 187
Child, Childe, 189, 190, 311
Childers, 178
Chisholm, 377
Chivers, 92
Choice, 323
Cholmondely, 27
Chope, 323

Chowen, 215
Christie, 54
Christison, 54
Christmass, 213
Christopher, 54
Christopherson, 54
Chubb, 92, 323
Churchill, 257, 392
Churchward, 120
Churchyard, 120
Clack, 187
Claridge, 61
Clarke, Clark, 136
Clavell, 257
Claver, 106
Claverhouse, 91
Claye, 120
Clayer, 120
Clayman, 120
Cleave, 161
Cleaver, 106
Clements, 55
Clemo, 55
Clerkson, 65
Cliffe, 161
Clifford, 396
Climpson, 55
Clive, 161
Clobbury, 365
Close, 57, 161
Clowes, 57, 161
Clutterbuck, 14, 375
Clymo, 55
Coates, 167
Coatman, 116
Coaker, 130
Cobb, 38, 161
Cobbett, 55
Cobbler, 136
Cobett, 55
Cobley, 161
Cock, 107
Cocker, 130
Cockayne, 310
Cocks, Cox, 107, 323, 387
Cockrell, 19, 120, 326
Codd, 92
Codner, 92
Cody, 38
Coffee, 257
Coffin, 363
Cogger, 137
Cohen, 20
Cokeman, 107
Cole, 13, 57, 187, 410
Colburn, 410
Coleville, 216
Collard, 326
Collett, 57
Colley, 391, 410
Collier, 137
Collis, 57
Colson, 57
Colt, 93
Colthard, 120
Columb, 90, 216
Colquhoun, 372
Columbell, 216
Combe, 161, 307
Comfort, 363
Comper, 137

Comings, 217
Comyns, 217
Conder, 137, 143
Condy, 257
Conquest, 257
Constable, 106, 393
Constantine, 55
Conry, 387
Conyers, 216, 270
Coode, 91
Cooke, Cook, 107, 137, 149, 150, 323
Cookson, 65, 107
Cooming, 217
Cooper, 137, 149, 150
Cope, 161
Copeland, 161
Copley, 161
Copperfield, 404
Copps, 161
Corbett, 83, 217
Corbyn, 83, 217
Corder, 137, 143
Cordery, 143
Cornelius, 387
Corney, 407
Cornish, 178
Cornwallis, 178
Corser, 141
Cork, 386
Cosens, 61, 65
Cossentine, 55
Costello, 387
Coster, 137
Cotter, 116
Cotterell, 116, 170, 326
Couch, 137
Coudray, 254
Couper, 150, 254
Coutts, 187
Coverer, 137
Coverley, 257
Coward, 120
Cowland, 326
Cowley, 137, 391
Cowper, 137, 148
Cox, 107, 323, 387
Coxwell, 327
Coxwold, 327
Crabbe, 92
Craddock, 13
Craig, 161
Craike, 161
Crane, 90
Cranmer, 120
Crawford, 382
Crayke, 161
Creale, 226
Creamer, 120
Creasy, 257
Creech, 162
Crespigny, 281
Cressy, 257
Crevelli, 335
Crewdson, 55
Cricket, 217
Cricklade, 162
Crisp, 55
Crispin, 55
Cripps, 55
Croft, 163
Crofton, 163

INDEX

Crocker, 137
Crockett, 137
Croker, 137
Crole, 226
Crommelin, 283
Cromwell, 174, 364
Crookes, 187
Crookshanks, 310
Cross, 95
Crosskeys, 95
Crossthwaite, 173
Crosswell, 174
Cruden, 120
Crudener, 120
Crytoft, 217
Cudliffe, 182
Cudlip, 365
Cuff, 257
Cullen, 178
Cully, 214
Cumberledge, 163
Cummins, 217, 375
Cundy, 257
Cunninghame, 382
Curle, 226
Curtain, 410
Curtis, 254
Curzon, 217
Cussack, 259
Custance, 257
Cutbeard, 55
Cutcliff, 182, 365
Cuthbert, 55
Cuthbertson, 55
Cutts, 55
Czerny, 325

Dabernon, 217
Dacre, ix
Dainty, 96
Dakins, Dakeyne, 55, 207
Dale, 162
Dalhousie, 343, 382
Dalmahoi, 343
Dalton, 162
Dalziel, 343, 382
Dames, 207
Dampierre, 258
Dance, 55
Dancer, 137
Dancet, 55
Danes, 178
Daniel, 55, 287
Danson, 55
Danvers, 319
Darcy, 207, 319, 387
Darell, 218
Darke, 258, 309
Daubeny, -igny, 207, 217, 290, 319
Dauber, 138
Daubuz, 287
Davers, 258
David, 55
Davitt, 55
Davey, Davie, 55
Davis, Davies, 55
Davison, Davidson, 55, 380
Dawe, 55
Dawes, 55
Dawkes, 55
Dawkins, 55

Dawney, 208, 319
Dawson, 55
Dawtrey, 218
Day, Daye, 120, 258, 312, 410
Dayman, 120
Dayson, 55
Deadman, 121, 327
Dealchamber, 363
Deamer, 138
Deane, 163
Dearden, 163
Dearmer, 138
Death, 312
Deeman, 107
Deemster, 138
De la Laund, 202, 218
Delany, 387
De la Pole, 97, 218
Delmar, Delamare, 169, 218
Dempster, 138
Denis, Dennis, 55, 178, 219, 387
Denman, 163, 178
Dennison, 55
Denny, 55
Denyer, 163
Depledge, 163
Despenser, 102, 107
De Trafford, 393
Deuce, 62
Deval, 19
De Vere, 396
Deverell, 219
Devereux, 219, 319
Deville, 219
De Villiers, 393
Devonshire, 181
Dewhurst, 168
Deyman, 120
D'Eyncourt, 207
Dick, Dicks, 58
Dickens, 55, 58
Dickenson, Dickson, 57
Dickman, 58
Diggenson, 55
Digges, 55, 120
Diggles, 362
Diggons, 55
Digman, 55
Digory, 55
Dilly, 96
Dimond, 258, 407
Dingle, Dingley, 163
Dinham, 258
Diprose, 258
Disney, 219
Ditcher, 100
Dixie, Dixon, 58
Dobbs, 58
Dobie, 58
Dobson, 58
Dodd, Dodds, 55, 121, 187
Dodge, Doidge, 58
Dodson, 55, 58
Doke, 90
Dolling, 67
Dolman, 177
Dolphin, 92, 188

Doyle, 220
Domville, 258
Donald, 55
Donaldson, 58
Donkin, 55
Donne, 187
Doser, 138
Douce, 178, 254
Doughty, 310
Dove, 90
Dovey, 187
Dowch, 178
Dowse, 62
Dowson, 62
Drake, 90
Draper, 138
Dresser, 106, 107, 138
Dressincourt, 287
Drew, 250
Drinkwater, 181
Driver, 121
Druce, 258
Drummond, 377, 407
Dubber, 138
Ducie, 258
Duck, 91
Duckworth, 121
Dudgen, 58
Dudman, 121
Dudney, 258
Duffy, 258
Dufour, 285
Duke, 310, 403
Du Laing, 387
Du Maillet, 387
Dummerel, 308
Dunbar, 382
Duncalf, 315
Dundas, 382
Dunn, 163, 187
Durant, 220
Durdon, 258
Durward, 111
Dust, 361
Dustan, 274
Dyatt, 55
Dye, 62
Dyer, 88, 131, 150
Dyett, 55
Dykes, 120
Dyot, 62
Dyson, 58

Eagle, 91, 410
Eales, 67
Eames, 62, 65
Easton, 410
Eaton, 363
Earl, Earle, 178, 310
Easterling, 178
Eave, 62
Ebbott, 61
Eccles, Eckles, 144, 163
Eden, 62
Edes, 62
Edkins, 62
Eddison, 62
Edmunds, 62, 63
Edmundson, 62
Edwards, Edwardes, 55
Eeles, 67
Egerton, 392

421

INDEX

Elbow, 326
Eldrich, 308
Elgar, 410
Elias, 55
Ellet, 67
Ellicock, 67
Ellicott, 67
Elliot, Eliott, 67, 319
Ellis, 67
Ellison, 67
Elkins, 67
Elwes, 62
Ely, 163
Eme, 91
Emery, 206, 250
Emmott 62
Empson, 61
Emson, 61, 62
Enderby, 160
English, 118, 178
Entwhistle, 174
Enys, 168
Epps, 61
Ernshaw, 167
Esdaile, 285
Essex, 181
Etchells, 144
Etty, 62
Eugene, 387
Eustace 55, 67, 220, 251
Evercreech, 162
Everstaff, 365
Eves, 62
Eveson, 62
Evett, 62
Eville, 219, 258
Ewart, 121
Ewin, Ewins, 255, 410
Eyre, 258, 382

Faber, 27, 133, 138, 313
Fabricius, 133
Facey, 246, 323
Fair, 309
Fairbrother, 65
Fairchild, 322
Fairfax, 310
Falcon, 91
Falconer, Faulkner, etc., 108, 150
Fancourt, 220, 258
Fanner, 121
Faraday, 138
Farewell, Farwell, 266
Farfield, 266
Farman, 138, 316
Farmer, 121, 150
Farquharson, 372, 380
Farrer, Farrar, Farrier, 121, 132, 138
Farren, Fearon, Fiaron, 27, 133
Faucett, Fawcett, 55, 108
Fawkes, 55, 92
Fawson, 55
Fayle, Faile, 254
Fearon, Fieron, Farren, 27, 121, 133
Featherstone, 14, 410
Feldberger, 300
Fell, 133, 138
Fellowes, 187

Fenner, 121
Fermor, 121
Ferrar, Ferrers, Ferrier, 27, 121, 133
Ferron, Fearon, Fieron, Farren, 27, 121, 153
Fervour, 133
Feures, 27
Fewster, 138
Ffinch, 368
Ffrench, 368
Ffoukes, 368
Fichett, 231
Fiddle, 88
Fidgett, 231
Field, 163
Field-Flowers-Goe, 407
Fiennes, 221, 393
Filberd, Filbert, 258
Filliol, 221
Filliot, Filiot, 64, 202
Fillpot, Filpotts, 323
Filmer, 221, 366
Filson, 58
Finch, 91, 121
Fincher, 91
Finmore, 221
Finn, 187
Fippen, Fippon, 246
Firebrace, 67, 317
Firth, 165
Fish, 91
Fishacre, 362
Fisher, 251
FitzAlan, 221
FitzAleyn, 202
FitzBrian, 221
FitzJames, 43
FitzPatrick, 385
FitzRobert, 202
FitzRoy, 43, 391
FitzUrse, 77, 251
FitzWilliam, 44
Flamank, 14, 178, 180
Flanner, 138
Flaxman, 138
Fleet, 163, 308
Fleetwood, 164
Fleming, 14, 178, 338
Flesher, 138, 327
Fletcher, 138, 249
Flinders, 14
Fleury, 289
Florence, 62
Flowers, 96, 138
Floyer, 138
Flurry, Flory, 62
Foley, 221
Follett, 258
Folliot, 64
Fonnereau, 284
Fookes, Foulkes, 55, 251, 326
Foote, 96
Forbes, 343
Force, Forcer, 138
Ford, 164
Forester, Forster, Forestier, Forrest, 108, 149, 150
Forrest-Bell, 407
Fortescue, 336
Foster Forster, 108, 150
Fotheringay, 166

Fowell, 258
Fowle, 92, 121
Fowler, 92, 121, 150
Fox, 55, 92, 387
Francis, 55, 252
Francombe, Frankham, 115
Franklyn, 115
Franks, 55, 115, 252
Franson, 55
Frayle, 254
Frazer, 221, 275
Free, 113
Freebody, 113, 159
Freeman, 113, 410
Freestone, 410
French, 178, 180
Frere, 65
Freyne, Freine, 254
Freyson, 56
Frieze, 130, 222
Frobisher, 110
Fromisher, 136
Froude, 410
Fry, 113
Fuller, 131, 138
Furneaux, 212
Furness, 399
Furnivall, 222
Furrier, 138
Furse, 258
Fust, 139
Fuster, 139
Future, 108, 113
Futurer, 108
Fyers, 254
Fyler, 113
Fynnes (see also Fiennes), 335
Fysh, 92
Fyshour, 251

Gabb, 55
Gabe, 407
Gabel, 55
Gable, 55
Gabriel, 55
Gage, 139, 222
Gager, 139
Gale, 108, 178
Galightley, 315
Galland, 57
Gallon, 62
Galt, 93, 410
Gam, 308
Gamage, 174-5
Gambier, 286, 290
Gamell, Gammel, 186, 187, 308, 410
Gamelcarle, 186
Gans, 86
Gant, 178
Garde, 113, 218
Garden, Gardener, Gardner, 108, 113, 149
Garrett, 53
Garrick, 53
Garrod, 53
Garlick, 97
Garth, 165
Gascoyne, 178
Gaskin, 178
Gastigny, 285

INDEX

Gates, 147, 165
Gatacre, Gattacre, 156, 159
Gatishill, 112
Gatherd, Gateard, 121
Gaud,
Gaunt, 178, 222, 312
Gaunter, 139
Gauntlet, 97
Gawthorpe, 172
Gay, 226
Gayer, 410
Gaylord, 259
Gaze, 222
Geer, 410
Geldart, 121
Gellot, 62
Gent, 178, 254
Geoffrey, 55
George, Georges, 55
Gerard, 55, 251
German, 178, 259
Gerry, 274, 410
Gibbings, 55
Gibbons, 55, 224
Gibbs, 55
Gibson, 55
Giddy, 251
Giffard, 222, 310, 367
Gilbard, 55
Gilbert, 55, 251, 306
Gilbertson, 55
Gilbey, 222, 259
Gilcock, 56
Giles, 56
Gill, 23-6, 165, 382, 410
Gillard, 142
Gillchrist, 382
Gillespie, 382
Gillett, 56
Gillie, 382
Gillott, Gillot, 56, 59, 62
Gillow, 62
Gilpatrick, 382
Gilpin, 56
Gillman, 327
Gilson, 57, 62
Giltpen, 315
Girdler, 139
Ginn, 107
Ginner, 107
Glanville, 267
Glascock, Glasscock, 57, 323
Glazier, 139
Glede, 91
Gledhill, 91
Gledstane, 91
Glover, 139
Gloyne, 267
Glyn, 165
Goad, 59, 259
Goatcher, 251
Goatherd, 121
Gobbett, 56
Gobbo, 224
Goch, 308
Godard, Goddard, 56, 59, 121
Godden, 59
Godfrey, 56, 67
Godkin, 59
Godliman, 182, 315
Godon, 59

Godrich, 59
Godwin, Goodwin, 13, 59
Goff, 55
Golding, 407
Goldring, 325
Goldschmidt, 306
Goldsmith, 88
Golightly, 315
Golland, Goland, 57
Gooch. See Goch
Good, 259
Goodacre, 159
Goodbody, 56, 181
Goodchild, 59, 310
Goodenough, 167, 310, 362
Goodfellow, 56, 310
Goodlad, 315
Goodlake, 56, 410
Goodly, 410
Goodluck, 56
Goodman, 304, 310, 410
Goodrich, 13, 59, 410
Goodridge, 59
Goodwin, Godwin, 13, 59
Goodyear, 59
Gordon, 375, 329
Gore, 165
Gorell, 168
Gorges, 222
Gorham, 165
Gorman, 327, 410
Gorwyn, 306
Goschen, 20
Gosling, 92, 259
Gospatrick, 382
Goss, 62, 92, 187
Gossett, 82
Gotobed, 56
Gott, 165, 179
Gould, 394, 466
Gower, 222
Goz, le, 83, 299
Gozzard, 122
Grace, 223
Graham, 380
Grandisson, 223
Granger, 108, 165
Graine, 410
Grant, 223, 254, 374
Granville, 276
Graunt, 223
Graves, 122, 165
Gray, 223
Greatrakes, 315
Greave and Greaves, 109, 122, 165
Green, 96, 307
Greendon, 176
Greenfield, 363
Greenhill, 176
Greenslade, 172
Greenwell, 174, 176
Greenwood, 42, 176, 291
Gregory, 56
Greely, 223
Grendon, 223
Grenville, 223
Gresley, 223
Gresson, 56
Greville, 223
Grey, 223
Greygoose, 315

Greyson, 56
Gribble, 187
Grice, 254
Grierson, 109
Grieve, 109
Griffinhoof, 328
Griffith, 13
Griggs, 56
Grindon, 176
Grize, le, 83, 93
Grocer, 139
Grosser, 139
Grosteste, 283
Grosvenor, 102, 392
Groves, 165
Grundy, 62, 410
Gruyelien, 19
Grymes, 14, 410
Gubbins, 224
Guelf, 79
Guest, 410
Guiness, 259, 387
Guise, 397
Guliver, 222
Gull, 92
Gulley, 92
Gunn, 109, 378, 410
Gunning, 325
Gunstone, 410
Gurdon, 223-4
Gurney, 224
Guscott, 116
Guthrie, 344, 410
Gwyllim, 251

Hacket, 56, 253, 364
Hackman, 122
Hadleigh, 169
Haigh, 166
Haire-Fowler, 407
Hake, 410
Halbert, 5-6
Haldane, 14, 225, 410
Hales, 265
Halfnaked, 315
Halford, 411
Halfpenny, 399
Halket, 56
Hall, 56, 165-6, 411
Hallet, 54, 56
Halley, 166, 324
Halse, 56
Halwell, 174
Ham, 166
Hamilton, 379, 392
Hamley, 56, 250
Hamlyn, 56, 224
Hammet, 56
Hamper, 139
Hampson, 56
Hand, 96
Hancock, 57, 107
Handcock, 148
Handel, 326
Hanger, 165
Hankey, 325
Hannah, 179
Hansard, 179, 224, 326
Hansom, 57, 61
Hanway, 179
Harbottle, 159
Harcourt, 224

INDEX

Hardgripe, 187
Harding, 325
Hardman, 109, 122
Hardy, 109
Hargreave, 122
Harman, 306
Harness, 139
Harper, 109
Harriman, 56
Harris, 56, 225
Harrison, 56
Harrow, 88
Hart, 93, 109
Hartman, 109
Hartopp, 167, 172
Harvey, 14, 411
Haseler, 110
Haskell, 410
Hassell, 411
Hastings, 202, 224
Hassard, Hazzard, 290
Hatch, 165, 176
Hatchard, 165
Hatchman, 165
Hatte, 22-3
Haughton, 166
Haverfield, 163
Hawes, Hawis, 56, 166, 176
Hawk, 91
Hawker, 122
Hawkes, 122
Hawkins, 56
Hawkinson, 57
Hawley, 202, 225
Hawson, 56
Hay, Haye, 166, 218, 331, 377
Haybiddle, 122
Hayes, 166
Hayman, 67, 122
Haysler, 110
Hayward, 122, 225
Hayter, 122
Hazlehurst, 168
Hazzard, Hassard, 13, 290
Head, 90, 167
Heale, 165
Heard, 122
Heath, 167
Heathman, 327
Hebblethwaite, 226
Hebblewhite, 226
Hebburn, 167
Hedgeman, 122
Hedger, 122
Hellcat, 85
Hellier, Helyer, 139
Helliland, 355
Help, 187
Helps, 187
Hemming, 411
Henderson, 54
Henry, 56
Henson, 54
Hepworth, 174
Herder, 110
Herice, 225
Hermon, 411
Heron, 93, 225
Herne, 93, 167, 225
Hernshaw, 93
Herrick, 226, 258

Herries, 226, 393
Herring, 92
Hersee, 226
Hewer, 122
Hewett, 56
Heyman, 327
Hickes, 56
Hickson, 56
Hide. See Hyde
Higgs, 56
Higgins, 56
Higginson, 56
Highstreet, 291
Higman, 56
Hilary, 56
Hilson, 56
Hinchman, 110
Hinksman, 110
Hird, 172
Hirschell, 326
Hiskison, Hiskinson, 56
Hitchcock, 58
Hitchens, 58
Hoarder, 110
Hoare, 307
Hobbes, 58
Hobbie, 56
Hobbins, 58
Hobbler, 110
Hobbs, 58, 58
Hobbson, Hobson, 56, 58
Hockaday, 313
Hodder, 363
Hodge, 58
Hodges, 58
Hodgkin, 58
Hodgman, 58
Hodgson, 58
Hody, 257
Hogarth, 123
Hogg, 93
Hoggart, 123
Holcroft, 161
Hold, 190, 366
Holder, 139
Holiday 313
Holker, 411
Holland, 179
Holmes, 167, 259
Hollet, 74
Hollick, 74
Holroyd, 171
Holst, 179
Holybone, 360, 411
Holzapfel, 20
Homer, 116
Honey, 119
Honeybun, 362
Honeyman, 119, 123
Hood, 251
Hoodwall, 251
Hooker, 139, 306
Hooper, 139
Hope, 167
Hopgood, 366
Hopkins, 58
Hopkinson, 58
Hopton, 167
Hopwood, 366
Horden, 110
Horder, 110
Hore, 307

Hornblower, 134
Horne, 139
Horneman, 106]
Horner, 139
Hosier, 140
Hostler, 142
Houblon, 281, 290
House, 168
Houseman, 327
Howard, 202, 225
Howell, 13, 226
Howett, 56
Hozier, 90, 140, 411
Hubbard, 56
Hubert, 56
Hudson, 56
Huggins, 56
Hugh, 56, 387
Hughes, 56
Hughes-Death, 407
Huish, 168
Hullin, 285
Humfine, 299
Humphrey, 411
Hund, 80
Hundredpounds, 307
Hunt, 110
Hunter, 110
Hunt-Grubb, 407
Hurd, 110
Hurst, 168, 392
Husband, 123
Hussey, 218, 310
Hutchins, 56
Huxter, 122
Hyde, 167, 392, 411
Hynde, 110
Hyne, 110

Ians, 57
Ibbott, 61
Ibsen, 61
Ide, 67
Idson, 62
Image, 97
Ince, 168
Inchbald, 411
Ingersoll, 171
Ingham, 259
Ingle, 411
Ingledew, 411
Inglis, 178
Ingram, 251, 411
Inkpen, 316
Innman, 124
Iremonger, 130
Irons, 130
Isaac, 56
Isaacson, 56
Isbel, 61
Ivers, 56
Ivey, 251
Ivison, 56
Ivory, 259
Izzard, 62, 219
Izod, 61, 397

Jackman, 110
Jacks, 56
Jackson, 86
Jacobs, 56
Jacobson, 56

INDEX

Jacox, 56
James, 187
Jameson, 56
Jane, 179
Janssen, 289
Janway, 179
Jacques, 56, 251
Jardine, 108, 150
Jarman, 178
Jarratt, 55
Jarred, 55
Jaye, 225
Jayne, 179
Jeames, 56
Jefcott, 322
Jefcock, 55, 322
Jefferson, 55
Jeffrey, 55
Jeffries, 55
Jeffs, 55
Jeffson, 55
Jekyll, 14, 411
Jelf, 187, 411
Jelly, 56, 108
Jellicock, 56
Jellicoe, 326
Jenkins, 57
Jenner, 107
Jennings, 57
Jephson, 57
Jepson, 55
Jerold, 55
Jerome, 288
Jesse, 140
Jessop, 57
Jeune, 290
Jevons, 57
Jewell, 57
Jillard, 19
Jimpson, 56
Jimson, 56
Jobling, 259
Jobson, 56
Johns, 57
Johnson, 57, 195
Joiner, 140
Joliffe, 310, 326
Joll, 13, 62, 187
Jones, 306
Jonson, 57
Jope, 56
Jopling, 56
Jordan, 19, 57, 250
Jortin, 289
Jose, 57, 62
Josephs, 57
Joskin, 57
Joule, 57
Jowett, 62
Jowle, 57
Joyce, 60, 254
Joynes, 57
Jubb, 322
Judd, 57
Judkin, 57
Judson, 57
Jukes, 57
Jule, 57
Julian, 57
Jury, 55, 243
Justel, 284
Juxon, 57

Kalkreuth, 336
Kaye, ix, 187
Keates, 54
Kebroyd, 171
Keeler, 143
Keep-Wells, 407
Kelson, 54
Kemble, 137
Kemster, 137
Kendrick, 327
Kenn, 90
Kennard, 310
Kennedy, 57
Kenneth, 57
Keppel, 19
Kerr, 375
Kersford, 366
Kerslake, 366
Kerswell, 366
Kettle, 14, 411
Kettlewell, 174
Kewe, ix
Key, 95
Keyes, 95
Keysar, 54
Kidd, 92, 123
Kidder, 123
Kiddle, 411
Kidner, 123
Kildare, 173
Kilkenny, 387
Killick, 168
Kilner, 123
Kilson, 57, 327
Kimber, 18, 137
Kimmeridge, 170
Kinch, 140
King, 96, 310
Kingstone, 387
Kinsman, 327
Kirkupp, 172
Kissack, 259
Kisser, 140
Kitchen, 107
Kitchener, 107, 140
Kite, 91
Kitson, 57
Kitts, 54, 92
Kitto, 54
Knapman, 168
Knapper, 111
Knapton, 168
Knibb, 61
Knight, 110, 310
Knollys, 57, 168
Knopps, 168
Knott, 338, 411
Knowles, 57, 168, 260
Knowlman, 168
Kyrle, 226

Labett, 57
Labouchere, 154
Lacer, 140
Lacey, 226
Ladbrook, 168
Lade, 168
Lafayette, 397
Laight, 168
Lake, 169
Lalleman, 177
Lamb, Lambe, 94, 411

Lambert, 57, 281, 306
Lambet, 57
Lambson, 57
Lambkin, 57
Lammas, ix
Lamoureux, 19
Lampert, 57
Lamprey, 365
Lancey, 344
Landseer, 367
Landor, 140
Lands, 169
Lane, 168
Laner, 140
Langstaffe, 364
Langtree, 173
Larder, 123
Lardiner, 140
Lardner, 124, 140
Larke, 94
Larkin, 56, 57, 94
Larpent, 281
La Saca, 338
La Scala, 338
Lassels, 226
Lathe, 168
La Touche, 290
Latimer, 140, 226
Latoner, 140
Laud, 266
Laund, 169
Launder, 140
Laurence, 57
Laurie, 57
Lavelle, 387
Lavender, 96, 140
Law, 57, 169
Lawes, 57
Lawson, 57
Layman, 140, 190
Lea, 169
Leach, ix, 141
Leadbeater, 141
Leader, 141
Leaper, 141
Leapman, 141
Leason, 57
Le Breton, 18
Ledbitter, 141
Lee, 169
Leech, 141
Leef, Liefe, 141
Le Fanu, 290
Lefevre, 290
Lefroy, 290
Legard, 320
Legatt, 320
Legge, 95, 179
Legh, 169
Le Goz, 83, 299
Leicester, 392
Leigh, 169
Leman, 181
Lemon, 367
Lempole, 18
Le Neveu, 320
Lennox, 391
Le Noir, 320
Lepell, 336
Le Roy, 400
Leslie, 219, 376
L'Estrange, 220, 320, 387

425

INDEX

Le Tablier, 289
Letts, 54, 62
Lettson, 54, 62
Levermore, 176
Levi, 20, 57
Levison-Gower, 27
Lewis, 57
Lewson, 57
Lewin, 187
Ley, 169
Leyton, 169
Liall, 260
Lias, 351
Liberty, 141
Libby, 61
Liefchild, 311
Liffard, 227
Ligonier, 281, 288
Lilienthal, 306
Lilley, Lilly, Lily, 94, 95, 219, 260
Lillicrap, 163
Lilywhite, 173
Limmer, 141
Lindau, Lindow, 162
Lindhurst, 168
Lindsay, 228, 375
Line, Lyne, 141, 260
Linsale, 386
Lintott, 260
Lion, Lyon, 83, 94, 380
Lipman, 141
Lipson, 58
Lipton, 58, 365
Liremont, 282
Lisle, 219, 260
Lister, 141, 148
Littleboys, 315
Lloyd, 393
Locke, 141
Lockhart, 332
Lockyer, 141
Locock, 57
Loder, 141
Loftus, 168
Lombard, 283
Lomond, 280
Long, 309, 319
Longfellow, 260
Longman, 315
Longshanks, 260
Longthwaite, 173
Longville, 227
Lopes, 20
Loreyne, 179
Lorimer, 141
Loring, 179
Louvain, 227
Love, 95
Loveday, 227
Lovelace, 322
Loveless, 322
Lovell, 82, 227
Lover, 411
Loveries, 227
Lovering, 227
Lowndes, 169
Lowrie, 260
Luard, 290, 411
Lubbard, 179
Lubbock, 179
Luce, 94, 228

Luckman, 315
Lucy, 94, 228
Luke, 57
Lukin, 57
Lukiss, 57
Lukitt, 57
Lund, 169
Luny, 228
Luxon, Luxton, 57
Lyas, 251
Lynch, 169
Lyne, 141, 260
Lynn, 165
Lysons, 272
Lyte, 141, 368
Lyteman, 141
Lyttleton, 363

Mabb, 62
Mabbot, 63
Maberley, 63
Mably, 63
MacAlister, 43, 54, 380
MacAlpine, 380, 399
MacAulay, 372
MacBean, 372, 380
MacCalummore, 380
MacCarthy, 384, 385
MacCheyne, 43
MacDermot, 43, 385
MacDonald, 377
MacDougall, 378
MacDuff, 372, 381
MacFarlane, 381
MacGarry, 372
MacGrath, 43
MacGregor, 372, 381-2
MacInlay, 381
MacIntosh, 372
MacIver, 56
MacKaye, 381
MacKenzie, 57, 381
MacKinlay, 381
MacKinnon, 381
MacLachlan, 381
MacLaine, 381
MacLean, 381
MacLennan, 373
MacLeod, 372, 378
MacMillan, 381
MacMurrough, 384
MacNab, 372-3
MacNaughten, 381
MacNeil, 57, 381, 385
MacPherson, 43, 373
MacPhie, 372
MacQuarrie, 281
MacQueen, 373
MacShane, 43
Maddison, 57
Magnag, 260
Magnall, 260
Magnus, 57, 411
Mahew, 57
Maidgood, 316
Mailer, 141
Maine, 179, 228
Mainwaring, 27, 261, 394
Maire, 261
Maitland, 376
Majendie, 288
Major, 67, 251

Makin, 63
Malberg, 228
Malby, 228, 362
Malborough, 228
Malet, 228
Malevrier, 230, 331
Mallison, 63
Mallory, 261
Maloysel, 316
Malster, 141
Maltby, 160
Malthus, 168
Maltravers, 232
Mandeville, 229
Mann, 117, 118
Manners, 229
Manney, 230, 262
Mansell, 229
Manson, 57
Mant, 261
Manville, 229
Manwell, 261
Mapleson, 63
Mappowder, 173
Marcett, 57, 324
Marchant, 142, 252
Marcock, 57
Marcheson, 57
Margetson, 63
Margotson, 324
Mariner, 141, 229
Mariott, Marriot, 63
Marjoribanks, 27
Marks, 57
Markham, 387
Markson, 57
Marney, 141, 229
Marshall, 233, 261
Martin, 57, 229
Martineau, 290
Marvell, 233, 261
Mason, 141, 357
Maskelyne, 142
Massenger, 110
Massey, 229
Master-Whittaker, 407
Mather, 123
Matheson, 57, 373
Mathews, 57
Matson, 57
Maturin, 289
Maude, 63, 230, 261
Mauger, 67
Maule, 229, 378, 411
Maulay, 229
Maunder, 141
Maunney, 230, 262
Mauregard, 342
Maurice, 57
Mawson, 57
May, 63
Maybrick, 261
Maynard, 228
Mayne, Maine, 179, 228
Maxwell, 378
Medlar, 315
Medlicott, 176, 358
Meek, 65
Mellor, 141
Melonie, 19
Melville, 229, 375
Memory, 272

INDEX

Mendel, 326
Menzies, 378
Mercer, 88, 142
Merchant, 142, 252
Merrick, 250
Merriman, 63, 327
Merrit, 261
Merry, 261
Merton, 169
Metcalf, 365
Meynell, 230
Michael, 57
Michaelmass, 313
Micklethwaite, 173, 326
Middlemas, 176, 313
Middleton, 176, 358
Midlane, 169
Midnight, 110, 315
Midwinter, 315
Miles, 57, 69, 251
Mill, Mills, 69, 150
Miller, 262
Millet, 57
Milman, 110
Milner, 110
Milsom, 57
Milson, 57
Milward, 110
Minter, 142
Mitchell, 57
Mitchener, 142
Mitcheson, 57
Moggs, 62
Moggsson, 63
Mogillapatrick, 385
Mohun, 97, 230, 262
Moll, 229, 411
Mompeson, 231
Monceaux, 231, 392
Moncrieff, 382
Monday, 262, 313
Money, 142, 262
Monier, 142
Monk, 233, 367
Monkey, 315
Monro, 282
Montague, 231
Montandre, 283
Montceau, 231, 392
Montfichet, 231
Montgomery, 203, 283
Montmorency, 392
Montmorris, 333
Montolieu, 288
Monyer, 142
Moody, 310
Moon, 197, 231, 262
Moore, 169
Moorhayes, 169
Mordaunt, 253
More, 169
Morgan, 13
Morell, 254
Morley, 18, 169, 222
Morrell, 290
Morres, 92
Morris, 57, 232
Morse, 57
Morshead, 96
Morson, 57
Morteville, 233
Mortice, 262

Mortimer, 233, 307, 387
Morton, 169, 232
Moses, 183
Moss, 183
Mossop, 14
Mostyn, 394
Motlawe, 183
Motley, 183, 309
Mott, 262
Mounce, 233
Mounsell, 232
Mounseer, 231
Mounsey, 233
Mount, 169
Mountain, 169
Mountford, 231
Mountfort, 231
Mowat, 279
Mowbray, 230, 390
Mowcher, 315
Moyne, 233
Moxon, 57, 63
Muffet, 272
Mules, 226
Mullens, 262
Mumfey, 231
Mummery, 363
Munday, 262, 313
Mungay, 362
Murray, 382
Murrell, 233
Muschet, 379
Musgrave, 233
Musgrove, 233, 343
Mussard, 233
Musset, 233
Musselwhite, 326
Mustard, 142
Musters, 233
Mutton, 183, 253
Mytton, 254

Naesmyth, 150
Nangle, 159, 387
Nankivel, 93, 170
Napier, 103, 111, 149, 330
Nathan, 20
Nation, 96
Nayle, 361
Neale, 57
Neames, 64
Neaves, 64, 253
Needler, 142
Neeves, 320
Neilson, 57
Nelson, 57, 392
Netherton, 176, 358
Nettleship, 160, 326
Neville, Nevill, 234, 262, 392
Nevins, 65
Nevinson, 65
Newbert, 234
Newbottle, 159
Newburrow, 234
Newcastle, 176
Newcome, Newcomen, 118
Newell, 262
Newers, 262
Newman, 118
Newmarch, 234
Nibbs, 61
Nicholas, 57

Nichols, 57
Nicholson, 57
Nihil, 57
Nixon, 57
Noel, ix, 213, 262
Nollekin, 57
Norfolk-Howard, 396
Norman, 179
Norrice, 179, 252
Norries, 179
Norton, 358
Notschaft, 338
Nott, 411
Nourse, 252
Nugent, 262
Nurse, 252
Nurse-Rivers, 411

Oastler, 142
Oates, 250-1
O'Brian, 36, 384
O'Caroll, 54
O'Connor, 384, 385
Odger, 67, 251, 411
O'Donohue, 384
O'Donovan, 384
O'Dugan, 384
Ody, 257
O'Faelan, 284
Offer, Offerer, 142
Ogle, 316
O'Laughlin, 385
Oldcastle, 176
Oldcorne, 182
Olde, 190, 366
Oliphant, 63, 235, 375
Oliver, 57, 69
O'Mahony, 384
O'Malbrogi, 385
O'Melaghlin, 384
O'Neil, 57, 384-5
Onion, 97
Ore, 170
Orme, 411
Ormrod, 171
Ormroyd, 171
Orsini, 77
Osbald, 58
Osbert, 58
Osborne, 58, 187, 332, 411
Osegood, 411
Oseler, 123, 135
Osmund, 58, 411
Ostler, 142
Oswald, 411
Otley, 336
Otter, 363
Ouvry, 290
Over, 170
Overbury, 176
Overman, 170
Overton, 176
Owen, 58
Oxenden, 163
Oysterman, 178

Pack, 142
Packer, 142
Packman, 123, 327
Padman, 123
Padson, 58
Page, 111, 316

INDEX

Paget, 111, 392
Painter, 142
Palfrey, 93
Palfreyman, 111, 327
Palgrave, 165
Palk, 58
Pallen, 319
Palliser, Paliser, 54, 10:
Pantler, 111
Papillon, 235, 290
Paramore, 169
Pargiter, 147
Parish, 311
Parke, Parkes, 19, 111, 149
Parker, 103, 111, 149
Parkinson, 58
Parkman, 111
Parminter, 142
Parnell, 63
Parr, 58
Parrot, 94, 322
Parry, 56
Parsons, 58, 311
Partrick, 94
Partridge, 94
Pask, ix
Patey, 58, 253
Patner, 142
Patrick, 58
Patrickson, 58
Patterson, 58
Pattison, 58
Patton, 58
Paul, Paull, 58, 284
Paulet, 58
Paulson, 58
Pavey, 179
Pawley, 324
Pawson, 58
Paxman, 123
Payne, 235
Paynter, 142
Peach, 235
Peachy, 235
Peacock, 75
Pearce, 251
Peascod, 377
Pearman, 123
Pechill, 281
Peddar, 123
Pedlar, 123
Peer, 50
Peggoty, 254, 324
Pellew, Pellow, 210
Petter, 138, 142
Pempol, 18
Pendennis, 170
Pender, 150
Penington, 307
Penlee, 150
Pennant, 170
Pennell, 235, 264, 302
Penninger, 111
Penny, 111
Pennyfather, 305, 310
Penrose, 171
Pepper, 58, 97, 142
Percy, 73, 391
Perkins, 58, 325
Perks, 58, 325
Pernell, Parnell, 63
Perowne, 263

Perrier, 123
Perrin, 58
Perrott, 38, 236
Perriman, 123
Perry, 236
Pertwee, 19
Peterkin, 325
Peters, 58
Peterson, 58
Petherick, 58
Pethick, 58
Peto, 179
Pettifer, 317
Pettit, 290
Pessoner, 142
Phayre, 14
Phelan, 384
Phelps, 58
Philbrick, 58, 160, 323
Philipson, 58
Phillimore, 221, 323, 366
Phillips, 58
Phillipson, 58
Philpott, Phillpots, 58, 253
Phinn, 187
Phipson, 58
Physick, 362
Pickard, 179
Pickersgill, 323
Pickman, 123
Pierce, 58, 251
Pierrepont, 236
Pierson, 58
Pigeon, 90
Pigg, 93
Piggot, Pigott, 64, 93, 238, 324
Pigman, 123
Pigou, 296
Pike, Pyke, 92
Pilcher, 142
Pillsbury, 323
Pimple, 18
Pinch, 263
Pinchard, 237, 263
Pinel, 263
Pineton, 283
Pinkerton, 263
Pinkney, 236, 263
Piper, 316
Pitt, 170
Place, Plaice, 237, 263
Plaister, 142
Plantagenet, 96
Platner, 143
Platt, 143, 170
Player, 143, 311
Plimsoll, 171
Plough, 88, 97
Plower, 124
Plowes, 124
Plumer, Plummer, 143
Plunket, 237, 263
Podger, 363
Poggis, 238
Pointer, 131, 150
Poins, Pointz, 179, 237
Poitevin, 179
Poland, 174
Poldue, 170
Poley, 254
Pollock, 179

Polwheel, 170
Pomeroy, 267-8
Pope, 310
Popgay, 94
Popjoy, 94
Porcher, 249, 252
Porson, 58
Portal, 284
Porter, 111, 355
Portman, 327
Portwine, 179
Pothecary, 132
Potter, 143
Pottinger, 111
Potts, 143
Poulter, 143
Power, 237, 362
Powlett, 58
Powlson, 58
Powter, 143
Poynder, 111, 150
Poyser, 143, 264
Prevost, 286
Price, 323
Prickard, 111
Prickett, 111
Prickman, 111
Primrose, 96
Prior, Pryor, 236
Probert, 58
Probyn, 58
Procter, Prockter, 111
Prodger, 43, 361
Prosser, 179
Prouze, Prouse, 253
Province, 179
Pruss, 179
Prust, 179
Pudsey, 263
Pugh, 56
Puissard, 285
Pulman, Pullman, 119, 327
Punchard, 237
Puncheon, Punshone, 264
Pulter, 143
Purcay, 236
Purkis, 58
Purser, 143
Purseglove, 334
Pursey, 264
Pusey, 263
Puttenham, 325

Quesne, 285
Quick, 174, 308
Quiller, 112, 143
Quilter, 143, 150
Quintin, 244

Radman, 115, 143
Radmore, 176, 188
Raffles, 143
Raffson, 58
Raffman, 143
Raikes, 315
Rainbow, 97
Raine, Rayne, 170
Ralph, 58
Ram, 95
Ramsbottom, 160
Ramsey, 163

428

INDEX

Randal, 58
Randers, 58
Ranson, Ransome, 58
Raper, 143
Rapson, 58
Raven, 411
Rawes, Rawe, 58, 264
Rawkins, 58
Rawle, 58
Rawlins, Rawlings, 58
Rawlinson, 58
Rawson, 58
Rayne, Raynes, 170
Rayner, 14, 264, 411
Read, 310
Reader, 124
Redcliff, 176
Redcock, 307
Redhead, 310
Redhill, 176
Redman, 115
Redstone, 176
Reed, 310
Reeder, 129
Regnard, 92
Reid, 310
Renaud, 92
Rennell, 58, 92, 251
Rennie, 58
Renshaw, 362
Renson, 58
Reuse, 52
Reve, 111
Reynolds, 411
Rhodes, 171
Richard, 58, 67
Richardson, 58
Richenough, 362
Richfield, 264
Rickards, 58
Ricketts, 58, 264
Rickson, 58
Ridell, 238
Ridler, 316
Ridge, 170
Ridgeway, 170, 357
Rigge, 170
Ritson, 65
Rivers, 238
Riviere, 290
Robartes, 58, 392
Robbins, 58
Roberts, 58
Robertson, 58, 382
Robethon, 283
Robins, 58
Robinson, 58
Robson, 58
Rock, 143
Rockster, 143
Rockstro, 143
Roe, 93
Rogers, 58
Rogerson, 58
Rohaut, 264
Roland, 58, 69
Roley, 58
Rolf, 58, 411
Rolle, 58, 251
Rollson, 58
Romer, 264
Romilly, 284, 286

Ronald, 411
Rooke, 95, 142
Rookard, 143
Rooker, 143
Roope, Roupe, 238
Rooper, 238
Roosmale-Cocq, 407
Roper, 143, 149, 238
Roscoe, 264
Rose, 88, 96, 239, 382
Rosenberg, 306
Roskelly, 171
Rothschild, 28, 306
Rouse, Rowse, 179, 239, 254, 261
Rouvigny, 281
Rowe, 264
Rowlandson, 58
Rowlett, 58
Roye, Roy, 246, 282
Rudall, 58, 272
Ruddiman, 171
Ruddle, Rudell, 58, 273
Rudyard, 171
Rugby, 176
Rugeley, 176
Ruggles, 264
Rule, 264
Rumbelow, 264
Rumbold, 264
Runciman, 143, 150
Rupell, 171
Rush, 124, 179
Rushman, 124
Russell, 239, 353, 354
Ryder, 149
Rye, 171, 239
Rymer, 112

Sacheverel, 260
Sacker, 143
Sackville, 240
Sadler, 143
Sagar, 124
Saggerson, 65
St. Amary, 239
St. Armand, 400
Ste. Barbe, 239
St. Chevrol, 266
St. Clere, 239
St. John, 243
St. Leger, 266, 393
St. Lo, 266
St. Marte, 266
St. Ville, 266
Sales, 253
Salmon, 59, 411
Salmons, 187
Salt, 143
Salter, 143, 253
Saltman, 143
Salvin, 240
Salwyn, 240
Samms, 58
Sampson, 58
Samson, 58
Samuel, 20, 58
Samuelson, 58
Sandercock, 54
Sanders, 54
Sanderson, 54
Sandford, 240

Sandiman, 110
Sandman, 110
Sands, 172, 368
Sandys, 368
Sanger, 403
Sangster, 144
Sankey, 325
Sanson, 58
Sarell, Sarel, 59, 241
Sarson, 179
Sartres, 288
Saunders, 54
Saunderson, 54
Saurin, 289
Savage, 96
Saville, 266
Savory, 96
Sawner, 252
Sawyer, 144, 327
Saye, 240
Sayer, 59, 105, 124
Sayler, 253
Saxton, 144
Scales, 171
Scales, 171, 214
Schelm, 329
Schenk, 329
Scholey, 264, 411
Schomberg, 19, 281
Sclater, 124
Scofield, 264
Scorey, 411
Scribner, 112
Scrivener, 112
Scroggs, 172
Scott, 180
Seabright, 59
Seager, 59
Seale, 144, 171
Sealey, 171, 181
Seamer, 131, 144, 243, 249
Seamore, 258
Searle, 59, 241
Sears, 59
Seaward, 59, 187, 411
Secker, 59, 143
Seeley, 171, 181, 265
Seguin, 240
Selby, 171
Sellars, 106, 143
Senior, 121
Sergeant, 145
Serle, 59, 241
Serleson, 59
Service, 265
Seward, 59
Seymour, 243, 358
Sexton, 144
Shailer, 144
Shakelady, 327
Shakespeare, 366
Shand, Shandy, 265
Shaper, 145
Shayler, 144
Sheepshanks, 320
Sheller, 144
Shepherd, 124
Sheppard, 124, 145
Shield, 97
Shillitoe, 173
Shillson, 327
Shipman, 144

429

INDEX

Shore, 172
Short, 309
Shorter, 309
Shovel, 264, 363
Shower, 112
Shufflebottom, 160
Shutter, 174
Sibbald, 59
Sibbaldson, 59
Sibbson, 59
Sibthorpe, 172, 361
Sidebottom, 160
Siggers, 59
Silke, 144
Silliman, 181
Sillitoe, 173
Simbarbe, 266
Simcoe, 59
Simcox, 59
Simkin, 59
Simmens, 59
Simonds, Symonds, 59
Sims, 59
Simper, 266
Simple, Simpole, 266
Simpson, 59
Simson, 59
Sinclair, 240, 378
Sinclere, 240
Singer, 144
Sison, 63
Skene, 343, 382
Skinner, 144
Skrimmiger, 107
Skrimshire, 107
Skryne, 386
Slade, 172
Slater, 124
Slatter, 124
Slaughter, 144
Slayer, 144
Slee, 172
Sleeman, 172
Slodger, 266
Sloper, 144
Slow, 266
Smale, 411
Smaley, 411
Smart, 266
Smith, Smythe, etc., 27, 133, 144, 148, 150, 195, 368
Smithson, 65, 148, 391
Smollett, 58
Snake, 97
Snell, 310, 411
Snooks, 329
Soaper, 144
Sobey, 59
Soley, 172, 241, 411
Somerfield, 163
Somerlid, 411
Somers, 241
Soper, 144
Sordwell, 241
Soules, 241
Souter, 144
Southcott, 358
Sower, 112
Sowerbutt, 160
Spain, 180
Sparrow, 88
Sparke, 91

Sparshot, 167
Spencer, 102, 107, 220, 392
Spenser, 108, 220
Sperling, 290
Spicer, 144, 150
Spiller, 144
Spillman, 141
Spittle, 315
Spooner, 145
Spratt, 92
Spurrell, 108
Spurrier, 145
Squeers, 108
Squire, 108, 310
Squire-Bancroft, 403
Stabler, 112
Stace, Stacey, 55, 220, 251
Stag, 93
Stallard, 124
Staller, 112
Stammers, 145
Stamper, 145
Stanhope, 167
Stanley, 169
Staples, 145, 265
Starke, Starkie, 145
Starre, 97
Stayner, 14, 179
Stead, 172
Steadman, Stedman, 172
Stebbing, 59
Stenson, 59
Stephens, 59
Stephenson, 59
Sterne, 97
Sternhold, 366
Stevens, 59
Stevenson, 59
Stewart, 112
Steyner, 145
Stibbs, 59
Stier, Steer, 187, 411
Stiff, 57, 326
Stiggins, 360, 411
Stomer, 243
Stone, 172, 307, 411
Stoneman, 327
Stoner, 14, 307, 411
Stonewig, 328
Stormey, 220
Stowe, 172
Straker, 148
Stranger, 220, 320
Street, 172
Strutt, 152
Stuart, 102, 112, 376
Sturgess, 323, 411
Sturmer, 220
Sturt, 148
Stutfield, 265
Such, 272
Suckbitch, 329
Suckerman, 113
Suckman, 113
Suffield, 163
Sugden, 93, 163
Sugg, 93
Sulley, 241
Summers, Somers, 149, 312
Sumner, 145
Sunday, 313
Sutherland, 382

Sutton, 358, 386
Swan, 98
Swaine, Swayne, 59, 411
Swainson, 59
Swayneson, 59
Swier, 108
Swinburn, 411
Swinherd, 124
Sydenham, 326
Syer, 59
Sykes, 172
Symes, 59
Symonds, 411

Taberner, 124
Tabor, Taborer, 124
Taburner, 145
Tackle, 241
Tadman, 113
Tagg, 63
Taggett, 63
Tahel, 241
Tailor, Taylor, 131, 145, 249
Tait, Tate, 96
Talbot, 241
Tallboys, 254, 307
Tallis, 254
Tancock, 53
Tanner, 145
Tapling, 59
Tapson, 59
Tapster, 145
Tardew, 19
Tasker, 124
Taverner, 124
Tays, 241-2
Teale, 265
Tebbits, 59
Tegg, 63
Tenant, 307
Tennison, Tennyson, 54, 55
Tentor, 145
Terell, 59
Terry, 59
Tessier, 281, 286
Tester, 145
Thacker, 124
Thackeray, 174
Theed, 59
Thellusson, 289
Theobald, 59
Thirlwall, 333
Thoms, Thomson, Thompson, 38-9, 196
Thorburn, 411
Thoreau, 83
Thorley, 244, 411
Thorne, 88
Thorney, 242
Thorold, 59, 411
Thoroldson, 59
Thoroughgood, 59, 174
Thorpe, 172, 207, 326
Thorzeau, ix
Thrale, 117
Thresher, 124
Thrupp, 326
Thurell, 59
Thurkell, 59, 411
Thurlow, 115, 187
Thynne, 115, 190, 308
Thwaites, 173

INDEX

Tibbald, 59, 254
Tibbets, 251
Tibbs, 59
Tighe, 174
Tiler, Tileman, 124
Tilewright, 124
Tillett, 63
Tillotson, 63
Tillie, Tilly, 124, 241
Timble, 254
Timbs, 59
Timcock, 59
Timkins, 59
Timson, 59
Tindall, 163
Tingler, 146
Tinker, 145-6
Tipkin, 59
Tippets, 59, 251
Tiptoft, 242
Tireman, 146
Tittler, 147
Toby, Tobey, 59
Todhunter, 113
Todman, 112
Toeni, 217, 269
Toft, 173
Toller, 148
Tomkins, 39
Tomling, Tomlyn, 39, 59
Toms, 59
Tomson, 54
Toney, 54
Tonkin, 54
Tonkinson, 325
Tonks, 54, 325
Tonson, 54
Toogood, 59, 310
Tooke, 273, 411
Tootle, 272
Toots, 265
Toovy, 187
Toplady, 180
Torre, 187, 242
Torrens, 265
Totman, 327
Tottenham, 325
Totthill, 181
Tower, 145
Towers, 265
Towler, 145
Townend, 163
Townsend, Townshend, 163
Towzer, 131, 146
Toye, 258
Tozer, ix, 131, 145
Tracy, 242
Trant, Tranter, 124
Travers, 173, 265
Travis, 173
Treble, 243
Tree, 173
Trefry, 173
Tregoz, 242
Trelawney, 173
Trench, 281, 289
Treville, 243
Triggs, 170, 411
Trimmer, 131, 146
Trist, 254
Trowbridge, 160
Trotman, 310

Trotter, 113
Trower, 145
Truebody, 181
Tubbs, 59, 146
Tucker, 131, 147
Tuckett, 244
Tuer, 148
Tuggett, 59
Tuke, 273
Tupman, 146
Tupper, 146, 150
Turnbull, 334
Turner, Tourneur, 147
Turney, 266
Turpin, 14, 69, 411
Turton, 290
Twopenny, 266
Tye, 174
Tyler, 124, 147
Tyrell, 59, 244
Tyson, 242
Tyzack, 182

Udall, 266
Uhtred, 411
Umfraville, 244, 271
Underwood, 357
Upcott, 358
Uphill, 307
Upperton, 358
Urquhart, 382
Ussher, 113, 411

Vache, la, 83
Valence, 244, 275, 306
Vandeleur, 14
Vansittart, 19
Varville, 266
Vaudrey, 266
Vautier, 59
Vaux, 55, 219, 245
Vavasour, 104, 244
Vaville, 245
Veale, 105
Veitch, 272
Velayne, 246
Venables, 245, 266
Veness, 180
Venner, 105, 245
Verdant, 266
Verderer, 245
Verdon, 245, 266
Vere, 246, 266
Verney, 266
Vernier, 105
Veysey, 306
Vickary, 411
Vile, 19
Villane, 246
Villiers, 266
Vipont, 271
Vivian, 67
Vizard, 266
Vokes, 55, 323
Vowell, 306, 323
Vowler, 323
Vowles, 266
Voysey, 246
Vyner, 147

Wace, 246, 308
Waddilove, 187

Wade, 174, 252
Wadman, 147
Wadster, 147
Wager, 113
Waggoner, 124
Wagner, 18
Wagstaff, 180, 365
Wakeman, 147
Wakling, 252
Waldegrave, 165
Walker, 147, 150
Wallace, 247
Waller, 141
Wallis, Walleis, 180, 355
Walmsley, 247
Walrond, 59
Walters, 59
Ward, 113, 218-9, 247
Warder, 113
Wardroper, 113
Waring, 59, 70
Warley, 247
Warne, 113
Warson, 59
Warren, 59, 247, 392
Warrener, 113
Waterer, 147
Waterfield, 247
Waterman, 147
Wath, 174
Watkins, 59
Watson, 59
Watts, 59
Way, 252
Wayburn, 411
Wayland, 197-8, 246, 411
Wayman, 124, 147
Waymund, 411
Waynwright, 147
Wayte, 147, 252
Weaver, 130, 147
Webbe, 130
Webber, 130, 147, 306
Webster, 130, 147, 150
Weekes, 174
Weewall, 367
Weir, 379
Welcombe, 181
Welland, 197
Wellesley, 391
Wellings, 59
Wellstead, 172
Welsh, 180, 247
Wemys, 382
Wenman, 124
Westcombe, 161
Westcott, 358
Westhead, 172
Wesley, 169, 391
Weston, 338
Wheatman, 148
Wheeler, 147
Whewell, 367
Whiffler, 147
Whistler, 123
White, Whyte, 305, 307, 368, 386
White-Bell, 407
Whitelamb, 94
Whiteslade, 172
Whitburn, 176
Whitby, 176

INDEX

Whiting, 92
Whitmore, 176
Whitstone, 176
Whitster, 147
Whitwell, 176
Whitwood, 176
Whittier, 148
Whittington, 355
Wicks, 174
Widdop, 167
Wigglesworth, 174
Wight, 180
Wightman, 140
Wigram, 363
Wilcox, 107
Wilde, 96
Wilkie, 325
Wilkinson, Wilkins, 59
Willard, 252
Willett, 59, 251
Williams, 59
Williamson, 59
Willon, 116, 246
Wilmot, 251
Wilson, 59
Wimbold, 59

Windsor, 170
Wingate, 253
Winnifrith, 26
Winterbottom, 160
Winthrop, 172, 326
Winson, Winston, 55
Wirer, 148
Wiseman, 125
Wishart, 113
Wolfe, 20, 95
Wollacombe, 366
Wood, 174, 254, 357
Woodcock, 95, 323
Woodhouse, 168
Woodman, 124, 327
Woodreve, 124
Woodrich, 327
Woodrow, 111, 124
Woodville, 245
Woodwall, 95
Woodward, 111
Woodyat, 175
Woodyer, 124, 327
Woolaston, 366
Woolcombe, 366
Wooller, 148

Woolner, 148
Wordsworth, 174
Wormall, 266
Worth, Worthey, 174
Wrath, 411
Wrenches, 362
Wright, 124
Wroe, 764
Wroth, 411
Wyatt, 361
Wyeman, 124, 327
Wyke, 174, 266
Wyld, 96
Wylie, 59
Wynne, 13
Wyon, 266
Wyvill, 245, 411

Yates, 147, 165, 175
Yeatman, 124, 165, 327
Yelland, 323
Yole, 57
Yorkshire, 181
Young, 187
Younghusband, 123

THE END

www.ingramcontent.com/pod-product-compliance
Lightning Source LLC
Chambersburg PA
CBHW052129010526
44113CB00034B/1028